Bachata and Dominican Identity /
La bachata y la identidad dominicana

Bachata and Dominican Identity / La bachata y la identidad dominicana

JULIE A. SELLERS

Foreword by Darío Tejeda

McFarland & Company, Inc., Publishers
Jefferson, North Carolina

Photographs are by the author unless otherwise indicated

LIBRARY OF CONGRESS CATALOGUING-IN-PUBLICATION DATA

Bachata and Dominican identity / La bachata y la identidad dominicana /
Julie A. Sellers ; foreword by Darío Tejeda.
p.   cm.
English and Spanish.
Includes bibliographical references and index.

ISBN 978-0-7864-7673-2 (softcover : acid free paper) ∞
ISBN 978-1-4766-1638-4 (ebook)

1. Bachata—Dominican Republic—History and criticism.
2. Popular music—Social aspects—Dominican Republic.
I. Title.   II. Title: Bachata y la identidad dominicana.
ML3486.D65S45 2014   781.64—dc23   2014031550

BRITISH LIBRARY CATALOGUING DATA ARE AVAILABLE

Front cover: Bachatero and producer Davicito Paredes
(photograph by Julie A. Sellers)

Printed in the United States of America

*McFarland & Company, Inc., Publishers
Box 611, Jefferson, North Carolina 28640
www.mcfarlandpub.com*

To my husband,
P.J Vaske,
and in memory of
Rupert,
a good and faithful dog

Table of Contents

✑ ENGLISH ✑

✑ ILLUSTRATIONS ✑ ILUSTRACIONES ✑

✍ ESPAÑOL ✍

English

Foreword by Darío Tejeda

I assume the reason Julie Sellers invited me to write this foreword is because of my works related to bachata, beginning with my 1993 biography of Juan Luis Guerra. That text includes my first writings on that style of Dominican music, and I detail the artist's ties to the musical genre, as well as the stories behind each of his first bachatas in the tone of a fictionalized biography. I followed this work with my 2002 book, *La pasión danzaria* (The Passion for Dance), an academic study in which I dedicated a chapter to bachata; this same chapter was later published separately as a bilingual offprint under the Spanish title, *La bachata: Su origen, su historia y sus leyendas* (Bachata: Its Origin, Story, and Legends).

Here, I will provide the reader with some ideas to help understand the importance of this book, in which the author discusses the aforementioned topics, bachata and Juan Luis Guerra. Her work fits within the framework of what, since 2007 and in a work in progress, I have termed bachatology. I use this concept to refer to a way of thinking about bachata within the context of Dominican and Caribbean culture, and its ramifications around the world, such as its impact in the United States, as Sellers studies in this book, and also in Europe. The author's interest in Dominican music was first revealed in her 2004 book, *Merengue and Dominican Identity: Music as National Unifier*, and has continued to grow since then. This book is the best evidence of that interest.

A journalist once asked me during an interview what gave rise to my studies of music, an understandable question in a country such as the Dominican Republic that has always allowed itself to enjoy musical expressions almost exclusively in terms of sound, song, and dance. My response was clear: they arise from an interest in thinking about music, and thus, moving beyond merely hearing, singing, or dancing it. For that reason, I began to talk about bachatology, describing it as an exercise in thinking about bachata as a musical and cultural phenomenon.

Indeed, that is what bachatology is about: focusing on bachata as a culture. I would call it bachata culture. This concept could be misleading for the very reason bachata was scorned at first: because it corresponds to a way of being among its musicians and fans who come from the poorest social classes in Dominican society. For that very reason, they are depicted as being—or almost being—illiterate (which includes lacking formal studies of music or voice), and often black or mulatto.

Bachata musicians—*los bachateros*—were, and are, bearers of a combination of economic, social, political, racial, and educational conditions that defined their profile as those excluded or marginalized from systems of decorum, wealth, power, knowledge, status, and refinement, all variables that intersect with classicist and racial criteria in the Dominican Republic. In bachata, the poor speak, as does the peasant, the black, the urban underprivileged, the forgotten one—in sum, he who is oppressed by economic, social, political, and cultural inequalities. This is the "*Pobre Diablo* (Poor Devil)" in the bachata by Teodoro Reyes, or the "*Juancito Nadie* (Johnny Nobody)" in the song of the same name by Elvis Martínez.

That "nobody" from the Dominican countryside came dressed as the agricultural day laborer, the small landholder, the farm laborer; and in the city, he was the guard, the watchman, the servant; abroad, he was the *cadenú*—a reference to the Dominican migrants who returned home wearing chains as physical decorations. Their poverty swept all of them along to a state of indignity (and often, social ruin), which included a poor education that unfairly depicted them as ignorant. For more than half a century, American anthropologist Oscar Lewis's studies have portrayed like none other the circumstances of the poverty-stricken who frequently descends into indigence and is down on his luck.

From this state of poverty, blackness, illiteracy, exclusion and oblivion—that is, of being nobody— there arose another state even more sorrowful: one of degradation and discrimination. The bachatero was the victim of a social stigma and cultural prejudice inherited from the long-standing membership of such people in second- or third-rate society in a hierarchy of power. This structure was established by the "fashionable set" who called themselves the First Class Society until well into the twentieth century.

These autodidact musicians—almost completely without musical or academic schooling—produced lyrics that were often lewd and full of sexual double entendres and phallic symbols. They sang these lyrics in an unrefined way and to a rustic musical accompaniment, and what's more, with a beat that was danced in a sexually inciting way in the squalor of rural cabarets and urban suburbs. When confronted with its supposed barbarism, the vigilant gaze of the gods of civilization determined that bachata must have been born in sin. Bachata was born under a pejorative sign as its own name shows. It was music of the common folk, such as that seen in Mexican cinema of the 1940s and 1950s. The musicians themselves, panic-stricken when faced with the social criticism accompanying the stereotypes associated with bachata, were reluctant to accept the name imposed by adversarial voices. Although they tried to make other names popular, they were unable to change the fact that the dominant, mainstream culture named them.

As Sellers emphasizes, "Bachata's association first with rural migrants to the city, then with the brothels, and later, with the lower-class domestic workers who listened to it as they did their work, marked it with a stigma that was difficult to overcome." Thus, musical taste became "a way to mark class lines," as musician Vicente García states in this book.

The obstacles were difficult. Bachata lacked social recognition. It did not possess that quality of social distinction, as observed by Pierre Bourdieu, which served as a sign of a privileged social status linked to society's power structure. The bachateros reacted to this state of being a "nobody" by means of what Gramsci would have called a war of position, fighting to come out on top in the genre and gain social prestige.

They left behind those names that nicknamed them *el Añoñaíto* (The Crybaby), *el Solterito del Sur* (The Bachelor of the South), or *el Chivo sin Ley* (The Lawless Goat), none of which helped them achieve greatness. Instead, they adopted other names, ones of higher social standing. While José Manuel Calderón was called the "Father of Bachata," Antony Santos became "*el Mayimbe* (The Cacique)." Luis Vargas was "*el Rey Supremo de la Bachata* (The Supreme King of Bachata)," and Raulín Rodríguez was *el Cacique*. The members of the band Aventura—the most notable bachata group from among the Dominican diaspora in the United States until they broke up—called themselves "The Kings of Bachata." When Aventura's members went their separate ways, lead singer Romeo Santos became "The King of Bachata," now in the singular form. Frank Reyes was "*el Príncipe* (The Prince)," and Linar Espinal, "*El Chaval* (The Kid)." As Sellers's analysis reveals, Romeo Santos's iconic bachata, "*Debate de 4* (Debate Among Four)," reflects this struggle for distinction within the genre among four of its principal leaders.

Bachateros assimilated reluctantly after being dubbed with such names, when other social processes reduced their negative associations and reduced the degree of intolerance and discrimination that weighed on the genre, as Sellers notes. The public university itself refused its entry. Music awards never took it into account until it was accepted as a category in the Casandra Awards, the most important in the Dominican Republic, in 1995. By that time, Juan Luis Guerra had won several Grammy Awards, been number one on Billboard charts several times, and toured on both sides of the Atlantic.

It is amazing that so great a paradox still exists in such recent times, at the very turn of the century, and the turn of the millennium: that a music belonging to the majority of the population was not accepted because it did not represent the minority. Bachata was not peripheral to the culture of the average Dominican or the common person, but it had not been legitimized by the mainstream, dominant culture, or filtered through the mass media controlled by the ruling classes. En *La pasión danzaria*, I established that the polarization between the elite and the common people in Dominican society is one of the keys to understanding bachata's social and cultural evolution.

Similarly, one of the cruxes of understanding bachata is its system of polarities, one of which is precisely that of the elite versus the common folk. The contrast of above/below serves to reveal the Dominican imaginary regarding decorum, wealth, power, status, and distinction, all of which are intermingled in the notions of social class and race; the pair above/below depicts the extremes of this social stratification with a spatial image and in a functionalist code. The lower class is below, and the upper class is above: upper/above, lower/below. Bachata is the music of the underdogs. It is in this way that bachata emerged as a music of the margins, as Deborah Pacini Hernandez, a pioneer in the academic study of the genre, called it in her 1995 book, *Bachata: A Social History of a Dominican Popular Music*. While Pacini Hernandez centered her attention on the ties between bachata and social exclusion, Sellers focuses on bachata's relationship to Dominican identity in this book.

Bachata's rise and conversion into a musical symbol of Dominican identity were parallel processes occurring simultaneously with the uprooting of a high proportion of smallholder peasants who became agricultural laborers, and by means of internal immigration, their entry into the urban proletariat or the urban down-and-outs, and into a state of informal underemployment, known on the island as *chiripeo*. These workers had no fixed job or stable income, and their life revolved around mere survival strategies. In other words, bachata was part of the development of rural capitalism in the second half of the twentieth century, which the peasants carried with them to the cities, thus creating an urbanization of poverty. Bachata was there, on the fringes of the cities, becoming part of the new urban imaginary, first in the barrios, and later at a transnational level, as Sellers's book shows.

Bachata culture had an urban space within the barrio, the habitat of laborers, and its special niche was the *colmado*, or corner store—the urban equivalent of the rural local store or *pulpería*. The *guagueros* (bus drivers) who transported people from the city to the country and vice versa became important agents in bachata's movement, as did the drivers of the small, public transportation cars known as *conchos* in the big cities such as Santo Domingo and Santiago de los Caballeros. The colmado replaced the rural cockpit and *enramada* (a thatched-roof construction without walls that featured a dance floor of packed soil, lime, and water) as the site of musical pre-eminence, just as the cities supplanted the countryside in importance.

It was there in the urban world that bachata was finally legitimized by the main-stream, the dominant mentality. This process began in the 1980s and crystallized, although somewhat unfinished, in the last decade of the twentieth century. There were three important milestones in its journey to legitimacy. First, the popularity of bachata pioneer, Luis Segura's "*Pena* (Sorrow)" in 1983 opened the doors to *los centros cerveceros* (small establishments selling beer) for the first time. These had come into full swing in the lower class neighborhoods to serve an impoverished clientele who had seen their buying power diminish, and to serve the cadenú—migrants returning from the North—when they came home for Christmas. Secondly, the so-called tecno bachata movement (which I called "neobachata") arose in 1984 with Luis Días's exper-imental album, *Luis Dias amargao* (Luis Dias, Embittered), recorded on cassette. Later, Sonia Silvestre, Juan Luis Guerra, and Víctor Víctor joined this movement and contributed in their own ways. This school of music infused the genre with musical and literary sophistication and reaped its greatest results in the 1990s, reaching its recording pinnacle with Guerra's *Bachata rosa*. Thirdly, Antony Santos's song, "*Voy pa' llá* (I'm Going There)," was so popular that this recording became a veritable bachata hurricane—that is, it surpassed all the records set by traditional bachateros and became a mass phenomenon.

Bachata's conversion into a legitimate music occurred at the same time as the impoverishment of the middle classes in what the economic organizations in the region have called the Lost Decade. This period saw the industrialization of the free trade zones, the rise of a new social class called the Dominican Yorks and their demon-stration effect—especially for Christmas and New Year's—who attracted a broader audience to bachata, a phenomenon that Dr. Sellers also studies. Thus, the Dominican overcame his ambivalence toward bachata during the transition phase towards its legitimization as an emerging identity of the new Dominicanness, both urban and transnational (and commonly bilingual, at least in the United States).

In light of these changes, it is understandable that identity is disputed territory: the modern is in conflict with the traditional, literate with illiterate, elitist with popular—just to stay within the sphere of those dichotomies typical to bachata culture. This culture is steeped in series of conflictive relationships. In fact, one could present an entire theory about Dominicans' ideas about our intrinsic conflictive nature: conflicts of love, intrigues, infidelity and betrayal, internal and external conflicts, disputes between the masculine and feminine, with the peculiarity that—in this case—the feminine generally prevails. Woman tends to be victorious because of masculine victimization, an immanent effect in bachata derived from one of its distinguishing traits, the inversion of reality—and specifically, of gender roles—to turn it into fantasy. The Romantic Movement's legacy to bachata is clear.

This legacy pervades the subject matter, lyrics, and interpretive style that characterize bachata culture: singing about disillusionment, indifference, and *amargue* (bitterness), the lament of oppression or human unhappiness in a quavering voice overcome with emotion, full of sadness and pain—including a helping of sadomasochism. Just like the bolero and the soap opera, the ballad and the tango, bachata is a melodrama, filled to the brim with weeping and tears. Bachata is a tearjerker by nature.

One of the great merits of Julie Sellers's book is that she details many of these elements in the voices of the bachateros themselves. From now on, this book will become an indispensable text for an intimate understanding of this emerging Caribbean music known as bachata.

Darío Tejeda
Santo Domingo

Darío Tejeda holds a degree in political science and a master's degree in Caribbean studies. He is a member of the Academy of Sciences of the Dominican Republic and director of the Institute of Caribbean Studies (INEC). His book La pasión danzaria *(Havana, Cuba: Casa de las Américas) was awarded an International Prize of Musicology in 2001.*

Preface

My interest in the Dominican Republic and its culture began in 1993 when I first traveled there as part of Kansas State University's International Community Service project. I little suspected that spending a summer working in two preschools in a marginalized barrio in Santiago de los Caballeros would have such an impact on my life. Each day, the teachers, children, and their parents taught my teammates and me about their culture, history, and what it meant to be Dominican. That summer was my first introduction to a culture and people I love, and I've been going back ever since.

I am an amateur musician and a hopeless music lover, thanks to fifteen years of piano lessons, playing flute and piccolo in the school band, and the influence of my grandfather, the late Benard Stromberg, who dearly loved to sing. Music has always seemed to me a profound form of communication, another language unto itself. This same ear for sounds and communication was what led me to study languages: I love words, and above all, their musicality. The combination of these two passions drew me to Dominican music, and eventually, to this research. While the Dominican national music, the playful merengue, was the music that most attracted me in those college days, bachata, bittersweet and nostalgic, speaks more to me as an adult.

This book is my effort to write a history of bachata and to describe how that genre has evolved to become a symbol of Dominican identity. The reader will learn not only about bachata's history, but also about Dominican history and worldviews, and how they are so intricately intertwined. This study is based on research and my personal understandings of the Dominican Republic—its people, culture, history, language, and its music. Most importantly, my interviews with bachata musicians and producers themselves provide astute, articulate, and poignant insights into what bachata is and what it means to be a bachatero. My selection for these interviews was based on my ability to obtain contact information, candidates' availability, and their response to my requests to speak with them. I am unable to include every individual who has influenced bachata due to space constraints. Although I do not directly quote lyrics for copyright reasons, I have carefully listened to, transcribed, and studied the lyrics of each song I discuss.

Although this is a scholarly study, my goal has been to make it accessible to anyone who is interested in bachata. From the very beginning, it has been my intention to write a bilingual book so that I could return it to the hands of all those who have contributed to it along the way; in the end, it is their story. I am a Federally Certified

Court Interpreter (English<>Spanish), and I have translated all material myself, unless otherwise noted.

To date, little has been written about bachata, although Deborah Pacini Hernandez's social history of the genre marked a milestone in 1995. Dominican journalist Carlos Batista Matos's *Bachata: Historia y evolución*, available in the Dominican Republic and in Spanish, provides historical references without a discussion of identity. Darío Tejeda's offprint, *La bachata: Su origen, su historia y sus leyendas* (Bachata: Its Origin, Story, and Legends), represents a brief, bilingual overview of bachata. Several documentary films have taken up the topic of bachata. Adam Taub's *The Duke of Bachata* primarily highlights Joan Soriano's career, while Alex Wolfe's *Santo Domingo Blues* and Giovanni Savino's *Bachata: Music of the People* integrate commentaries from various bachata musicians. None of these films specifically treats the relationships between the genre and Dominican identity, nor do they consider modern and urban bachata, products of Dominican Americans in the USA. This study thus provides a broader understanding of bachata and the historical, social, and political processes at work, first in its discrimination and later, in its acceptance as a symbol of Dominican identity, in both English and Spanish.

I could not have begun, much less completed this project without the assistance and support of a number of people. Darío Tejeda helped me make contacts for a first round of interviews in New York and accompanied me to them, and he and Dixa D'Oleo welcomed me into their home during my stays. Alexis Méndez likewise helped me arrange interviews in Santo Domingo, and he accompanied me around the city and even through a tropical storm. These friends have answered questions and supported my work throughout its course. I appreciate the assistance of Ray Acosta, Marti Cuevas, Mark Hason, Gilberto Vidal, and Rafael Zapata in arranging contacts for other interviews.

I am grateful to the bachata musicians and producers who gave of their time to talk with me and answer my questions: Julio Ángel, Mayra Bello, Rafy Burgos, José Manuel Calderón, Gerson Corniel, Vicente García, Toby Love, Elvis Martínez, Leonardo Paniagua, Davicito Paredes, Edilio Paredes, Ray Santana "el Pollito del Cibao," Henry Santos, Lenny Santos, Tony Santos, Susana Silfa, and Joe Veras. I especially thank Henry Santos for answering my follow-up questions, and Joe Veras and el Pollito del Cibao for staying in touch and checking in to see how my project was going. I would also like to recognize Isidoro "Chichí" Aponte, Luis Aquino, Rubén Darío Aponte, Guillermo Cano, Crispín Fernández, Tommy García, Máximo Jiménez, Francisco Medina, Xiomarita Pérez, and Alex Sanche for sharing their expertise in their respective fields, and Máximo Jiménez and Cynthia Staley for helping me obtain and edit photographs. My friend, Dr. Susan Kelley, generously read my original proposal, and I appreciate her comments, not to mention her moral support. Alexis Méndez has been a careful and articulate proofreader, and I appreciate his insights.

Several friends have supported and encouraged me. Annette Starr has faithfully prayed for me as I travel and work. Carmelinda Chilelli and Rosalba Ovalle have constantly cheered me on. My *concuñada* (husband's sister-in-law) and a sister to me, Deisy Vaske, not only supported me with words of encouragement, but also by helping me obtain hard-to-find articles. I am also grateful to Brettney Cole for patiently tagging along with me through the hot streets of Santiago in search of a music store.

Bachata is about love, and I am blessed to have the love and support of my husband, P.J Vaske. He has encouraged my research and travels, and he listened to my rants about what I consider good bachata. I am especially thankful that he agreed that we could be "in the New York area" when I won passes to the world debut of Henry Santos's second album at Sirius XM, and that he accompanied me on that trip. I dedicate this book to P.J.

Bachata is also about loss, and in the course of this project, I lost a dear friend to cancer, my faithful dog, Rupert. Rupert and I spent many an hour listening to bachata as he stretched out behind me on his bed while I worked. Rupert kept me grounded with morning walks and a gentle nudge at mealtimes to remind me that dogs, and even writers, need breaks. I also dedicate this book to Rupert, a beloved and loving friend.

Introduction

Searching for the ties between bachata and Dominican identity is much like asking for directions in the Dominican Republic: everyone is eager to help, and everyone has his own idiosyncratic way of telling you where to turn and what landmarks to seek. I especially remember searching for a home in Villa Mella, a suburb of Santo Domingo, that almost drove my friend, Alexis, and me to desperation. We bounced through the potholes of rain-soaked, muddy streets in a taxi, looking for the hardware store that figured prominently in the directions telephoned to us earlier. Once we found the store and made the turn, we discovered that none of the streets were marked. Not to be bested, the taxi driver stopped and asked a group of *motoconchistas* (public transportation motorcyclists) gathered around their motorcycles in the park if we were on the right track. They weren't sure, but suggested hopefully that we continue on.

We forged ahead, up one street, down another, honking at people in businesses or on front porches, beckoning them to come out and add their insight to our growing body of directions. Finally, honing in on our destination, we stopped at a *colmado*, or neighborhood store, and this time the response seemed to indicate that we were on the right street—which of course curved and dipped. After a few more turns, we honked at a barbershop, and someone came out to confirm our success.

"Just keep going till you see the blue colmado," he explained. "Then turn right and look for a big yellow house."

"How many streets from here?" asked the taxi driver.

"I don't know how to tell you by counting streets, but look for the blue colmado, and then the big yellow house. You can't miss it."

We thanked him and continued on. This time, the directions were accurate, and we arrived without any further misdirection.

Much like this hunt for an elusive house, my studies of bachata revolved around the perspectives of Dominicans themselves, and I followed their directions along the way. My journeys took me across spaces and distances of various natures: geographical, historical, psychological, sociological, political and transnational. I spoke with Dominicans of different classes and backgrounds, and heard as many diverse opinions as voices. Still, one thing is certain: anything that has elicited such strong reactions on both ends of the spectrum—from utter adoration to utmost scorn—throughout its existence is, without a doubt, something powerful.

Music and Identity

In studying the role of music as a symbol of identity, it is necessary to consider the essentialist and constructivist notions of individual and collective identities. Essentialists argue that identities arise naturally out of some inherent and "real, tangible mass base."[1] This foundation is seen as something inherent to a people and a point of departure for understanding the essence of who they are. Dominicans have long employed essentialist claims about music, first by linking merengue inherently with *dominicanidad* (Dominicanness) as a rhythm they insist they carry in their blood.[2] These same explanations have also come into use to identify bachata as symbolic of dominicanidad. In describing bachata as a Dominican genre, singer Mayra Bello observed, "Bachata is inside of me.... Each of us has a little bit of bachata inside of us, as we have merengue."[3] Bachata musician Gerson Corniel[4] reiterated this same argument of nature over nurture, maintaining that bachata was inside of him. The view of the seemingly naturalness of bachata is further solidified among musicians and fans alike by the common characteristics they have shared for many years: rural or lower-class origins, migration, limited formal education, and discrimination.

In contrast to such essentialist claims, constructionist views of identity posit that intellectuals and those in positions of power actively work to create national identities that benefit their own projects and plans. There exists no pure, core element of national character, but rather, ideologies and political agendas are at the heart of the identities that are forged. Still, it is wise to remember that "nationalists cannot, and do not, create nations *ex nihilo*. There must be, at least, some elements in the chosen population and its social environments who favour the aspirations and activities of the nationalist visionaries."[5] As we shall see, those in power across the history of the Dominican Republic have contributed to the creation, propagation, and acceptance of such elements both to retain power and to project a desired identity. These official identities, often constructed against an identified Other, contributed to the discrimination against early bachata.

Music has long played an important role in identity processes, and "[t]hroughout the world music has been used to express and help create, contest or dissolve the identity of social groups."[6] Music is not merely a reflection of a group's preference or taste, but also a player within broader social, political and historical processes: "music is not only the product of a specific social reality: it also contributes to the production of realities."[7] As Seeger aptly points out, "[i]f we are to understand music we must understand the processes of which it is a part. If we are to understand those processes, we would do well to look to the music."[8] These observations are especially germane in the Dominican context where one musical genre, the merengue, has long held center stage as a symbol of Dominican identity. Dominicans embraced merengue as a reactive identity marker during the Untied States Marines' occupation of the nation (1916–1924). Later, Rafael Trujillo appropriated merengue as a symbol of dominicanidad during his thirty-year dictatorial rule (1930–1961). Trujillo hired musicians to modernize the traditional version of the genre and convert it into a progressive-sounding music more appropriate to his nation-building agenda, using it to spread propaganda about his greatness as well. When bachata arrived on the Dominican musical scene in 1962, it faced many challenges in the face of merengue's broad appeal as the official national music. Fifty years later, many Dominicans embrace both genres as symbols of identity. Bachata's trajectory from the countryside to the urban shantytowns and then abroad and its journey from discrimination to international popularity emphasizes the fluidity and malleability of both music and identity.

"Knickknack Music": Discriminating Against Bachata

Bachata's original discrimination resulted from the intersection of the historical moment of its origins and the deeply rooted ties between social class and race. Bachata was born in the shifting sands following Trujillo's assassination, a time marked by dread and uncertainty for many.[9] Although repressive and violent, the Trujillo regime had provided the scaffolding for Dominican identity and existence for three decades, and many clung to established markers of identity. Bachata did not present itself at a time propitious to accepting anything new, and the original discrimination against it arose in part from this uncertainty. Dominican constructions of race also contributed to bachata's original rejection by the middle and upper classes. Dominicans have long embraced a Hispanic identity stemming from historical practices and events. As a colony, Santo Domingo suffered because of out-migration to more profitable colonies, and colonial authorities adopted a broader definition of white to accept those of mixed race into the ruling group. Two Haitian invasions during the nineteenth century strengthened the division between black and white. Still, race is not static in the Dominican Republic, for it is tied inexorably to social class. Thus, one can progressively lighten his race with each rung of the class ladder that he scales.[10]

The longstanding split between the city and country also contributed to the discrimination against bachata. The Dominican middle and upper classes have long held contradictory and at times conflicting views of the Dominican *campesino* (peasant). In some cases, the campesino is judged as the purest representation of all things Dominican, especially when compared to the Haitian or U.S. Other.[11] From this angle, the campesino served as the embodiment of a Creole identity—the racial classification of *indio* that allowed Dominicans to disassociate themselves from both Haiti and Haitian rule, as well as Spain and the nation's brief return to Spanish rule (1861–1865).[12] In practice, however, the Dominican campesino came to be treated as a backwards, unmannered hick who did not understand or contribute to national progress.

The large influx of poor, rural migrants to Santo Domingo following Trujillo's assassination brought with them their tastes for romantic guitar music, often adapting popular Latin American boleros to their own unique interpretive style. These lower-class musicians, largely self-taught and without the financial backing of the entrenched merengue, had limited access to recording and production opportunities. These pioneers of bachata sang emotionally of suffering and in the vernacular of the marginalized barrios, often painting with their lyrics the realities of barrio life for audiences in the city and in the country. Bachata was not discriminated against at first, but later, its critics portrayed it as the uncultured black sheep of the Dominican musical family because of its association with lower-class (read "black") rural and urban musicians and fans.

"Señora Bachata"[13]: Bachata's Acceptance

Bachata's eventual acceptance and reception as a symbol of Dominican identity resulted from what Slobin has termed "validation through visibility" by which "a higher profile causes a local or regional population to reconsider its own traditions."[14] Bachata's increased visibility beyond its original audiences arose from the convergence of several factors. Its fan base continued to grow and listen to bachata on the radio and on records played in public places. Some of those fans, notably young women who were forced to leave their barrio homes to work as domestic workers for the bourgeoisie and elite, played their music within earshot of their employers, thus exposing others to the music, regardless of the latter's real or feigned criticism of it. The ongoing economic crises also continued to broaden the reaches of the lower class, as more and more Dominicans knew the realities of living below the poverty line. As Fiske reminds us, music must be "above all, *relevant* to the immediate social situation of the people."[15] The growing expanses of poverty thus provided a broader group of people who could relate to bachata. As Luis Días notes, misery gives rise to bachata "because it is the people's voice, blues, agony, desperation, and wail."[16] Additionally, innovations to bachata, such as the tecno bachata ventures of Luis Días, whose primary catalyst was singer Sonia Silvestre, and the efforts of Víctor Víctor and Juan Luis Guerra made further inroads into new audiences among the middle and upper classes.

The rapid growth of the Dominican transnational community in general, and specifically migrants' experiences living in the urban setting of marginalized barrios in New York City have created new audiences for bachata. In addition to Dominican migrants themselves, both Spanish- and non–Spanish-speakers are exposed to bachata, and, unaware of the existing prejudices against the genre, many have embraced it. A new generation of Dominican Americans has transformed the genre by complementing it with rhythms such as blues, pop, rock and reggaetón along with a signature Spanglish. This modern and urban bachata still represents what it means to be Dominican, but within a transnational context. Modern bachata has carried the genre as a whole worldwide and also brought it back with migrants' visits home. The disposable income available to these migrants contributed to bachata's economic viability and also its reach into Dominican society.[17]

This Book

This book considers bachata within its historical and social framework. Chapter One situates bachata in relation to its musical predecessors, and other international genres, highlighting its humble beginnings, musical characteristics and dance step. This chapter also describes and discusses the meaning of the word "bachata" and how it has evolved. I explain the origins of other names for bachata, including knick-knack music, guards' music, and *canciones de amargue* (songs of bitterness). Merengue's and bachata's roles as symbols of Dominican identity reiterate the importance of music in identity processes. Dominicans' distinctions between merengue as their musical preference for fun and bachata as their romantic music of choice underscore essentialist ties to these genres. The guitar-based version of merengue that many *bachateros* perform reinforces the ties between the two genres as well as their links to Dominicanness.

Chapter Two interprets key elements of Dominican identity. Dominican understandings of belonging, articulated by the notion of *cultura*, are reflected through imagined geographies of identity that highlight ethnic and racial purity. Such geographies infuse geopolitical borders with significance. The Dominican-Haitian border serves as a political and psychological divider between Dominicans, who see themselves as Hispanic, Catholic, and Spanish-speakers, and Haitians, whom Dominicans view as black, Vodouisants, and Kreyol-speakers. National borders are also definitive in United States–Dominican relations following the eight-year U.S. occupation (1916–1924). In light of this breach of the border, Dominicans responded by embracing nationalist symbols such as the merengue. This chapter further explains the historical threads of racial identity and how it is interwoven with social class. Likewise, it discusses the dichotomy between the Dominican city and countryside.

Rafael Leonidas Trujillo Molina's aggressive nation-building projects during his thirty-year dictatorship are the topic of Chapter Three. Trujillo's agenda focused both on notions of belonging and a modern plan of progress. Trujillo actively worked to construct a desired national identity by drawing on Dominican Hispanicism. Given the country's long history of regional strongmen and uprisings, a solidified national identity helped to strengthen Trujillo's position and to project a national image of solidarity. Trujillo presented merengue as a symbol of this nationalism and as an essential element of Dominicanness.

Chapter Four details bachata's birth and first years on the musical scene. Born on May 30, 1962,[18] one year after Trujillo's assassination, bachata emerged in the unsure setting of political upheaval and the changing social fabric of the Dominican Republic. The influx of rural migrants to the Dominican capital that followed the end of the dictatorship brought with it self-taught musicians who played their own interpretations of popular Latin American boleros of the era. Originally produced as romantic guitar music, bachata was not discriminated against at that time.

Chapter Five discusses bachata trends and innovations following its initial wave. Double entendre bachata, so popular during the 1980s and early 1990s, gave way to experiments with tecno bachata and more romantic themes. Topics continued to reflect the desperate economic and social conditions of many bachata musicians and fans, including the increased participation of women in the workforce and the Dominican diaspora. Traditional bachata topics, such as love, deception, and love lost, continue to figure among the most popular lyrics.

The increasingly popular trend of romantic bachata is the topic of Chapter Six. In the early 1990s, bachateros such as Joe Veras began to bring new audiences to the genre with their romantic bachata. Their lyrics run the gamut of falling in and out of love, as well as social topics and other types of relationships. Their interpretations are still heartfelt, although they are less bitter overall. This variety in content and romantic approach continued to help erode discrimination against the genre.

Chapter Seven considers typical bachata's role within the Dominican transnational community. Rural migrants flooded the capital following Trujillo's assassination, exacerbating an existing lack of jobs and pushing increasingly more Dominicans below the poverty line. Relaxed migration policies both at home and abroad fueled the growing out-migration, especially to New York City. Ongoing economic woes across the decades have continued to encourage migration, contributing to a significant Dominican transnational community. Bachateros living abroad, such as Rafy Burgos, Gerson Corniel, and Ray Santana "el Pollito del Cibao" (The Cibao Chick) deliver bachata to an audience seeking ties to home and a genre that is the "music of the uprooted."[19]

Chapter Eight presents the transnational phenomenon of USA modern and mainstream bachata. A product of the Dominican diasporic community in New York, modern bachata complements the typical bachata sound with R&B, rock, pop, hip-hop and reggaetón. Lyrics commonly feature Spanglish and effortless code-switching, and they portray the realities of Dominicans abroad as well as traditional bachata themes. The tensions and traumas of migratory dislocation, discrimination, and economic hardship made bachata a propitious language to express migrants' situations and realities. Modern and urban bachata have played a key role in increasing bachata's visibility, and thus its validation as a uniquely Dominican music and symbol of national and transnational identity.

Women's participation in bachata production is discussed in Chapter Nine. The gendered and separated spaces of the *casa* (home) and the *calle* (street) traditionally place the home as the sanctuary of all respectable women. In contrast, the street is a place of uncertainty and danger where anything might happen to besmirch a woman's virtue. As a popular music of the cabarets, bachata became linked to prostitution and women of the streets, distancing many female fans and musicians from the genre. Similarly, the social constructions of *machismo* and *marianismo* contributed to these notions. While macho men were viewed as victors of many romantic conquests, women were expected to remain in the home and be an exemplary model of suffering in the image of the Virgin Mary. Although these constructions contributed to a reduction in women's participation in bachata, some women did dare to record bachata, singing the genre's common themes from a woman's point of view.

The Pulse of a Nation

Music is an integral part of Dominican daily life, so much so that Dominicans draw on essentialist imagery to describe it as a genetic trait that pulses through their veins,[20] beating in time to individual needs and national and international realities. This study proposes to track bachata's pulse across the years of its history, drawing ties to historical and social undercurrents that affected both its rejection and acceptance. Originally scorned by the middle and upper classes as "knickknack music" or a product of little musical value, bachata is now embraced by Dominicans at home and abroad as a symbol of identity that is, for many, merengue's equal. Essentialist arguments maintain that Dominicans carry both genres in their blood and that they complement each other as the two ends of the emotional spectrum. Dominican constructions of race and class have long influenced the acceptance or rejection of musical genres, and bachata's rural and lower class roots branded it early as the black sheep of the Dominican musical family. Still, economic hardship became a daily reality for a growing number of Dominicans, broadening the audience listening to bachata.

Dominican migrants abroad embraced the genre as representative of their experiences, and a new generation left their mark by melding bachata with sounds from rock, blues, pop and reggaetón to create modern and urban bachata. Over five decades after bachata was born, it continues to keep pace with the sentiments of Dominicans around the world, beating in time to the pulse of the nation.

ONE

Situating Bachata: Naming and Claiming a Genre

My first interview in Santo Domingo was, appropriately, with the very first bachatero, José Manuel Calderón. "The phenomenon that we call bachata today was born with me," Calderón reminisced, although when he began his career, his style of music was not identified as different from guitar boleros. Calderón and other early bachateros saw themselves as performers of romantic songs, and commonly, remakes of popular Latin American boleros of the time. In the contested space of Dominican musical identity, the Dominican middle and upper classes became increasingly critical of this new genre, and the names they gave it condemned the music as bitter and unrefined, and the dance step as erotic. These were the same detractors who used name-calling to christen the genre as "bachata," indicating a knickknack or something of little worth, and later, *música de amargue*—music of bitterness. With time, some musicians embraced the latter as a preferable name.

Bachata musicians (*bachateros*), mostly self-taught and of rural and humble origins, tend to embrace the essentialist qualities of being a bachatero. These musicians emphasize the bachatero's innate gift for interpreting pure sentiment and transforming it into music. Nevertheless, the influence of the bachatero's social environment cannot be overlooked as a component in the making of a musician. Although bachata's critics clung to the merengue as the national music, distancing it from bachata, many of these first bachateros performed both bachata and *merengue de cuerdas* (merengue on string instruments), establishing early on the interconnectedness of these two pillars of Dominican musical identity.

Bachata's Roots

Bachata is descended from the Cuban bolero, a genre that was born in the late nineteenth century and spread across Latin America in the decades that followed. Bolero musicians from across the region made it the most popular romantic dance music in Latin America in the years preceding bachata's birth. A uniquely syncretic New World product of the Antilles,[1] the bolero was born of the fusion of "the Spanish bolero, mixed with the *danzón* and reinforced by the blues."[2] From its origins in the Caribbean, the bolero moved fluidly and easily throughout Latin America due to its universal themes (often romantic) and rhythmic base, which made it an extremely mobile and adaptable music.[3] As a genre, the bolero was not only a favorite form of music in the Dominican Republic, but also an integral element of Dominican identity.[4]

In addition to the universality of themes, bolero lyrics are imprecise and often consist of a first person singing voice (*yo*/I) that directs him or herself to an indeterminate second person (*tú*/you).[5] These romantic lines expressed a gamut of emotions, from the pain of love lost to declarations of new love. Love, a universal element of the human experience, is both abstract enough to contribute to a sense of collectivity among bolero listeners and specific enough to inspire individual identification.[6] Dominican archaeologist, anthropologist and author Marcio Veloz Maggiolo observes that bolero lyrics form part of a literary heritage that extends back to the image of the unattainable woman of medieval courtly love to romantic novels of the nineteenth century and popular poetry of the twentieth century.[7] The serenade as an expression of love is similarly a part of this tradition, "a combination of poetry and music ... telling the heart's truth or lies through song."[8] In much the same way, boleros were "an erotic crutch"[9] for those who felt inhibited or could not find the words to speak their true feelings. Both listeners and composers implicitly understood the ties that joined them—the former in need of words to express themselves, and the latter a type of Cyrano de Bergerac speaking on their behalf.[10] This romantic atmosphere of boleros provides a socially acceptable setting in which macho men are allowed to be sentimental and express their feelings, even if that expression is through the words of another.[11]

When combined with the universality and familiarity of romantic themes and formulaic situations, the bolero's lack of specificity facilitates individual identification. The listener feels a personal connection with the lyrics while at the same time recognizing, either consciously or subconsciously, the body of listeners who experience the same feelings of connection. As a "cultural product,"[12] this contributes to feelings of community, and, by extension, the formation of a group's collective memory among its listeners, while at the same time infusing the individual with a sense of uniqueness and individuality.[13]

Vanessa Knights identifies the bolero as a response to the changes experienced with urbanization:

> It is music for the masses ... who have been relegated by the radical transformations of a modernization associated with speed and fragmentation, it is a counter discourse to the official history for the subaltern classes who have been denied social representation. The urban masses do not fit in traditional social structures and in some way the new mass culture is a response to their need to express the basic ways of feeling.[14]

In this way, the bolero serves as both an individual and a collective space of escape from the overwhelming changes and challenges within the modern urban world. It is no coincidence that bolero's growing popularity ran parallel to the advent and growth of mass media as part of that world.[15]

As a genre, bolero was by no means uniform, and its subgenres varied both in content and rhythm.[16] The bolero fused with other genres, such as mambo, son, tango, chachachá, the Mexican ranchera, and Andalusian flamenco (*bolero moruno*) as it moved throughout Latin America. Bolero consumption also varied by social class: while the upper class listened to bolero orchestras in the finest venues, the lower class might hear the same music in more humble locations as performed by a trio or on jukeboxes.[17] In the cabarets and brothels, where the jukebox was king, "boleros that revealed betrayal, bitterness, indifference and death were more highly esteemed in these places than the typical poetic ... or bucolic boleros."[18]

Boleros easily entered the Dominican Republic over shortwave radio stations from places such as Cuba and Mexico, and later, through Mexican cinema, a medium that was a primary exporter of popular Mexican boleros and boleristas such as Los Panchos and Agustín Lara.[19] Bolero's golden age (1950s) coincides with that of the Mexican cinema, a time when those films portrayed scenes and characters from the cabarets and lower classes.[20] The very act of going to see these movies also contributed to a sense of shared experience and similarity, since moviegoers might come from a variety of backgrounds to share in the common story and songs that accompanied the film.[21] The jukebox as an essential element of locales across class lines also helped determine which songs were popular. In addition to repetitions of favorite songs, some owners accepted monetary incentives not to play a record.[22]

Bachata inherited a number of elements from the bolero tradition. The instrumentation of the smaller groups or trios, the centrality and picking of the guitar in *bolero picado*, the dialogistic paradigm between an indeterminate singing *yo*/I and an indeterminate *tú*/you, and romantic themes of both love realized and love lost, all carried over into bachata. Like bolero, bachata would quickly become a cultural product of the masses, borne across radio airwaves, on jukeboxes, and the voices of live performers in small venues. Nevertheless, bachata differed from bolero in its underlying sentiment. While bolero was primarily nostalgic, bachata expressed melancholy, "which means *a vague, deep, calm, and permanent sadness, born of physical or moral causes, which makes it impossible for anyone who suffers from it to find any pleasure or fun in anything."*[23] As Juan Miguel Pérez observes, melancholy is not a passing phase, but rather a lingering state, brought on, in the case of bachata fans, by social factors.[24]

Definitions of "Bachata"

Bachata[25] was not distinguished as a new genre of music when José Manuel Calderón recorded the first bachata in 1962, or indeed, until the 1970s. Instead, this style of music was lumped into the broad grouping of *música de guitarra* (guitar music), *bolero campesino* (peasant bolero), and *bolero de guitarra* (guitar bolero). In the beginning, bachateros, radio announcers and fans referred to this style of music simply as bolero de guitarra.[26] This was in large part because the original meaning of the word "bachata" was quite different. Dating from the nineteenth century, "bachata" referred to fun, carefree times and informal gatherings in the countryside and later, in the marginalized barrios of the city.[27] There, musicians played stringed and percussive instruments, many of which they fabricated themselves.[28] Edilio Paredes differentiates between a *fiesta* (party) where more established or well-known musicians would play, drawing people from around the area, and a *bachata*—an informal get-together where friends could hang out and sing, chat, and dance.[29]

The guitar-based music's growing popularity among the urban *barrios populares* (lower-class neighborhoods) caused those of the middle class to call it many things in the early years: *música de guardia* (guard's music, with reference to low-ranking military men) because it tended to be played in cabarets and brothels they frequented, and *música de cachivache* (knickknack music) because of the comparatively poor quality of recordings, most of which were produced completely out of pocket by musicians who did not enjoy the financial backing of a record label or agent.[30] Indeed, the name "bachata," commonly employed by middle-class detractors, was meant as another insult. Edilio Paredes situates the christening of bolero de guitarra as bachata in 1969, when more hopeful musicians were beginning to record their romantic guitar music.[31] At that time, a recognized Dominican musician appeared on the popular *Show del mediodía* television program and shared his opinions of the music, claiming it was of poor quality and associating it with the barrios populares. To sum up, the musician insulted the music by calling it "una bachata," something of little worth, a music "of peasants, of people without cultura who have no manners."[32] As the show's name suggests, it was broadcast at noon (*mediodía*), a time when families gathered around the table to have lunch together. As a result, this program had a broad audience to hear the musician's condemnation, and soon thereafter, the middle class began to refer to this music as bachata.[33] On the lips of the middle class, however, the term "bachata" ceased to refer to an informal, enjoyable get-together, but rather, expressed a scathing condemnation of poverty, lack of refinement, and poor-quality music: "No one played a record of that guitar music at home anymore. They played them in the barrios, and when you heard the song, the people said, 'there's a peasant.' That meant someone without cultura."[34] This association with the campesinos who labored in the countryside was later used to distinguish traditional bachata from tecno, modern, and urban bachata by insisting that its essential representation always had *"grajo"*— underarm odor.[35]

Many bachateros resisted the bachata label and sought others. For example, Leonardo Paniagua did not like the name "bachata" because it was a derogatory term imposed from the outside on the type of music he was making: "I've never wanted to accept the word 'bachata.'"[36] Edilio Paredes reported an equally visceral reaction to the name-calling: "A knickknack! It made me furious when I heard them call my record a knickknack. It was the same as saying it was garbage."[37] Paniagua observed that the same style of romantic guitar music was being produced in other countries where it was never called bachata: "That same genre was being recorded in Ecuador, in Puerto Rico and they didn't call it bachata. You only heard talk of 'bachata' in the Dominican Republic. And it was the same instrumentation."[38] Bachata, then, was a term unique to the Dominican Republic,[39] where it did not so much refer to a genre of music as it communicated scorn. Years after his first recording in 1973, Paniagua is still bothered by the name "bachata" because of its original connotations.[40] Others, however, eventually appropriated the name of bachata through a process of name-claiming that infused the term with pride. Now, the name that was once an insult has invested musicians with their own power.

For bachateros, defining bachata as a genre and style usually goes far beyond a mere description of its 4/4 time signature, instrumentation and sound. For most, it also involves a foundation in emotions. For José Manuel Calderón, the Pioneer of

Bachata, bachata is pure emotion and capable of representing not only bitterness and love lost—common themes of bachata—but also a whole gamut of emotions, making it a true message of the people: "Bachata also sings of love. Bachata sings to God, to mothers. It sings to nature. Because its message really gets to people, and that's what's made it more popular."[41] Susana Silfa describes bachata as something that comes from deep within, full of emotion, a natural, uncontrollable response. Silfa goes on to define bachata as "the campesino's cry" that sings precisely what one experiences.[42] For bachata musician and producer Davicito Paredes, bachata is a tapestry of different emotions, and all the things one might want to say to a significant other but does not dare.[43]

The appeal of this guitar-based music in the rural areas and poor barrios is not surprising, given the longstanding importance of music and dance in the country-side,[44] as well as the popularity of its ancestor, bolero. Bolero found a following among Dominican rural musicians, a great many of whom were self-taught. In rural areas, guitars were a relatively inexpensive instrument to purchase, and musicians themselves fabricated many of their own percussive instruments. In contrast to the larger merengue bands, local musicians could easily form a small group of one or two guitars, bongos and *güira* (scraper). These rural musicians strove to imitate the popular boleros, although their emotionally charged, plaintive interpretations and tones with which they interpreted the songs was what eventually differentiated their music and led bachata to its own name. Musicians learned songs by ear from others, off of the radio or jukebox, and they passed them on orally, as was common to the local oral tradition, and they performed these versions at local gatherings and events. This form of bolero consumption and subsequent reinterpretation was happening across the country without any unified intention.[45] Following the assassination of dictator Rafael Trujillo in 1961, the huge wave of rural migrants who came to Santo Domingo brought with them not only these early interpretations of what would become bachata, but also a new audience who was already consuming this style of music.[46]

As bachata evolved and took on its own form and name as a separate genre, it came to be defined by its basic instrumentation of five instruments: requinto, second guitar, bongo, güira, and bass. The guitar was, and continued to be, central to the expressive quality of bachata, and often singers called on the guitar to cry along with or for them. As Henry Santos explains, the singer's performance results from this interaction with the guitar: "You need to understand ... the feeling, the guitar—how it cries, where it cries, where it's supposed to cry.... And whenever you're signing, the guitar in bachata has to complement whatever you're talking about."[47]

The first bachatas relied on nylon-stringed guitars, though later bachateros, following Luis Vargas's lead, replaced these with steel-string instruments and inserted a microphone into the sound hole of the guitar. The result was a strong, sharper sound. Although innovators have played bachata rhythms using different instrumentation, bachateros describe this five-instrument combination as the recipe for creating the essence of bachata.[48] Davicito Paredes emphasizes this basic instrumentation as essential: "for it to be bachata in its essence, you need those five basic instruments. From there, you can enrich it and mix it with whatever you want. But you have to have the basics of bachata. If not, it's not bachata."[49]

Songs of Bitterness

Bachata is a genre that speaks of love and suffering in every facet. A product of marginality and poverty, bachata lyrics often reflect the disillusionment of those who know the realities of loneliness and living in poverty. Dominican musician Crispín Fernández places this suffering in the broader context of Dominican history: "Our people have suffered plenty and can sing their bachata to pain."[50] Bachata's 4/4 ballad style is punctuated by emotional lyrics sung in a plaintive voice that often appears to be truly weeping. The bachatero sings of love—and often love lost, unrequited love, indifference, heartbreak, and betrayal—in the common vernacular of everyday life. He portrays the bitter difficulties of love and life, lacing each word and every cry of "*¡Ay!* (Oh!/Ouch!)" with emotion. *Desamor*—"coldness, indifference, lack of affection" or heartbreak—in general, the opposite of love—is a common descriptor of bachata content.

Bachata's prevalent sense of bitterness contributes to yet another name: *música de amargue*. In fact, bachata is commonly referred to as a Dominican form of the blues[51]: "it's total blues—it's Dominican blues."[52] Bachata's interpretive style and content reflect those of the blues and other genres that arose out of marginality, such as the Mexican ranchera and Argentine tango.[53] Bachata's content, its origins within the marginalized segments of society, and its singers' highly emotional style of interpretation are indeed reminiscent of the blues. As Crispín Fernández observed, "Bachata … is a Latin form of the blues, and the blues is a song born of social treatment."[54] The sincerity with which bachateros sing of the difficulties of living in poverty, their suffering, and the fact that the only option is to sing about these problems are common elements of bachata. The depths of despair expressed in bachata also contribute to another common descriptor of its tone as "*cortavenas*"—figuratively, extremely depressing, and literally, something that makes you want to slit your wrists.

Some bachata musicians themselves embraced this name, música de amargue, in the 1980s when bachata had made some inroads into middle-class popularity. In keeping with their newfound appeal, musicians saw this name as preferable to the then-common term imposed upon them by the middle class.[55] One group of bachateros purposefully embraced amargue to describe their music as a way to confront the term "bachata." Edilio Paredes, along with Leonardo Paniagua, Augusto Santos, Ramón Cordero, and Isidro Cabrera ("el Chivo sin Ley") decided to collaborate on a regular show at a Santo Domingo restaurant. They secured a location, the El Túnel restaurant, and began their series, originally referred to as *el Show de los Lunes* (the Monday Show). Soon after starting, however, Paredes overheard someone refer to him and the other musicians as bachateros in an utterly disparaging tone: "To me, that sounded the same as saying, 'there are the dogs.' That was what you felt when they said 'bachateros.'"[56] Offended, Paredes called the group together, and they tossed around ideas for a new name for their show that would distance them from the discrimination associated with the name "bachata." One of the wives in attendance suggested *Lunes de amargue* (Amargue Mondays), and the name stuck.[57]

Amargue is not easily limited to a one-word definition of "bitterness," and for musicians and fans alike, it means much more. In much the same way that *saudade*—the sentimental essence of Portuguese *fado* music—does not have a one-word translation, amargue encompasses a broad spectrum of emotions and associations, including much of the same melancholy, nostalgia, loss, longing, and desire that comprise saudade.[58] Richard Elliott has proposed that the longstanding insistence on the untranslatability of the word "saudade" may exemplify the belief that the lack of an exact equivalent in other languages "would mean the impossibility of the conditions to describe an appreciation of fado by a non–Portuguese speaker,"[59] thus emphasizing the essential Portugueseness of both the sentiment and the musical genre. Similarly, "amargue" may underline the singularity of both the sentiment and bachata as uniquely Dominican. Regardless of the translation woes related to saudade and amargue, Elliott maintains that anyone who is fluent in what he calls the "grammars of nostalgia"[60] can understand these emotions.

Just as "fado … is about the longing of saudade, expressing what is lost and might never be found, what never has been but might be,"[61] bachata is about conveying the many facets of amargue. Thus, amargue is an essential ingredient in bachata, and the bachatero must feel that sentiment to truly interpret it.[62] Both Gerson Corniel and Rafy Burgos emphasized the need to feel and express a sentiment of whining.[63] Joe Veras described amargue as "that moment of sadness, in the case of a lost love, or that moment of happiness, in the case of a love you hope to have."[64] For Mayra Bello, "Amargue is personal. It's when a person is expressing herself, for example, falling in love, or an unrequited love."[65] Modern bachatero Henry Santos defined amargue as "a combination of really sorry feelings … and a really sad guitar."[66] For Toby Love, amargue is "that deep talk, that talk that comes from within."[67] Bachatero Elvis Martínez also emphasizes the sincerity of word choice as musicians sing about topics to which their audiences can relate: "We're very direct when we sing … with straightforward words that are understood."[68] Still, Martínez does not agree with the association between bachata and amargue, since one could have a drink and identify with any romantic song.[69] Lenny Santos believes, "whether it has to do with a girl leaving you or it has to do with infidelity, that's basically it: you're crying out your heart. And it has to do with the lyrics of the song, and it has to do with the guitar, the instrumentation of the song."[70]

The individual voice sings a song that metonymically represents the feelings of many, allowing listeners to relate for their own individual reasons. Paniagua reiterates this connection between the amargue expressed in a song and what one is experiencing in his own life: "If the lyrics tell me what's happening to me, I'm going to get bitter."[71] Rafy Burgos observes that "when you go somewhere to have a drink because you're feeling a little down, you hear that song that relates exactly the same thing that's happening to you."[72] Toby Love reiterated this type of connection: "It's the concept that connects us, or the sorrows of amargue…. Everybody *se identifican*—they identify themselves with it … especially because of the literature or the concept when it comes to being in love and being out of love."[73] According to producer and musician Davicito Paredes,[74] one might become bitter, for example, if he could not articulate his feelings for a woman. In those cases, the *amargado* (embittered) could listen to a bachata that expressed these same feelings, or even play it in hearing distance of the woman. As he observed, "you can say things that are hard to say by singing them— that's bachata."[75] At times, one's amargue might reach such depths that the amargado might cry along with the song or even more: "I know people who have hugged the jukebox, listening to a song ... because they thought they were embracing the woman, that they were talking to the woman."[76] Bachata can also have a cathartic effect on its listeners. As Ned Sublette points out, amargue "can be a nostalgic, melancholic pain that makes you feel better, like the blues."[77] Rafy Burgos reiterates this view that bachata has the power to convert suffering into something to be enjoyed and thus, to alleviate the blues: "Then, the sadness is gone, and you start enjoying it."[78] Likewise, Lenny Santos observes, "You don't have to dance to bachata all the time. You just listen to it and cry. It's also healing."[79]

Bachatero Gerson Corniel told me, "They say that you have to have amargue to be a bachtero."[80] He described amargue as an interpretive style of crying out while singing the melody, and then offered to give me a demonstration to better illustrate. He picked up his guitar and sang the same portion of a song first as a ballad, and then as a bachata. As he sang with amargue, Corniel's face, voice and posture reflected suffering and pure emotion. Corniel's demonstration reiterates the ties within saudade identified by Leal and Féblot-Augustins that "joined a physical or material element, desire, with a spiritual element, sorrow, and at the same time returned to the past, sorrow, and memory, and to the future, desire and hope."[81]

Dancing Bachata

Although it descended from bolero, bachata's dance style differed considerably from its predecessor. Bachata's faster pace lent itself to a new dance style that drew from both bolero and son.[82] Bolero, son, and bachata are couples dances, but couples held each other closely and danced smoothly to the bolero. This embrace was central to the experience of dancing bolero, which "sought, above all, nothing more than the deepest embrace between a couple."[83] In contrast, son's embrace is tighter and more provocative, and there is more hip movement as the male traces intricate figures with his feet as he dances. These sensual elements also carried over into bachata. Xiomarita Pérez, the first National Director of Folklore in the Dominican Republic (2004–2012) and dance instructor, observes that early bachata dancing began as a bolero but with slight contortions and the addition of the son's sensuality.[84]

Bachata consists of four steps, with the fourth being danced in such a way that the same foot is used for the next step, thus alternating between the right and left foot on the first count.[85] Originally, bachata's signature step included three steps forward or to one side with a slight lifting of the foot or little hop, followed by three steps backward or to the opposite side and the same lift or hop. Over time, the fourth beat has evolved, sometimes being marked with a tap, and others, as a pronounced hip check to mark time.[86] As Francisco Medina, dance instructor and owner of Pasos Dance Academy in Santo Domingo notes, however, there is no one single way to dance bachata, and the liberty of the fourth step lends itself to freedom of expression.[87] Carlos Andújar Persinal also points to this pause on the fourth beat as the unique ingredient that differentiates bachata's movement from its nearest cousins, bolero, son, and salsa.[88] Medina uses the treatment of this fourth step to differentiate between "popular or street bachata" with a more pronounced hip movement, and "classical or ballroom bachata."[89] The growing popularity of the Dominican carwash as a gathering space to socialize, drink, and dance, whether one's car is being washed or not, has created a new space for bachata innovation. There, dancers have incorporated more patterns adopted from the footwork of the son and cha-cha-chá, and from the hand positions and turns from salsa.[90] The options available to the bachata dancer are not limited: "You go somewhere and you're going to see everyone dancing differently, but they're doing it based on the moment with which they identify."[91] Bachatero Lenny Santos reiterates this freedom of individual expression: "People always just want to add a little extra sauce to the same type of dish.... As long as you're keeping that one, two, three, four count, it doesn't matter what you're doing in between."[92]

For sociologist Tommy García,[93] the increasingly innovative nature of bachata steps establishes dancing skill and ability as a form of social power and thus, a reflection on the dance floor of the posturing of power in the national government. As a result, the acts of dancing and asking a woman to dance must follow their own protocol to recreate in miniature both political paternalism and cultural machismo. To play out his role as *galán* (suitor or leading man) in the emerging world of bachata, a man paid special attention to his attire—clothing, shoes and hat—and made certain he arrived impeccably dressed. This attention to detail was meant to underscore that the man was a complete gentleman, regardless of his social position or job status. The elaborate ritual of dance began when the galán approached a table and asked a woman to dance; if men accompanied her, he asked for their permission to dance with the woman.

Out on the floor the man dominated the act of dancing as well. Men held their dance partners in traditional form, by the waist, and determined the steps, direction and turns the couple would take. Some dancers showed off their footwork by dancing elaborate figures and steps around their female dance partner, a practice typical of the son. Just as a cockfight requires the reigning champion to continually better his opponents, the dance required the hopeful dancer to continually improve his steps in a constant effort to prove himself the most adept dancer.[94]

Today, bachata continues to be a male-dominated dance, although the couple's position in relation to each other has changed. Now, many couples dance only holding hands, and the movement of the couple's hands becomes part of the showiness of the dance along with their footwork. Women are now as likely as their male dance partners to decide when and how they turn. Thus, if the early bachata reflected the national power play, this evolution towards equality among dance partners has become more democratic as bachata has become more socially accepted.[95]

Bachateros: Born or Made?

An interesting theme arising from my interviews with bachata musicians was that of the essential nature of being a bachatero. The majority of bachata singers and musicians have little to no formal musical training, and many of them had limited access to formal education. As Rafy Burgos points out, bachata continues to be "a music that isn't written down on paper. It comes out of your head. It's all by ear."[96] Certainly, these musicians' musical skills and resulting success stories are remarkable, and considering whether a bachatero is born or is made (*nace o se hace*) is insightful to understanding the content and interpretation of bachata as well as its initial discrimination and eventual acceptance as a symbol of identity.

According to Davicito Paredes, "the bachatero is a bachatero from birth."[97] Although artists of other genres may have the musical skill to sing and perform bachata, they will lack the ability to interpret its emotions if not a born bachatero.[98] José Manuel Calderón likewise considers that a bachatero is born, not made: "To be able to give it that swing, that feeling ... you have to feel it to be able to communicate it."[99] Edilio Paredes reiterates this primacy of feeling: "the first thing is to feel."[100] Bachatero Elvis Martínez adds that you have to be born with that feeling: "The bachatero is really born.... Bachata doesn't accept imposters because you really have to be born with that feeling, with that desire to sing.... You have to carry that romanticism inside you."[101] Likewise, Susana Silfa (Mariíta), a trained musician, believes that bachata has an essential quality to it. For Silfa, "you have to be very sensitive to interpret it if you aren't from the country or don't have those roots."[102] Similarly, Rafy Burgos emphasizes, "not everyone is born to sing bachata." For Burgos, a true bachatero has to have feeling and his "voice has to be sweet, almost crying"[103] to communicate that feeling. Crispín Fernández also emphasizes such sincerity of expression and links it to the economic and social milieu of economic distress and indigence in which bachata was born.[104] Just as American blues rose out of the economic and racial sufferings of U.S. Southern blacks, bachata arose among the Dominican poor (also read "black")[105] in the marginalized barrios inhabited by new and recent migrants to Santo Domingo. Thus, for Fernández, it is one's social position that makes him a bluesman or a bachatero.[106]

Leonardo Paniagua, who had no formal training, does not read music, and plays entirely by ear, insists that one is either born with the swing of bachata in his blood, or he is not: "This isn't something you can learn; you're born with it. You have to be born with that gift."[107] According to Paniagua, one's music will never make it big without this birthright of swing, no matter the quality of the music or lyrics. Paniagua also cites his own case as support for the essential nature of being a bachatero, since no one in his family had been a musician, and he had no illusions of becoming a singer of any type. Paniagua points to the Pioneer of Bachata, José Manuel Calderón, as someone born to sing bachata, and to the Dominican American bachata band, Aventura, as having bachata in their blood.[108] Ray "el Pollito del Cibao" Santana likewise believes that "music is in one's blood," and Tony Santos describes the bachatero who plays by ear as "the greatest musician in the world" because his talent comes from within.[109]

Joe Veras, who comes from a musical family—his mother sang and his father played accordion—but has no formal studies of music, echoes this sentiment, emphasizing that he was born into bachata and is a "born bachatero."[110] Veras, who is from the small town of Cevicos, describes bachata as its own geography, thus emphasizing his roots and the music's origins in the countryside: "I'm from there, from bachata.... I'm a born son of bachata."[111] Modern bachatero Henry Santos reiterates this view: "I've always been proud of being a bachatero, because it's something that I can proudly say I was born to be.... There's no one in my family who's a musician.... I never took a class in music."[112]

Bachatero Lenny Santos believes that the bachatero is both born and made. On the one hand, Lenny believes that a bachatero is born: "*Nace porque*—you're born in DR, you listen to bachata everyday. *Tú naces con ese ritmo*.... But I never had a bachatero in my family."[113] Lenny described the effort it took to learn to play guitar as a teenager and the amount of time, effort, and practice he had to dedicate to develop his skills. For those reasons, Lenny believes that he made himself the bachatero that he is today.[114]

In contrast, sociologist and former director of the Museum of Dominican Music in Santo Domingo, Tommy García, sees the bachatero as a socially constructed figure and music as a socially constructed phenomenon. Although García admits that a musician must have some natural ability to succeed, he sees no genetic essence to being a bachatero; rather, the work, training and desire to act on those natural tendencies and abilities are what ultimately contribute to being a bachata musician.[115]

Such discussions reiterate the question of whether identities are inherent or constructed. Those who back an essentialist stance—the born bachatero—interpret musical talent as something innate and pure that pulses through the musician. It is precisely this view that is behind the common explanation that Dominicans have merengue and bachata in their blood.[116] This understanding also serves as an explanation for why musicians with no formal training can write and perform music that becomes widely popular. In contrast, the constructivist view takes into consideration the broader social, historical, and economic milieu of the musician. The bachatero who is made is the product of experiences that contribute to his musical formation, even if it occurs wholly informally. He may learn to play by ear or by imitating another's sound or style, but he is still acquiring and developing a skill as opposed to simply being born with those abilities. Additionally, the social realities and economic straits of the bachatero serve as building blocks of his construction, and they contribute to his preference for a genre that sings of those difficulties.

The debate about whether a bachatero is born or is made reiterates the centrality of music in Dominican identity processes and pits life experience versus musical training. In discussing the blues, Julio Finn differentiates between the "bluesperson" and the "blues performer"; for the latter, "the blues is not something they *live* but something they *do*—which makes all the difference in the world. What separates the bluesperson from the blues performer is cultural-racial make-up."[117] Such differentiations, ultimately linked to race and class, will continue to come into question among bachata musicians and fans as the genre's appeal steadily grows across class lines.

Bachata and Merengue: Music and Dominican Identity

The distinction between merengue as Dominicans' music of choice for fun and happiness and bachata as their preference when feeling romantic or depressed is common among Dominicans.[118] They also emphasize that musical choice sometimes revolves around a change in emotional states: if one is feeling down and sad, he may listen to merengue to raise his spirits, whereas if one is feeling too euphoric, a bachata will bring him back down to earth.[119] Whatever the emotional state in question, these common references to the ties between music's influences on emotion reiterate an essentialist view of their role in Dominican life. For many, they are just as Crispín Fernández describes them: "Our emotions are merengue and bachata. They compliment each other."[120] Mayra Bello reiterates this essentialism when she says, "There's bachata inside of me. Each of us has a little bit of bachata, as we have merengue."[121]

Although there are still those who want nothing to do with bachata, Crispín Fernández believes it is currently the most popular Dominican music, even in Santiago de los Caballeros and the Cibao Valley, the area known as merengue's birthplace.[122] Nevertheless, Fernández sees bachata and merengue as a couple in a well-functioning marriage that joins these two Dominican genres in harmony. Merengue, the husband, is the Dominicans' music of choice for happiness and fun, the preferred music for raising one's spirits. Bachata, which Fernández describes as merengue's wife, is Dominicans' romantic music—their own bolero—and it speaks to love, forgiveness, and heartache, all with the utmost sincerity.[123]

Joe Veras, who also plays merengue, does not believe bachata will replace merengue; rather, he sees both genres coexisting and remaining emblematic of Dominicans.[124] Susana Silfa likewise believes that "merengue is what truly identifies us" as Dominicans.[125] Similarly, Davicito Paredes and social communicator Guillermo Cano believe that each genre, merengue and bachata, has its own space; Cano likens the situation to the way *vallenato* and *cumbia* both represent Colombia.[126] Nevertheless, Paredes says that he measures popularity by taking his "thermometer" out as he travels from his home into the capital. According to his readings, the nation's temperature is rising for bachata, the music he hears being played predominantly along his route.[127]

In contrast, music promoter Isidoro "Chichí" Aponte believes that bachata can eventually surpass merengue since merengue has lost some of the ground it previously held. According to Aponte, bachata is already above merengue in terms of popularity worldwide. For Aponte, "Bachata has something you can't avoid. It's something that comes in through your feet, goes up to your head, and you want to dance."[128] Radio announcer Rubén Darío Aponte agrees that more people are listening and dancing to bachata than merengue.[129] Santiago record storeowner Alex Sanche maintains, "Bachata has gone where merengue has not" because of its romanticism.[130] Modern bachatero Toby Love notes, "bachata is the music that's dominating right now."[131] Love attributes this popularity to the ease of dancing bachata and its universal content: "Who doesn't like a romantic song?"[132] Leonardo Paniagua believes that some of the original and continued criticism of bachata resulted from merengue investors', musicians' and fans' fear that bachata, with its large lower-class fan base, could easily come to surpass the merengue.[133] A common topic among many Dominicans is the perceived decay of merengue due to its increasingly fast beat and lyrics deemed of poor quality, both at the expense of musicality and meaning.

Merengue de cuerdas—merengue played on guitars rather than accordion, in the case of *merengue típico* (typical merengue), or saxophones and synthesized instruments, in the case of *merengue de orquesta*—has long been a staple for many bachateros who also played merengue on their guitars.[134] This combination of musical styles is another inheritance from bolero orchestras who included merengues "[s]o that couples wouldn't perish from so much love set to bolero."[135] As they began to perform bachata, the practice of including merengue de cuerdas continued due to the very real necessity of not losing an audience to other venues. Producer and bachatero Davicito Paredes explains that including guitar-based merengue in bachata shows was a way to add equilibrium to performances.[136] Merengue represented a happy, playful contrast to the bachata numbers, and some of those in attendance wanted only to have fun, not to relate to or be brought down by bitterness.[137] In both their bachata and their merengue de cuerdas, bachata guitarist virtuosos imitated the merengue's *jaleo* section, performed in merengue típico by the accordion and on the saxophone in orchestra merengue.[138] Some bachata bands also incorporated saxophones for their merengue numbers, later including them in their bachatas, and thus lending those numbers a new sound.[139]

Eladio Romero Santos played a central role in the evolution and popularization of merengue de cuerdas. Romero Santos had begun recording bachata bolero in the early 1960s. His first release, "*Por ti* (Because of You)," in 1964 was very much in line with the style and content of other romantic bachatas of that time, with the male voice blaming the female for all the heartache he feels. Romero Santos and his band played a primarily rural circuit centered mostly in the area of the Cibao Valley in the north. As a result, his audience was primarily rural and his music did not carry with it the negative associations of the cabarets and brothels. These venues were also conducive to a broader array of musical styles, including merengue de cuerdas, to meet this audience's tastes.[140] Although Romero Santos and his band routinely played guitar-based merengue along with their bachata and other popular dance forms, he had not considered its possible commercial appeal until Edilio Paredes paved the way by recording the first merengue de guitarra.[141] Taking the cue for Edilio Paredes's success with guitar-based merengue, Romero Santos recorded an LP featuring many songs in this style; the title number, "*La muñeca* (The Doll)," was hugely successful.[142] As the title suggests, the singer likens his beloved to a doll, who has gotten lost in the city. He begs his listeners to return his doll, insisting that he is her owner and won't loan her out. Despite the sweeter tone of this merengue de cuerdas, as contrasted with the overtly sexual double entendres of later bachatas, the doll lost on the streets lends itself to the interpretation of a woman who has left her mate and must seek income on the streets through prostitution.

Blas Durán, who had begun with bachata, also experimented with merengue de cuerdas, bringing a new, modern sound to guitar-based merengue by including electric guitars. Durán's landmark release of the 1980s, "*Consejo a las mujeres* (Advice to Women)," set a new path for guitar merengue both in terms of its electric, modern sound, and its production technique of recording the song on multiple tracks, thus improving sound quality.[143] Once the commercial value had been made clear, other bachateros followed suite, and merengue de cuerdas became a common fixture of their recordings. These guitar-based merengues may be erroneously identified as bachatas solely based on the fact that they were produced by bachateros. Nonetheless, they played an important role in helping expose a broader public to bachata and reiterate the interconnectedness of the two genres.

Conclusion

The contested turf of naming the new genre of romantic guitar music and the derogatory names attributed to it are reminiscent of human name-calling. As James

Valentine observes, "[n]aming is central to questions of identity" for names "can be forced on recipients against their will." Names identify us not only as individuals but also in our relationship to others as a contrasting form of identification. The ability to christen someone or something with a name denotes power, but not all have equal access to that power. Indeed, those with the least amount of power and thus, least access to naming, are often the recipients of less than desirable monikers. Such "marginal people are too close for comfort and close enough for contempt. Here the power of the mainstream is orchestrated by using expert authority to define the marginal and thereby the boundaries that contain those who fully belong."[144] Thus, naming can serve as a form of "agency constraining" that limits individual actions in order "to protect and promote beliefs and practices which those in power see as representing the society as a whole."[145] Name-claiming of an imposed label can conversely empower those who were named. This appropriation subverts the original intent of the term and invests it with pride and at times, defiance.[146]

Such was the case with naming the romantic guitar music that was born in Santo Domingo around 1962. Musicians playing this offshoot of the Latin American bolero often remade popular boleros, interpreting them in an emotionally charged style. These early musicians had to pay out of pocket to record, press, and distribute their records. Without the financial backing of the entrenched merengue, these recordings did not enjoy high-quality production, leading its middle- and upper-class detractors to label it a bachata, or something of little worth. The plaintive, sobbing timbre of the music contributed to bachata's criticism as music of bitterness. These offensive names effectively aimed to promote one image of dominicanidad over that of rural and lower class Dominicans. Bachateros and their fans, however, have since claimed these names as their own. Fans and performers have infused the names that once served as the basest insult with pride. Their original offensiveness is being subverted as bachata's global popularity continues to grow.

Two

Interpreting Dominicanidad

My friend, Belkys, gave me my first introduction into the complexities of defining race and social class in the Dominican Republic. Belkys, a teacher in the preschools where I was volunteering that summer, along with two other students from my university, had come calling one Saturday to take us shopping. She stopped first at one host family's home, only to have the door slammed in her face because she was from Pekín, a marginalized barrio, and was, therefore, black. Belkys was in tears by the time she arrived at my home, and even though I understood the words she told me, I didn't yet grasp how intricately related race and social class were.

Feelings of belonging have come to be articulated in Dominican understanding by the concept of *cultura*, which "measures who or what belongs to the Dominican Republic and who or what belongs to the United States or Haiti, the two defining 'others' in the construction of Dominican Nationhood."[1] This vision of cultura was linked to Dominicans' Spanish heritage as the source of refinement, although originally, there was no racial connection. By the early 1900s, cultura referred to race and national identifiers of dominicanidad, all of which retained their Hispanic roots, and later, it differentiated between social classes.[2]

This mode of differentiation contributed to a practice of defining belonging by contrasting oneself or group with the Other. As a social construct, the Other can be abstract or concrete, interior or exterior, individual or a group, close or far away. Sometimes, the Other is remarkably similar: "beings whom everything links to me on the cultural, moral, historical plane."[3] In other instances, the Other is so remarkably different that self-identification with him is impossible: "unknown quantities, outsiders whose language and customs I do not understand, so foreign that in extreme instances I am reluctant to admit they belong to the same species as my own."[4] Faced with this other entity, we judge his value and proximity to us, and finally, we either chose to embrace or reject him. This very type of accepting or rejecting others as part or representative of our group would influence bachata's original discrimination.

Imagined Geographies

The Dominican Republic and Haiti, two nations destined to share the same island, have had a contentious history. Spanish colonial authorities depopulated the island's western region in the seventeenth century to try to halt the lucrative contra-band trade centered there. Soon, French settlers from the nearby island of La Tortuga filtered into the former smuggling lands, and by the late 1600s, plantations owned by French-speaking slaveholders filled the region. The border between the two regions of Hispaniola was a hazy construction, and French-speakers so outnumbered the Spanish that Spain eventually waived its jurisdiction of the island in 1795.

Spanish-speakers in the east held at best a tenuous peace with their neighbors in Saint-Domingue where there had been considerable racial mixing. Although slavery was abolished and mulattos were officially equal to whites in Saint-Domingue,[5] whites still discriminated against them. Slavery in the east made for an uneasy relationship, and in 1801, western forces under Toussaint L'Ouverture invaded and captured Santo Domingo. Toussaint abolished slavery and took steps to unify the island politically and economically. These policies had little time to take effect, for the French ousted Toussaint in 1802.[6]

It is telling that the residents of Santo Domingo preferred European rule to a Creole government headed by a black ruler. Approximately seventy-five percent of Santo Domingo's inhabitants were free blacks or mulattos who supported themselves with subsistence farming and saw themselves as Creole because they were not enslaved, and by extension, not black.[7] This self-identification reflects the construction of race in the Dominican Republic as something that is not solely dependent on phenotype. As Candelario notes, in the eighteenth century, "Dominican whiteness was an explicitly achieved (and achievable) status with connotations of social, political, and economic privilege, and blackness signaled foreignness, socioeconomic subor-dination, and inferiority."[8] The Dominicans' worldview, which included the long-held practice of a broader definition of white ethnicity, made rule by those they saw as black undesirable.[9]

These tensions continued to grow following Haiti's declaration of independence in 1804 as the world's first black republic, and a second Haitian invasion (1822–1844). During this longer period of Haitian rule, President Jean Pierre Boyer abolished slav-ery across Hispaniola and used revenue from the eastern lands to help reimburse France for territories seized during the revolution.[10] Culturally, Boyer alienated the Spanish Haitians by setting limits on the amount of time devoted to religious cele-brations and outlawing the national sport, cockfighting.[11] Dominican collective mem-ory remembers this second occupation as violent, repressive, and denigrating. From that point forward, "the national memories of all things Haitian were grounded in the twenty-two years of the Haitian occupation."[12] The date when Dominicans won their independence from Haiti (February 27, 1844) marked a dividing point in Dominican nationalism. Although this was not the last time Dominicans won their independence, it is recognized as Dominican Independence Day.

Given this conflictive history, it is not surprising that Dominican identity has long been partially contrasted across the border with Haiti. Sarah Radcliffe and Sallie Westwood associate the concept of the Other with "geographies of identity" or "the sense of belonging and subjectivities which are constituted in (and which in turn can constitute) different spaces and social sites."[13] As Anderson accurately notes, "a nation is imagined as *limited* because even the largest of them ... has finite, if elastic bound-aries, beyond which lie other nations."[14] Similarly, borders serve an important function in these imagined geographies for "they reinforce notions of purity and sameness within the territory, and difference and impurity outside the territory."[15] Thus, geographies serve as "symbolic anchors of identity" by linking identities to "a sense of belonging to a specific territory."[16] This linkage between self and place strengthens and reinforces boundaries:

> Not only do communities with hard boundaries privilege their differences, they tend to develop an intolerance and suspicion toward the adoption of the Other's practices and strive to distinguish, in some way or the other, practices that they share. Thus, communities with hard boundaries will the differences between them.[17]

Dominicans envision dominicanidad in contrast with Haitian ethnicity in terms of race, language, and religion. Whereas Dominicans consider themselves Hispanic (white), Spanish-speaking, and Catholic, they see Haitians as black, Krèyol-speaking Vodouisants. These two opposing identities are reinforced through stereotypes and flexible boundaries. As Sander Gilman observes, such stereotypes

> perpetuate a needed sense of difference between "Self" and the "object," which becomes the "Other." Because there is no real line between the Self and the Other, an imaginary line must be drawn; and so that the illusion of an absolute difference between self and Other is never troubled, this line is as dynamic in its ability to alter itself as is the self.[18]

We imagine borders as protective and impervious, and they solidify the perceived link between "'race' and 'place.'"[19] Dominicans' racial and cultural identification with a predominantly Hispanic identity gives the border with Haiti an even greater significance: it serves as the imagined barrier, keeping in what is Dominican, and keeping out what is not.

The Dominican-Haitian border is a longstanding concern for Dominicans, much in the same way that the U.S. border with Mexico has come increasingly into the limelight in recent years. Official histories and nation-building efforts have heightened the preoccupation with Haitian encroachment on Dominican soil as a silent invasion. Labor questions have contributed to this sense of invasion since sugar producers first looked to Haiti for cheap labor in the early decades of the 1900s. Since then, Haitians continue to migrate to the Dominican Republic in search of jobs, working at tasks that Dominicans consider beneath them. In economic downturns, Haitians bear the brunt of the blame, making them a convenient scapegoat.[20] The "generations of official vilification of Haitians"[21] have helped create ties of identity among Dominicans based on understandings of who they are not.

This same understanding of purity within boundaries is equally important in the construction of the United States as Other, first during the eight-year Marine occupation of 1916–1924. This occupation was the result of both economic and political factors, including the Dominican Republic's increasing indebtedness to foreign powers, among them Germany, and the country's ongoing political instability. The occupying forces dissolved the Dominican cabinet and earmarked funds formerly of the Customs Receivership for government use and public works projects to better unify the country. Economic measures provided incentives to American-owned sugar companies to facilitate their expansion at a time when world sugar prices soared. Bustling cities exploded where mere villages had been before. Violence and repression were also common elements of the occupation. U.S. forces censored the press, disarmed the population, and formed and trained the Dominican National Guard to suppress regional uprisings once the occupation was over.

The U.S. occupation was a stinging affront to Dominican sovereignty, and nationalists responded with an essentialist return to the meaning of domnicanidad. This involved, in part, the idealized image of the Dominican campesino as the essence of a Hispanic Dominican identity.[22] The peasant was seen as innocent and pure, "clever and honorable yet duped by crafty and rapacious Yankees."[23] Although Dominicans had shied away from Hispanicism and associations with Spain during a brief period of Spanish reannexation (1861–1865), they embraced them anew during the U.S. intervention.[24] Cultural resistance to the occupation opposed the intrusion of uncouth North American culture and glorified all things Dominican.

In spite of such strong feelings of nationalism, Dominicans' outward-looking gaze switched once and for all from Europe to the United States at that time. Previously, consumers preferred European products,[25] but during the occupation, U.S. products flowed into the country for the Marines' and local consumption. The eight years of occupation "left behind a very pronounced taste for the consumption of North American ... goods."[26] Baseball supplanted cockfighting as the Dominican national sport, and Dominican Spanish adopted numerous loanwords from English.[27] Another byproduct was the widening chasm between the vast majority of Dominicans in the lower class and the elite. Distinctions became increasingly precise in light of the elite's loss of political power, and the upper class took refuge in a cultural elitism that highlighted their ability to consume high-class products.[28]

Race and Identity

Some one-half million indigenous people, the Taíno, inhabited the island they knew as Quisqueya when Christopher Columbus arrived in 1492. This population dwindled swiftly as the Taíno fell victim to European diseases and the harsh conditions of forced labor. Spanish colonists began to import slaves from Africa in the 1530s to work in the mines and fields.[29] At this time, many colonists were leaving for Mexico and several South American colonies, enticed by the discovery of silver. This outmigration far outweighed the influx of slaves, and by 1546, slaves outnumbered their masters by a ratio of almost 2.5 to 1.[30]

Although racial mixing had been common in Santo Domingo, colonists did not openly acknowledge this *mestizaje* (racial mixing). This was partially due to the practice of recognizing persons of mixed race as Spanish (read "white") that colonial authorities adopted as a way to increase the official count of citizens in light of the dwindling European population.[31] This practice marked the beginning of an intricate linguistic system for identifying race in the Dominican Republic. Dominicans' association of all things evil with Haiti further distanced them from identification with their African heritage. As Frank Moya Pons observes, Dominicans "had come to believe that only the Haitians were black."[32] Although Dominicans now acknowledge mestizaje, the weight they attribute to each of the three ethnicities that comprise domincanidad—Spanish, indigenous, and African—is re-imagined. Within this pyramid, Dominicans view their European heritage as the broad, influential base, and see

African ethnicity as contributing the least. The heritage left by the Taíno people—who were decimated early during the colonial period—was the ideal solution to recognize racial mixing without acknowledging blackness, for the Taíno "represented a category typified by non-whiteness as well as non-blackness."[33] Dominicanidad became the amalgamation of indigenous racial and cultural Hispanic identities,[34] a self-identification that evokes roots predating the Haitian and U.S. invasions.

Although African influences and contributions have been officially downplayed or discredited across Dominican history, they are not fully ignored. Ginetta Candelario references a common joke among Dominicans that the eighth wonder of the world is a white Dominican.[35] In the title of her study, Candelario recalls another Dominican saying, "Tenemos el negro detrás de las orejas [We have the black behind the ears]."[36] This saying reiterates the criticism of Juan Antonio Alix's 1883 poem, "*El negro tras de la oreja*," in which the poetic voice pokes fun at Dominicans who try to claim a Hispanic identity and criticizes their loss of good judgment when trying to pass as white:

Cómo hoy la preocupación	Since nowadays so many people
A más de una gente abruma,	Are overwhelmed with worry,
Emplearé mi débil pluma	I will use my weak pen
para darle una lección;	To give them a lesson;
Pues esto en nuestra Nación	For what's going on in our Nation
Ni buen resultado deja,	Doesn't even work,
Eso era en la España vieja	That was in old Spain
Según desde chico escucho	Or so I heard as a child
Pero hoy abunda mucho	But today, there's no shortage of
"El negro tras de la oreja."	"The black behind the ear."[37]

As the poetic voice insists, the African heritage of many Dominicans is always "just behind the face of Dominican national and individual bodies."[38]

Dominicans have long used selective word choice to more precisely define and blur the boundaries between races. As early as 1549, racial categories were specifically defined in Santo Domingo, dividing inhabitants among seven different groups: black (African slaves or their descendants); white (Spaniards or their descendents); mulatto (the child of one black and one white parent); mestizo (the child of one indigenous and one white parent); *tercerón* (the child of one mulatto and one white parent); *cuarterón* (the child of one tercerón and one white parent); and *grifo* (the child of one indigenous and one black parent).[39] This tendency to specify and differentiate has continued across Dominican history, with language helping to articulate subtle racial variables. Dark-skinned Dominicans of the nineteenth century adopted the habit of calling themselves *blancos de la tierra* (whites of the earth).[40] In the 1920s, the term *indio* (Indian) began to be used as an inoffensive identifier of people of color; this same term, modified by numerous differentiating descriptors, went on to emphasize belonging during the thirty-year dictatorship of Rafael L. Trujillo.[41] As Dominican poet and essayist Blas Jiménez notes, even those Dominicans who wished to self-identify as blacks on their official documents were recorded as some form of indio, such as *indio oscuro* (dark Indian).[42]

Dominican racial identification is both highly specific yet equally indeterminate. A popular decoration and souvenir, the Dominican faceless doll, concretely exemplifies this tendency to include and exclude at the same time. These ceramic dolls hold flowers or baskets and wear long, flowing dresses, some of which are intended to appear folkloric while others are distinctly European and colonial in nature. Dominicans explain the dolls' defining characteristic—their lack of facial features—as being indicative of the essence of dominicanidad, for just as the dolls, the Dominican is a mix of three different ethnicities and has no single face.[43] Notably, the dolls' skin tone, a bronze color, is reminiscent of an indigenous identity. Whether they are carried home as a souvenir or adorn a Dominican home, the faceless dolls are a subtle reminder of the understandings of dominicanidad.

Dominicans continue to employ an intricate yet specific set of terms to identify a broad spectrum of racial differentiations. Daysi Josefina Guzmán's study in the early 1970s considered the vocabulary residents of Santiago used to define race and racial characteristics, including hair type, skin, hair and eye color, and facial and body features.[44] Among those interviewed, Guzmán found that participants were able to identify fifteen categories of hair texture and nine hair colors. They also specified six body types, ten facial features, and five racial shades or hues.

It is interesting to note that the characteristic with the greatest number of categories—hair type or texture—continues to be the primary determinant of race among Dominicans, "followed by facial features, skin color, and last, ancestry."[45] Juan Antonio Alix's aforementioned poem also emphasizes the incriminating role of hair.[46] *Pelo bueno* (good hair)—soft, straight, Caucasian hair—and *pelo malo* (bad hair)—kinky, coarse, Negroid hair—mark the two extremes of a long list of hair types.[47] Ginetta Candelario's ethnographic study of a Dominican beauty salon in Washington Heights (Upper Manhattan, New York) reiterates how hair as a racial marker plays out daily on the bodies of Dominican women who straighten and alter their hair to embody an imagined (to use Anderson's term) national identity. This insistence on hair as a racial signifier is as ambiguous as it is important, given that kinky or curly hair can be straightened, and hair color can be altered.[48]

Race is also linked to social class, making it an alterable and achievable category. The bond between class and race is indivisible and the two support each other reciprocally.[49] As one improves his class, his race may whiten; similarly, if one loses his social position, his race may consequently darken.[50] The link between race and social class heightens divisions; as Lauren Derby has pointed out, race is so interwoven with social class that it functions as its principal indicator.[51] Conversely, class can eclipse race in certain cases as, for example, in the case of dark-complexioned, white-collar, educated Dominicans.[52]

The relationship between race and class goes hand in hand with cultura, which Dominicans use to differentiate between social classes: those with refinement, and those without. Thus, while "race may be based on a metaphor of blood lineage ... it is fundamentally achieved in part by social class and in part by style and manners."[53] For this reason, "middle-class and poor Dominicans tend to express their identities in terms of race as cultura, rather than race as a social community determined by color."[54] Cultura unites people of different phenotypes under a broader blanket whose threads are woven of elements reaching back to the Spanish colonial era and its more contemporary understandings as a marker of social class, and by extension, race.[55]

The Dominican Peasant

The opposition between the city and country is a longstanding tradition in Dominican thinking and politics. The division between these two arose from a lack of geographic unity that contributed to deeply rooted, fiercely regional loyalties. This regionalism added to ongoing political instability and conflict following Dominican independence from Haiti. A lack of internal infrastructure separated the nation's population centers both geographically and politically. Without a sense of national identity, regional identities solidified around local *caudillos* (strongmen) who raised their own peasant armies. This model dominated Dominican politics during the latter half of the nineteenth century and the first years of the twentieth, and the peasants' participation in these armies convinced the liberal nationalists that the campesino was the primary obstacle to their goals of a centralized, democratic, and educated nation.[56]

Nationalists represented and understood these campesinos in contrasting ways, on the one hand, backwards and uncivilized, and on the other, the bearer of the essential elements of dominicanidad. Campesinos were largely independent well into the 1800s, living off the land, and nationalists pointed to this connection with the land as symbolic of their rootedness or purity—the essence of dominicanidad. This view of the campesino situated dominicanidad in a location somewhere between the black slave of Haiti and the European conquistador of Spain.[57] In the face of U.S. intervention, nationalists increasingly viewed the campesino as the essence of a Dominican Hispanic identity.[58]

Despite ties to the land and agriculture, the campesino was, without question, poor. These were not the large landholders of the haciendas, but rather, subsistence famers who made do by cultivating enough land to survive and hunting whatever game was available.[59] This manner of survival was completely unfathomable to city dwellers, and the campesino's lifestyle, so rooted in years of traditions, did not fit into a model of progress and modernity. This view of the campesino led to strict migration policies meant to keep him out of the cities and safely tucked away in the countryside. Laws aimed at controlling the influx of rural migrants to urban centers were first passed following the San Zenón hurricane of September 1930, although they remained in effect for many years after the disaster.[60] In 1953, it was decreed illegal for peasants to move to urban areas without first obtaining the permission of local authorities.[61] As a result, the majority of Dominicans continued to live in the countryside, even as Rafael L. Trujillo embarked upon his agenda to modernize the nation during his thirty-one-year dictatorship (1930–1961).

Merengue and Dominican Identity

Historic events contributed to merengue's eventual rise to its position of Dominican national music in much the same way that those events led to the construction of a fluid racial identity for Dominicans. Merengue's precise origins are unknown, and other Caribbean countries have also claimed to be its birthplace. One early legend told that the original merengue was created and performed after the Dominicans' defeat of Haiti in the Battle of Talanquera. As the story goes, a faint-hearted Dominican flag-bearer ran from the battle with the national colors in tow, and Dominican troops commemorated both their victory and the flag-bearer's cowardice that evening in the first merengue.[62] This unsubstantiated legend cements the national music, merengue, with national independence[63] and reiterates Dominicans' essentialist ties to the genre as their national music.

The first reference in print to merengue occurred when Dominican intellectuals launched a passionate literary campaign against it, publishing a series of articles condemning the genre. These criticisms portray the merengue as uncouth and inappropriate for refined society and attack it as the instigator of misconduct among those who danced it. Others launched attacks against merengue because they feared it would become more popular than the national dance of the time, the *tumba*.[64] Author Manuel de Jesús Galván rails against the merengue in his poem "*Queja de la tumba contra el merengue* (The Tumba's Complaint Against the Merengue)." In Galván's poem, the tumba mourns its forced exile by the merengue and accuses Dominicans of turning their backs to serve Satan.[65] Merengue's swinging hip movement and the proximity in which couples danced were also a source of concern. Galván's tumba insists, "Where is modesty, where is morality...?" and demands that men consider how they would feel if they thought their sister or daughter were so "agile of hips."[66] Although this style of dance worried those concerned about propriety, they also likely condemned it because of hip movement's association with African music. Dominicans' recent independence from Haiti contributed to a rejection of all things associated with the black republic. Such a heated debate illustrates the prominent role that music plays in Dominican culture and identity processes. For merengue's critics, the European-influenced tumba was a better representative of dominicanidad than merengue.

The passionate campaign against the merengue is indicative of the following it was gathering in the Dominican Republic, especially among those who lived in the countryside. This fan base was not insignificant, considering that 425,000 of the overall population of 435,000—some ninety-eight percent—lived in rural areas.[67] Cultural traditions of African origin remained strongest in the campo, and music and dance were important cultural and social practices among peasants.

Although merengue's instrumentation varied by region, it most commonly included string instruments, a *tambora* or goatskin drum, and the *güiro*—a scraper fabricated from a gourd. These instruments purportedly reflected the ethnicities of dominicanidad: the string instruments were of Spanish origin, the drum is common to African music, and the güiro was attributed to the Taíno.[68] The one-row accordion, imported from Germany, eventually replaced the string instruments in the 1870s. Intellectuals launched another literary campaign against the merengue at this time, with former president Ulises Francisco Espaillat at its head. Espaillat condemned the merengue for its negative influences on those who heard it, maintaining that it "affected the nervous system too much and that it resulted in the *ailment of being unable to control the imagination*."[69] The accordion became the whipping post for merengue's detractors because it had allegedly ousted so-called typical instruments such as the *tres, cuatro,* and *seis*; this dislike may lie in the fact that the accordion's sharp sound accentuated the rhythmic aspects of merengue, and thus, its ties to African influences. In Juan Antonio Alix's "El cuatro y el acordeón," the cuatro accuses the accordion of being a short-lived fad and prophesies that worse will befall it "if something better comes along."[70] Alix's décima now seems prophetic, considering the twentieth century tirades launched against bachata.

Merengue in its different regional forms continued to gain a following, in spite of the intellectuals' literary tirades. In the Cibao region, the *merengue cibaeño* was solidifying in form on the eve of the U.S. occupation. This twentieth century invasion served as an impetus for Dominicans to seek out a defining cultural element to embrace in the face of this new foreign Other. Nationalists embraced the merengue in its different variations from across the nation as a symbolic tool of resistance. Specifically, they promoted the Cibao variant, the merengue cibaeño, as a national symbol of Dominican culture as contrasted with U.S. musical forms of the time that had become popular among the upper class prior to occupation. A group of composers worked with traditional music such as merengue, modifying the rural form to make it more appealing to upper class tastes.[71] By embracing merengue, these nationalists set the music on its path towards helping to unify and strengthen a sense of national identity.

It is important to note that Dominicans embraced a Creole musical form as the basis for their musical resistance to the U.S. occupation.[72] Forms of popular culture such as merengue have served Dominican nationalists across the years as they idealized folk and traditional cultural forms as the essence of dominicanidad.[73] The choice of merengue as a tool to emphasize a Hispanic identity in opposition to the U.S. invaders "represents a sort of reinterpretation of *hispanidad* as a creole identity."[74] Additionally, the importance of dance as a social practice within Dominican culture provided yet another point of contrast: Dominicans' ability to dance merengue fluidly as opposed to Americans' jerky attempts. Dancing therefore instilled Dominicans with a sense of dominance over their own individual bodies as well as their own music.

Conclusion

Interpreting dominicanidad reveals a complex construction of identity that has both fluid and rigid boundaries. On one hand, racial categories have been imprecise since colonial times to broaden the reach of the Hispanic group. Race and nationality overlap, as Haitian has come to equal blackness, and Dominicanness is its own unique category that emphasizes racial mixing without specificity. In spite of detailed racial differentiations, race is not fixed and can change because of its ties to social class. Nationalists saw the Dominican campesino as the essential bearer of all things Dominican when desired, or as the uncultured obstacle to modernization and progress. This same tendency for imprecision lent itself to merengue's acceptance across diverse groups of Dominicans during the U.S. occupation. In contrast, national borders are seen as rigid. The heritage of attempting to draw strict boundaries where none—or at best a very hazy one—existed would continue following the U.S. Marines' departure in 1924. By 1930, a modern-day Dominican caudillo, Rafael L. Trujillo, would capitalize on old patterns of identification to solidify a sense of national identity, and through it, his own power.

THREE

Dictatorship
and Nation-Building:
The Era of Trujillo

"That's where they killed Trujillo," Alexis pointed out as we passed the Monument to the Heroes of May 30 on our way back from an interview. I glanced at the rapidly disappearing monument. Fifty years had passed since the fateful night in 1961 when the dictator was assassinated, and yet it was impossible to forget his influence.

The thirty-year dictatorship of Rafael Leonidas Trujillo Molina marked the consolidation of a national identity based in Dominicans' Hispanic roots and an aggressive modernization. Trujillo's nation-building agenda was founded in the concepts of cultura and *progreso*. In Trujillo's nationalist project, cultura emphasized Dominican Hispanicism, as contrasted in part to the Haitian Other. Progreso, which originated as part of nineteenth-century liberal jargon, is "an idea of historical change: over time, things get better.... Progreso is how things ought to work."[1] Trujillo called for constant progress to modernize and urbanize the country; progreso likewise became analogous to social betterment, and by extension, whitening.[2] Himself a social climber of humble origins, Trujillo established a new social order in which class (and thus race) could be achieved, becoming the embodiment of both cultura and progreso.[3] These two concepts were reflected throughout Trujillo's thirty-one-year dictatorship in key areas that had long-lasting effects on the birth, growth and reception of bachata.

Trujillo's Rise to Power

Rafael Trujillo, an uneducated, former telegraph operator, rose swiftly through the ranks of the National Guard from his role as informant to an officer in little time. He was head of the National Police (formerly the National Guard) when the U.S. evacuated in 1924. Trujillo publicly supported Horacio Vásquez, but privately, he groomed the Dominican military to be loyal to him. When Vásquez fell ill before the 1930 elections, Trujillo advantageously masterminded a coup with Santiago politician Rafael Estrella Ureña. Trujillo then ran for president in the May 1930 elections, winning with a reported forty-five percent of the vote. In typical caudillo fashion, Trujillo used intimidation and violence to win; threat and fear of harm would run as underlying currents throughout the thirty years of Trujillo's regime.

Only weeks after Trujillo took power, the San Zenón hurricane of September 1930 razed the capital and devastated the country. This natural disaster inadvertently contributed to Trujillo's consolidation of power and his modernizing strategy. Trujillo emerged out of the rubble as a solid, dependable head of state in this time of need,[4] thus turning some former opponents to his favor. San Zenón's voracious appetite had destroyed much of Santo Domingo, providing Trujillo with a blank page to design the modern capital city he desired.

The San Zenón hurricane was also significant in its sudden destruction of the physical boundaries that separated lower class neighborhoods from the bourgeoisie and elite. Before the hurricane, the poor barrios were literally out of sight; after the storm, they were openly on display, and their inhabitants mingled with those of the middle and upper class barrios in public spaces. For many of the bourgeoisie and elite, "the erasure of the signs through which social identities were represented in the city was as much a part of the terror of the event as the deaths and devastation to property."[5] These classes supported Trujillo's plan to rebuild the capital as a modern urban center because it would reestablish these physical boundaries. This emphasis on urbanization and modernization established progreso as desirable; the countryside and peasant were presented as its polar opposites.[6] Both campesinos and the urban poor became viewed as an impediment to progreso, a stumbling block over which it was necessary to prevail.[7]

Reconstruction after the hurricane heightened the contrast between the city and country. Those who had come to the capital when communal lands were dissolved or seeking aid after the storm rebuilt in shantytowns known as *ranchitos*—little farms.[8] Trujillo's urban designers also underscored the ties between ramshackle housing, poverty, and moral turpitude.[9] The ranchitos bore the brunt of the upper classes' scorn because they so concretely introduced the country into the city.[10] This perceived chasm between rural and urban continued a long tradition of the conflictive images of the uncultured campesino on one hand, and of the peasant as the repository of dominicanidad on the other. Following San Zenón, the government approved legal measures to bind the campesinos to the countryside and prohibit their migration to the city.[11]

Trujillo continued to project the image of protector of the Dominican nation following the hurricane. He actively solidified the image of himself as the stalwart presence upon which progreso was dependent. This perception was made concrete through his impeccable dress, including a military dress uniform covered with medals and awards,[12] many of which were created solely for the purpose of bestowing them on the dictator. The numerous titles granted to Trujillo also reiterated his centrality to all aspects of Dominican life.[13] Trujillo was early recognized as the "Benefactor of the Fatherland" in 1932, and two years later, he was awarded an honorary doctoral degree, despite his almost complete lack of formal education. Trujillo was recognized as the "Father of the New Fatherland" in 1955, a title that emphasizes the commonly propagated belief that Trujillo had, indeed, fashioned a new nation and identity.[14]

As Hartlyn notes, Trujillo's regime did not have a concrete political ideology; instead, it was based upon the caudillo precedent of rule for personal wealth and power.[15] Trujillo exploited the strongman tradition of maintaining ties through personal loyalties and exploiting the nation as a private industry to fill his personal coffers. The spoils of the nation fell to the Dominican government as Trujillo created monopolies on numerous industries such as sugar, rice, livestock, salt, and even shoes.[16] The economy was so interwoven with the nation's political life that it was synonymous with Trujillo himself. At the time of his assassination, Trujillo controlled approximately 80 percent of industry, his firms employed 45 percent of the work force, and the state employed another 15 percent.[17] The growth and development of industry filled Trujillo's own pockets and went hand in hand with the state agenda of modernization and progress.

Forging a Dominican Identity

The identity that Trujillo actively presented joined Dominicans through a sense of belonging at a national level for the first time. Historically, regional loyalties and identities had contributed to ongoing political instability. Trujillo took advantage of notions of belonging—cultura—to purposefully sow a national sense of identity as a tool to retain power. Astutely, Trujillo drew upon the Hispanic identity articulated throughout history, heightening Dominicans' sense of belonging by aggressively opposing that identity against the Haitian as Other. Trujillo exacerbated the deeply entrenched view of Haiti and its citizens as the root of all national problems. His anti–Haitianism is, nonetheless, ironic considering that his maternal grandmother was Haitian and he was rumored to resort to divination.[18] Nonetheless, Trujillo wore his Hispanicism openly, masking any ties to Haiti just as he attempted to lighten his complexion behind the pancake make-up he wore throughout his dictatorship.[19]

In the early years of the regime, this supposed difference was played out on the contested stage of the border. In October 1937, Trujillo sanctioned the massacre of Haitian citizens on Dominican borderlands, ordering Dominican soldiers to use machetes to carry out the deed so that it would appear to have been primarily a peasant uprising.[20] Internationally, the ghastly attack was met with outrage; nationally, the Trujillo regime portrayed it as a justified act in the face of Haitian encroachment on Dominican lands, thus playing out the Spanish medieval practice of *limpieza de sangre* (blood cleansing) on New World soil.

Trujillo also solidified feelings of belonging to the regime through gift-giving, official appointments,[21] and by extending family ties through *compadrazgo*. By the latter, he became godfather of numerous Dominican children, including those of the lowest social echelons.[22] Such practices created a sense of indebtedness in recipients that precluded them from acting against the dictator.[23] Appointments to official government or military assignments also provided poorer Dominicans with the opportunity to scale the social ladder, and by extension, allowed them access to the whitening mechanism of social privilege. Conversely, Trujillo exploited others' fear of exclusion. Those in official posts feared any perceived shortcoming or accusation that would strip them of their position. Dominican citizens likewise worried over public denouncements in the *Foro Público* (Public Forum) column of the *El Caribe* newspaper. These written snippets of gossip criticized individuals for both their acts and their omissions, since insufficient praise of the dictator or regime was sufficient to label one as unpatriotic.[24]

Consequences of falling out of Trujillo's graces ranged from social ostracism to physical danger. Trujillo established threats, fear, and brutality as underlying foundations of his power. Trujillo relied on a group of organized thugs, *La 42*, and an elaborate network of spies, the *Servicio de Inteligencia Militar* (Military Intelligence Service—SIM) to report, threaten, and punish. Together, the real and imagined threats produced a pervasive sense of terror reflective of Bentham's proposed model for the ideal prison, the Panopticon. This design highlights the role of the guard/observer who watches isolated prisoners from a tower where he cannot be seen himself. The observer has the advantage of knowing each prisoner's actions while they never know if he is actually present to see them. This lack of certainty is what makes the Panopticon effective, for it produces

> a state of conscious and permanent visibility that assures the automatic functioning of power.... [T]he surveillance is permanent in its effects, even if it is discontinuous in its action.... Power should be visible and unverifiable ... the inmate must never know whether he is being looked at any one moment; but he must be sure that he may always be so.[25]

Trujillo also interwove a series of symbolic keys to access participation in the New Fatherland. He reconfigured the nation's geographic features by renaming the capital *Ciudad Trujillo* (Trujillo City) and changing the name of the highest mountain in the Caribbean, Duarte Peak, to Trujillo Peak. Slogans, poetry, and songs reiterated Trujillo's presence and kept his name literally on the tip of every Dominican's tongue.[26] Each home featured a prominently displayed picture of the dictator with the motto "God and Trujillo."

One of the most pervasive and powerful tools of repression and identity construction at Trujillo's service was the merengue. A number of reasons have been posited for Trujillo's obsession with merengue, ranging from propagandistic aims to antagonism of the elite classes and the dictator's personal musical preferences.[27] In truth, Trujillo turned his attentions to the merengue as a way to build a stronger sense of belonging among Dominicans and to control and replicate the regime on an intimate, daily level.[28] Trujillo tapped into the merengue's potential as early as his first campaign when merengue bands travelled with him to perform the merengue "*Se acabó la bulla* (The Racket Is Over),'" which celebrated his rise to power as an end to constant caudillo uprisings.[29] Trujillo's choice of merengue drew upon his first-hand knowledge of how it had served as a nationalistic symbol of resistance during the occupation and the merengue's history of documenting historical and current events.[30]

In much the same way that he gave a facelift to the capital after the hurricane, Trujillo sought to transform merengue "into a symbol of the power and modernity of his regime."[31] The dictator hired Luis Alberti and his ensemble as his personal band, and this renowned musician made several significant changes to the merengue to reflect the new image of *progreso* and to make it more palatable to the Dominican elite. These changes in instrumentation—the guitar and accordion were replaced with the saxophone, clarinet or trumpet—and the inclusion of a *paseo* section to allow couples to strut across the dance floor in their finery caused a fissure between it and the traditional merengue típico.[32] While the latter remained popular among the campesinos and lower classes, the new salon or orchestra merengue (*merengue de orquesta*) was the choice of the elite. Both genres were represented as essentially Dominican, and merengue was proclaimed the national dance.[33] This cooption of a popular music accentuates the intentionality of choice underlying it:

> the fact that elite nationalists deploy the idea of cultura popular to represent national identity does not mean that they always accept and celebrate the actual cultural practices of the Dominican poor. It means rather that nationalist intellectuals on both the left and the right frequently regard the popular customs they like as truly Dominican.[34]

The alterations made to merengue de orquesta are an accurate reflection of the dictator himself: "a dance of the *campo* with African elements covered over with lighter make-up."[35] Composers churned out merengues in honor of Trujillo and all of his acts and attributes,[36] serving as a constant flow of propaganda about his presence and greatness.

Mass media furthered merengue's penetration, allowing Trujillo vastly more possibilities for control than his caudillo predecessors of the nineteenth century. Censorship determined what was broadcast and consumed, and the dictator's brother, José "Petán" Arismendi Trujillo, founded his own radio station, *La Voz del Yuna*, in 1942.[37] Petán's radio programming, and his later incursions into television and recording, transmitted state-sanctioned news and his own musical preferences.

The Final Years

In 1955, the Dominican Republic hosted the *Feria de la paz y confraternidad del mundo libre* (Free World's Fair of Peace and Confraternity) in honor of 25 years of Trujilloism. The country served as the stage on which Trujillo could perform as the ultimate benefactor, the man who had brought peace, prosperity, and progreso to the island nation.[38] The dictator's address at the fair's dedication reiterates the role he played in the construction of dominicanidad since his rise to power in 1930: "There was delivered to me a people with a weak sense of identity, with their territory still undefined, and today I offer to my fellow-citizens a country the demarcation of whose frontiers has been completed."[39]

Despite its grandiose claims of progress and prosperity, the 1955 fair did not generate the anticipated revenue to offset its construction projects, and the same degree of financial stability would never again be attained under the regime.[40] Other events contributed to a growing dissatisfaction, such as the allegedly state-sanctioned disappearance of Jesús de Galíndez, who wrote his doctoral dissertation about the regime, and the coldblooded murder of the three Mirabal sisters who were involved in opposition activities. Although various groups contemplated the overthrow of the government, one band of primarily upper-class men eventually obtained CIA backing and weapons. These men did not embrace any particular political ideology, but rather, they were bound by ties of compadrazgo and compelled to act out of unsettled accounts and concern for future violence.[41] Even with the loss of U.S. support, the conspirators moved forward with their plan, and they ambushed and assassinated Trujillo on the night of May 30, 1961, as he made his weekly drive to his hometown.

Conclusion

The Era of Trujillo was violent and repressive. Still, Trujillo had become such a part of everyday life that many Dominicans were left adrift when the regime at last came crashing down. The end of Trujillo's rule represented far more than a change in leadership; rather, it signaled the end of an entire way of living, thinking, and being that had been mostly unchanged for thirty years. As a result, "[t]he end of the Trujillo era also provoked tremendous popular dread about the future that verged on the apocalyptic for many."[42] Clinging to the old anchors of identity provided a point of certainty for those Dominicans who were apprehensive about an uncertain future.

Trujillo solidified a sense of dominicanidad, and he recast the interwoven understandings of class and race through the lens of progreso and cultura. By doling out official positions and gifts, and by serving as an example of upward social mobility himself, Trujillo embodied the markers of whiteness and the belief that lower-class Dominicans could transform themselves racially as their social position improved.[43] In light of these wrenching changes, many Dominicans clung to the signs of identity that Trujillo had provided, including merengue as their national music. Merengue's official backing and entrenchment in the Dominican national mentality privileged it for years to come, even at the expense of the growing popularity of the guitar-based music later known as bachata.

FOUR

The Dawn of Bachata

Bachatero Edilio Paredes remembers the first bachata "*Condena* (Conviction/ Sentence)," recorded by José Manuel Calderón: "In 1962, the first recording of what we now call bachata was made. Then, it was called 'bolero de guitarra.' Everyone called it that. At that time, it wasn't called bachata."[1] Ironically—or perhaps, poetically—Calderón debuted what was later recognized as the first bachata single on May 30, 1962—one year to the day after Trujillo's death. Hindsight's clarity allows us to trace bachata back to this song, recorded on that specific date. In an interview with the *Listín Diario* to commemorate bachata's fiftieth anniversary, Calderón noted the date's significance and observed that it is no coincidence that bachata's birth coincides with the new era following Rafael L. Trujillo's assassination, since bachata helped lighten the load of those difficult times.[2]

The First Bachateros

José Manuel Calderón, the pioneer of bachata, was born August 9, 1941, in San Pedro de Macorís. After a brief stay in the capital when Calderón was 10, his family settled in Santo Domingo in 1954. Calderón's mother, who also played guitar, was his first musical influence. He recalled, "So my mother bought me a guitar, and when my father came home, that guitar was hidden so he wouldn't see it."[3] Calderón's father held a poor view of musicians, and it was only after Calderón's songs were given airplay and people began to talk that his father learned the truth. Fortunately, his father was supportive and even congratulatory.[4]

As a young adult, Calderón worked as a messenger in Santo Domingo and pursued music on the side. He formed the Trío los Juveniles, with Andrés Rodríguez on first guitar and Luis Pimentel on second guitar; in addition to the vocals, Calderón played third guitar. Together, the group began to learn by doing: playing among themselves and for local gatherings and serenades.[5] When they decided to record the demo of "¿Qué será de mí?,"[6] the trio, along with the addition of marimba, bongo and maracas, rented time in the studio at La Voz del Trópico. Ironically, Radhamés Aracena, the man whose name came to be synonymous with bachata, originally discouraged the young Calderón, at that time seeing little future in his style of music.[7] Fortunately, Calderón paid no attention and persevered. Calderón's disc jockey friends, César Bobadilla Rivera and Marco Antonio Rojas (a.k.a. Papá Rojita), made sure the demo was given airtime, and soon requests came in for Calderón's song.[8] These DJs suggested he rerecord the single using the modern studios at Radio Televisión Dominicana. Unsure if he would even be allowed to use the facilities, Calderón inquired and was allowed to rent the space and equipment. This time, the musicians exchanged the marimba for an upright bass and the maracas for a güira.[9]

Acting upon the advice of Atala Blandino, owner of the Salón Mozart, Calderón paid out of pocket to have 100 records pressed in the United States. When the records arrived, Calderón distributed half of them directly to the radio stations and sold the other half himself for two pesos each.[10] Calderón managed every aspect of his musical endeavor: "I was the producer, the salesperson, the public relations director, I was everything because ... this was something new."[11] This first release featured two remakes: the popular bolero "¿Qué será de mí?" written by Bienvenido Fabián under the original title, "*Condena*,"[12] and the B-side bolero waltz "*Borracho de amor* (Drunk on Love)." In the voice of Calderón's trio, the songs took on a new flavor, and as airplay increased, "¿Qué será de mí?" reached new levels of popularity.[13] Soon, Calderón had sold the entire first batch of records and sent to have more made.[14]

As sales continued to rise, Calderón began work on another record. His second production featured two of his own compositions, "*Lágrimas de sangre* (Tears of Blood)" and "*Muchachita linda* (Pretty Girl)."[15] Titles of other releases in the next several years (1962–1964) highlight the tone that bachata's critics later identified as "bitter": "*Quema esas cartas* (Burn Those Letters)," "*Te perdono* (I Forgive You)," "*Serpiente humana* (Human Snake)," "*Vano empeño* (Vain Endeavor)," and "*Llanto a la luna* (Crying to the Moon)."[16] Calderón's songs continued to grow in popularity, and in 1963, he signed with Kubaney Records. At the same time, contacts and travel to Puerto Rico helped spread the enthusiasm for Calderón's music abroad.[17]

Other musicians soon followed in Calderón's footsteps, attracted by the new sound: "They started joining us because it's contagious."[18] Then, bachata was still considered bolero de guitarra or romantic guitar music and "at that time, it wasn't discriminated against."[19] Singing in a similarly plaintive, emotional style reminiscent of sobbing, Rafael Encarnación debuted in October 1963 with a recording of his own compositions, "*Muero contigo* (I Die with You)" and the B-side "*Pena de hombre* (A Man's Pain)." Encarnación's "Muero contigo" contained the hallmark themes of many a bachata: abandonment, desamor, and in the face of it all, undying love. Of humble beginnings, university student Rafael Encarnación offered a new possibility to bachata. Tommy García remembers that Encarnación dressed formally in a suit and tie, a look akin to bolero tradition. Encarnación died tragically in a traffic accident in March 1964 after recording only eleven songs of his own composition.[20]

Inocencio Cruz's 1964 debut recording, "*Amorcito de mi alma* (Sweet Love of My Soul)" continued in the same vein of sentimiental voicing. Punctuated by cries of "¡Ay, ay, ay, ay, ay!," the lyrics promise eternal love. Cruz's second hit, "*Mal pago* (Poor Recompense)," was a remake of the bolero "*Amor gitano* (Gypsy Love)" whose lyrics incorporated ever more vivid images of pain and suffering. This song paints the bitterness of the narrator's discovery that his beloved has been unfaithful. After reproaching her heartless treatment in return for his undying love, he begs her to slit his wrists, since life has no meaning without her.

Bernardo Ortiz also released a popular romantic bachata in 1964, "*Dos rosas*

(Two Roses)." This song's sweet lyrics inextricably link bachata with emotion, presenting the two roses as a song in and of themselves. Throughout the song, the roses speak for the narrator, expressing his love and adoration, and begging his beloved not to disappoint him. Given that the title and content of the song focus specifically on two roses, the implication is that they carry a secondary message—likely, "I love you," which is only two words in Spanish: *Te amo.* The sentiments expressed in *"Dos rosas"* could well be the content in the minds of those who say that bachata was a way to communicate feelings that one did not dare say for fear of rejection. Producer and musician Davicito Paredes notes, "you can say things that are hard to say with song. That's bachata."[21]

Raffo el Soñador's (the Dreamer, Rafael Alcántara) songs were among the saddest of this early wave of musicians. From the beginning, Raffo's bachatas projected a certain fatalism reflective of the difficulties and debilitating blows he was dealt in life. As a child, Raffo shined shoes; as an adult, he would lose his wife and child in a traffic accident in New York.[22] Although Batista Matos maintains that Raffo's songs are more rhythmic boleros than bachata,[23] the bitterness expressed in them is certainly in line with the emotions of other early bachatas. In *"No me hablen de ella* (Don't Talk About Her to Me)," the narrative voice begs his listeners—likely a group of friends—not to speak of his lost love, preferring to weep undisturbed. *"El soñador* (The Dreamer)" centers on the common bachata theme of *desengaño* (disillusionment).[24] In this bachata, the singer contrasts his dreams of love and happiness with the emptiness and solitude he feels when fate unexpectedly steals his love. Raffo's lyrics were genuine, born of his life experiences. As the title of one song reveals, he had suffered a *"Cadena de tragedias* (Chain of Tragedies)." Toward the end of his life, Rafael Alcántara would wander aimlessly through the streets of Santo Domingo; in 1985, at the age of 41, he took his own life.[25]

Production and Consumption of Early Bachata

Although this emotional guitar music had a significant following, it enjoyed neither the popular support of the middle and upper classes nor the financial backing of the already-entrenched national music, merengue. Merengue, which had enjoyed the official backing of the Dominican state under the three decades of the Trujillato, had a broad national following and a long history with record labels. Merengue reached across lines of social class, age, and gender with its two different styles, merengue típico and merengue de orquesta. Further, merengue enjoyed the support of investors. Some of bachata's original criticism and discrimination arose from those who had a vested interest in merengue. Realizing that bachata had a significant following among the masses, "those who had invested a lot in merengue spoke harshly about bachata to stop it, so it wouldn't continue."[26]

Bachata was associated with and consumed by the inhabitants of the barrios populares and the campesinos who had migrated to them.[27] As musician Vicente García observes, musical tastes became "a way to mark class lines."[28] Seen by the middle class as backward, uncouth and without value, live performances of bachata were usually in small venues such as neighborhood gatherings or bars. Record play was likewise relegated to a limited scene that included jukeboxes in cabarets, brothels, and colmados. Although bachata was barred entrance to the large-scale venues available to merengue, it was not without a significant fan base. Bachata musicians catered to their audience's taste for guitar music, and often remade popular boleros or ballads.[29]

Calderón describes the production of early bachata as very personal,[30] in large part because record companies were not interested in it. Without the equipment, advice, or financial support of a label, musicians found themselves responsible for every aspect of recording, promotion, distribution, and sales. Lacking professional backing, the music was produced, performed and distributed wholly within the informal sector. All costs were paid out of pocket, which in turn affected the quality of the records. Musicians had to rent time and space in recording studios, where they would lay down their production on a single track; retakes in such a setting were costly. Since musicians paid for studio time, they tended to release only singles and rarely produced long plays. Musicians did not earn royalties, as their counterparts in merengue did, and payments usually consisted of a small sum paid only once.[31]

Musicians were also responsible for distributing records themselves by selling them on the street corner or for play on jukeboxes. In those years, an average sale of 7,000 to 8,000 records for jukebox play was common.[32] The Trujillo family had inadvertently contributed to these jukebox sales, since the dictator's brother, José "Petán" Arismendi Trujillo, imported them in the 1950s. Petán made his profits off the machines by placing them in local colmados and collecting fifty percent of the profits.[33]

Barrio life often revolved around these small corner stores where local residents purchased food and household supplies and exchanged news and gossip. The colmado's proximity coupled with the need to purchase just enough to get by made it a center of social and commercial exchange in the barrios.[34] Here, merchants understood the economic plight of their clients, often selling them only the amount they needed of a product for a few cents or *cheles*.[35] The colmado was much more than a place for doing business. It was the social center of a neighborhood, a place for sharing news, having fun, getting to know and know about other members of the community.[36] Already a center for congregating and inexpensive socializing, the colmados became a primary distributor of the new sound of bachata as it played in the background for clients, passersby, and everyone in earshot.

Even before this romantic *música de guitarra* had its own name, it had its own following among residents of the poor, urban barrios and shantytowns. Bachata was also a staple in the bars, cabarets, and brothels of these neighborhoods, all venues that did not endear it to the middle and upper classes: "people criticized it before because it was bar music."[37] In addition to the guardias (low-ranking military men) referenced by one of its names, bachata was popular among many whose harsh realities and disillusions were often portrayed in its lyrics. These associations with the lower class contributed to its discrimination "because it came from so low."[38]

Because of this popularity base, bachata was present in the servants' quarters in more affluent homes of the middle and upper classes. Young women, leaving their homes in search of work as domestic workers in middle-class homes, took the music with them. These women "basically made it a condition to have a radio ... in the kitchen so they could work comfortably. So, in all of the middle-class homes, chores were done listening to the music of the marginalized."[39] Across the country, housework and chores were done to an ongoing soundtrack of bachata. The family could and did hear the music over the radio as their domestic help listened. Susana Silfa recalls that as a child, "I would go to a place behind the house and I'd start daydreaming and singing there.... The servants' quarters was close by and I listened to Radio Guarachita."[40]

Middle-class Dominicans, however, criticized the music and its performers as backward and tasteless. Bachata's association first with rural migrants to the city, then with the brothels, and later, with the lower-class domestic workers who listened to it as they did their work, marked it with a stigma that was difficult to overcome. Playing bachata in earshot of others was likely to have middle-class Dominicans accused of being a peasant. Edilio Paredes remembers that people would say, "'That's peasants' music, the music of people without cultura or manners."[41] Similarly, Gerson Corniel relates that others said to him, "Oh, you're a peasant—you play the guitar."[42] This is not to say that there were no bachata aficionados among the middle and upper classes; rather, they were closet fans of the music, listening out of earshot[43] and "clandestinely."[44]

The style of dancing bachata—couples held in close embrace with the lights down low, much as the bolero was danced—also contributed to the middle class's rejection and condemnation. At that time, a woman might hesitate to dance a bolero unless her partner were her fiancé or husband, since doing so was practically "a declaration of love."[45] Given that this was the reaction with bolero, the even stronger reaction to bachata is not surprising, considering its associations with Santo Domingo's brothels.[46]

In those times, bachateros also ran the risk of being openly scorned by the music's critics.[47] Bachatero Eladio Romero Santos vividly remembers being called a *comesopa* (soup-eater), a reference to the only staple a poor musician could afford, and also *pasacantando* (one who spends his time singing), a valorization of someone's activities as having no future.[48] Similarly, Gerson Corniel remembers being called "mediocre" because he performed bachata.[49] Luis Segura recalls having to hide his guitar when he was walking down the street to avoid the ridicule of others.[50] Leonardo Paniagua was insulted with *dañadiscos* (record ruiner) because his first recording had been a bachata remake of a popular ballad, something seen by bachata's detractors as ruining a perfectly good song.[51] Edilio Paredes relates that both eggs and insults were hurled at him while performing, and his son, Davicito Paredes, shared a story that another musician told about being asked to get off public transportation when others found out he was a bachatero.[52] The derogatory terms used to refer to their bolero de guitarra were just as insulting. Edilio Paredes admitted that he stopped recording for a time after hearing his record referred to as a cachivache (knickknack), which carried the connotations of something worthless.[53] Susana Silfa's sister remarked to her "that it was good I'd changed my name so she wouldn't have to say she was my sister."[54]

This aggressive vocal discrimination and recrimination of bachata was based on far more than musical preferences. Such a visceral reaction can be attributed in part to the degree to which Dominicans' musical identity had been bound to merengue. As we have seen, many Dominicans felt adrift when the world as they knew it under Trujillo came crashing down. Strong opinions about musical preference and which genre should be considered the national music had a long history in the Dominican Republic, as evidenced by the nineteenth century's heated literary campaigns against the merengue's potential to displace the tumba. Given the uncertainty of Dominican politics in the early 1960s, and later, of the Dominican economic and social situations, it is not surprising that many clung to the merengue as a symbol of their Hispanic identity.

The passionate campaign against bachata also arises from questions of race and class. Cultura as a measure of belonging had deep roots. Although cultura originally was linked to all things Hispanic, over time, it came to be a marker of social class and a mechanism for distinguishing between social classes.[55] Similarly, lower- and middle-class Dominicans tended to use the construct of cultura as a marker of racial community, instead of seeing race as determined by phenotype or skin color.[56] Trujillo had exploited this sense of belonging by embodying the myth of social advancement (and thus whitening),[57] which some may have seen as threatened by the arrival of a rural, lower-class (read "black") music.

Cultura was easily recognizable in those with *buenas costumbres*—respectable people—and was utterly lacking in those without. Different spaces within the nation or even a given neighborhood could either edify buenas costumbres and cultura, or be quite the opposite: centers of perdition.[58] These were the very locations where bachata was being played. Such a polarizing distinction contributed to divisions of identity based not only on questions of class and race, but also on this notion of respectability. Describing the bolero de guitarra as "una bachata" was meant to be an insult, and the intended message was that it was peasants' music and without cultura.[59] Rural musicians' mispronunciation of words or inarticulate diction also fueled the middle and upper classes' disdain of bachata: "the diction and word pronunciation were wrong. So, it bothered an educated person to hear a recording with mispronunciations."[60] Through their harsh criticisms of bachata, middle- and upper-class Dominicans were essentially defining who they were by maintaining who they were not: lower-class, black, and unrefined. For the new migrants to Santo Domingo, the identification process was quite the opposite. Bachata's audience, drawing from the poor sectors of society both in rural and urban settings, saw itself reflected in the songs and lives of bachata musicians. For these people, the bachatero "was the mirror that reflected the face of amorous afflictions, the faces of misery and the value of life."[61]

Radio Guarachita

Despite his initial rejection of bachata and refusal to include it on his radio programs, producer and radio announcer Radhamés Aracena's keen sense of business and promotion eventually led him to reconsider. Aracena realized that there was a massive audience listening to the increasingly popular genre. Tommy García emphasizes the mutually beneficial relationship between Aracena and the new style of music: "What makes it popular? This businessman's realization that it's easier for him to compete with a new station when he already has this new massive audience inhabiting the city."[62]

Since even poorly produced bachata records sold well, Aracena opted to capitalize on the broad consumer base and current Dominican musical preferences. In 1964, Aracena installed his second-hand equipment and debuted his new station by playing nothing but popular music—until ordered by the government to at least identify the station—to stimulate interest and to grow audience expectations. Aracena took his station officially on the air in March 1965, but it suffered a setback that same year when civil war erupted and sent it off the air. When Radio Guarachita reopened for broadcasting in 1966, Aracena discarded his earlier model and instead, dedicated his station to the Dominican guitar-based music and its constantly growing body of consumers.[63] Radio Guarachita became "the first and only station at that time that played bachata."[64]

Aracena not only featured the guitar music on Radio Guarachita, he also recorded it. Aracena was involved in each phase of the recording and distribution process of his label, Discos la Guarachita, to produce what he deemed a quality product. Aracena auditioned potential musicians himself, recording the songs he liked. Later, Aracena transcribed the songs' lyrics and corrected grammatical errors and any linguistic links that might belie the singers' social class or regional origins.[65] He then required the artist to learn the song again in its corrected form before recording it for release. In this way, the music produced by Aracena, while retaining the style and emotion of bachata, was more accessible to the diverse fan base from different regions of the country.[66] Radio Guarachita was a well-played business venture. Aracena was an astute businessman, and his station featured only those artists whom he himself produced and those productions to which he held distribution rights. Bachatero Tony Santos recognizes Aracena's business savvy: "I have to admit he was a businessman. Because he looked for singers. I mean, if you took him a record, he wouldn't play it. You had to record it with him."[67] The increased visibility effectively created a demand, and Aracena profited from supplying it.

Radio Guarachita not only played bachata, it also entrenched itself in all aspects of its audience's lives. For one, Aracena's recognition of these new migrants as a viable audience gave them a presence in an atmosphere where they were marginalized. Additionally, Radio Guarachita very swiftly became the link, both concrete and symbolic, between migrants to the nation's cities and those who remained behind in the countryside. Aracena promoted and facilitated interaction between listeners and the station by installing a telephone in the booth. Listeners could call in with requests, or to broadcast a message to friends and family over the radio. These messages, known as *servicios públicos* or public service announcements, were especially important in maintaining ties to home at a time when the Dominican Republic had limited and questionable telephone and mail services.[68] These messages were often very personal and specific in nature, ranging from a notice that a migrant would be returning home for a visit on a certain date and the family should meet him at a given location, to the newly-arrived campesino's attempts to locate a relative in Santo Domingo.[69] Similarly, a popular program on Sundays was the *programa de saludos*, a show dedicated to sending out *saludos* (greetings).[70] In addition to telephone interaction, Radio Guarachita opened its doors to listeners. The station allowed the audience to come and watch broadcasts from the DJ's booth, which was elevated for better viewing.[71]

As a whole, this style of programming helped cement feelings of unity among listeners, fulfilling much the same role as other "cultural product[s]"[72] that join individuals by linking their actions with the awareness that others are consuming the very same product. Anderson describes this consumption as a "mass ceremony":

> It is performed in silent privacy, in the lair of the skull. Yet each communicant is well aware that the ceremony he performs is being replicated simultaneously by thousands (or millions) of others of whose existence he is confident, yet of whose identity he has not the slightest notion. Furthermore, the ceremony is incessantly repeated ... throughout the calendar. What more vivid figure for the ... imagined community can be envisioned?[73]

Thus, listening to bachata "became both a social and an individual act."[74]

Radio Guarachita helped spread bachata's popularity quickly and effectively[75] and lent itself to feelings of belonging while easing the alienating sense of the anonymity of urban life: "it was their link to all they'd left behind."[76] Similarly, the station contributed to a sense of community among listeners of different geographical locations by joining urban and rural patrons across the nation as they listened to the same music and messages. Radio Guarachita, with its mechanisms for linking the city with the countryside and providing a growing audience with the music it preferred, transformed its audience into both consumers of music and producers of their life stories, giving voice to a population that, in many ways, was silenced.

Recognition of a New Genre

Although bachata was not recognized as a separate genre until the 1970s, it increasingly developed its own style in the 1960s as artists continued to produce their romantic music, infusing their songs with their own style. This was especially the case with the bachata boleros sung by Luis Segura, known as *"el Añoñaíto"*—"the crybaby." This name referred to Segura's interpretive style, which seemed to those who were not fans as the sound of a whiner (*ñoño*). For Segura, he was a romantic singer and his style was merely the way he expressed himself and "sang delicately."[77]

Like many bachateros before him, Luis Segura was born in the countryside (Mao) and later moved to Santo Domingo. A self-taught musician, Segura's model was the popular bolero trios and singers of the time whom he sought to imitate.[78] These early influences remained with Segura throughout his career, and he has and continues to be a singer of romantic bachata, or bachata boleros. Segura's first recording, *"Cariñito de mi vida* (Love of My Life)" (1964), emphasized the singing voice's suffering and the woman's guilt for withholding her love. His emotional singing style and lyrics made Segura a hit with this and subsequent recordings.[79]

Bachata guitarist and singer Edilio Paredes first recorded with Luis Segura as part of this early bachata. Born in the countryside near San Francisco de Macorís in 1945, Edilio Paredes was only four when he first picked up a stringed instrument, the *tres*, in the local colmado. This self-taught musician left for Santo Domingo at the age of thirteen, where he found work in singer and musician Cuco Valoy's record store.[80] Valoy also produced and recorded artists on his own label, and Paredes began to play guitar on these productions. Not long thereafter, Paredes recorded for Rhadamés Aracena, playing first guitar for many of the big names on the Guarachita label and also recording his own songs.[81]

Edilio Paredes's unique style of playing was influential in the evolution of both bachata and merengue de cuerdas. Paredes artfully imitated the voices of the merengue's accordion on the guitar, increasing the tempo and making the rhythm more marked and conducive to dancing.[82] In Paredes's dexterous hands, the intricate figures borrowed from merengue and interpreted in the voice of the guitar lent a new sound to bachata, contributing to its distinction from the bolero.[83] Edilio Paredes was also influential in opening bachata to a more diverse audience through the *Lunes de amargue* shows that he helped launch, along with other renowned bachata artists Augusto Santos, Leonardo Paniagua, Ramón Cordero, and Isidro Cabrera "el Chivo sin Ley."[84] The show's format and venue brought in audiences from different social classes. It contributed to bachata's move into a broader consumer base and began to erode the stigma that had been associated with it.[85]

Leonardo Paniagua Alberto, who recorded some eight hundred romantic bachatas, describes his career as beginning by chance.[86] Born on August 5, 1950, in Las Yayas, La Vega, Dominican Republic, Paniagua had begun working as a messenger for the National Institute of Potable Water (*Instituto Nacional de Aguas Potables—INAPA*) at a salary of just 58 pesos and 80 cents.[87] One afternoon in 1973, Paniagua went for a haircut, and his barber, Danilo Rodríguez, invited him to stay for a musical rehearsal he was hosting that afternoon. Once the group had finished rehearsing, Rodríguez invited his guest to sing. Paniagua sang the only song he knew, the popular "*Amada amante* (Beloved Lover)." Impressed, Rodríguez asked Paniagua to accompany him the following day to Rhadamés Aracena's studio where he had an appointment to record.[88]

The next day, Rodríguez had to ask Aracena's permission so Paniagua could even be present in the studio. Aracena consented, but with a warning not to make a sound: "Rhadamés let me in and let me sit at a little table, but told me not to make a sound while he was recording."[89] Paniagua sat motionless throughout the recording process, and at its conclusion, Rodríguez asked Aracena to listen to Paniagua sing. Again, Aracena agreed, and Paniagua sang Roberto Carlos's "Amada amante" accompanied by Rodríguez's band. Unbeknownst to Paniagua, Aracena had left the recording equipment running. Dually impressed, Aracena asked him to sing another song, and Paniagua had to admit that he'd already sung the only one he knew. He offered to sing "Amada amante" a second time, but Aracena liked the first take, and he insisted Paniagua sing something else. Paniagua repeated again that he didn't know another song, but Aracena was adamant that he had to have a side B. According to Paniagua, "we stayed and it was three in the morning. He wouldn't let us leave; he had the key. And I said, 'Well, I've heard a song....' It was called '*Insaciable* (Insatiable)' ... [Rhadamés said].... 'I have that on a record. I'll copy it off.' So he put the lyrics on the stand and I recorded it by reading them."[90]

The romantic "Amada amante," which sings of the beauty of unselfish love, was an instant hit. Paniagua continued recording romantic bachatas, following his first hit with "*Un beso y una flor* (A Kiss and a Flower)" (1973), a remake of a ballad by Spanish pop singer, Nino Bravo. Paniagua had numerous hits over the next several years, and was invited to appear on Yaqui Núñez del Risco's *Show del mediodía* television program. Despite his success, Paniagua did not enjoy significant income from his work at that time due to a combination of factors, including merengue's domination of the music market, and bachata's production and distribution within the informal sector.[91]

In 1979, Paniagua's popularity skyrocketed with his bachata remake of the Swedish group ABBA'S hit, "*Chiquitita.*" This song reached new levels of national and international popularity and earned Paniagua a nomination for the El Dorado Prize's Singer of the Year.[92] More than one Dominican friend has shared with me a favorite story based on a play on words with the title of the song, a diminutive of "little girl." According to the story, a fan was listening to Paniagua's hit on a jukebox and liked it so much that he loudly stated, "Play me '*Chiquitita*' until she grows up!" The song was such a hit that it was given airplay on radio stations that had not included bachata before. In spite of such popularity, bachata as a genre continued to be marked and criticized as a lower-class music of little artistic value. "Bachata was considered bad for the country. Including a song with that sound was seen as bad for society."[93]

Conclusion

Bachata dawned at a crossroads in Dominican history. Borne on the wave of rural migrants to the capital city, the early bachatas were commonly guitar remakes of popular Latin American boleros interpreted by primarily self-taught musicians. Bachata was not discriminated against in its early years, although its principal audience consisted of the rural and urban lower classes. Later, as its presence grew with the continued influx of rural migrants to the city and the outreach of Radio Guarachita, bachata increasingly became the target of middle- and upper-class criticism and scorn. Early interpreters of the romantic guitar music did not enjoy equal access to recording opportunities in the shadow of the national music, merengue. This was reflected in the sound of their recordings, which contributed to criticisms of poor quality.

Longstanding constructions of race and class also ran as strong undercurrents in the discrimination against bachata and highlighted the ongoing tensions between rural and urban areas. Many of the peasants flocking to the capital from the southern regions of the country were dark-skinned, and therefore seen as backward and poor. These peasants did not have a place in the essentialists' view of the Dominican campesino as the purest essence of dominicanidad. The ties between race and social class reflected blackness upon the poor musicians who played and recorded bachata. The word "bachata" was originally an insult of the urban middle and upper classes, reflecting their opinion that it lacked artistic value.

The unsure footing following Trujillo's assassination also contributed to the early rejection of bachata. In the face of the uncertainty of that time, many Dominicans clung to the identity anchors that Trujillo's nation-building agenda had provided, among them the national music, merengue. The debates about bachata and the offensive insults directed at it and its interpreters reiterate the tradition of perceiving musical identities as unchangeable. Just as merengue's critics condemned it when it threatened and eventually replaced the tumba, bachata's detractors went on the offensive against its growing popularity. Embracing bachata at this time would have constituted an open acknowledgment of blackness, of a worthy contribution by the rural and urban poor. Bachata's critics instead opted for the heritage of progreso and modernization, seeing the campesino and poor as obstacles. Rather than fly in the face of the imposed national music, merengue, the Dominican bourgeoisie and elite instead attempted to maintain the status quo.

FIVE

Bachata's Many Faces: From the Red-Light District to Rose-Colored Bachata

We had seen the same shoeshine boy, Eduardo, every day on our afternoon trek home from the Santiago preschool where we worked that summer. Once he accepted the fact that we didn't want to have our tennis shoes shined, he asked us other questions: where were we from? What was it like? What were we doing in the Dominican Republic? When we mentioned the name of the preschool where we were volunteering, he nodded in understanding. "Oh, I used to go there to eat when I was a kid!"

Looking back on Eduardo's comment, it gives a personal face to the ongoing undercurrent of need and unemployment that continued in the Dominican Republic across different administrations. Across the years, economic crises have pulled increasingly more Dominicans into the lower class. Rates of poverty continue to be high, with over 40 percent of Dominicans falling below the poverty line.[1] These crises also contributed to the growth of the Dominican transnational community with the ongoing migration of significant numbers abroad. As a result, more Dominicans at home and abroad became familiar with the conditions, suffering, and longing for times past represented in bachata. Although double entendre bachata was popular in the 1980s and early 1990s, softer, romantic lyrics coupled with innovations and experimentation with instrumentation and lyrical content and interpretation helped bachata reach new fans.

Singing the Blues

The worsening economy of the late 1970s and early 1980s pulled more rural women to the cities and encouraged more women to work outside the home. Women commonly found work more readily than men, since they were paid a lower wage. Their involvement in the public workplace affected the traditional Dominican family and marriage practices, and their financial solvency meant that they did not have to depend on a husband.[2] Consensual marriage became more common and gave women more decision-making responsibility within a couple or family.[3] Women's participation in the workplace made them essentially street-walkers, "*mujeres de la calle* as they enjoyed increased access to … public spaces,"[4] and the government was quick to blame the nation's high birthrates on female barrio residents' consensual relationships (often serial in nature) and men's failure to recognize their offspring.[5] This shift in roles also contradicted the long-standing Dominican machista "notion of what it means to be a good man … [that accepts] … that the man has to be a good father, providing for his *mujer*, or woman, and children."[6] Now, many economically independent women found themselves supporting men who discovered themselves adrift in this new reality.

Bachata kept pace with these changes. Lyrics increasingly depicted men searching for solace outside the home and family nucleus, in the bottom of a bottle or the one-night-stand relationships of the brothels.[7] Lyrics also portrayed conversations among male friends as they commiserated in bars. Pacini Hernandez's review of bachata lyrics shows that the narrative voice of most early bachatas spoke to a second-person listener; in contrast, 1980s bachata lyrics tended to talk about the woman indirectly through use of the third person.[8] Bachata's lyrics and tone were so bitter that its detractors called it música de amargue.

Luis Segura figured prominently in bachata's history in 1983. That year, Segura released the album *Pena* (Sorrow) with his signature weeping style of interpretation. The title song, in which the narrator bemoans his love's lack of understanding, marked the first mainstream bachata hit on a broad scale. Suddenly, bachata was in the lime-light and in a positive way. Such was the sudden interest in the genre outside of the lower classes that it produced something equivalent to bachata fever.[9]

Segura and bachata became the center of national attention when students at the Universidad Autónoma de Santo Domingo (UASD) invited him to perform in 1983, and university president, Joaquín Bidó Medina, forbade bachata performances on campus,[10] an action reminiscent of nineteenth-century attacks on merengue's supposed indecency. The resulting scandal criticized the president and university as out of touch with the Dominican people and especially, the large percentage of UASD students who came from the countryside.[11] Sergio Reyes, writing in *Fuero* (the University Employees Association's publication), maintained that such individual and cultural tastes "are carried within, like one's own blood."[12] In Reyes's opinion, bachata's message was superficial, but he insisted, "we should never deny its cultural and popular worth, as that would be like denying who we are to ourselves."[13] The UASD scandal brought national attention to bachata and questions of musical identification.

Double Entendre Bachata

Bachata's lyrics grew increasingly racy in the 1970s and 1980s. While musicians such as José Manuel Calderón, Luis Segura, and Leonardo Paniagua continued to record romantic bachata, others began to introduce highly suggestive and thinly veiled double entendres in cabaret bachata. Tony Santos, the most popular double entendre bachatero of the 1980s, left the countryside and moved to Santo Domingo at age 18 with the dream of being a romantic singer. Santos emotionally recalls the opportunity Marino Pérez gave him to record in 1977. Late one Sunday afternoon, Santos approached Pérez and explained that he liked to sing. Pérez told him to come the following day to sing for him, an offer that seemed almost unbelievable: "I was trembling because someone wanted to record me!"[14] Santos admitted he didn't have the money to pay for a recording, but Pérez insisted, and once he heard Santos, asked him to sing a second piece.

After this fortuitous start in 1977, Santos became the leader of double entendre bachata in the 1980s, employing sexually charged plays on words and theatrical, suggestive dance steps on stage. Santos, along with Julio Ángel and Blas Durán, became the favorites of this lucrative style of bachata. One of Santos's best-known songs, *"Mamá me lo contó"*—literally, "Mother Told Me"—was a crafted play on words charged with sexual overtones. When the individual words of the title are run together as *"mámamelo con to,"* it means something more along the lines of "suck it with everything you've got."[15] Despite criticisms of what was diplomatically labeled as double entendre or cabaret bachata, and more often identified as obscene, Santos's 1986 hit *"Amarilis, échame agua* (Amarilis, Pour Water on Me)" proved that this kind of bachata sold. In this number, the singer begs Amarilis to cool him off by dousing him with water, a double entendre for sexual relations. All outcries of indecency aside, this song earned Santos airplay on mainstream radio stations and television spots.

Julio Ángel is another singer from the countryside[16] who made it big with the double entendres of cabaret bachata. Ángel, who remembers going hungry more than once as a youth, was enthralled with the music he heard on the radio and from live trios, and he remembers one of the first bachatas he heard, Raffo el Soñador's *"Tiniebelas* (Darkness)."[17] Ángel purchased his first guitar for eleven pesos using most of his winnings from the *quiniela* lottery. Although he gave his mother two pesos from his windfall, Ángel didn't admit how he got them, nor that he had purchased a guitar, claiming instead that someone loaned it to him. After several days and at his mother's insistence that he return the guitar to its rightful owner, Ángel took a stroll through town, lingering as long as possible. When he returned, he told his mother that the guitar's owner said he could borrow it a while longer. Ángel was thrilled: "So I kept my old guitar. I didn't know how to tune it or anything else."[18]

Eventually, Ángel decided to try his luck in the capital. He arrived in Santo Domingo with only a vague idea of how to locate an uncle there. His uncle's situation was little better, and he told Ángel he would have to leave, loaning him four pesos for bus fare. Fortunately, Ángel found work and stayed. During this time, he listened to Radio Guarachita and dreamed of singing. He eventually saved enough money to record his first record in 1971.[19] Ángel continued to record thereafter, and his 1983 hit, *"El salón* (The Salon),"* is another example of none-too-subtle double meanings. This song relies heavily on rhyme and word similarity; for example, the word for comb, *peine*, sounds very similar to the word for penis, *pene*. The title and setting for the song, the salon, also rhymes with *pajón*, which in this case referred to the woman's pubic hair or "bush." Indeed, the association with the latter meaning led many to refer to the song as *"El pajón."*

Singer Blas Durán started his career singing bachata boleros, but he became better known for his double entendre bachatas and merengues de cuerda. His 1970 *"Clavelito* (Little Carnation)" featured the narrator's sweet comparison of his beloved's mouth to a red carnation. Durán's subsequent songs of the 1970s and early 1980s reflected the changing social realities. The narrative voice of *"Equivocada* (Mistaken),"* for example, portrays a machista point of view—he has many lovers but loves none of them—and emphasizes that the woman erroneously believed she had broken his heart. Given the limited opportunities available to bachata because of merengue's dominance of the market, Durán began to pursue the more profitable merengue genre in the early 1970s. Durán sang for several different bands and singers, including top merengueros such as Johnny Ventura and Joseíto Mateo.[20]

Durán also recorded his own cabaret bachata. "*El huevero* (The Egg Vendor)" portrays a man who is unable to find work and as a result, has to sell *huevos*—eggs— slang for testicles. In addition to having to sell eggs (i.e., prostitute himself), his sweetheart is demanding, and in a role inversion, he must feed his ravenous lover who wants nothing but eggs—hard (boiled) and big. Durán's 1986 merengue de cuerdas, "*La arepa*," centers around the same theme of a vendor selling his wares, in this case, *arepas*, sweetened cornmeal cakes. This narrator calls to his neighbor to come get a piece of his *arepa*, but then warns her not to handle it too much or his sales will go down. In addition to the popularity of such sexually overt double entendres, these songs also present the social realities of men in desperate search of work.

The Changing Sound of Bachata

In the mid–1980s, Blas Durán began experimenting with his sound and style. His 1986 cabaret bachata, "*El motorcito* (The Little Motorcycle)," was the first to feature an electric lead guitar playing repetitive lines at a faster tempo.[21] The narrator explains that he bought a motorcycle since he doesn't have a car. The economic implications of this statement are clear: a motorcycle is all he can afford. This mode of transportation, however, is completely acceptable and appropriate for the woman in his life, since she always likes to have his motorcycle running and to ride it.

Durán continued to experiment with these new sounds in his smash hit, "*Consejo a las mujeres* (Advice to Women)." This merengue de cuerdas marked a significant milestone, since its innovations were carried over to bachata. Most notable was the instrumentation featuring an electric guitar and the inclusion of merengue's güira instead of bachata's usual maracas.[22] Recording on multiple tracks improved production and sound quality.[23] "Consejo a las mujeres" was also a hit because of its cheeky double entendres. This song inserted itself into everyday speech with its shouted first words directed to women to catch their attention: "*¡Mujeres hembras!* (Female Women!)" The phrase stuck as a secondary title to this popular merengue, which "transcended all sectors of Dominican society."[24] Durán integrated these same innovations to his bachata, and his "success helped bring bachata's popularity to a level where the mainstream media had no choice but to embrace it."[25] Durán's style laid the foundation for a new generation of bachateros to build upon it.

Tecno Bachata

Nueva Canción Influence

Several Dominican musicians who influenced bachata in the 1990s had their roots in *Nueva Canción* (New Song), a movement that originated in the South American

Southern Cone region in the late 1950s and early 1960s as a renewed interest in folk music. Middle-class students fused a variety of styles with traditional folk forms and instruments, brought to the cities by indigenous and rural migrants seeking improved economic and social conditions. Nueva Canción lyrics challenged political and social ills throughout Latin America, and thus this movement was "a dual project of roots recovery and social criticism."[26] Throughout the region, it served as a lens through which to examine everything from traditions to the current social, political, and cultural condition, and as an avenue for change.

Convite, a group of Dominican politically active academics, musicians and folklorists, embraced Nueva Canción and its premise of social change through music. As in other parts of Latin America, the return to folk forms and their use as the basis for experimentation was central to Convite's mission. Musically, Convite was particularly opposed to the commercialization of popular culture and how financial interests deformed the nature of this music. Therefore, members of Convite participated in research and fieldwork to uncover the roots of folk and traditional musical forms, with the intention of preservation, experimentation, and education of the general public.[27]

Yo quiero andar

Composer and musician Luis Días was a member of Convite and the Dominican Nueva Canción movement. Días's musical experimentations included the blending of elements of Dominican folk music with genres such as jazz, rock, and blues. Días recorded little, dedicating his time primarily to composing and to exploring musical fusions during the 1970s and 1980s.[28] Like other bachateros, Días recognized the possibilities available to the guitar by imitating the role of the saxophone in merengue. Tommy García, who knew Días, relates that he once discovered him practicing a saxophone methods primer. When pressed, Días explained that he first had to understand the saxophone technique to be able to do the same on his guitar.[29]

Días's musical exploration ventured into bachata, and he introduced its musical and lyrical elements into several compositions performed at that time but never recorded.[30] Días also embraced the streets and life of those who consumed bachata, and he moved into a brothel to live within the atmosphere of cabaret bachata.[31] This experiential knowledge combined with Días's musical studies placed him in a unique position to significantly alter bachata's path. In 1988, producer Cholo Brenes approached Días with the idea of collaborating on a production with Sonia Silvestre, a popular ballad singer. Días agreed, provided that it was a bachata production.[32] This was a daring project, given the still-prevalent discrimination against bachata. Nevertheless, Brenes and Silvestre accepted and began work with musician Manuel Tejada to produce the long play, *Yo quiero andar* (I Want to Walk) (1989), which included five bachatas. In addition to the better recording options available to these artists, the album's instrumentation was entirely produced by synthesizers. This unique electronic sound inspired its creators to christen it with a new name: *tecno bachata* or *tecno amargue*.[33]

In contrast to the sound of tecno bachata, the album's lyrics were similar to bachata boleros that had been sung for almost thirty years. The title song, "Yo quiero andar," expresses the female narrator's wish to leave her lover and travel to a place where he cannot find, hit, or abuse her. "Andresito Reyna" relates how the title character's gambling and alcohol addictions lead to his demise. "*Mi guachimán* (My Watchman/Guard)" tells of the dangers faced by a woman who likes to go out and have a good time when preyed upon by men with bad intentions. The Días/Silvestre/Tejada collaboration marked the first big break for bachata into a broader audience that crossed social and class lines. Without a doubt, bachata was already highly popular and had a large fan base,[34] and the efforts and innovation of these musicians lent themselves to bachata's diffusion to a broader audience.

Because of its importance in bachata history, *Yo quiero andar* was included in the 2013 list of 100 Essential Albums compiled by the Dominican *Asociación de Cronistas de Arte* (Association of Arts Journalists, ACROARTE). This list aims "to identify those albums that paved the way for new styles to emerge, which, over time and due to their quality, achieved the level of a classic."[35] Certainly, this collaboration's importance cannot be overlooked, for it contributed to the erosion of the social stereotypes associated with bachata.

Juan Luis Guerra

In 1990, Juan Luis Guerra released his album, *Bachata rosa*, a title that distanced his pink (*rosa*) bachata from that of the red-light district. Guerra, who was also involved in the Dominican Nueva Canción movement, studied at the Berklee College of Music in Boston. Although Guerra's first compositions reflect more of a pop influence, he later returned to Caribbean rhythms to create a refined merengue de orquesta. Guerra applied a similar approach to bachata to compose songs that were soft, smooth, and definitely pink.

Despite its name, *Bachata rosa* included only four bachatas. Their titles—"*Como abeja al panal* (Like a Bee to Its Honeycomb)," "*Estrellitas y duendes* (Little Stars and Elves)," "Bachata rosa," and "*Burbujas de amor* (Bubbles of Love)," contrast with the bitter thread woven through traditional bachatas. Their themes are indeed romantic; for example, "Como abeja al panal" features an exchange between a male and female in which he begs her to accept him, and in "Estrellitas y duendes," the singer regrets his beloved's departure, admits his jealousy, and claims he cannot live without her. Despite the surface level similarities to bachata themes, Guerra's poetic lyrics reveal none of their directness or starkness. In Guerra's world, the wounds of separation are temporary and show the possibility of being overcome, as in "Como abeja al panal." Similarly, the narrative voice of "Burbujas de amor" is impatient and begs his lover for one night together. Although the narrator claims he will die without his beloved in "Estrellitas y duendes," he does not ask her to slit his wrists, as in Inocencio Cruz's "Mal pago." Instead, this wounded lover vows to live on in her memory as a rain shower, a storm composed of the titular elves and stars. "Bachata rosa," as its name indicates, is the sweetest bachata of the album, an expression of love through delicate tropes and poetic device.

While Guerra's bachatas still included double entendre, their poetic quality smoothed the edges considerably. The narrator of "Burbujas de amor," for example, wishes he could be a fish so he could touch his nose on the woman's fishbowl and blow bubbles of love. Although the sexual double entendres are clear—the fish's nose as a phallic symbol penetrating the contained world of the fishbowl—they are indeed expressed in shades of pink rather than red. Guerra's world of bachata is refined and sanitized—the mineral water setting of "Bachata rosa" and not the interior of a seedy bar, a red-light district brothel, or the bottom of a bottle.

Although Luis Días and Sonia Silvestre had introduced bachata to a broader national audience through their tecno amargue, Juan Luis Guerra's *Bachata rosa* took the genre to a global audience.[36] *Bachata rosa* did exactly what it was meant to do: it sold internationally, making the album a hit and earning Guerra a 1991 Grammy in the Latin Tropical category.

Víctor Víctor

Singer-songwriter Víctor Víctor's roots were also in Nueva Canción. From the beginning, Víctor Víctor's music had strong social ties, and it is no surprise that his interests eventually led him to bachata. A formally trained musician, this singer-songwriter embraced various musical influences, including those of the Caribbean, such as bolero, son, and bachata, and others, such as rock and Brazilian music.[37] Víctor Víctor had been working with bachata before releasing his 1990 album, *Inspiraciones* (Inspirations), with its bachata hit, "*Mesita de noche* (Bedside Table)."[38] This song incorporates the common bachata themes of love and an imminent break-up, but the lyrics, while heartfelt, are not cortavenas. In this song, the narrator paints the image of the woman's love as a guiding light that he leaves burning on his bedside table. Later, he extends a parallel between the bedside lamp and her love as a light glowing in the center of his heart. In addition to its lyrical imagery and tempered vocal interpretation, the song's synthesized instrumentation replaced the sharper sound of the plucked guitar and infused this bachata with a softer, ballad-like quality. This take on bachata resulted in a hit that crossed class and national lines, helping introduce bachata to a wider audience and making it one of the most important Dominican albums since 1950.[39]

Víctor Víctor's bachata came more fully under the national spotlight in December 1993, when he organized two concerts, *De bachata en bachata*, featuring Sonia Silvestre, Luis Segura, and rising star Raulín Rodríguez, along with himself. The concerts, held in Santo Domingo and Santiago de los Caballeros, the nation's second-largest city, included popular bachatas across the years as well as hit bachatas of the moment, thus uniting the old school with the new. The concerts also exposed new audiences who came for the techo bachata to the traditional style that had been produced for three decades. Víctor Víctor expressed his respect for these predecessors in the genre and points to them as his inspiration.[40] He has continued to record bachata, along with other genres, although none of his subsequent bachata productions equaled "Mesita de noche's" success.[41]

What's in a Name?

These successes of non-traditional bachata musicians have led many to identify them, and in particular, Juan Luis Guerra and his *Bachata rosa*, as the silver bullet that made bachata palatable for a new audience. In fact, this overlooks the significant fan base that bachata already had among its original followers, and the fact that this base was simultaneously growing with the popularity of other young bachateros such as Antony Santos and Luis Vargas,[42] as we shall see below. Additionally, Víctor Víctor's work in the genre plus the success of *Yo quiero andar* had already established bachata's possibilities among the middle class.[43] Still, the popularity of their work gave bachata national and international exposure and contributed to the genre's "validation through visibility."[44]

Because of their poetic lyrics and softer style, some bachateros do not consider Juan Luis Guerra or even Luis Días, Sonia Silvestre, or Víctor Víctor to be true members of their ranks.[45] They did not grow up in the social atmosphere of the lower class, and they had educational opportunities and musical training unknown to bachateros. Víctor Víctor and Guerra have continued to record bachata across the years; still, Guerra reiterates that he is not a bachatero, but rather someone who experimented with the genre.[46] For many of those who have always known, played, and listened to bachata, Guerra and his manager, Bienvenido Rodríguez, entered the world of bachata in much the same way that Rhadamés Aracena originally did: as a business venture.[47]

This debate reflects another question: what to call this style of bachata. Without a doubt, these artists altered bachata's sound significantly; in fact, it could be likened to the way in which musician Luis Alberti experimented with and changed elements of merengue típico to make it more appealing to an urban audience.[48] Although Días, Silvestre and Tejada named their experimental creation "tecno bachata" or "tecno amargue," that term is no longer commonly used, since the international appeal of bachata has influenced the lumping of it all into the broader, simpler name of bachata. Some refer to all tecno bachata as bachata rosa, using the title of Guerra's album.[49] For bachata pioneer José Manuel Calderón, bachata is still the roots of Guerra's music, and one cannot see it in its context without looking back down the long line of bachateros who preceded Guerra, including the *Pionero* himself.[50]

Bachateros from the Borderlands

Three musicians from the northwest border region were also developing their own sound and style at the same time that tecno bachata was evolving. These bachateros—Luis Vargas, Antony Santos, and Raulín Rodríguez—continued Blas Durán's innovative work with the electric guitar. They also added patterns borrowed from merengue and an instrumental mambo section.[51] These musicians carried bachata to new listeners, and later, inspired new generations of bachateros both at home and abroad.

Luis Vargas

Luis Vargas continued Blas Durán's tradition of double entendre bachata and a more modern sound. Vargas's recordings of the 1980s met with little success, and they included more merengue de guitarra than bachata. This original focus on merengue is not surprising, given the popularity of merengue típico in the borderlands where Vargas was born.[52] Still, bachata was also a part of Vargas's upbringing, and from an early age, he listened to música de guitarra: José Manuel Calderón, Luis Segura, and Paniagua.[53] Inspired by the sound of the electric guitar in Blas Durán's band, Vargas replaced nylon-strung guitars for steel-strung instruments, inserting a microphone into the guitar's sound hole to achieve a sharper timbre; he also definitively included the güira, and gave the other instruments—the requinto, bongo, and upright bass— a more prominent, rhythmic role.[54]

Vargas first caught the public's attention in the late 1980s with his popular merengue de guitarra, *"La maravilla* (The Wonder)."[55] Vargas's sound differentiated his music from previous guitar-based merengue, merengue de orquesta, and merengue típico. His lyrics also took the double entendre tradition to new levels. The sexual double meanings continued to sell, and Vargas's 1990 merengue *"El tomate* (The Tomato)"* was a hit, despite its overt suggestiveness, which likened the female sex organ to a tomato through the rhythmic emphasis on the first syllable of the word *"tomate," "to."* The quick repetition on the strong first and third beats of the song essentially rendered the word *"toto"*—Dominican slang for vulva. These innovations were also present in the bachatas on Vargas's album of the same name. In Vargas's bachata, this new approach included a more pronounced rhythm, patterns, and an accelerated tempo inherited from merengue.[56] Vargas carried this musical innovation into bachata along with the traditional style of emotional vocal interpretation.

The taste for double entendre began to wane in the face of censorship and criticism. In response, Luis Vargas took his new style of bachata and merengue down a different path in his 1994 album, *Loco de amor* (Crazy About Love). The bachatas of this recording returned to the genre's roots in both subject and interpretation. In a voice oozing with emotion, Vargas sings of desamor, abandonment, and the bitterness of being alone. This formula, which combined Vargas's danceable rhythms, innovative sound, and traditional bachata themes, proved an accurate recipe for success.

Luis Vargas's lyrics cover a wide array of themes. Love is a constant, as in *"Simplemente te amo* (I Just Love You)."* The narrator of this song overcame others' doubts about his beloved's future with him. Although he has nothing of monetary value to offer her, she is his greatest treasure. The narrator of *"Loco de amor* (Madly in Love)"[57] is, as the title suggests, crazy about the woman. He spends so much time in her neighborhood that the neighbors fear he is casing the place to commit a robbery. He enumerates all that he will do to win her love, and hopes that a doctor will diagnose his lovesickness and prescribe her as the cure. Some songs deal with impossible love. The narrator of *"Carta final* (Last Card)"* regrets that fate prevented him from meeting the woman of his dreams earlier. Although she is already with someone else, he intends to play his last card—his feelings for her—and has no doubt that he'll win. Likewise, the narrative voice of *"No puedo vivir sin ti* (I Can't Live Without You)"* falls for a woman who is with another. Although he proclaims in a sobbing voice that he is unable to live without her, he does not fight for her love.

Indifference and suffering take on various forms in Vargas's bachatas. The narrative voice in *"Veneno* (Poison)"* has suffered for years at the hands of a heartless woman, who he describes as venom itself. In *"Volvió el Dolor* (The Pain Returned)," the narrative voice suffered until love came into his life. Then, when his beloved betrayed him, his pain returned. The narrator of this bachata takes the high road, forgiving her and encouraging her to do the same should her new love ever betray her. The narrator of "*Yo mismo la vi* (I Saw Her Myself)" falls from the heights of love to the depths of despair when his beloved is unfaithful. For this narrator, the worst part of her infidelity is not that others told him, but rather, that he witnessed it with his own eyes.

Vargas reiterates the ties between desamor, drinking, and the bar in several songs. In "*La mesa del rincón* (The Corner Table)," the narrative voice sits alone at the corner table, drowning his sorrows in rum. Although the table itself reminds him of his sweetheart, he intends to continue drinking at it. The chorus alternates between the narrator's comments and the back-up singers' responses, thereby depicting the bachata tradition of men sharing and singing their emotional troubles with other men in the bar.[58] "*Dos hombres bebiendo* (Two Men Drinking)," a duet with merengue star Sergio Vargas, portrays this male camaraderie. When one man attempts to intervene in his friend's three-day drinking binge, the other explains that his woman betrayed him and that he doesn't want advice, only more alcohol. His friend agrees, and decides it's best to join the party. A palm reader reveals a fate of betrayal and alcoholism to the narrator in "*Yo no muero en mi cama* (I Won't Die in My Bed)," a fate he unflinchingly embraces. He informs the seer that he'll die drinking and states that friends should commemorate his death with alcohol.

Known as the "*Rey Supremo de la Bachata* (The Supreme King of Bachata)," Luis Vargas was among the first to show that bachata could be lucrative,[59] and he continues to be a favorite among bachata fans. Still, Vargas remembers when things weren't so easy for him. As he noted in the 2004 documentary, *Santo Domingo Blues*, "How wonderful to be a bachatero now ... but *now*. Back then, it wasn't very good."

Antony Santos[60]

Antony Santos—"*el Mayimbe de la Bachata* (the Cacique of Bachata)"—is also a product of the borderlands. Santos began his career playing the güira for Vargas, but left the band after a falling out, releasing his own album in 1992.[61] Of the bachatas on this album, "*Voy pa' allá* (I'm Going There)," became the best known. The song took a roundabout path to fame for Santos when Las Chicas del Can, a female merengue group, helped propel "Voy pa' allá" to popularity on mainstream radio stations.[62] The remake, which included both a bachata and a merengue section, brought visibility to the song and its origins as a bachata. Fans of the bachata/merengue fusion sought out the original, and Santos's sales shot up.[63]

Antony Santos's "Voy pa' allá" kept with bachata tradition in terms of lyrics and interpretive style: the singer's voice is filled with sadness and emotion as he vows to look for the love of his life against all odds. What made this song such a pivotal one in bachata history, however, were Santos's musical innovations. Santos created a rhythmic, distinct, sharp sound on his guitar by playing with a thumb pick and a downward motion, often incorporating merengue patterns and figures; similarly, Santos included the merengue's mambo section—an instrumental interlude, often marked by improvisation.[64] The result was highly danceable, and bachata began to make inroads into sectors that had previously rejected it.[65]

Antony Santos continues to successfully release bachata, remaining among the top names of bachateros.[66] Across the years, Santos has interpreted common and innovative bachata themes with his unique sound. For example, the narrator in "*Qué plantón* (What a Way to Stand Someone Up)" suffers the heartache of constantly being stood up by an indifferent woman. He decides to get drunk and threatens to kill himself if his love goes unrequited. In "*Lloro* (I Cry)," the narrative voice relates his suffering and abandonment in a sobbing, plaintive tone. In contrast, the narrator of "*Vete y aléjate de mí* (Leave and Get Away from Me)" decides to end a forbidden relationship with a woman who toyed with him, preferring to feel pain for a short time so that his story will have a better ending. Similarly, the narrator of "*Yo quiero* (I Want To)" tries in vain to forget the woman he loved. Santos interprets this song, which paints love as an all-or-nothing venture, in a softer style that is yet filled with emotion.

Love is often portrayed with a twist in Antony Santos's bachatas. For example, the narrator in "*Corazón culpable* (Guilty Heart)" claims he didn't want to fall in love and places all the blame on his wayward heart. Love hangs in the balance in "*Por mi timidez* (Because of My Shyness)." The shy narrator risks losing the woman he's loved since childhood. When faced with her impending marriage, he vows to fight for her at all costs. "*Ay de mí, ay de ti* (Woe to Me, Woe to You)" is a dialogue between a male and female voice. She claims the narrator has not appreciated or loved her, and he tries to convince her not to let their love die. "*Creíste* (You Thought)" depicts a narrator boasting of his new love to a former one. He reminds his ex that she thought he would never make it over their breakup and explains how his new romance has erased all that she did to him. This 2013 single provides a good example of how Antony Santos continues to be a leader in bachata innovation. Santos blends the traditional bachata instrumentation with electronic instruments, an upbeat tempo, and chord progressions among the song's sections. This successful recipe earned Santos the 2013 Bachata of the Year (Premios Soberano).

Today, Antony Santos ranks among the most popular bachateros in the Dominican Republic and abroad.[67] ACROARTE (Association of Arts Journalists) recognized Santos's pivotal role in helping erode the discrimination against bachata by including his first album, *La chupadera*, in its list of 100 Essential Albums (*Cien discos esenciales*) from 1950 to 2010.[68] ACROARTE specifically highlighted Santos's album in a sample of ten, noting that songs such as "Voy pa' allá" helped the genre "begin to break down the barriers of opposition among some groups."[69] His style and innovations have served as an inspiration to other musicians, including many modern bachateros abroad, as we shall see in Chapter Eight.

Raulín Rodríguez

Bachatero Raulín Rodríguez had his start as a signer with Antony Santos shortly after Santos left Vargas's band. Rodríguez, who dropped out of school because it would have been too far and expensive to attend high school in another community, taught himself the basics of the guitar.[70] In 1992, Rodríguez, the Cacique del Amargue, formed his own band and launched his solo career. Soon thereafter, his composition "*Qué dolor* (What Pain)," with its sweet lyrics regretting the singer's actions towards a lost love and sung in Rodríguez's tempered yet still mournful voice, became a hit across class lines.[71] Raulín Rodríguez's cleaner, romantic lyrics and his contemporary sound, professional dress, and managerial support made bachata palatable for many who had previously disdained it.[72] This allowed Rodríguez access to larger venues, play on FM radio, and television spots previously unavailable to bachata musicians.

Rodríguez's success is not limited solely to his look or management. Rather, he has continued to treat the traditional bachata themes of love and love lost with innovative lyrics, his tender voice, and a danceable beat. The message is simple and repetitive in *"Mi morenita* (My Sweetheart)"*: the narrator reminds his former sweetheart how much he loved her and insists he'll never forget her. The lyrics of *"Medicina de amor* (Love Medicine),"* one of his best-known songs, are more varied. This narrative voice suffers from love cancer because his sweetheart left him, and he begs her to return to cure him. The narrator of *"Mujer infiel* (Unfaithful Woman)"* also suffers at the hands of a treacherous woman. He warns her that someday, she will be treated in the same way and will understand how he feels. In *"Ay hombre* (Oh, Man),"* the narrative voice speaks to his blooming yellow-elder tree, asking it to carpet his beloved's path with its flowers. This speaker recognizes that he lied to her and that she has every right to leave him. Still, he is unable to forget her and hopes she will hear his song and understand his anguish.

Rodríguez also sings of the different shades of love. The narrative voice of *"Me la pusieron difícil* (They Made It Hard on Me)"* intends to marry his sweetheart against all odds. He reveals that her family thought he was fickle and a womanizer, and he suffers from their opposition. Still, he is determined to prove that he will make her happy, and eventually, they run away together. In contrast, the narrative voice of *"Culpable* (Guilty)"* begs his beloved not to feel guilty because she is in a relationship with him when she belongs to another who does not love her and is unfaithful. He urges her to give him a chance to love and be loved. Rodríguez's 2013 hit, *"Esta noche* (Tonight),"* is a tender declaration of love. The narrator, unable to rein in his passion for the woman he loves, promises an unforgettable night for them both.

Raulín Rodríguez continues to be one of the most popular bachateros both at home and abroad. At the time of this writing, "Esta noche" ranks among the top ten most popular songs in the Dominican Republic.[73] Although styles and sounds have changed since Rodríguez made his debut in 1993, he continues to be a trendsetter with his hip look, bachata themes and sound.

Conclusion

As the Dominican economy progressively worsened, bachata continued to represent the realities of a growing body of fans both at home and among Dominicans who migrated abroad. The popular double entendre bachata of the 1980s and 1990s was followed by tecno bachata, and innovations to sound, style, and lyrical content. Pedro Antonio Valdez, author of the novel *Bachata del ángel caido* (Bachata of the Fallen Angel), observes that bachata of this time was a staple among "the people of the barrios and countryside, that is, the majority of the Dominican people ... it wasn't a marginalized expression but rather, an esthetic sample of the collective being of our country."[74] Bachata's fan base grew with the increasing number of Dominicans who experienced the realities depicted in bachata and the new listeners attracted by its innovations.

SIX

Romantic Bachata

When I asked romantic bachatero Joe Veras to define amargue for me, he explained that "every song has a bit of amargue," or an emotional spark.[1] Veras differentiated between the "amargue of years gone by, and today's amargue," describing the former as "cortavenas."[2] For Veras, one of the first bachateros to successfully write, produce, and perform a more romantic bachata, amargue is still present in his bachata—"but it's more poetic."[3]

The 1990s saw a number of bachateros such as Joe Veras come onto the music scene just as the genre was making significant inroads into the tastes of the middle and upper classes. These musicians by and large represent the same characteristics as their predecessors—a rural or lower class upbringing, largely self-taught, and often with limited access to formal education. The bachata they produced, however, was almost overwhelmingly romantic, focusing on the various facets of falling in and out of love. As David C. Wayne notes, the ballad's influence on this style of romantic bachata is evident, especially considering that some bachateros recorded ballads on their albums.[4] Content and images continued to evolve. Now, male narrators might wish their exes well, admit a fear of falling in love, brag about overcoming heartache with a new love, or admit their mistakes. The lyrical depth, softer musical texture, and tempered singing style from these romantic bachateros debuting in the 1990s and new millennium helped erode prejudices and increase bachata's mainstream airplay.

Joe Veras

Joe Veras was among the first to turn to romanticism with the release of his first album, *Con amor* (With Love), in 1993. Veras listened to both merengue and bachata as a child, and he continues to play and record both; nevertheless, he describes bachata as always being the center focus of his life.[5] Veras's lyrics—many of his own composition—align with the romanticism of bachateros such as Luis Segura, although his voice is softer and less mournful. The standard bachata themes of despecho and desamor are still present in the bachatas of *Con amor*, but Veras's lyrics and interpretive style treat them with more romantic nostalgia than sobbing. Veras's "*Te necesito* (I Need You)," for example, is reminiscent of doo-wop music of the 1950s, even including the rhythmic doo-wop vocals in the lyrics. In this song, the male voice nurtures his memories of the place of the first kiss he shared with his sweetheart, although he no longer knows where she is. Similarly, the voice of "*Sonámbulo* (Sleep-walker)" is unable to sleep because he cannot stop remembering the woman he loved, despite his best efforts to forget her. Rather than drown his sorrows, he pledges to keep looking for her until he finds her.

Across the years, Veras's bachatas continue to depict love in its many facets. The philosophical "*En el amor* (When It Comes to Love)" contemplates both the beautiful and the devastating emotions related to falling in and out of love. This bachata reminds listeners that everyone has his own love story and can relate. "*Chiquilla Chiquita* (Little Girl)" portrays an enamored narrator who feels the heat of love's flames and longs to see his beloved. Unrequited love is the theme of "*Por tu amor* (For Your Love)," and the narrator insists that he will do anything—from household chores to an extravagant vacation—for the woman he loves. The speaker in "*Pido auxilio* (Help)" also suffers from unrequited love, and calls for help because he is dying.

Others' murmurings can also influence love. In Veras's "*El hombre de tu vida* (The Man of Your Life)," the narrator begs his beloved not to listen to others' lies about his supposed carousing and womanizing. He reminds her that he is the man about whom she has always dreamed. In contrast, the narrative voice of "*El cuchicheo* (Whispering)" recognizes that he turned a deaf ear to the rumors about his sweetheart's unfaithfulness. In fact, he maintains that what hurts him most is not her infidelity but rather, others' whisperings about it. The speaker in "*Cartas del verano* (Summer Letters)" deduces from others' hints that the woman he loves no longer cares for him. Now that he knows the truth, the narrator finds himself alone in his hometown and still in love with her.

Several of Veras's bachatas contrast interior and exterior beauty. In "*Tu belleza interior* (Your Inner Beauty)," the narrator emphasizes that he has fallen in love with the inner beauty of the woman he loves. In contrast, the male voice of "*Cirugía en el alma* (An Operation of the Soul)" criticizes the woman's obsession with her physical appearance. He maintains that she needs a change of heart—an operation on her soul—to win back his love. Veras's endearing classic, "*El molde* (The Mold)," joins interior and exterior beauty through the notion of "they broke the mold when they made you." This narrator enumerates the physical characteristics, as well as the angelic and divine qualities of the woman he loves, insisting that her creator broke the mold he used to make her so there would be no imitations.

Veras's bachatas also consider the other side of love: indifference and heartache. The narrator's inability to forget his sweetheart in "*Inténtalo tú* (You Try)" convinces him that she will not succeed in forgetting him either. In "*Duele* (It Hurts)," the narrative voice complains about his beloved's treatment, observing that he knows many animals that fare better. He emphasizes how much he suffers and warns her that she will learn how it feels someday. In contrast, the narrator of "*Sobreviviré* (I Will Survive)" is confident that he will forget his former love. He enumerates all that he and others have already overcome—including his father's ability to survive Trujillo's regime—and vows he will forget, even if it means he must learn to love again. "*Te solté* (I Cut You Loose)" portrays the narrative voice's almost euphoric joy at being free of the woman who made him suffer. Now, he no longer loves her and plans on living for himself.

Joe Veras's place among bachata greats is indisputable and, to use the word often heard in his songs to describe his bachata, "unmistakable." His album, *Carta de verano*, ranks among ACROARTE's top 100 Dominican albums since 1950.[6] Past-president of ACROARTE and head of the committee who created the list, Máximo Jiménez, observes, "We couldn't leave Joe Veras off of this list, and without a doubt, *Carta de verano* is the album that best defines his style: romantic songs, successful arrangements, and a collection of songs that were able to gauge his career both within and outside of the Dominican Republic. Veras's contributions in this album are an important reference point within the genre for his peers."[7] His romantic lyrics and refined arrangements also inspired new generations of bachateros.[8] Veras's bachatas continue to be among the most popular on the radio[9] and to be included on compilation albums highlighting top bachatas of a given year.

Frank Reyes

Frank Reyes, "*el Príncipe de la Bachata* (The Prince of Bachata)," was one of the most successful bachateros who originally embraced romanticism and a broad range of topics in the early 1990s. Like many other bachateros, Reyes left a life in the country for Santo Domingo at age twelve, working at a number of odd jobs before he was able to start his own colmado; there, he eventually met producer Juan Genáo, who recorded Reyes's first album, *Tú serás mi reina* (You'll Be My Queen), in 1991.[10] Reyes's songs on this and subsequent albums skyrocketed to popularity. He firmly established his foothold in the world of bachata with *Cuando se quiere se puede* (Where There's a Will, There's a Way) in 2004, an album that won him four Premios Casandra in 2005.[11] Reyes continues to be one of the most popular bacahteros[12] and is counted among those bachateros with the greatest number of hits.[13]

Reyes's bachatas encompass the gamut of emotions and topics. One of his earlier hits, "*Se fue mi amor bonito* (My Darling Left)," reveals a less dramatic take on love and love lost. This narrator relates a tale of unrequited love and abandonment. His sadness at his beloved's departure is evident, but the overall tone and word choice are less cortavenas. This narrative voice holds no grudge against his sweetheart and wishes her well, for letting her leave is his own way of loving her. This same topic of unrequited love goes from the personal to the global level in "*A quien tú quieres no te quiere* (The One You Love Doesn't Love You)." Although the narrator shares his own story of love and abandonment, he contemplates his suffering within the universal mystery of why we love those who don't love us. "*Princesa* (Princess)" portrays the sweet story of a schoolboy romance all grown up. As a man, the narrator is overcome by the woman's beauty and asks her to let him make her his queen.

Desamor and conflictive relationships continue to be popular topics in Reyes's bachata, although the plots are more complex than earlier bachatas. "*Cuando se quiere se puede* (Where There's a Will There's a Way)" combines an apparently motivational saying with the speaker's inability to forget the woman he loves. A woman's double betrayal is the topic of "*Tú eres ajena* (You Belong to Another)." This narrator learns too late that he has fallen in love with a taken woman. Although he loves her and feels betrayed, he wisely observes that she could easily betray him, too, and he renounces the relationship. "*El alcohol* (Alcohol)" portrays the narrator's drunkenness as the culprit who destroys his relationship. He begs the woman to forgive him for the harsh things he said, insisting that it was the alcohol talking. Reyes's romantic bachatas also reveal that some relationships are better off ended. In "*Nada de nada* (Nothing at All)," the narrative voice explains how he suffered when his sweetheart left him. Now, he is completely over her, and she has decided too late that she was wrong. Reyes's hit "*24 horas* (24 Hours)" also portrays a man who is ready to end a corrosive relationship. This narrator tells his beloved to go her own way, and he gives his heart a period of twenty-four hours to move on.

Reyes's music has also taken up the realities of the Dominican transnational community. "*Extraño mi pueblo* (I Miss My Home)" emphasizes the loneliness of being separated from one's homeland and family in the hopes of building a better life for his children. Reyes's vibrato promises to come home one day struck a chord with many Dominican and other Latino migrants who have lived this very situation themselves; the universality of this theme was one of Reyes's inspirations for the song.[14] Although Reyes's "*Amor a distancia* (Long Distance Love)" does not specifically mention the diaspora, its plot—one party forgets the love left behind—is not uncommon to migrants. Santiago record store owner, Alex Sanche, points to the relevancy of the topic of long distance love combined with Reyes's bittersweet interpretation as the ingredients that made "Amor a distancia" one of the most popular bachatas of 2012–2013. As we listened to the song in his shop, he observed, "This song is really good. It has a good melody, good lyrics. It's a bachata about someone who lived abroad, that's the distance … and they broke up."[15]

In addition to his varied content, Reyes has also experimented with bachata's sound. In the early years of the new millennium, he embarked on an ambitious project: orchestral bachata. Reyes played to a sold-out crowd at Santo Domingo's Hotel Jaragua in his 2002 Bachata de Gala concert. This historic event marked the first time that bachata had been performed with a full orchestra and is indicative of bachata's growing acceptance and popularity among a broader target audience. Frank Reyes's bachatas continue to top the charts,[16] and Cruz Hierro points to him as one of ten key figures of bachata's first fifty years.[17]

Yóskar Sarante

Yóskar Sarante was born in 1970 and raised in Villas Agrícolas, a Santo Domingo barrio. Sarante worked as a shoeshine boy, and as a young man, in construction.[18] He sang in several merengue bands before launching his solo career in bachata in 1994.[19] For several years, Sarante kept his construction job to help make a living before his 1999 hit, "*La noche* (The Night)."[20] Sarante's emotive voice and interpretation have contributed to his ongoing success not only in the Dominican Republic, but also in Europe, the United States, and worldwide.

Sarante's bachata covers a variety of romantic themes, all sung in his clear, tremulous vibrato. His aforementioned hit, "La noche," revolves around a series of antitheses that contrast the night—when the narrator remembers his love and dreams of happier times—with day—when all is clear and he remembers his anger at her for leaving.

His articulation of "la noche" and the guitar accompaniment lend a mysterious tone to the song and emphasize the contrast of what he believes in the darkness with the stark reality of the light of day. "*No tengo suerte en el amor* (I'm Unlucky in Love)" is a contemplative soul search that paints love as an uncontrollable force and contrasts love's beauty with the pain it can bring. Although this narrator has suffered from unrequited love, he is hopeful that he will someday find true love. The narrative voice of "*He tenido que llorar* (I've Had to Cry)" also recognizes that love goes hand in hand with pain. He accepts that he must cry because he still loves and misses his sweetheart, and he is unable to forget. "*Llora alma mía* (Cry, My Soul)" is a conversation between the narrator and his soul. This sufferer weeps from loneliness and his inability to change things, and he implores his soul to cleanse him of his beloved's poisonous goodbye. "*Guitarra* (Guitar)" is an apostrophe directed to the guitar. The narrator asks the instrument to speak for him and convince his sweetheart to return. These lyrics reiterate the connection between singer, sentiment, and instrument so often articulated with a bachatero's plea for the guitar to cry for him.

Yóskar Sarante sees himself essentially as a romantic, and links his subject matter to bachata's predecessor, bolero. For Sarante, there will always be a place for love songs as long as love exists.[21] His formula for romantic bachata continues to produce hits in his homeland and worldwide.

Luis Miguel del Amargue

Luis Miguel del Amargue appeared on the bachata scene with his first album in 1994. Ironically, Luis Miguel first enjoyed his greatest success in Europe, and especially in Spain, before rising to the top of the charts in his homeland and the United States.[22] His romanticism wraps traditional bachata themes in gentle images. For example, loneliness is personified in "*Se acabó lo bonito* (The Good Times Are Over)" and mocks the narrative voice, who mourns the passing of all the beautiful aspects of his relationship. In contrast to earlier bachata, this narrator blames no one for the growing indifference. "*Abrázame amor* (Hold Me, Dear)" depicts a woman who plans to leave to follow her own dreams and a narrator who will not stop her. Still, he begs her to hold him and make love to him one last time. The narrative voice of "*De rodillas* (On Bended Knees)" emphasizes his sincere regret for cheating on his beloved, begging her on bended knees to forgive him. Similarly, the narrator in "*Télefono ocupado* (The [Telephone] Line's Busy)" admits he made a mistake. He insists that he is useless without his sweetheart's love—just a busy telephone line that can't be reached. "*Sal de mi vida* (Get Out of My Life)" presents the opposite paradigm: this narrator rebukes his beloved for disrupting his life, first with her love and later, with her betrayal.

Luis Miguel del Amargue's sweet voice, romantic lyrics, and sentimental interpretation continue to bring him international success. His trajectory is indicative of the growing and different markets worldwide for the genre. Luis Miguel has starred in European concerts and festivals, such as the Latin American Festival in Milan and El Gran Bachatazo in Madrid, both in 2008.[23] He was recognized for his work in the genre during the Dominican Heritage Festival (New Jersey) in 2012,[24] and he was named the 2011 Bachatero of the Year in his homeland.[25]

Zacarías Ferreira

Another newcomer in the 1990s, Zacarías Ferreira continued the romantic trend, extending its reaches with the depth of his lyrics and arrangements.[26] Ferreira was raised in the country in the Cibao region, but unlike the vast majority of his bachata predecessors, he did study music formally in the National Conservatory in Santo Domingo before joining the Brugal (rum) Company's orchestra.[27] Ferreira's nickname, "*la Voz de la Ternura* (The Voice of Tenderness)," is an accurate description of his interpretive style. Ferreira released his first solo album, *Me liberé* (I'm Free), in 1997, a Casandra Award-winning production.[28] Ferreira's 2000 release, *El triste* (The Sad One), affirmed his place among the romantic bachateros of the new millennium, a position that he has maintained with successive hits.

Although Ferreira's bachatas continue to deal with different aspects of falling in and out of love, the listener often finds the male narrative voice tentative about love or wishing a former sweetheart the best after they part ways. For example, the narrator of "*No hay mal que por bien no venga* (Every Cloud Has a Silver Lining)" contrasts his pure love with the woman's insincerity. Although she did not fully appreciate his emotions, he still wishes her well and hopes she will be happy. "*La avispa* (The Wasp)" also portrays an understanding narrator who wishes a heartless woman the best. The narrator of "*Es tan difícil* (It's So Hard)" reiterates that he is unable to forget his former love. His efforts to replace her are equally futile, although he admits he is unsure of whom to blame for their failed romance. "*Quédate conmigo* (Stay with Me)" presents an impending break-up. Still, there is a glimmer of hope as the narrative voice begs his beloved to tell him she does not plan to leave, or that she will return— even if it is untrue in the end.

Amorous relationships are multidimensional in Ferreira's bachata. The narrator of "*Me ilusioné* (I Got My Hopes Up)" describes the love he felt at first sight. He begs the woman he loves to give him a chance and ease the suffering that kills him little by little. In "*Me sobran las palabras* (Words Are Unnecessary)," the narrative voice celebrates his growing love. The direct and unadorned lyrics of this song parallel its title, and Ferreira's romantic interpretation makes it clear that an excess of words is, indeed, unnecessary to express love. Unrequited love is the focus of "*Dime qué faltó* (Tell Me What Was Missing)." This narrator does not blame his former love for leaving, but rather, recognizes that she has a right to be free and do as she pleases. The question he poses, then, serves as his goodbye to her. This romantic bachata contrasts with earlier songs that railed against women and presented them as men's property.

In other songs, the narrator makes a conscious decision to reject love. "*Como amigo sí pero como amor no* (I'll Be Your Friend but Not Your Lover)" presents a narrator who insists he is better off as the woman's friend. He believes he will find true love one day, but admits that he is afraid to fall in love now. Similarly, "*Un buen amigo que un mal amor* (Better a Good Friend Than a Bad Lover)" asks which is better: a good friendship, or a romantic relationship gone wrong. The narrator references the wisdom shared by those who've suffered for just such a mistake, and he opts for the freedom of friendship rather than the imprisonment of a bad relationship.

Ferreira's popularity has not waned since his first release. His 2007 album, *Dime que faltó* (Tell Me What Was Missing), solidified his position as a romantic bachatero and established his signature interpretive style. This album, one of ACROARTE's 100 Essential Albums, was a hit not only with Ferreira's fans but with the musical critics as well.[29] His romantic interpretations of diverse topics continue to draw crowds worldwide, in person and on the radio.

El Chaval de la Bachata

Linar Espinal, *El Chaval de la Bachata* (the Bachata Kid), is a product of Santiago's Pekín barrio whose interest in bachata grew from listening to Blas Durán. After recording two albums with other bands, El Chaval released his first solo album in 1997. Since then, he has interpreted bachatas covering a wide range of topics in his unique, somewhat husky voice.

Espinal's bachata covers the spectrum of romantic themes. His 2011 bachata remake of "*No molestar* (Do Not Disturb)" sings the narrator's plea for his sweetheart to come away with him where naysayers won't disturb them. Several of El Chaval's bachatas serve as observations of human nature and relationships. In "*¿Dónde están esos amigos?* (Where Are Those Friends?)," the narrator explains how his supposed friends and the women he loved abandoned him after his economic stability disintegrated. The narrative voice also bemoans the evils of money in "*Por el maldito dinero* (Damned Money)," blaming his lack of funds for his lost love. In "*El golpe avisa* (You'll Learn the Hard Way)," the narrator warns his listeners to pay attention to avoid catastrophe in love and life, although they may have to learn the hard way. "*Maldita residencia* (Damned Residency)" reflects the sentiments of a man left alone in his home country when his wife migrates to New York with their children. In addition to familial separation, this song paints other realities of many migrants: the woman is able to migrate because she has been sponsored by a family member, her mother, and he is unable to follow because he does not have a visa. The man is further unsatisfied by the options available to stay in touch with his family—an occasional phone call or interaction through Facebook—and begs her not to forget him in New York. This song, inspired by the real-life events of a friend, became a hit within only its first month on the air and an anthem for many.[30]

Espinal's lyrical variety and individual sound have made him popular both at home and abroad. He has toured extensively in Europe, Spain and non–Spanish-speaking countries such as France, Italy, Germany, and Holland.[31] The topics he depicts are pertinent to audiences worldwide who relate to the situations they represent. His "¿Dónde están esos amigos?" earned El Chaval a Casandra for Bachata of the Year, and an ASCAP (American Society of Composers, Authors, and Publishers) Award in 2009.

Elvis Martínez

Bachata exploded onto mainstream radio in the United States in 1998 with Elsido "Elvis" Martínez, *el Camarón* (The Shrimp) / *el Jefe* (The Boss). Martínez, a native of San Francisco de Macorís, grew up in a musical family and performed in local

bands before forming his own group. In 1998, his song "*Así fue* (That's How It Went),"
became the first bachata to be programmed on mainstream tropical radio in the
United States.[32] Martínez describes the song's broad popularity as "an international
scandal," and guitarist Lenny Santos, who played on the song, points to it as the turning point for bachata's entrance into mainstream radio programming.[33] "Así fue" interweaves the two themes of love and love lost. In this song, the male voice explains to
a former love that he has forgotten her and found a new love. Both the song's content
and Martínez's tender interpretive style made this song approachable across a diverse
audience and eventually, it lead the way for others to follow.

Martínez's bachatas portray a wide array of themes. Romantic love continues to
be a common topic, but from multiple points of view. For example, the narrative voice
of "*Yo te voy a amar* (I'm Going to Love You)" proclaims his feelings and promises of
undying love with conventional images: for him, the woman is his breath, soul, present, and future. In contrast, the narrator of "*Así te amo* (That's How I Love You),"
confronts the stereotypes associated with his urban look of jeans and earrings that
are frowned upon by his beloved's parents. He emphasizes the difference between
the exterior world and the interior realm of his feelings for her, which are more powerful than his outward appearance. In other compositions, the narrative voice declares
his love and tests his footing in a new relationship. The narrator of "*La luz de mis
ojos* (The Light of My Eyes)" emphasizes his feelings and asks his beloved to reveal
her own. Similarly, the voice of "*Dime* (Tell Me)" openly expresses his love and insists
that the woman tell him why she hides her feelings for him. A pair of Martínez's
bachatas represents an initiation into the art of loving. His 2001 hit, "*Maestra*
(Teacher)," portrays a young man begging an older woman to teach him the art of
making love. "*Profesor* (Professor)" plays intertextually on the content of the former
song. Now, the young man is an expert—a professor—in the ways of love, and he
offers to teach a young woman all that he knows.

Martínez's bachatas describe desamor in both traditional and innovative ways.
In "*Tú sabes bien* (You Well Know)," the narrative voice insists that he will not be able
to go on if his beloved leaves him. He uses traditional images of tears, emptiness, and
solitude to emphasize his desperation. In contrast, the prevailing sentiment of "*Amada
mía* (My Beloved)" is anger as the narrator curses an unfaithful woman for her betrayal
with his good friend and his own blindness to her acts. "*Ambición* (Ambition)" depicts
an ambitious woman who preferred material riches to true love. "*Yo no nací para
amar* (I Wasn't Born to Love)" intensifies the themes of indifference and loneliness.
In this song, the narrative voice describes how he watched all of his friends fall in
love, never to find it himself.

Separation from a loved one during the holidays and the resulting loneliness are
the topics of two Martínez bachatas. "*Esta Navidad* (This Christmas)" and "*Triste
Navidad* (Blue Christmas)" depict distance, separation, and solitude. Although these
songs do not specifically state that one party lives abroad, the emphasis on separation
and the tendency of many Dominican migrants to return for the holidays is evident
and make migration a plausible context for these songs.

Martínez's "Juancito Nadie (*Johnny Nobody*)" introduces a unique character: the
palomo (kid from the barrio). This underprivileged child narrates a common day in
his life, which includes selling flowers on the street and an occasional sniff of rubber

cement to escape his harsh reality. Videogames and superheroes are not a part of this child's reality, although missed meals and the thrashings his mother's boyfriend gives him are. The figure of Juancito Nadie, an eight-year-old going on eighty, reminds listeners that the reality of this child becomes the reality of the country's future. In the end, Juancito Nadie, the kid from the marginalized barrio, can no more be ignored than bachata itself.

In addition to the thematic variety of his bachata, Martínez varies his performance according to his intended audience:

> I can't make music just for one audience. The bachata that's enjoyed in the Dominican Republic is a hot bachata, a danceable bachata…. In other markets, they like romantic, smooth, quiet bachatas…. In Europe, you have to make music with a little bit of tecno…. You have to sing and do arrangements for different markets.[34]

Martínez likewise reiterates the importance of evolution within the genre. Originally attracted to bachata by what others were doing in the 1990s, Martínez points back across the fifty years of bachata's history to see his influences as well as the music's future:

> People like Calderón, Luis Segura, like Paniagua, all those singers … Antony Santos … Luis Vargas, Raulín, among others … they also did a great job. But if they'd stayed there, I'm one hundred percent sure that bachata wouldn't have kept growing…. There has to be a changing of the guard so that genres keep growing. If not, I can assure you that the genre will come to a halt right where it is.[35]

This natural process of change has lead Martínez to experiment with varied instrumentation and to mix in others genres such as tecno, hip-hop, and cha-cha-cha. Together, Martínez's sound, content, and tender interpretive style have contributed to his international popularity.

Monchy y Alexandra[36]

The romanticism of the early 2000s found a popular voice in the mixed duo of Monchy y Alexandra, who figured prominently in bachata's acceptance outside of the Dominican Republic. Monchy (Ramón Rijo) and Alexandra Cabrera debuted with their 1999 hit, "*Hoja en blanco* (Blank Sheet of Paper)," a bachata remake of a popular Colombian vallenato that narrates the tale of lovers whose lives take separate paths. This and subsequent releases were international hits that helped carry bachata far beyond Dominican borders.[37]

Although some criticized their music as being more akin to ballad than bachata, their central themes are in the amargue tradition, though presented from the point of view of dialoguing male and female voices. In this way, situations are portrayed as two sides of the same coin. For example, the narrators of "*Dos locos* (Two Crazy People)" proclaim that they must be crazy to be with others when they still love each other. In contrast to this story line, the couple in "*Te quiero igual que ayer* (I Love You Just as Much as Yesterday)" admits that they still love each other as much as they used to, finding forgiveness and harmony by singing together. Similarly, the couple of "*No es una novela* (This Isn't a Novel)" vows to defend their love from naysayers who try to write their love story for them. Forbidden love also continues as a theme in the duo's songs, as in the case of the couple of "*Perdidos* (Lost)" who must see each other secretly and lose themselves in their own world of love.

Monchy y Alexandra's romantic bachata rapidly gained an international following, and others followed their lead. Their 2002 album, *Confesiones* (Confessions), made them a point of reference "for the best bachata produced in the first decade of the 2000s."[38] Although the duo disbanded in 2009, they significantly affected bachata production and acceptance with their romantic lyrics, duets, and fusions of other sounds and rhythms.

Héctor Acosta "El Torito"

Héctor Acosta "El Torito" (The Little Bull)[39] began his career in merengue as lead singer with the popular Los Toros Band in 1990. Fifteen years later, he launched his solo career, recording both merengue and bachata. Acosta's bachatas continue the thematic tradition of love and love lost, as depicted with refined images. For example, the narrator of "*Tu primera vez* (Your First Time)" euphemistically describes the sex act through the image of a boat that drops anchor in the woman's body. Their lovemaking is not a fit of unbridled passion, but rather, a conscious decision based on true love. "*Primavera azul* (Blue Spring)" presents a narrator suffering from unrequited love, but his pain is mitigated by images of love as a guiding light and the idyllic springtime he promises the woman he loves. Natural images almost make suffering seem bearable in "*Perdóname la vida* (Spare My Life)." Nature's unity reminds the narrator of his own solitude when the shore and sea embrace and the birds kiss the sky after a storm breaks. The passing hours of the day bring him no relief, and he begs his sweetheart to spare him.

Guilt and a request for forgiveness are common themes in Acosta's bachata. In "*Sin perdón* (Unforgiven)," the narrator admits his mistakes and seeks forgiveness. His beloved lectures him about love and faithfulness, and although she forgives him, she no longer trusts him. The narrative voice of "*Me duele la cabeza* (My Head Hurts)" likewise recognizes he made a mistake by lying to, cheating on, and leaving his sweetheart. Now, he suffers the physical pain of his emotional distress. In "*No soy un hombre malo* (I'm Not a Bad Man)," the narrator admits his unfaithfulness, but he insists he does not deserve his beloved's indifference and that she'll be responsible for his death if she leaves him.

While a number of merengueros have recorded bachata, few have had as much success as Acosta in being accepted as a bachatero. Although Acosta continues to record both merengue and bachata as a solo artist, more than one Dominican informed me, "he's a bachatero now." In fact, bachatero Henry Santos pointed to Acosta as an example of a born bachatero: "Héctor Acosta, el Torito—he was born a bachtero. He was just doing merengue. But when I heard him, I was like, this guy sounds like a bachatero.... Voice, feeling, a way of singing ... he sounds like a bachatero.... Then he started doing bachata, and look where it got him."[40] Acosta's outstanding work earned him the 2013 Gran Soberano, the most prestigious of the Soberano Awards.

Conclusion

The romantic bachata of the 1990s and new millennium continues to depict the different angles of love and love lost, although now with gentler lyrics and from more varied points of view. Bachateros have expanded their content and consider relationships in general, social topics, and what it means to be part of a transnational community. More complex arrangements and musical fusions have accompanied this sentimental approach. This breadth of content and softer interpretive approach contributed to bachata's growing popularity, helping undermine the discrimination against it. By 2003, bachata's reach had extended so far that the Dominican National Symphony highlighted the genre in a special production, *Bachata sinfónica*, under the direction of William Liviano. These romantic bachateros' work fostered the genre's acceptance within the country and abroad and would serve as a point of departure for a new generation of bachateros in the Dominican transnational community.

Seven

The Dominican Transnational Community and Bachata Típica

My friend, Darío, and I had stopped at a street vendor's stall in Washington Heights, Upper Manhattan, for *majarete* on a cold December afternoon. As we indulged in the sweet, creamy corn pudding, I tapped my toe in time to the bachata I heard in a nearby business. Looking around with a shiver, it seemed that the only thing that really separated the scene before me from a street in the Dominican Republic was the bitter cold and the snow that threatened. There, in the midst of this scene so reminiscent of the Dominican Republic, it was concretely evident what it meant to be part of a transnational community.

Dominican Migration Abroad

Dominican out-migration was selectively limited under Trujillo, but migration trends shifted significantly following his assassination. The United States, and principally New York, became Dominicans' primary destination. In addition to political upheaval following the dictator's fall, changing U.S. immigration policy encouraged migration. The 1965 Hart-Celler Immigration and Nationality Act abolished the system of quotas based on migrants' national origins that had been in place since the 1920s, but required immigrants to present evidence that they filled a labor need.[1] Dominicans continued to migrate in unprecedented numbers thanks to exemptions to this regulation granted to immediate relatives of established migrants. This laid the foundation for networks of kinship as an essential element of Dominican migration.[2] Approximately 75 percent of these early migrants were from urban areas,[3] and the majority of those migrating to New York in the 1960s and 1970s came from the lower-middle, working class.[4] During that time, the Dominican population in New York grew by more than 400 percent.[5] The 1990s saw a sharp climb from 348,000 to 695,000 Dominicans in the U.S.; numbers skyrocketed again between 2000 and 2004 to approximately one million.[6] Presently, Dominicans constitute the fourth largest U.S. Hispanic group, outranked only by Mexicans, Puerto Ricans, and Cubans.[7] While New York City remains the primary U.S. destination, significant Dominican communities can also be found in New Jersey, Massachusetts and Florida. Puerto Rico is also a common destination for Dominican migrants, and especially, illegal

immigration by crossing the dangerous Mona Passage in makeshift boats known as
yolas.[8]

Dominican migrants to the United States retain strong ties to their homeland at
the same time that they integrate into a life in the U.S. Dominicans thus exemplify
the common characteristics of transnationalism with its "constant flow of people in
both directions, a dual sense of identity, ambivalent attachments to two nations, and
a far-flung network of kinship and friendship ties across state frontiers."[9] Concurrently
living with one foot in two different worlds has contributed to a fluid sense of identity
among these migrants. These two realities are mutually important, for Dominican
migrants "became simultaneously incorporated into two national communities ...
ties to home were part of the process of becoming New Yorkers, and the process of
becoming New Yorkers helped constitute ties to home."[10] Economic transactions, and
especially remittances, real estate and small business investments in the Dominican
Republic, and dollars spent on trips back home help strengthen these transnational
ties.

Dominicans' dual participation in two worlds contributes to a psychological and
verbal distinction between the two overlapping sites. Many migrants originally left
the island with the intention of staying only temporarily in the United States and
eventually returning home to stay. Although this is not often the case, migrants' emotional ties to the homeland remain strong and are reiterated through the verbiage
they employ to describe their home and host nations, contrasting the U.S.—*aquí*
(here) or *este país* (this country)—with *allá* (there) or *mi país* (my country).[11] Such
nostalgic ties to the homeland remain strong, even among Dominican Americans
who were born in the United States, thus revealing how "[d]iasporas always leave a
trail of collective memory about another place and time and create new maps of
desire and attachment."[12]

Dominicans' intimate bonds with the homeland are reinforced through dreaming
about and making visits home. The Dominican Tourism Office in New York contributed to these trips by advertising for Christmas visits. All aspects of the tourist
industry were reimagined and represented with images considered typically Dominican, serving as a magnet to pull on the heartstrings of homesick migrants.[13] Numerous
Dominican-owned and operated travel agencies in U.S. Dominican communities facilitate migrants' travel home by providing economic flights and thus, increasing the
frequency of migrants' visits.[14]

Ties to home are solidified in U.S. Dominican neighborhoods such as Washington
Heights and the Bronx. Colmados sell Dominican products, restaurants serve typical
food, street vendors offer Dominican wares, and merengue and bachata filter out of
businesses and homes into the streets. Newspapers and media also keep Dominicans
up to date. Early on, Dominicans abroad constructed an elaborate exchange with
national newspapers. Not only did they read the newspapers hot off the press each
morning, they contributed to them by writing home. As Hoffnung-Garskof has
pointed out, the representations of Dominican migrants sent home and printed often
left out much of the actual hardship they faced, instead emphasizing opportunities
and success stories.[15] Migrants also became the storytellers of their own Horacio
Alger–type tales of making it big in the U.S., stories played out by the actors themselves who returned home bearing gifts and wearing the outward appearance of

upward mobility. Bestowing these gifts to friends and family members asserted not only success but also the ongoing ties to the homeland.[16] Unfortunately, success stories are not the norm for many Dominican migrants whose economic situation has not greatly improved in the U.S. Although many migrants remain below the poverty line, their compatriots continue to leave the island in search of a better life.

Dominican laws have encouraged political ties to home. In 1996, the new constitution granted those who obtained a second citizenship the retention of full rights as Dominican citizens. The constitution allows those born to Dominican parents in other countries to enjoy the full benefits of Dominican citizenship.[17] The Dominican National Congress's 1997 decision to allow those who resided abroad to run for office and vote in presidential elections has encouraged even greater participation in national politics.

Regardless of these ties, some in the homeland believe migrants lack cultura or authenticity. The distinction between island Dominicans and migrants is made through the disparaging term, *Dominican York*, or *domínican*—those who lose their cultura by being inundated with American culture.[18] The term *dominicano ausente* evolved to reference those Dominican migrants who had not lost their cultura and essential Domincanness. Others scorned migrants' remittances and gifts with another disparaging term, *cadenú*, with reference to the *cadenas* or gold chains that many returned wearing. This term "referred specifically to cultural artifacts, to symbols of consumer power ... and more broadly for the foreign-inspired class pretensions of Dominicans with no real cultura."[19]

Dominican migrants to the U.S. are often lumped into the general group of people of color, or associated with or mistaken for Puerto Ricans as Spanish-speakers. Although Dominican migrants face many of the same challenges as these groups, they tend not to align with them.[20] Dominican migrants distanced themselves from other minority groups, and language and music became common tools for marking those boundaries. First merengue, and later bachata, served as musical signs of identity for Dominicans, differentiating them from other groups and helping them face the anxieties of migration by reinforcing nationalistic ties to home. The growing number of working-class migrants who came to New York in the 1980s significantly increased the audiences already familiar with bachata to expand its fan base abroad.

Migrants not only imported these genres from the island, they also incorporated the rhythms and life experiences of their own realities into these two quintessentially Dominican forms. Bachata, with its tradition of suffering, spoke especially to Dominican migrants in New York City:

> If bachata's low-class associations had formerly rendered it anathema to anyone with middle-class aspirations, in New York, where immigrants of diverse social backgrounds were sharing similar experiences of economic hardship and social dislocation, such social pressures began to lose ground to immigrants' powerful desire for more "authentic" sounds of home.[21]

Bachata's sentimental repertoire expressed all angles of suffering and longing, and it became a powerful magnet for Dominicans abroad, especially among women.[22]

Bachata and the Transnational Community

The presence of the large Dominican transnational community in the U.S. offers new opportunities to traditional bachateros who live in those areas. These musicians perform and record their own and others' songs in venues that run the gamut from birthday parties to bars and concerts. Income differs by event and varies from a flat fee to a cover charge.[23] A given song's potential also depends on the market, and "If it's not a hit there, it might be here. It's local."[24] This section serves as a snapshot of three New York-based bachateros who continue to perform and produce traditional bachata outside Dominican borders.

Ray Santana "el Pollito del Cibao" was born in Dajabón in 1967. Pollito's life story reflects common themes among bachateros: his family worked the land, and from the early age of seven or eight, he was running the rice farm. He remembers listening to bachata greats such as Eladio Romero Santos and Luis Segura, and this instilled in him a curiosity for music. Pollito's musical path took him from playing local parties and events in Dajabón, to Santiago, then Santo Domingo, and finally New York where he has lived for over a decade. Now, Pollito performs in New York, Boston, and wherever he is invited to play.[25]

Pollito has seen the number of bachata bands explode during his time in the U.S. "Now," he says, "there are more bachata groups than places for them to play."[26] Despite this increase in bachateros, bachata has been lucrative for Pollito: "I've been making my living off of music, off of bachata, for several years now.... Thank God, I could buy a house for my mother because of bachata."[27] Pollito has been recognized with a Premio Too Much Award as the Bachata Artist of the Year, and a nomination to Los Premios Latinos in 2010.[28]

Rafy Burgos "*el Cupido*" comes from a modest rural family. He grew up listening to bachata with his family: "My family always liked bachata. We always listened to it."[29] Burgos also noted that merengue's doors were closed to him because of a lack of financial backing: "I barely had enough to buy myself a guitar. Merengue comes with a lot of expensive instruments. The only guys who could buy those were the ones whose parents said, 'here, go by yourself an instrument.' I didn't have that kind of support."[30] As a teen, Burgos moved to his godmother's house in San Francisco de Macorís so that he could finish high school. He worked in a small store during the day and took classes at night, and in between, he joined a friend's band as a back-up singer.[31]

Burgos joined the band Tropical in 1997 and toured with them abroad. He came to the U.S. to perform in 1998 and stayed to pursue his solo career. He released his first album, *Flechando corazones*[32] in 1999; his second release, *Con el corazón flechado* (In Love), included a popular remake of the 1980s merengue by Sandy Reyes, "*Enamorar* (Falling in Love)." This song helped earn Burgos a nomination for Premio Lo Nuestro's Best New Artist in 2003.

Bachatero and producer Gerson Corniel, a native of Salcedo, comes from a rural family that worked the land. At the age of 12, Corniel moved to Santiago with his family where his father began his own business. Corniel described his father, who played the accordion, and his uncle as his first musical influences. His mother supported his musical inclination from an early age by constructing makeshift instruments for him to play.[33] Corniel dropped out of school around the age of 15 to work and dedicate more time to music. From Santiago, he went to Santo Domingo and continued to play with different groups, working his way up: "I kept climbing. I started out playing second guitar, and later, first guitar."[34]

Corniel remembers the discrimination bachata suffered and how it was branded as lower-class music. Detractors' insults didn't sway Corniel, though: "I didn't feel badly; I enjoyed my bachata ... because that's what was inside of me. I was proud to be a musician."[35] He also recalls the challenges of recording bachata without access to the best studios: "Now, it's really easy to record. Before, everyone was stuck in a room with only one microphone."[36]

These musicians' songs continue the bachata lyrical tradition of painting the many hues of love and suffering. In Gerson Corniel's "*Ante una flor* (Before a Flower)," the narrative voice recognizes that he must give his sweetheart her freedom and that she will return to him if her love is true. Meanwhile, he pledges to love and never forget her. The narrator in Rafy Burgos's "Enamorar" refuses to give up his quest to win his beloved's heart, regardless of how much she resists. He offers her his heart and begs her to end his suffering with her love.

Desamor continues to be a prominent theme, too. The narrator of Pollito's "*Corazón enamorado* (A Heart in Love)" maintains that his heart, not he, is in love. His capricious heart refuses to forget his sweetheart, even though she is with another, and it speaks her name in each heartbeat. Gerson Corniel's "*Ella no me quiere* (She Doesn't Love Me)" relates the narrator's decision to leave rather than continue to suffer from unrequited love. Rafy Burgos's "*Romeo y Julieta: La historia* (The Story of Romeo and Juliet)" turns the story of Romeo and Juliet on its head and mourns the disillusionment of romantics worldwide who learn that the legendary couple's love was not eternal.

Rafy Burgo's 2010 hit "*Dame cabeza*" returns to the tradition of double entendre bachata. This song revolves around the double entendre in the title, which can mean either "think about it" or "give me head." In this bachata, the narrator admits that he once fell in love and suffered from his sweetheart's infidelity. Now, he isn't looking for a serious relationship, and tells the woman with whom he's speaking, "*dame cabeza*," to be interpreted as one sees fit.

Pollito's "*La travesía* (The Crossing)" interweaves love, abandonment, and migration. The narrator in this song begs his sweetheart to take him with her wherever she may go. Later, he observes that no one seems to be happy in his homeland and that everyone believes the grass is greener elsewhere. The narrator finally reveals that she was ambitious and unhappy with what he had to offer, so she attempted to migrate to Puerto Rico in a yola and died in the crossing. The narrator vows to live a good life so that he might someday be reunited with his beloved in heaven. This bachata tells a story that speaks to many aspects of the Dominican experience: love, separation, ambition or that the only hope for a better future is found by migrating, sometimes at any cost.

Conclusion

Relaxed immigration restrictions and continuing economic and political instability contributed to Dominican migration abroad, while networks of kinship and ties to the homeland reinforce dominicanidad. "Bachata is a music of the uprooted,"[37] and it gave voice to the experience of learning to live, work, love, and dream in a new and unknown setting. Many of these immigrants faced similar social conditions as those who had first moved to the Dominican cities following Trujillo's assassination: low-paying jobs, poverty, discrimination, conditions all that are magnified by the sense of being out of one's element—the "product of the insurmountable and irrevocable cognitive dissonance of living where *'I don't know how to live.'*"[38]

New York–based bachateros deliver bachata to a growing audience looking for those ties to home or simply a fun time. As Rafy Burgos observed, "Music is an international language"[39] and bachata's popularity across class, national, and linguistic boundaries speaks for itself. Migrants' disposable income facilitated their access to music consumption, and this encouraged bachata's potential for economic viability. As migrants' social position improved, so did the social position of bachata. Migrants played bachata from new vehicles on return trips home, arousing the middle and upper classes' curiosity and helping bachata gain a following and improved status.[40]

EIGHT

United States and
Mainstream Modern Bachata

The street in front of the Bronx address I'd been given was dark and deserted when the taxi dropped my husband and me off at almost 10:00 p.m. In the distance, I could hear sirens, and up above, bachata's unmistakable pulse beating out onto the still, night air. Moments later, producer and bachatero Lenny Santos explained that this setting was integral to the modern bachata he helped bring to life and continues to play and produce: "I was born and raised in the Bronx, actually two, three blocks from here. I live upstate now.... But I've got my studio here in the Bronx, because that's where all the ideas ... everything comes from. I can't do music in front of deer and squirrels. I need to hear the sirens and the noise."[1]

In just such a setting, bachata has evolved to express the realities of these new generations of Dominican Americans. It is a fusion of languages—lyrics are an interplay of Spanish and English—and musical influences such as R&B, pop, rock, and reggaetón that complement bachata. Later, musicians emphasized the R&B "musical progressions ... and R&B infused sound effects" with a bass "drum kick throughout the whole bachata"[2] in urban bachata. The international popularity of modern and urban bachata helped carry the genre around the world.[3] This modern and mainstream bachata, representative of what it means to be Dominican within a transnational setting, was also influential in rethinking the genre within its traditional context.

Bachata in the Diaspora

Although children often snub their parents' music as out of style, young Dominican Americans increasingly listened to bachata.[4] Often, these were closet fans, just as in the Dominican Republic. Modern bachatero Henry Santos, who graduated from a U.S. high school in 1996, remembers, "You would see my friends in school listening to bachata, but hiding. They would be hiding! ... Even in my house, I remember that my father ... would tell me, '*En mi casa no se escucha bachata* (We do not listen to bachata in my house).'"[5] These young Dominican Americans increasingly embraced bachata as symbolic of their ethnic roots in the 1990s,[6] listening to and collecting recordings of bachateros such as Antony Santos, Luis Vargas, Joe Veras, and Frank Reyes.[7]

These young fans were not only consumers, they became bachateros themselves, and in their hands and voices, they transformed typical bachata with the musical and linguistic influences around them to create modern bachata. Although these musicians did not come from privileged families in the American sense, they had access to opportunities unavailable to their counterparts on the island,[8] including linguistic advantages that helped carry bachata to a wider market: "they were born and raised in the United States. They speak English and know a lot of refined words that those guys from the countryside don't."[9] In their hands, "bachata molted ... but with the awareness of what original bachata is."[10] The bachata they made was based in their understanding and interpretation of the genre's musical essence.[11] As Henry Santos affirms, "In order to do modern bachata, you have to know the soul of traditional bachata."[12]

Life for these migrants was also a blend of languages, and Spanglish in modern bachata lyrics is much more a fact of life than a marketing venture. Lenny Santos described this blend of Spanish and English as representative of who band members are: "we want to show the people that we're both. We're Americans and Latinos. And we want to show where we're from, how we were raised, our culture. You know, I speak Spanglish."[13] Lenny reiterates that this type of code-switching—"the alternate use of two languages"[14]—is done with the intended audience in mind: "since you speak Spanish, too, I'll flip Spanish and English.... So we do it with the music."[15]

Code-switching in music, just as in literature, "represents a reality where segments of the population are living between cultures and languages."[16] These switches are not the result of sloppy language use, but rather, reflect the realities of bilingual speakers who move from one language to another for a word or phrase that best expresses a thought or concept.[17] As Grosjean observes, code-switching "is also used as a communicative or social strategy, to show speaker involvement ... [and] ... mark group identity."[18] For many second and third-generation Dominican migrants, English is their dominant or base language, and Spanish is a second language. Bachatero Toby Love observes:

> I guess that's how we're raised—with our families we'll speak Spanish, and being in the street with our friends, we'll speak more English.... You know, a lot of my Latino friends, they don't speak Spanish fluently, so I have to speak English.... I wanted to give music back to my people, where I'm from.... That's the way we talk normally.[19]

Singer-songwriter Henry Santos describes the use of Spanglish as the result of the rhythmic and melodic quality of words. According to him, fitting words to a certain melody is "like a puzzle ... the melody tells me certain things.... And if it's English or Spanish, I cannot really sit down and tell you, 'I'm going to write you an English song right now.' Because it doesn't work that way.... It is born by itself."[20] Fitting the words to the rhythm in the melody is a natural, organic process, and not forced.[21]

All of these innovations came with their own dose of criticism and discrimination from bachata purists. Some fans and musicians criticized the modern bachateros for ruining their music with their inclusion of English, other instruments, and different genres,[22] just as bolero aficionados had done of the first bachatas. Others thought it too refined and lacking "grajo," an essential rustic element.[23] Regardless, modern bachata rapidly drew a large and faithful following among Dominican American and

Dominican youth, and also among audiences worldwide. Modern bachata's growing international popularity circled back to the Dominican Republic via transnational routes, and migrants' consumer buying power and practices helped push bachata into the forefront of the international music scene.[24]

Aventura

The four-member band, Aventura, offered the first major expression of modern bachata. These self-proclaimed "Kings of Bachata" or "K.O.B." gave bachata a new sound and face that is unique to the experience of Dominican migrants and their children in New York. Like many of their fans, lead singer Anthony "Romeo" Santos, guitarist and arranger Lenny Santos, and bassist Max "Mikey" Santos (Max Agende) were born in the Bronx, and singer-songwriter Henry Santos was born in Moca, Dominican Republic, and migrated to New York at thirteen. As teenagers, they were fans of bachata innovators Antony Santos and Luis Vargas, and of romantic bachateros such as Joe Veras and Raulín Rodríguez.[25] Lenny Santos recalls, "I started liking bachata after I heard Antony Santos and Luis Vargas storm the whole New York City area and the Dominican community. Already these guys did their job—Paniagua, Luis Segura, guys like that. But people were branded out here, not really mainstream yet."[26] The infamous rift between Antony Santos and Luis Vargas drew attention to bachata both at home and abroad. As Lenny listened to more and more bachata, he was especially drawn to the guitar, wondering how the bachateros brought those sounds out of their instrument.[27]

Lenny began to watch videos of his idol, Antony Santos, including home videos recorded by relatives who went to concerts on return trips to the Dominican Republic. Amazed by the sound of the guitar, Lenny bought a guitar for twenty-five dollars at a local pharmacy, and asked his cousin to teach him to play. Lenny practiced the three chords his cousin showed him and played them along with Antony Santos videos and records, and also those of other genres such as rock and heavy metal, always imitating what he saw. As Lenny's skills grew, so did his interest in performing. He formed his first band, *Sueños* (Dreams) while still in high school, along with his brother Max on bass, another cousin as lead singer, and several friends playing bongos, güira, piano and drums. At that time, Lenny considered his band a hobby, albeit an important one, but not a possible profession.[28]

The band practiced in a Puerto Rican social club and performed outside local businesses with a box on the street to accept any payments left by appreciative passersby. One day, Lenny's pianist approached him about bringing a new singer into the group. Lenny remembers that his friend insisted, "'he's always singing. I mean, he sounds like a bird.... He has this sweet voice.... He just sounds so unique.'"[29] So Lenny invited the singer, Anthony "Romeo" Santos, to practice, but first, Romeo visited him at his Bronx apartment. The two compared their bachata favorites on the stairs before Romeo offered a sample by singing an Antony Santos song. "I was shocked," recalls Lenny. "And with that reverb that hallway gives, I was like, wow! This guy sounds great. This kid is awesome!"[30] So Romeo joined the band.

The band's first performance was at the social club where they practiced. The event was informal, without advertising or a playlist, and the two lead singers took turns. Soon thereafter, Lenny's cousin left the band, and Romeo was left as the sole lead singer; Romeo's cousin, Henry Santos, came on board to sing as well. The band changed its name to "*Los Tinellers*" (a Dominicanization of "teenagers") and played well-known bachatas at local events. With time, they began to rehearse their own compositions, and eventually, they recorded their first album, *Trampa de amor* (Love's Trap). Although the album did not make a splash, it eventually opened the door for the group when Romeo played it for producer Julio César. He recognized their talent and signed with them, changing their name to Aventura to represent the new, fresh appeal of a group of young Dominican Americans making bachata. In 1999, Aventura released *Generation Next,* which included several remakes off of their first album.

Aventura's music reflects their experiences of growing up surrounded by multiple languages, cultures, and rhythms in the Bronx. For band members, life was always a collage of different sounds that surrounded them at home and on the streets.[31] Lenny Santos cites music's constant presence in his life as his motivation: "I got into music because all around me, all you hear is music. You go outside, you hear people pumping their cars with music ... hip-hop, R&B, rock.... But at home, I hear merengue and bachata music. And it was a blend."[32]

Aventura brings these innovative sounds to its bachata, largely inspired by guitarist Lenny Santos's arrangements: "The first person to really put sounds into the bachata and have the courage to change it all around, when it comes to implementing guitar effects, and hip-hop and R&B, was me—Lenny."[33] Lenny points to bachatero Antony Santos as his primary influence in creating the "poppy sound" of bachata by lowering the guitar strings and playing them with a thumb pick.[34] With this point of departure, Lenny experimented to create his own sound with the inclusion of electric guitars, wah-wah pedal (an effect that mimics the human voice), and tremolo.[35] Lenny identifies the new and innovative sounds, instrumentation, and topics as what truly set modern bachata apart from typical bachata: "We use a lot more harmonies ... there's more R&B, rock. We use a lot more instruments—synthesizers and strings— and rhythms inside the bachata.... We were the first ones to introduce social songs and what's happening in that moment."[36]

In addition to their musical and lyrical innovations, Aventura presented a contemporary, youthful face to bachata without losing any of the sentiment so crucial to the genre. The cover of Aventura's first album, *Generation Next* (1999), proclaimed that the band represented "*La nueva generación de la bachata* (The New Generation of Bachata)," and featured the group in jeans with Romeo in an unbuttoned, long-sleeved, white shirt, and Lenny, Henry and Max in sleeveless white T-shirts. This look contrasts with early bachata album covers in which bachateros such as Rafael Encarnación wore suits and ties. Aventura's typical wardrobe, both on album covers and onstage, reflects a contemporary look with an attire of jeans, T-shirts, hoodies, flat-billed baseball caps or stocking caps, informal jackets, and vests. When the group donned suits and ties for an album cover—*K.O.B. Live* (2006)—it was to emphasize their image as leaders of a youthful craze. This black and white cover featured the group in moptops, Beatles-era suits and thin ties, and it underlined Aventura's role as hip heartthrobs. The New York flavor of Aventura's bachata is also reiterated through album covers highlighting urban backgrounds and the New York skyline.

For some bachata purists, Aventura's instrumentation, plus its Spanglish lyrics and inclusion of other genres such as R&B and hip-hop, was worthy of criticism and complaints that the band was "'messing up our music.'"[37] Unfazed by claims that they were just a bachata boy band—a "'Dominicano N'Sync,'"[38] Aventura continued with their innovative style. The title of Aventura's second album, *We Broke the Rules*, is a response to those who saw them as somehow lowering or devaluing bachata.

Aventura's sound and look struck a chord with a younger generation of Dominican and Dominican American music consumers, and in a broader Latino and global audience. As Larry Rohter points out, "According to the 2010 census the Hispanic population of the United States is now more than 50 million, making Latinos the nation's largest minority group. Of those 18 or under ... more than 90 percent were born in this country, and many of them are bilingual and bicultural."[39] This connection to a multicultural and multilingual world is essential to Aventura's popularity in the Dominican American context. Leila Cobo of Billboard explains Aventura's appeal through a parallel to Tex Mex star Selena Quintanilla "'who was from Texas and spoke to people who were like her.... Romeo appealed to an audience that was like him and didn't see other people like them up on the stage.'"[40] Bachata's common themes of lost love, hardship, suffering, and longing for something better, seasoned with themes and realities of the twenty-first century, resonate with Spanish-speakers of varying origins. Played through the amp of the Dominican American experience, Aventura's unique sound speaks to migrants in general.

Despite Aventura's instrumental innovations and their blending of languages and genres, bachata's time-honored, emotional interpretive style and themes of love, heartache, and disillusion are still present. For example, the narrative voice in "*Cuándo volverás* (When Will You Come Back)"[41] sings of his unwarranted abandonment, wondering plaintively where his sweetheart is and when she might return. Similarly, the narrator of "*Por un segundo* (For One Second)" regrets his lost love, which he describes as a fairytale starring him as the king, and his beloved as the princess. The speaker in "*Dile al amor* (Tell Love)" converses with Cupid, criticizing the god for missing the mark with his enchanted arrows. "*Ella y yo* (She and I)" portrays the double betrayal of a woman and a male friend. In this reggaetón, which features that genre's Don Omar, one man must confront the bitter realization that his wife has been unfaithful to him with his friend. Until the truth is revealed, the husband excuses his friend's adulterous actions, reminding him that love is worth fighting for, especially if the woman's husband no longer loves her. Only when the friend admits the truth does the husband recant. This song, then, depicts a double standard of machismo: seduction and multiple lovers is acceptable up to the point that one's own woman is involved.

Love is the central theme of other Aventura songs. In "*Un beso* (One Kiss)," the narrator relates how Cupid's arrow found its mark in one kiss from his beloved. Similarly, the redemptive power of love is the central focus of "*Princesita* (Little Princess)." The narrative voice admits that he was formerly a shameless player. Now, in the face of the woman's purifying love, he vows to leave that life behind so that he can build a future alongside her. The narrator's love has become an obsession in the bachata of the same name ("*Obsesión*"). He has lost all friends and contact with reality, and although he insists that it is love, she is equally positive it is an obsession.

Aventura also sings of situations that reiterate gendered social roles, such as *machismo* and *marianismo*.[42] Aventura's merengue, *"Mujeriego* (Womanizer)"* epitomizes machismo's central elements. The narrative voice is the quintessential conquistador who admits to courting two women at the same time. As he speaks to an audience of male listeners, the narrator excuses his actions by claiming that he is a womanizer by simple virtue of being a man, and above all, a Dominican man. Claiming that God made him with this characteristic, he excuses himself by insisting that he does not lie to any of the women he seduces. When his listeners reproach him, he justifies his actions by pointing out that he is not the only man who has more than one woman, and proceeds to list off all of the guilty parties.

Aventura broke ground by treating social themes in their bachata. *"No lo perdona Dios* (God Doesn't Forgive It)"* relates the contemporary situation of a woman who has the freedom to opt to abort a child conceived out of wedlock and in poverty, while at the same time underscoring traditional family roles and values of the overarching importance of woman's role as mother. In this song, the narrator harshly criticizes his partner for choosing to abort their child, even though they are no longer together. The word choice describes her as ignorant, heartless and unfeeling. While the singer states that his former lover killed an innocent child who—true to many Dominican parents' hopes—might have grown up to be a baseball player or even a bachatero, the narrator emphasizes his own loss and missed opportunity to be a father. He challenges her reasons for aborting, which he labels as excuses: her regret over their failed romance and her desire not to have a child born into poverty. Therefore, although "No lo perdona Dios" presents a contemporary situation, it reinforces traditional social roles and values for both men and women.

"Amor de madre (A Mother's Love)"* upholds the construction of woman as a mother who suffers and endures all for the sake of her family. In this song, a single mother finds herself in financial straits. When welfare proves insufficient, she turns to prostitution—described as her only option—to provide for her son. The mother's efforts to ascertain that her son never lacks anything instead serve to spoil him: he drives a late-model car and wears Armani fashions. The mother's blind eye to his actions enables the son, who eventually is imprisoned for murder. In this song, the mother's actions are excused because of her mother's love, while her son is criticized for not recognizing her affection and sacrifice in time. Together, these representations reinforce traditional gendered values.

In contrast, *"Hermanita* (Little Sister)"* criticizes domestic violence. In this song, the male voice attempts to make his sister see clearly the reality of her situation. The word choice is stark and honest, portraying both the physical and emotional abuse the battered woman knows. The abuser is depicted as a monster, a rat, and a dog—a heartless drunk who cares nothing for his partner or their children. Despite this violent setting, this song still reaffirms family values: the narrator reminds his sister that they are family and offers to put the abusive partner in his place.

The theme of woman as a siren leading man astray and to his perdition is central to *"Su veneno* (Her Poison)"* and *"Peligro* (Danger)."* In the former, the male voice accuses his beloved of poisoning him through her kisses and ridding him of sound judgment and good sense. He no longer has control over his actions or decisions, and is unable to resist her venomous attraction. In *"Peligro,"* the unfaithful woman is described as a dangerous serpent, a devil in woman's clothing. She deceives the innocent narrator, taking advantage of both his sentiments and his bank account.

Aventura has been hugely successful in taking bachata to a broader, mainstream audience, including English-speakers. In September 2007, the group made history by being the first bachata band to play at Madison Square Garden.[43] Two years later, Aventura achieved another bachata first when they were invited to perform "*Su veneno*" before President and Mrs. Obama in the "Fiesta Latina" concert that formed part of the series, *In Performance at the White House.* Aventura highlighted both their Dominican roots—"We want to share with you our Dominican culture"—and their upbringing in the Bronx—"The Bronx is in the house!"[44] A unique product of the Dominican American experience, Aventura showcased the goal of Fiesta Latina: to "celebrate Latin music's place in the rich and colorful tapestry of American culture."[45]

At the time of this writing, Aventura is taking what has largely been called a "hiatus."[46] The four band members went their separate ways after their final album, *The Last* (2009), which ACROARTE identified as one of 100 essential albums[47] and described it as "the best album of their transcendental discography."[48] These artists forever changed the world of bachata: "We were the ones who came up with modern bachata. We made people around the world listen to this rhythm called bachata.... We showed bachata to the world.... We broadened the market; we broke it open."[49] Even though Aventura has disbanded, its founders continue to influence bachata, as we shall see below.

Toby Love

Octavio Rivera, who goes by the stage name Toby Love, is a Bronx native born of Puerto Rican parents. Love comes from a musical family, and he describes his family atmosphere as one where "there was always music, whether it be Christmas or a birthday.... That's just the type of family that we are."[50] Love began playing a variety of percussion instruments before his singing debut as a candlestick in a musical production of *Beauty and the Beast* at the age of nine.[51] Love's father had a merengue band, and Love accompanied him to gigs, playing bongos or güira even as a young child. Later, Love sang and played güira in his own merengue band.[52]

Love began his formal career at the age of 16 as a backup singer for Aventura before launching a solo career in 2006. Love admits that his first love was R&B and Michael Jackson pop, although his family listened to a variety of genres. For Love, bachata was the Dominican answer to the rhythm and blues he loved, and when his friend, Max Agende, invited him to be a part of the band, he joined without ever signing a contract, at his parents' request.

Love's bachata integrates soft rock, R&B and hip-hop with bachata and his tender voice. Love emphasizes that he wanted to differentiate himself from Aventura with something new, so when he recorded a single with rapper Pitbull, he christened it as "crunkchata."[53] Love describes this as "more street" than traditional and modern bachata.[54] According to Love, he first used the term "urban" to describe the fusions he brought to bachata in an interview, and the name stuck and is often used to refer to all modern bachata.[55]

Toby Love's bachata contains many of amargue's usual themes while his nickname—"*La voz de la juventud* (The Voice of Youth)"—and his hip attire reiterate a connection with a young, new generation of bachata consumers. Desamor continues to be a common theme, although Toby Love sings of it in both English and Spanish. The narrator of "*Lejos* (Far Away)" condemns the woman as a heartless seductress who bewitched him and took advantage of his love. Now, he orders her to save her crocodile tears and to go far away. In contrast, the speaker in "*Tengo un amor* (My Love)" follows the common bachata and bolero traditions of speaking directly to the woman to bemoan her abandonment. The narrator also suffers from love lost in "*Llorar lloviendo* (Crying in the Rain)." He reveals that men sometimes need to cry, no matter how tough they try to appear. Nevertheless, he wishes for a rainstorm to cover the evidence of his tears so that no one knows of his broken heart. "Llorar lloviendo" thus functions as a safe space in which it is socially acceptable for a man to cry—a bachata song—while at the same time reiterating that macho men veil their emotions.

Love and the possibility of love are also themes in Love's modern bachata. His 2013 bachata remake of "I Just Can't Stop Lovin' You (*Todo mi amor eres tú*)" celebrates the woman's attributes and the narrator's love for her. Although the narrative voice of "*Nueva York* (New York)" has lost his heart in some corner of the world, he still nourishes the hope that he will find her again in New York—the place where dreams meet and all paths cross. The speaker of "*Y volveré* (And I'll Return)" is similarly hopeful that a new day may bring an end to the couple's suffering and a new dawn to their love.

Uncertainty in love is the central theme in other Love bachatas. "*Casi, casi* (Almost, Almost)" portrays a timid man whose shyness prevents him from proclaiming his feelings. This narrator suffers not from love lost, but from love yet unrealized. In "*Te parece poco* (It Means Nothing to You)," the singer is also uncertain, although in this scenario, his confusion arises from the woman's seeming lack of appreciation for his love. He enumerates all that he has done for her, though she sees his actions as insignificant.

Although Love is now one of the biggest names in modern bachata, he admits that traditional bachata fans did not embrace his experiments: "In the beginning, the traditional Dominicans didn't really accept what I was doing as far as the whole fusion of hip-hop, R&B, with the bachata…. But the kids accepted it."[56] Still, Love does not complain about the criticism:

> The criticism's always going to be there, but without criticism, that means you're not doing your job…. When we started something different with this genre, it was hard to break the barrier. And right now, people are accepting it all over the world. It's just incredible because I've been there from the beginning, the transition, to where bachata is now.[57]

Xtreme

The bachata duo, Xtreme, composed of U.S.-born Dominican Americans Danny D and Steve Styles, likewise appeared in 2004 and had several hits before disbanding in 2011. Xtreme complemented bachata with hip-hop and R&B, along with sentimental interpretations of traditional bachata themes. For example, the narrator of "*Te extraño* (I Miss You)," expresses his tears and suffering directly to the woman, although she has left him and is no longer physically present. He reiterates his suffering with images of burning, pain and solitude. Desamor is also the main theme of Xtreme's collaboration with actress/singer Adrienne Bailon in "*No me digas que no* (Don't Say No)." This song features the duo as a single narrative voice who asks his beloved to explain why she intends to leave. The female voice enumerates the narrator's transgressions and disavows him of the notion that she loves him. The focus then shifts, and the narrator talks about his beloved in the third person, reiterating that she is leaving him in spite of his attempts to atone for his actions.

Xtreme's "Shorty, Shorty" represents the most fluid blend between bachata and hip-hop. This song, whose title incorporates a hip-hop technique of referring to a beautiful woman as "shorty" (or "shawty"), relies heavily on code-switching as the narrator relates his tale of trying to find the woman who left him. Throughout, he speaks directly to the woman, explaining that he has become an insomniac and is dying without her. These images of suffering intermingle with expressions of the woman's beauty in both languages. The combination was a hit, and "Shorty, Shorty" rose to number one in the Latin Singles category.

Xtreme also brought their own look to bachata with their youthful faces (both Danny D and Steve Styles were born in 1985), cornrows, baggy jeans, and Styles's common accessory of a sweatband. This look was reiterated by the duo's dance moves in their music videos. For example, in "Te extraño," they wear baggy jeans, white tennis shoes and T-shirts, and black leather jackets. They perform a choreographed hip-hop routine during the instrumental mambo section that highlights their moves.

Xtreme marked another bachata first by appearing in an eight-episode reality show, *On the Verge*, on the Spanish cable network Mun2. As the name suggests, the band was seen as being "on the verge" of making a big break, or not making it at all. In the spirit of reality television, the show highlighted the conflicts between the two as it followed them through their daily lives and musical careers in the Bronx and on tour. Although Xtreme ultimately disbanded after only a few years, their sound and look contributed to bachata's growing popularity among a global audience.

Prince Royce

Geoffrey Royce Rojas, who adopted the stagename Prince Royce, erupted onto the bachata scene in 2010 as a solo artist with his Spanglish urban bachata cover of Ben E. King's 1961 classic, "Stand by Me." Born in the Bronx to Dominican migrant parents, Royce's experiences are similar to other modern and urban bachateros, growing up with one foot in the music, languages and cultures of each of two worlds. With his bachata remake of "Stand By Me," Royce concretized this reality with his bilingual blend of bachata and a North American classic. His first hit was followed by others off his 2010 debut album, making it the number-one selling Latin album in 2011, and winning Royce Billboard's Latin Music Awards 2011 Best New Artist.[58] In his second album, *Phase II* (2012), Royce brings other sounds and styles to his bachata, such as

Mexican mariachi in "*Incondicional* (Unconditional)," and totally abandons the genre for pop and upbeat dance tempos in other songs. In the "Prelude" to the album, artist La Bruja chants over Afro-Cuban drums, telling of Prince Royce's rise to stardom from the Bronx and how he is a proud representative of dominicanidad. Royce has also pursued fusions with the Mexican rock band Maná in "*El verdadero amor perdona* (True Love Forgives)," salsero Luis Enrique in "*Sabes* (You Know)," and with Mexican pop star Thalía in "*Te perdiste mi amor* (You Lost My Love)"

Prince Royce, with his soulful voice, youthful face and stylish dress—he is often seen sporting a fedora or Gatsby—is the picture of sincerity as he interprets traditional bachata's romantic themes in his twenty-first century songs, many of whose lyrics he composes himself. In his hit "*Corazón sin cara* (Blind Love)," for example, the narrator scolds the woman he loves for worrying about her outward appearance, reminding her that true love is blind. Similarly, the narrator of "*Tú y yo* (You and I)" reminds his sweetheart that they are meant for each other and begs her not to listen to the lies her friends spread about his alleged unfaithfulness. As the title of "Incondicional" suggests, the narrator proclaims his unconditional love. He insists his love is real and selfless, and he will always fight for it. In much the same vein, "*Las cosas pequeñas* (The Little Things)" exalts the beauty of the little things that constitute love, such as a hug, kiss or glance.

Prince Royce also sings of love lost. In "*El amor que perdimos* (The Love We Lost)," the speaker is nostalgic about his former love. Similarly, "*La última carta* (The Last Letter)" is framed as the narrator's letter to his wife in a last-ditch effort to gain her forgiveness. The narrative voice of "*Mi habitación* (My Room)," alone in his room, mourns his lost love and her betrayal, while in "*Te me vas* (You're Leaving Me)" he recognizes that he hurt his beloved. The narrator of "*Memorias* (Memories)" remembers each aspect of a former love. The timbre of this song, which is as much soft pop as it is bachata, makes desamor sound almost painless.

Prince Royce's music also has a dose of machismo. In "*Su hombre soy yo* (I'm Her Man)," the narrator reminds his sweetheart that she belongs to him. He reprimands her, telling her to respect him. The pop rock dance track "Rock the Pants," primarily sung in English, is an urban machista statement of male dominance through its reference to the narrative voice wearing the pants in the relationship. In this song, the man declares he is tired of the woman's questions and plans to live out her worst suspicions. He rebukes her for not giving him enough space, and leaves for the club. Much like a strutting rooster, he intends to make the women at the club go wild with his dance moves.

Prince Royce continues to be one of the hottest modern bachata acts. His trendy look and sound have earned him nominations and awards, including Billboard, Premios Lo Nuestro, Premios Juventud, and Latin Grammy. Billboard's Latin Music Awards recognized the 22-year-old Royce as Composer of the Year in 2012, making him the youngest ever to receive this award.[59] Both of his albums have topped U.S. Latin and Tropical charts. Royce was the celebrity voice coach for the 2013 winning contestant, Paola Guanche, in *La Voz Kids*, a Spanish-language youth version of *The Voice*.

Romeo Santos

Aventura lead singer Romeo Santos was the first of the band to release a solo album in 2011, *Fórmula Vol. 1*. This album featured Romeo's unmistakable voice singing his trademark Spanglish bachatas along with several exclusively pop and rock songs and guest appearances by Usher, Lil Wayne, Mario Domm, rapper La Mala Rodríguez, and flamenco guitarist Tomatito. The album is bookended by two skits, an "Intro" and "Outro," that explain Romeo's musical formula as unique and confront his critics. Throughout the album, Romeo continues to refer to himself as the King (now in the singular) of Bachata.

Romeo's bachatas contain the common themes of love, suffering, and desamor. His first solo release, "You," celebrates love and its power to change a former player into a one-woman man. "Promise," featuring Usher, blends English and Spanish over a bachata base. This song portrays the narrator as a prisoner, condemned and held captive in the woman's body. Although the song is a duet between Romeo and Usher, the action is seen as from the point of view of a single male voice. Given the bilingual lyrics (Romeo sings in Spanish and Usher, in English), the duet can be read as one single person expressing himself in two languages. "*Mi santa* (My Saint)" depicts love as a religion. In this song, the narrative voice worships the woman and promises to prove his love through dangerous tests and valiant deeds. The song relies heavily on religious symbolism and language, such as prayers, lighting altar candles, fasting, and the sacrament of baptism. In contrast to a saint, the woman is portrayed as a she-devil in "*La diabla* (The She-Devil)." Although the narrator recognizes that he willingly took a risk, this femme fatale expertly outwits the unsuspecting man and beats him at the game of love. "*Soberbio* (Arrogant)" also makes use of fairytale imagery, for a wealthy man finds himself abandoned and alone in his castle without his princess.

The most interesting song on the album is "*Debate de 4* (Debate Among Four)," Romeo's collaboration with Luis Vargas, Raulín Rodríguez, and Antony Santos, which stages a showdown between the four bachateros to win a woman's love. Each states his individual virtues, emphasizing who they are within the world of bachata: Romeo, the King; Luis Vargas, the Rey Supremo de la Bachata; Raulín Rodríguez, the Cacique, and Antony Santos, the Mayimbe. In the chorus, they enumerate the weapons they brought with them to the debate, all of which are symbolic of bachata and its role as a romantic music: roses, a guitar, and a bottle of alcohol. The arguments that each singer presents reiterate his own qualities as a bachatero and his role within the genre, and they incorporate numerous intertextual references to their own music. Romeo sings in Spanglish and portrays himself as the unhappy, suffering King of Bachata. Luis Vargas is madly in love[60] yet sincere, and maintains that there is still a spark between him and bachata. Raulín Rodríguez emphasizes that he is a real man[61] and appeals directly to the woman/bachata,[62] claiming he no longer wants anything to do with solitude.[63] Antony Santos describes the woman/bachata as both beautiful and difficult,[64] admitting that his heart is guilty and he suffers because of her.[65] Nevertheless, he is certain he will win the battle.[66] Santos tells her to stop her little game and not to stand him up, even if it is a question of her shyness.[67] Although "Debate de 4" apparently is a showdown between four men vying for the same woman, this song can also be read on a different level in which each of the four singers seeks to dominate bachata. In the end, the winner is undecided. Bachata chooses none of them alone, and it could be inferred that she needs all of them together to be complete.

Romeo Santos's talent as a singer, composer, and producer has earned him nominations for Billboard, Billboard Latin, Premios Juventud, Premios Lo Nuestro, and the Soberano Awards. Romeo won the 2006 ASCAP Tropical Song of the Year, as well as another ASCAP award in the American pop market, becoming the first Hispanic composer to take home an ASCAP in the U.S. market.[68] He was recognized as Composer of the Year,[69] and "You" won him the 2012 ASCAP Tropical Song of the Year.

Henry Santos

Singer-songwriter Henry Santos, formerly of Aventura, has also released his first two solo albums, *Introducing* (2011), all bachata, and *My Way* (2013), which includes a merengue and dance numbers in addition to bachata. Santos's songs, many of his own composition, highlight the singer's interpretive sensibility. His first release, "*Poquito a poquito* (Little by Little)," is the male voice's plea for the woman to open her heart just a little bit to him. In addition to facilitating rhyming, the abundant use of the diminutive, *-ito*, communicates the same tenderness heard in Santos's voice. "*Dame una sonrisa* (Give Me a Smile)" expresses a similar situation in which the narrator finally overcomes his shyness and declares his love, encouraging the object of his affection to grace him with her smile and not to delay as she falls in love.

Henry Santos also sings of the tried and true bachata themes, desamor and desprecio. "*Por nada* (For No Reason)" questions the advisability of staying in a relationship in which two people intentionally hurt each other for no reason. Despite hurtful words and actions, the narrator admits that he is still in love and unable to forget her. In "*Mi adicción* (My Addiction)," the narrative voice describes his beloved and her love as an unbeatable addiction. Although she gives him momentary relief, he recognizes that she will eventually be his undoing.

In contrast to the suffering of these songs, the narrator of "*Deja de llorar (Mi desprecio)* (Stop Crying [My Disdian])" instigates the break-up. This song follows a skit, "Flippin' Channels," in which the narrative voice channel surfs, and we hear snippets of television ads and a brief weather forecast that situates the action squarely in New York. The skit ends with a short break-up scene from a Spanish-language *telenovela* (soap opera) in which the male character ends his romance with the sobbing female character, refusing to be convinced by her tears of remorse. "*Deja de llorar*" plays off this scene, and the narrative voice, just like the character in the soap opera, tells his former love to save her tears and forget him. The telenovela is interwoven intertextually into the song as the characters reappear in spoken parts, thus emphasizing the role of both genres in the Latin American romantic cultural paradigm. This interplay of cultural expressions nevertheless leaves room for interpretation, since the telenovela as a genre allows true love to win out and have a happy ending.[70] The possibility for reconciliation, then, is present, for one never knows what might transpire—just as the weather forecast in "Flippin' Channels" predicts a dry day but warns viewers to take an umbrella, just in case.

The strongest and most modern denunciation of the traditional theme of infidelity on Henry's first album is "Gotcha." In this case, the narrator reveals that he has known about his sweetheart's unfaithfulness for some time. Although he was blind to the deception at first, he plants cameras to test his suspicions and gives himself a second set of eyes that see more clearly than his own. He confronts his sweetheart with evidence that she was caught red-handed, informing her that he has also posted the videos on YouTube. Although the inclusion of video cameras and YouTube situate this song in the twenty-first century, its themes of desengaño, desamor and amargue follow longstanding bachata traditions.

Henry Santos's second solo album, *My Way* (2013), considers standard bachata themes within a broad cultural framework. In "*Mi poesía* (My Poetry)," the narrator defines his beloved as the muse of his music and poetry. She sticks in his thoughts, like an earworm from an oft-heard song, and she inspires him to great and valiant deeds, such as crossing the desert barefoot. His constant thoughts of her have made the narrative voice restless. In courtly tradition, love is a cult governed by Cupid, and an illness for which she is the only cure. The narrative voice of "*Vuelve conmigo* (Come Back to Me)" is also lovesick. This narrator admits he made a mistake, regrets his actions, and asks for forgiveness. He pleads with his beloved to return and save him from the death that awaits him without her love. When words fail, the narrator seeks an intermediary in the guitar, asking it to cry in his place. The instrumentation highlights the plucked guitar and imitates teardrops. In the end, the narrative voice again asks for forgiveness in both English and Spanish. "*No sé vivir sin ti* (I Don't Know How to Live Without You)," a duet with Tejano musician, Bobby Pulido, also represents love as an illness and insanity. This narrator mourns his abandonment and informs his ex that she is the only cure for what ails him. He is going crazy and insists that he is slowly dying without her. "*Preso en tu cárcel* (Your Prisoner)" brings to mind the medieval Spanish sentimental novel, *Cárcel de amor* (Prison of Love). While the lovesick prisoner of this 1492 bestseller allows himself to die from unrequited love, Santos's bachata portrays a narrator who is gladly and willingly held captive by his sweetheart's love. He is lovesick and madly in love with his jailer, and although he wasn't looking for love, he would fall prisoner to it again. This narrator is so enamored with his captor that he has no fear of marrying her and becoming her lifelong prisoner.

Other songs form part of musical traditions. "*Tango a la diva* (The Diva's Tango)" references the telenovela as a frame for understanding the twists and turns of love. This song blends bachata with tango, another genre originally of the lower class, to depict a heartless woman of venomous kisses. She is the protagonist of the narrator's own personal telenovela and the leading lady of his misfortune. The word choice emphasizes a theatric setting in which appearances deceive, and the woman's betrayal makes her deserving of the very song the narrator sings: a tango. The title of "*Bésame siempre* (Kiss Me Always)" brings to mind a classic bolero, "*Bésame mucho.*" The bolero, whose title is literally, "Kiss Me a Lot," carries with it more the idea of holding on to a moment—making the kisses and moment linger as if the two lovers were spending their last night together. Santos's "Bésame siempre" emphasizes the forever aspect of the kiss the narrator proposes, but it is in the singular—a deep, history-making kiss that will win over the woman's heart. Love is a religion for this narrator, and it inspires him to shed his timidity and risk everything for his beloved. In contrast, the urban bachata "My Way" focuses entirely on the moment. This song is the narrator's intimate, personal, and passionate invitation to his sweetheart and details all that he will do to give her an unforgettable experience. The chorus of this bachata, which was number one on Billboard's Tropical Songs chart, is an excellent example of code-switching in which the narrator moves effortlessly between English and Spanish to convince his beloved to let him demonstrate his feelings for her. "*Amor y dinero* (Love and Money)" turns the common bachata topic of suffering because of money on its head. In this song, a rich narrator questions whether the woman he loves would stay with him if he were poor. He uses fairy tale images of a castle and Cinderella, but observes that his princess was wearing name-brand labels and driving a Mercedes. This narrator's contemplative hypothesizing about his sweetheart's selfish motives convinces him that love that is untrue is not love at all.

Henry Santos has heightened bachata's visibility through other artistic activities, too. He was the musical director in the Dominican movie, *La soga* (The Rope). In 2012, he won the *Mira Quien Baila* competition—Spanish-language channel Univisión's answer to *Dancing with the Stars*. Santos, the first Dominican participant, was never nominated for elimination in the series, a testament not only to his dancing abilities, but also to his excellent rapport with his fans.

Henry Santos's refined bachata lyrics sketch the varied panorama of love in all its dimensions. Although he says that only some 20 percent of his lyrics are based on personal experiences,[71] Henry sings his bachatas with strong melodies and a heartfelt interpretation. For Henry, his bachata is the result of an intricate process and combination of elements, not least of which is the "soul" of traditional bachata. He explains, "It's not as simple as grabbing and putting music together because there is an unspoken chemistry that is born.... You need to understand the feeling, where it comes from, in order to understand bachata."[72]

Vena

Producer and guitarist Lenny Santos, along with his brother Max Agende, have joined with Steve Styles, former lead singer of Xtreme, to form Vena, a band that Jon Caramanica describes as a "Dominican Supergroup." The band draws its name from the essentialist view that bachata is in Dominicans' blood[73]: "Basically, Vena is the music running through our veins."[74] Despite their former successes with Xtreme and Aventura, Styles, Santos, and Agende emphasize that Vena is a new venture—"a new world," as they state in their songs—and that their goal is to constantly improve. "We're starting over again ... a new era, a new group, a new world," says Styles.[75]

Vena's four singles to date complement the emotional timbre and signature bachata beat with a blend of genres and Spanglish. Vena's first release, "Señora," portrays a narrator who finds himself incapable of forgetting the woman he loved, although he recognizes that he is responsible for her leaving. The speaker of "*Por mentiras* (Because of Lies)" likewise accepts responsibility for his lies that led to a relationship gone wrong. As he reflects back and agonizes over what might have been, he begs his beloved to return. In contrast, the narrative voice of "*Ya no* (No More)" is the victim of the woman's disdain, indifference, and insincerity. He questions how she could be unfaithful to him, since he was always true. Once her slave, he declares his freedom and ends the destructive relationship.

"*Sangre de mis venas* (My Lifeblood)" is a love song that makes use of essentialist images to represent the beloved as the narrator's lifeblood. She completes him, and their love will withstand all trials, including gossiping tongues. On a different level, this song can also be interpreted as a commentary on bachata itself. Just as the narrator's love courses through his veins, bachata courses through these bachateros' veins. The lovers in this song pay no mind to those who would destroy their love, and similarly, bachata fans and musicians ignore critics.

Lead singer Steve Styles believes "it's important for ... bachata to come from the heart,"[76] and Vena's music gives voice to a myriad of emotions. Vena's themes—love, love lost, and suffering—link their music to the bachata tradition while their innovative, fresh sound set them apart. Vena strives to give their fans a fun and unique experience at their live performances, and this brought them a large and faithful following even prior to the release of their first album. Several countries have Vena fan clubs, and the Vena Mamis—female fans—are diehard supporters. Vena's promising start bodes well for them to be the bachata supergroup they are billeted as.

Bachata's Crossover Potential

Romeo Santos's role as front man for Aventura, his success with his first solo album, and an upcoming television sitcom deal[77] have convinced many (e.g., Richards; Rohter "Crossing Over"; Rohter "Romeo") that he will be the face of bachata crossover. Prince Royce, with his hometown-boy look and chic image, along with his bilingual bachata cover of "Stand by Me," is also a prime candidate.[78] Indeed, bachateros and bands such as Aventura, Prince Royce, Toby Love, and Xtreme contributed significantly to bachata's spread to other Spanish-speaking countries outside of the Caribbean. Now, bachata forms part of the popular club sound in many locales throughout Europe and Central and South America. The unfortunate side effect of this popularity is that many in these locations know bachata only in its modern and urban forms.

So-called crossover musicians are those who were first successful in the Spanish-language market before crossing into the Anglo market with English-language recordings aimed at an English-speaking audience. The term "crossover," however, carries certain expectations and valorizations. Although the word implies a horizontal movement between musical genres, cultures, languages and consumers in which a Latin musical form "has merely changed lanes to enter into the North American mainstream," the term in essence carries with it a hierarchic ordering.[79]

Several Latin singers marked the first years of the new millennium with successful crossover careers. Ricky Martin erupted onto the English-language music scene in May 1999 with his (in)famous hit, "Livin' la Vida Loca." This single featured a fusion of rock, Latin-sounding beats, and Spanglish, along with Martin's hip-swaying, Elvis-style stage persona. Although Martin's Spanish-language albums had already brought him international renown, his English-language album, released on May 11, 1999, made him among the hottest acts of that summer. In only a few short weeks Martin's popularity had mushroomed to such a degree that he graced the cover of *Time* magazine.

Similarly, Columbian rock star Shakira crossed into the English-language market with her 2001 album, *Laundry Service.* For Shakira, crossing over meant more than a change of language; it also meant a new look. The blonde, seductive Shakira gracing her first English-language album is a far cry from the brown, stick-straight hair she has on her Spanish-language album of 1996, *Pies descalzos* (Barefoot), and the simple braids and long-sleeved shirt she wears on the cover of *Dónde están los ladrones?* (Where Are the Thieves?) of 1998. Shakira clearly reveals how not only the language of crossover music is whitened, but its face may be as well.

A review of crossover musicians who have been most successful in the English-language music industry reveals that they have been overwhelmingly "white, middle- and upper-class, educated musicians,"[80] such as Gloria Estefan, Juan Luis Guerra, Ricky Martin, Shakira, and Enrique Iglesias. As Willie Colón so aptly put it, "'black musics were accepted only in a white disguise.'"[81] This process of acceptance, which is also reminiscent of trends in rap and hip-hop, has occurred through what I describe as a process of filtration in which music is systematically whitened across time to create a product that appeals to new audiences among the dominant group.[82]

Modern and urban bachtateros, with their light complexion, crooning heart-throb voices, Spanglish lyrics, and bachata fusions make them the poster children for bachata's proposed coup of North American musical tastes. Royce has already included primarily or all–English songs on both of his albums, and is reportedly working with Atlantic to release an English-language album.[83] Romeo, however, says he is determined to cross over on his own terms: bachata and Spanish.[84] In contrast to artists such as Ricky Martin and Shakira, who shifted completely or almost wholly to English and mainstream pop or rock for their crossover albums, Romeo has stuck mostly with bachata and his Spanish-dominant Spanglish.[85] Romeo challenges the definition of crossover as one-way: "'I never liked the term crossover, or at least the definition that everyone has, that you record an album in English, and that's a crossover ... I just felt like that if I'm going to cross over, why not have the English audience cross over too, to my world?'"[86]

Thus, the demand for the crossover music produced by Latin artists should not be mistakenly construed as only coming from monolingual English-speakers. As Frances Aparicio notes, "crossing over has been made possible by a new emerging Hispanic audience 'increasingly imbued with Anglo culture and energized by its very own political and economic aspirations' rather than 'from an appeal to some new, largely Anglo audience.'"[87] Producer Sergio George reiterates,

> Whether they're Mexican Americans, Puerto Ricans, Dominicans, they don't care any more where the music's from.... These are fourth-generation Hispanic kids, they're American kids. Most of them were born and raised here. So they want to be hip but they still want to retain their culture, with the [Spanish] language.[88]

Bachata's so-called crossover success, then, may ultimately be tied to the very real face of American demographics in which Hispanics figure as the country's largest minority.[89] The first ten years of the new millennium marked a significant increase for Latinos in the United States with a 43 percent growth change.[90] Hispanics also constitute the nation's youngest minority group: one out of every four newborns in the United States is Hispanic, as is one out every five schoolchildren.[91] While Romeo's and Prince Royce's style, sound and look may appeal to an English audience, the fan base that helps carry them may well be Hispanic.

For English-speakers, bachata's projected crossover is viewed through the hegemonic lens of mainstream, English-language pop. Romeo is described as "largely unknown"[92] beyond the Spanish-language market, and "a secret hidden in plain sight."[93] Anglo writers portray bachata as a "slinky Dominican ballad ... seedy hick music ... a Caribbean folk music"[94] with "bawdy lyrics ... played at parties and seedy bar-brothels" by musicians wearing "gaudy outfits."[95] Modern and urban bachateros are conversely described as refining bachata by blending the genre "with R&B, hip-hop and big-city attitude ... [which] ... has created a swaggering, distinctly New York Style."[96] Cantor-Navas similarly credits "the heartthrobs in Aventura ... who have turned bachata from a Dominican barrio sound into the music of Pan-Latino youth." Similarly, the urban (read "black") nature of this Dominican American creation must be filtered out as well. Cantor-Navas acknowledges Prince Royce's former producer, Sergio George, for having transformed Royce "from an underground, baseball cap-wearing bachata artist to a well-dressed performer." These representations underscore the colonial gaze that is inherent to considerations of so-called crossover music and musicians, seeing them as somehow nonexistent or inferior until they are sifted through the filter of English-language, mainstream music.

Conclusion

The significant Dominican transnational community contributed to the growth of new audiences for bachata. This genre, which so often speaks to the life experiences of urban dwellers, was emblematic of the experiences of many Dominicans in large cities abroad, while a new generation of Dominican Americans interpreted bachata through the lens of their own realities. Their modern sound blends bachata with R&B, rock, pop, and even reggaetón, and code-switches between Spanish and English. This generation of Dominican Americans has adopted modern bachata as a distinctive representation of what it means to be Dominican within the transnational community. This unique combination reflects musical and linguistic realities of this group while still speaking to the musical heritage of Dominicans at home.

In Aventura's "*Mi niña cambió* (My Girl Changed)," the narrative voice observes that the saying, "New York changes one, even his skin," is true. This song reads on one level as the narrator's criticism of his girlfriend for thinking herself better than those in her homeland because she speaks English and has traveled to Europe. In keeping with the Dominican notion of progreso, he acknowledges that she progressed, but regrets that she has forgotten him and her roots. On another level, this song and saying reiterate the role modern bachata has played in the overall acceptance of the genre and how it symbolizes dominicanidad. Migrants embraced bachata as pertinent to their situation and as an expression of dominicanidad within the context of migration. They brought the music back home along with all of the trappings of social mobility to which they had access, thus disassociating it solely with the lower class. Dominican links between class and race are also reflected in this process: bachata's higher social position equaled its gradual whitening and enhanced its growing appeal.

Lenny Santos described this phenomenon as an uncontrollable force: "You couldn't stop it. At the end of the day, it's what people like. If you've got millions of people saying, 'No, this is what we want to listen to,' you're going to have to go with what the people say. So just don't try to control it—that Dominican culture will come get you!"[97] Henry Santos articulated bachata's validation at home by its international visibility: "It's kinda sad it has to go that way. It has to be accepted by the world before it's fully accepted. They hated us.... Then we got international fame, all over the world, and now they love us."[98] United States and mainstream modern bachata's innovations took the genre world wide, and its international popularity helped validate bachata at home.

NINE

Las Bachateras

A look back across the history of bachata reveals very little female participation in the industry. When I asked singer Susana Silfa why she thought this was so, she explained, "As a woman, finding a place in this genre…. It's not that it has been hard; it *is* hard."[1] This trend reflects the intersection of a number of factors, including gendered social expectations, bachata's locations of production and consumption, and the tendencies within the Dominican music business.

The historical delimitation between the *casa* (house/home) and *calle* (street) has deep roots in Latin America. These two contrasting spaces are opposing and gendered. The family is at the heart of the casa, which represents domesticity and a controlled respite from the world outside. This is an orderly space, where each member of the family has his or her own role. Here, the family as a collective whole takes precedence over the individual, and order is maintained. In contrast, the calle is the space of the individual. Roles are not clear at a casual glance, and because each person is looking out for his own best interests, the possibility of "deceit, deception and roguery" always exists.[2]

The casa/calle distinction is particularly important when applied to women's roles. Women are safely protected in the casa from all potential dangers and threats. At home, girls respect their fathers as children, and as wives, women raise families and meet the needs of their husbands. Out on the street, women are unprotected and exposed to any number of sinister dangers. Women of the street, as the name suggests, are not the pure, domesticated women of the home.

These two spheres parallel the social constructions of machismo and marianismo, which define acceptable and expected behavior for both genders. The macho man is the image of the original *conquistador* who conquers and dominates, not only his woman and children, but also other women. He is concerned with saving face and preserving his macho image at all costs, never revealing his emotions and always demonstrating and imposing a sense of masculinity. Marianismo—in reference to María, the Virgin Mary—posits that the ideal woman must be pure, humble and passive. Woman's highest calling is to be a mother, and she must sacrifice herself constantly, tolerating all of man's bad behavior. She must be long-suffering and prepared to endure everything, since life is martyrdom.

The casa/calle differentiation was made even more pronounced in the Dominican Republic under the Trujillo regime. Trujillo, the ultimate strongman, emphasized his masculinity, and thus macho control over the country, through the propagation of an official construction of gender that presented femininity as "ornamental, baroque, and saintly."[3] This ideal contrasted with Trujillo's own macho image, as presented through the numerous medals on his uniforms, his countless conquests and seductions of women, and the merengues that sang his many praises. Lauren Derby also points to the state's intentional representation of Trujillo's virility through the construction of a large obelisk to commemorate the one-year anniversary of the changing of the capital city's name to Ciudad Trujillo. The obelisk, which Derby describes as a "great phallic token of Trujillo's fecund and promiscuous dominion,"[4] was both a visual and psychological reminder of the strongman and his iron rule. The official vision of femininity propagated under Trujillo struck a chord with Dominican middle and upper class women, in part because it also contrasted with the image of the modern American woman whose independence was seen to have unsexed her and made her too individualized and brazen.[5]

The official image of women disseminated under Trujillo was unattainable for many rural and urban women of the lower class, especially in the shifting demographics following Trujillo's assassination. As we have seen, the influx of migrants to the capital resulted in increased numbers of women in the workforce. These women did not have the luxury of remaining within the safe walls of the casa, and instead, had to venture forth into the world outside the home to earn a living. Although not all of them were literally women of the street, some of them did work as prostitutes in the cabarets where bachata was consumed. This link between bachata and the brothels left an enduring tarnish on the music, and often led to the inaccurate assumption that any woman listening to bachata was, by extension, a prostitute.[6] From the brothels and bars, bachata made its way into middle-class homes through the lower-class domestic workers who came to work in them. This reality further linked bachata with the lower class and with women who had to work outside the home to survive.[7]

Being a musician was also considered an inappropriate profession for women, and many even believed that women simply lacked the capacity to play instruments well.[8] Among the rural and urban poor, musical education was primarily given and received informally, outside of the home—that is, in the calle. Musicians learned from each other informally and through hands-on experience, often in the very places where the music was performed and consumed.[9] In the case of bachata, this meant access to locations such as bars and brothels. Additionally, it was difficult for a woman to own and manage her own band in the machista context of Dominican music production.[10] Bachata's form of dance may also have contributed to stereotyping women who consumed and danced it. Although couples also danced merengue *pegados*—literally, stuck together—bachata's slight hop or emphasized hip check on the fourth beat while dancing so closely earned it many a censure from its detractors.

Together, these long-standing social constructions and practices preemptively kept many women out of the music industry. Indeed, even after fifty years of history, there have been very few female solo bachata musicians.[11] The small number of women in bachata has also contributed to confusion over what to call them. For some, using the feminine form of the word for a bachata musician, *bachatera*, carries negative connotations by associating women with the original derision and stigma with which the word bachata was laced. For others, a female bachata musician is such a new occurrence in a male-dominate profession that she falls into the same category of nomenclature applied to professions such as law enforcement, firefighting and the military. In these fields, new terms have come into Spanish that do not follow the rules usually used to denote gender[12]; instead, the word *mujer* (woman) figures prominently: *mujer policía* (policewoman); *mujer bombero* (woman firefighter) and *mujer soldado* (female soldier). In the case of female bachata musicians, this becomes *mujer bachatero*. As a whole, this indeterminacy underscores women bachata musicians' ambiguous place within the world of bachata.

Mélida "la Sufrida"

Although men dominated early bachata, a female bachata singer was also among the first recording wave. This woman, Mélida Rodríguez, quickly caught the attention of fans and critics alike with the stark themes and lyrics of her few songs. Rodríguez's bachatas, many of which she composed herself, were reminiscent of themes sung by Blanca Iris Villafañe, a popular Puerto Rican singer of guitar boleros: desamor, desengaño, and suffering, often from the point of view of the bar.[13]

Mélida Rodríguez, nicknamed *"La sufrida"*—"The Long-Suffering Woman"—after the title of one of her songs, openly presented many of these same realities as faced by women of the marginalized class. The narrative voice of "La sufrida" openly challenges middle class society's expectations of women. She insists that she doesn't care that people think she is a bad girl, for she is happy. This statement, which emphasizes the abyss between the expectations for men and women regarding sexual fidelity, is a bold declaration that challenges the social constructions of marianismo and machismo.

Many of Rodríguez's songs are situated in or make reference to bars and drinking, thus openly portraying a female narrator who flies in the face of middle class norms of social propriety. In *"Bebiendo y llorando* (Drinking and Crying),*"* the narrator turns to alcohol to help ease the pains of her broken heart. She tells others not to interfere in her life, and notes that if she drinks, she does so with her own money. This latter statement reiterates women's increased economic freedom and insinuates the condition of many men of the time who had migrated to the city in hopes of work, only to find none and have to live off what women could provide for them. In contrast, the narrator of *"Me quiero emborrachar* (I Want to Get Drunk)*"* states that she has a good man in her life, but she wants to get drunk to explore her options.

Love also figures as a theme in Rodríguez's music, though it is a love that must be defended against rumors. The female voice of *"No importa, vida* (It Doesn't Matter, Darling)*"* boldly proclaims that it does not matter that others say that her beloved is bad, nor what others say of their relationship. Their love brings happiness to both of them, and she would give her life for him. In contrast, the female voice of *"Incredulidad* (Incredulity)*"* must defend herself to the man she loves in the face of others' accusations. These two songs reiterate the power and influence of what others say, the ever-present concern with public opinion.

Both desamor and amargue figure in Rodríguez's lyrics. The female voice of *"Él me mintió* (He Lied to Me)*"* repeats the words of the title in a sobbing voice as she relates the betrayal of the man she loved. The song concludes with a brief spoken interlude in which the narrator insists that she will never forgive him, even if he returns. The song ends with the repetition of "él me mintió" interlaced with the sounds of weeping in the background. Similarly, the narrative voice of "*Cobardía* (Cowardice)" demands an explanation for the man's betrayal and abandonment. She insists he is a coward, since he will not answer for his actions.

Some of Rodríguez's songs gave a new twist to desamor, however, as the narrator not only related her pain and suffering but also took a stance of power by refusing to be the victim and articulating the man's actions as inappropriate. The titles and lyrics of these songs cut to the chase and leave no room for the man to defend himself or his actions. In "*Mal hombre* (Bad Man)," the narrator accuses her former love of cheating on her with a prostitute, noting that she shouldn't be surprised since he's a man. She goes on to say that she doesn't want him around and would rather forget him so that she makes no more mistakes. Similarly, the narrative voice of "*Traicionero* (Disloyal)" minces no words as she accuses the man of betraying her love. Still, she informs him that he shouldn't think she'll die of heartache, but rather, she will find a new love. The narrator of "*Lo peor de la vida* (The Worst Thing in My Life)" describes the man as ungrateful, reminding him that she gave him all he has. He is the worst thing that has happened to her, and insists she no longer cares if he leaves.

The narrative voice of "*La ley* (The Law)" combines several of these unique characteristics of Rodríguez's bachata. Although not directly stated, the action is understood to occur in a bar where the female voice states that she'll be singing in this location as she awaits the return of the man she loved and who betrayed her. She exerts her dominance over him by claiming that he cannot live without her kisses and insists that she will not give him a single kiss even if he begs her. The chorus reiterates that she is going to punish the man so that she cannot be toyed with, since she is the law. As a whole, this song's lyrics make it clear that the narrator is anything but heartbreak's victim.

Regardless of the popularity of Rodríguez's songs, she did not record again after these initial hits. Rodríguez moved from the capital and away from the nascent bachata industry, which also contributed to her lack of participation. She continued to sing occasionally until her untimely death of a heart attack in 1975.[14]

Aridia Ventura

In 1975, Aridia Ventura released her first recording, becoming the second woman to leave her mark on the world of bachata at the national level.[15] Ventura's first production was only mildly successful, but her second release, "*En la misma tumba* (In the Same Grave)," was a hit. This song, written as a Mexican ranchera waltz and sung in the same emotional style as male-produced bachata, proclaimed the singer's eternal love and likens the beloved to an angel sent by God. So great is this love, that only death will separate the couple, and the singer's final wish is to be buried with him in the same tomb. These themes resonated with bachata aficionados, and Ventura's success with "En la misma tumba" also caught the attention of bachata radio announcer and producer Rhadamés Aracena, who signed Ventura to a contract.

Aridia Ventura continued to record into the 1980s. She performed regularly in the Cibao region of the Dominican Republic, and was also a regular participant in Edilio Paredes's *Lunes de amargue* shows. Throughout her career, Ventura continued to release songs that portrayed the unique situations of women, highlighting their suffering as well as their anger in the face of betrayal. Ventura's strong lyrics earned her the nickname of "*La verduga*" (literally, "The Executioner," but figuratively used more in the sense of "The Torturer"), since the female voice in her songs showed little mercy to the unfaithful man depicted in them.[16] Ventura embraced the nickname, referencing it in the appropriately titled "*Vengo con el garrote* (I'm Coming with the Club)." In this song, the narrator declares that "la verduga" has arrived with her club in hand, and that she is prepared to beat the perverse man in her life. She then explains her suffering at his hands and how he spends all the couple's income on alcohol. She concludes by declaring that she intends to start drinking, just like him, since they have the same rights.

Ventura's lyrics do not mince words as they confront men in different roles. In one of Ventura's best-known songs, "*No eres varón* (You Are Not a Man)," the singer informs her former lover that she no longer loves him and has no intention of crying over him. Admitting that she suffered greatly when he abandoned her, she now refuses to forgive him, and she orders him to leave. In "*La hija abandonada* (The Abandoned Daughter)," the singer condemns her father for leaving her mother for no reason, provoking her untimely death. Although the mother figure worked to provide for her family, the father, a *canalla* (pig), did not fulfill his protective role.

Ventura continued to record and perform as a bachata favorite into the 1980s. Health issues limited her participation at the same time that bachata continued to evolve away from Ventura's traditional sound.[17] Ventura's place as a bachatera pioneer and a pillar within the genre is undeniable. Her lyrics cover the gamut of bachata themes, portraying and giving voice to them from a female perspective.

Mariíta

In the early 1990s, Susana Silfa appeared on the bachata scene as Mariíta. Silfa, who is from a Santo Domingo middle-class family and studied music and voice formally at the National Conservatory, chose her stage name because it sounded more authentic to the Dominican countryside of bachata's roots.[18] When she was first approached about the possibility of doing bachata, Silfa admits that she was unsure, given that her roots were not those of most bachata musicians and consumers. Nevertheless, Silfa tells of listening to bachata on Radio Guarachita as a little girl. Silfa, who had always dreamed of being a singer, would go to the back part of the house to pretend she was singing on stage, and overheard bachata on the domestic workers' radio as it spilled out of their room. She remembers that her favorite song when she was four years old was Bernardo Ortiz's "*Dos rosas* (Two Roses)."[19]

Silfa grew up surrounded by bachata, even though she did not belong to the social class most commonly associated with it. As a result, she was able to infuse all the sentiments expressed in bachata into her music as Mariíta. Silfa, who took Tejano music star Selena Quintanilla as a model, wanted to take a genre she saw as authentic to Dominicans and open it to new audiences by drawing on her own formal studies and experiences to look for the "other colors of bachata."[20] Mariíta's album, *Bachata amargue,* featured the tried and true themes of bachata (love and love lost, abandonment and prohibited love) interpreted in the traditional, emotional style. Although the lyrics of Mariíta's bachatas are not as stark as those of Mélida Rodríguez or as cutting as those of Aridia Ventura, they still offer a view of common bachata themes through the unique lens of a woman's point of view. In *"El que ríe último ríe mejor* (He Who Laughs Last Laughs Best)," Mariíta reproaches her lover for his betrayal and reminds him that she is brave and knows how to tough it out, even though he may be laughing at her suffering now. In contrast, Mariíta describes her relationship in *"Amor de novela* (Storybook Love)" as an enduring storybook love. In *"Lo buscaré* (I Will Look for Him)," Mariíta vows to look everywhere for the man who left her and to seduce him again once she finds him.

The title song of the album, "Bachata amargue," serves as a retrospective explanation of how Mariíta came to sing bachata. The song opens with a series of vocal runs that highlight the dexterity and skill of the trained artist behind the rural-sounding name. The lyrics go on to explain how the singer, born in the Dominican Republic, sought a way to connect with its people through a music that would get everyone to sing along with her. Mariíta emphasizes that bachata is in her blood, and that is ultimately why she sings it. Both in sound and in content, "Bachata amargue" underscores the uniqueness of Mariíta as a bachatera: a trained female singer from the middle class who yet feels an essentialist connection to bachata.

Silfa admits that being a female bachata singer presented its own set of challenges in a machista genre and male-dominated industry.[21] In addition to the stigma attributed to the usual locales of bachata consumption and performance, the lyrics of some songs railed against women, sometimes violently. Double entendre bachata was also still popular at the time that Silfa began her reign as Mariíta, *"la Reina del Amargue* (The Queen of Amargue)." Silfa accepted the challenge and found ways to meet this trend, too. Her highly popular merengue, *"El pullaíto* (Push Push)," proclaimed a new dance of the same name that was so popular it was danced at night in any dark corner. Mariíta claims the pullaíto as hers and encourages all men to dance it, instructing them that they must dance the pullaíto exactly as she tells them, thus exerting her dominance over them. For Silfa, this double entendre merengue was a response to the tastes of the time and its popularity showed that women could successfully produce this same type of tongue-in-cheek music.[22]

The machista tendencies of bachata were a challenge to Silfa, but not an obstacle. She recalls in particular how one journalist condemned her for singing bachata in one article, and later sang her praises when she was successful. She admits that she also heard some unpleasant and colorful things directed her way when performing live in certain locales.[23] As Mariíta, Silfa sang with bachata great Aridia Ventura, and other top musicians of the genre, including Paniagua, Luis Segura and Raulín Rodríguez. For personal reasons, she did not continue working in bachata, although she has produced some bachata under her given name, which she describes as more along the line of tecno amargue.

Mayra Bello

Like Susana Silfa, Mayra Bello was originally unsure about singing bachata because of the discrimination against it. Born in 1964, Bello grew up hearing that bachata was for people of a different social class—plebs' music and the preferred genre of prostitutes and low-paid guards. Bello remembers that her mother was adamant that no one play bachata in her home, although it was common in the streets. Bello distanced herself from bachata at first, listening instead to balada and bolero. Although Bello was drawn to music even as a child and participated in church choirs, she completed a university degree before launching her musical career. Bello sang with the Los Toros merengue band and later, with female merengue star Milly Quezada, as well as other international stars.[24]

When Bello's manager suggested that she consider recording bachata, Bello at first was uncertain, given her upbringing. Bello remembers that the machista view held of women bachata performers was very negative and closed the doors to women in the genre. Still, Bello recognized that she was drawn to the sound of bachata's guitars. Although hesitant at first, Bello recognized bachata's authenticity as a popular musical form from her homeland: "There is bachata inside of me. It's very much a part of us."[25]

Bello's lyrics range across the various facets of love and love lost, portraying them from a woman's point of view. In "*La infiel* (The Unfaithful Woman)," featuring female merengue star Milly Quezada, the narrative voice admits to her best friend that she had an affair with the friend's husband. Although she begs her friend to have compassion and to save their friendship, the other refuses to listen. Similarly, the narrator of "*El hombre casi perfecto* (The Almost-Perfect Man)" finds herself in love with a man who has all the traits she could desire except for one: he is married. Desamor is also the central theme of "*Pero me acuerdo de ti* (But I Remember You)." In this song, the female voice acknowledges repeatedly that she has overcome an unhealthy love. Although all seems to be going well for her, everything falls apart the moment she remembers her former lover. Love realized also figures in Bello's repertoire. Although the male and female voices of "*Sé que volverás* (I Know You Will Return)" (featuring Nacho Bianco) are separated, both reiterate their belief that they will be together again. Likewise, the female voice of "*Contigo* (With You)" is secure in her love and wishes to spend each moment of her life with the man she loves.

Bello describes her sound as "different" and points to Juan Luis Guerra as influential in directing bachata down a new path and making it possible for others to follow in this line. The instrumentation of Bello's bachata is more complex than the original five instruments, placing it more in line with Guerra's tecno amargue. As Bello admits, "I can't show up somewhere with two guys playing a guitar and a requinto, bongo and güira. Mine needs an acoustic guitar, a drum set ... maybe I won't have a violin, but I'm going to have a synthesizer with that sound."[26] Bello's bachata therefore combines the tecno amargue sound with tried and true bachata themes told in a woman's voice.

Leslie Grace

Leslie Grace Martínez made Billboard history in October 2012 when her bilingual rendition "Will U Still Love Me Tomorrow," a cover of the Shirelles' 1960 classic, reached number one on Latin radio charts. Leslie Grace, who was seventeen years and nine months old, became the youngest female singer to reach the coveted spot. Her adaptation of the classic is appropriate on many levels, not least the shared history of schoolgirls making it big in the music industry (the Shirelles were the first all-female band to reach number one), and their potential to influence other women singers. Leslie Grace's interpretation of these classic lyrics, which beg to know if the man's love will be true the morning after, captures traditional bachata sentiments in her bilingual rendition.

Leslie Grace's self-titled album (2013)—her first secular album following her start in Christian music[27]—includes a mix of urban bachata, pop, R&B and dance numbers. Her instrumentation is highly synthesized and in many cases, the guitar—so central to bachata típica and moderna—plays a less prominent role. Instrumentally, her bachata is heavily influenced by R&B. Her lyrics, though not complex, continue in bachata's lyrical tradition. "Day 1," another number one hit on Billboard's tropical chart, is about love at first sight. The narrator's love seems a fairy tale, and she fell for her sweetheart on the first day she saw him. Similarly, her bilingual remake of the Ronettes' 1963 "Be My Baby" describes a love at first sight. This narrator promises love and loyalty to her beloved, if he'll only accept. Sometimes, love must also confront criticism. In "*Hoy* (Today)," the narrative voice reaffirms her trust when others accuse her sweetheart. Her love is greater than her doubts, and she reiterates her belief in him.

Leslie Grace also sings of desamor, although it is far less cortavenas than in bachata típica. The narrator of "*Odio no odiarte* (I Hate Not Hating You)" is unable to forget a former love. Although she wishes she could hate him and move on, she cannot. "*Peligroso amor* (Dangerous Love)" relies on antitheses to describe the attraction of a love with no future. Although the narrator knows she is bound to lose, she is unable to avoid love's pull. The narrative voice in "*No me arrepiento* (I'm Not Sorry)" uses almost exclusively English to sing of desamor. She criticizes her sweetheart for not expressing his feelings, but insists she has no regrets.

"*A mi manera* (My Way)" varies most from bachata's traditional lyrical content. The narrative voice of this song is a young woman who is tired of how others try to tell her how to live. She maintains that she is old enough to choose her own path. Thus, this narrator will live her life according to her own plans and in her own way.

Leslie Grace is in the unique position of being the first urban bachatera to be aggressively promoted. Her releases from the United States could help erode barriers to female bachata musicians, since the tradition of discrimination against bachata is unknown among bilingual and other Spanish-speaking audiences internationally. It is still too early to tell what impact Leslie Grace's bachata will have.

Conclusion

Long-held views of the appropriate social spaces and roles for men and women have affected women's access to participation in bachata production. The two gendered and opposing spaces of the casa and the calle emphasize the purity and sanctity of the home as contrasted with the danger and exposure of the street. Women who must work outside the home to make a living were by extension suspected of being true women of the street. Bachata's early associations with the lower classes in general, and with cabarets in particular, tainted the genre and made it unacceptable both as a musical style to enjoy and as a genre to produce. Further, the informal musical training available to men outside of the home was unavailable to women precisely because of the locations where it took place.

Early female bachata musicians such as Mélida Rodríguez and Aridia Ventura co-opted the common themes and sounds of bachata, telling them from a woman's point of view. Later, trained musicians such as Susana Silfa and Mayra Bello took up those same themes with their own unique sound of the 1990s and early twenty-first century. Leslie Grace has launched her urban bachata from the United States, perhaps opening the gates to even more women bachata musicians. In spite of bachata's growing popularity, women's access to the music industry in general, and especially to bachata, has been more limited than that of men. Still, as the bachateras featured here remind us, love and love lost are equally poignant in both male and female voices.

Conclusion

Music enveloped the small table where I sat with my friend, Alexis, and other regulars who came to listen to music weekly at the Parada 9 on Sunday nights. Nearby, a couple dressed in matching white pants with lime green shirts and accessories danced in the minuscule space beside our table. The establishment's owner circulated among the tables with an ice-filled dishpan, deftly avoiding the flying hands and tongues as he refilled glasses in the sweltering night air. Some sang along to the lyrics like old friends, and another kept time on a güira. Outside, a man dressed out of season in the *diablo cojuelo* costume of Carnival celebrations walked by under a steady August rain.

When talk turned to my research, everyone present had his own grain of sand to add to my growing ideas and understandings of bachata. This had been a pattern whenever I mentioned my purpose for being in the Dominican Republic, the Bronx, and Washington Heights. From taxi drivers and utter strangers in neighborhood businesses to the owner of the place where I was staying, everyone was happy and willing to share opinions and personal experiences with me. Some remembered that it used to cost five *centavos* (cents) to play a bachata on the neighborhood colmado's jukebox, before they raised it to ten. Others portrayed local characters who would show up at a colmado with a roll of coins and play a favorite song repeatedly, often to the chagrin of other listeners. Many spoke the names of bachata signers and songs as if they were old friends, relating the history and stories from the genre's first five decades of existence.

Dominicans readily discuss musical preferences and histories with the same intensity and solemnity as political questions. This deference to music as a crucial element of daily life reiterates its central role in Dominican identity across the nation's history. Nineteenth-century intellectuals heatedly attacked the merengue when it threatened the tumba's role as the national dance at that time. Later, the accordion's growing presence in merengue came under fire when it threatened to replace stringed instruments deemed autochthonous. Dominican nationalists embraced the Creole merengue as a symbol of cultural resistance during the U.S. occupation, only to abandon it after the evacuation. Music's potential to unite disparate Dominican identities was unquestionable, and dictator Rafael Trujillo tapped into those possibilities by making merengue the national music and commissioning a refined orchestra version of the genre. Propagandistic compositions praised his greatness and helped cement a sense of national identity.

Born in the aftermath of thirty years of dictatorship and merengue's imposed status as the national music, bachata was viewed as challenging the status quo at a time when too much had already been overturned and uprooted. Bachata's original detractors scorned the music because of its rural and lower-class origins, and by association, the racial implications of these roots. Critics and those with monetary interests in merengue christened the romantic guitar music with derogatory names meant to confine it to a marginalized space. This imposition of power through name-calling relegated bachata production to the informal sector and its performance to small-scale venues. Nevertheless, musicians and fans have effectively claimed the imposed monikers of "bachata" and "amargue" as their own, thereby subverting the original offensive intent. Although merengue's dominance in the music industry closed many doors to bachata, amargue's broad fan base among the rural and lower urban classes consumed the music on economically produced records, as faithful listeners of Radio Guarachita, and in local colmados, bars and cabarets. Together, these factors contributed to the discrimination hurled at bachata that portrayed it as lower-class, unrefined music of low quality for so many years.

Still, as Tommy García accurately notes, "Rhythms can't be imposed from a position of power," and bachata was freely chosen.[1] Bachateros and those in the music industry tend to describe bachata's growing popularity as something unstoppable and in many ways, unavoidable. Promoter Isidoro "Chichí" Aponte identifies bachata's popularity as an unavoidable pull.[2] Edilio Paredes attributes bachata's success to the messages and stories it tells, and the sentiments it conveys.[3] For Paredes, bachata was like a river that starts up in the mountains and grows as it flows out to the sea— "but in the beginning, it's just a trickle of water."[4] Joe Veras also likens bachata to natural forces, describing it as "such a strong hurricane that nothing could stop it."[5]

Bachata's visibility continued to increase as its fan base grew in stride with the far-reaching stretch of poverty across repeated economic downturns. Modifications made to bachata's sound and content across the years—tecno bachata, innovations to instrumental interpretation made by figures such as Blas Durán, Luis Vargas, and Antony Santos, more romantic and varied lyrics, and eventually, modern bachata's new sound—also grew bachata's fan base. Dominican migrants, whose experiences of economic suffering and alienation were more akin to bachata than the increasingly fast-paced merengue, embraced the genre as reflective of their realities. These same migrants furthered bachata's reaches by bringing it back to the Dominican Republic through transnational routes of return trips and ongoing connections with friends and family at home. Modern bachata stepped into the international spotlight, and its global popularity opened doors for the genre as a whole. Bachata's increased visibility in addition to migrants' improved social (and by extension, racial) status slowly helped ease the former discrimination against it. As Henry Santos observes, "Sometimes ... something that is born in your own country, actually they're the last to *apoyarlo*—to support it. They're the last, until it gets international acceptance."[6]

Bachata offers a unique study of how musical genres evolve to represent national identities, and how individual and collective tastes grow to accept new rhythms and genres as symbolic. Bachata's rise to the hallowed position of national identifier is especially significant in light of merengue's longstanding position at the heart of Dominican musical identity and its official backing during the Trujillato. Now, bachata has joined merengue to form a second musical pillar of Dominican identity, representative of dominicanidad among Dominicans at home and abroad.

Bachateros are quick to reiterate these ties to Dominicanness. For Joe Veras, bachata and merengue contribute to dominicanidad and pride in the homeland, and he points to both, along with baseball, as being recognized internationally as Dominican.[7] Davicito Paredes echoes this point of view, expressing pride in the national collective ownership of the genre.[8] José Manuel Calderón, the very first bachatero, believes bachata's growth and acceptance lie in the support and backing of a large fan base that represented the majority, even if they were not as vocal as the genre's detractors.[9] Fans' ability to relate to bachata has helped convert it into a mechanism of identification on such a large scale internationally.

Since its birth among the lower urban classes of Santo Domingo in 1962, bachata has beat along with the heart of the Dominican nation, even when the middle and upper classes vehemently criticized it, condemning the genre as cheap and devoid of musical value. Now, spread far and wide on the tastes of Dominican migrants, bachata has gained a solid international foothold. "Bachata is speaking for itself," maintains Henry Santos. "It's there, it's powerful, it's gonna continue growing. It speaks for itself."[10] Today, bachata can be heard both at home and among dominicanos ausentes —played from a CD in a neighborhood *colmado*, in a live performance, or over local or satellite radio. Whether it is loved or abhorred, at home or abroad, bachata has been and is an integral part of the Dominican experience—an accurate measure of the pulse of the Dominican nation.

Notes

Introduction

1. Smith 107.
2. Sellers 2.
3. Bello interview.
4. Corniel interview.
5. Smith 108.
6. Seeger 451.
7. J. M. Pérez 386.
8. Seeger 459.
9. Derby 240.
10. Derby 185; Candelario 26.
11. Hoffnung-Garskof 1.
12. Candelario 59.
13. "Señora Bachata," a collaboration among bachata stars José Manuel Calderón, Blas Durán, Leonardo Paniagua, Ramón Cordero, Ramón Torres, and Luis Segura on the 2009 CD of the same name, personifies bachata and relates its path from a discriminated fixture of the bars to a dignified woman whose beauty is admired by the very ones who formerly criticized her.
14. Slobin 11.
15. Fiske 25.
16. Días 407.
17. *Santo Domingo Blues.*
18. José Manual Calderón debuted what would later be recognized as the first bachata single on this date.
19. J. M. Pérez 391.
20. Sellers 2.

Chapter One

1. Veloz Maggiolo 19.
2. Zavala 190.
3. Knights 8–9; Veloz Maggiolo 70–1.
4. Veloz Maggiolo 15.
5. Knights 11; Veloz Maggiolo 70.
6. Zavala 192.
7. Veloz Maggiolo 26–9.
8. Veloz Maggiolo 30.
9. Veloz Maggiolo 73.
10. Veloz Maggiolo 71.
11. Knights 12.
12. Anderson 33.
13. Knights 5.
14. Knights 5.
15. Knights 3, 7; Delgado Malagón 219.
16. Veloz Maggiolo 167.
17. Veloz Maggiolo 137.
18. Veloz Maggiolo 138.
19. Calderón interview; T. García interview.
20. Veloz Maggiolo 121.
21. Veloz Maggiolo 133.
22. Veloz Maggiolo 129.
23. J. M. Pérez 390.
24. J. M. Pérez 390–1.
25. Although this style of guitar-based bolero music was not considered its own genre until the 1970s, the author will refer to it as *bachata* for ease of identification.
26. E. Paredes interview.
27. T. García interview; E. Paredes interview; Tejeda *La pasión* 129–30.
28. Corniel interview; T. García interview; Batista Matos; Pacini Hernandez *Bachata.*
29. E. Paredes interview.
30. Calderón interview.
31. E. Paredes interview.
32. E. Paredes interview.
33. E. Paredes interview.
34. E. Paredes interview.
35. H. Santos interview; Cáceres.
36. Paniagua interview.
37. E. Paredes interview.
38. Paniagua interview.
39. Love interview.
40. Paniagua interview.
41. Calderón interview.
42. Silfa interview.
43. D. Paredes interview.
44. Veloz Maggiolo 22.
45. T. García interview.
46. T. García interview.
47. H. Santos interview.
48. Burgos; Paniagua; Santana.
49. D. Paredes interview.
50. Fernández interview.
51. *Santo Domingo Blues.*
52. H. Santos interview.
53. Burgos interview.
54. Fernández interview.
55. E. Paredes interview.

56. E. Paredes interview.
57. E. Paredes interview.
58. Gray; Leal & Féblot-Augustins; Van Vleck.
59. Elliott 29.
60. Elliott 30.
61. Gray 107.
62. Corniel interview; Burgos interview.
63. Corniel interview; Burgos interview.
64. Veras interview.
65. Bello interview.
66. H. Santos interview.
67. Love interview.
68. Martínez interview.
69. Martínez interview.
70. L. Santos interview.
71. Paniagua interview.
72. Burgos interview.
73. Love interview.
74. D. Paredes interview.
75. D. Paredes interview.
76. D. Paredes interview.
77. Qtd. in *Bachata Roja: Amor y amargue.*
78. Bugos interview.
79. L. Santos interview.
80. Corniel interview.
81. Leal and Féblot-Augustins 181.
82. Veloz Maggiolo 189.
83. Veloz Maggiolo 189.
84. X. Pérez interview.
85. Medina interview.
86. Santana interview.
87. Medina interview.
88. Andújar Persinal 72.
89. Medina interview.
90. X. Pérez interview.
91. X. Pérez interview.
92. L. Santos interview.
93. T. García interview.
94. T. García interview.
95. T. García interview.
96. Burgos interview.
97. D. Paredes interview.
98. Although a number of artists of other genres have experimented with bachata, few have switched equally or predominantly to the genre. The most notable exception is merenguero Héctor Acosta "El Torito" who more than one Dominican described to me as "now a bachatero."
99. Calderón interview.
100. E. Paredes interview.
101. Martínez interview.
102. Silfa interview.
103. Burgos interview.
104. Fernández interview.
105. Candelario 26.
106. Fernández interview.
107. Paniagua interview.
108. Paniagua interview.
109. Santana interview; T. Santos interview.
110. Veras interview.
111. Veras interview.
112. H. Santos interview.
113. L. Santos interview.
114. L. Santos interview.
115. T. García interview.
116. Sellers 2.
117. Qtd. in Adelt *Blues Music* vii.
118. Batista Matos 16.
119. Fernández interview.
120. Fernández interview.
121. Bello interview.
122. Fernández interview.
123. Fernández interview.
124. Veras interview.
125. Silfa interview.
126. D. Paredes interview; Cano interview.
127. D. Paredes interview.
128. I. Aponte interview.
129. R. D. Aponte interview.
130. Sanche interview.
131. Love interview.
132. Love interview.
133. Paniagua interview.
134. Paniagua interview.
135. del Castillo 296.
136. D. Paredes interview.
137. D. Paredes interview.
138. Fernández interview; T. García interview.
139. Méndez interview.
140. "Eladio Romero Santos."
141. D. Paredes interview.
142. "Eladio Romero Santos."
143. Wayne "Sexual Double Entendre."
144. Valentine.
145. Allen 166.
146. Valentine.

Chapter Two

1. Hoffnung-Garskof 11.
2. Hoffnung-Garskof 12.
3. Todorov 3.
4. Todorov 3.
5. Moya Pons *Dominican Republic* 95.
6. Moya Pons *Dominican Republic* 107–8.
7. Candelario 99.
8. Candelario 5.
9. Moya Pons *Dominican Republic* 109.
10. Wucker 38–9.
11. Balaguer 15.
12. Crassweller 149.
13. Radcliffe and Westwood 27.
14. Anderson 7.
15. Radcliffe and Westwood 23.
16. Radcliffe and Westwood 22; 16.
17. Duara 169.
18. Gilman 18.
19. Radcliffe and Westwood 33.
20. Derby 18.
21. Torres-Saillant "Tribulations" 1104.
22. Hoffnung-Garskof 24.
23. Derby 35.
24. Derby 57.
25. Derby 35–6.
26. Moya Pons "Modernización" 222.
27. Moya Pons *Dominican Republic* 338.

28. Derby 37.
29. Derby 12–13.
30. Moya Pons *Dominican Republic* 40.
31. Wucker 75.
32. "Modernización" 245.
33. Torres-Saillant "Tribulations" 1104.
34. Derby 2.
35. Candelario 29.
36. Candelario 1; her translation.
37. Alix 15–17.
38. Derby 2.
39. Guzmán 4–5.
40. Wucker 33.
41. Derby 200.
42. *Mirrors of the Heart.*
43. *Sábado Gigante.*
44. Guzmán 6.
45. Candelario 223.
46. Alix 16.
47. *Mirrors of the Heart.*
48. Candelario 223.
49. Derby 185.
50. Candelario 26.
51. Derby 150.
52. Derby 202.
53. Derby 159.
54. Hoffnung-Garskof 13.
55. Hoffnung-Garskoff 12; 21–3.
56. Hoffnung-Garskof 18–19.
57. Torres-Saillant "Tribulations" 1104.
58. Hoffnung-Garskof 23.
59. Hoffnung-Garskof 17.
60. Derby 107.
61. Hofnung-Garskof 29.
62. Henríquez Ureña 147; Arzeno 127.
63. Sellers 64.
64. Tejeda *La pasión* 38.
65. Galván, qtd. in Rodríguez Demorizi 114.
66. Qtd. in Rodríguez Demorizi 115.
67. Moya Pons "Modernización" 213.
68. In truth, there is no evidence to support the indigenous roots of the güiro, and both it and its later metal equivalent, the *güira*, are believed to be of Dominican or Puerto Rican origin.
69. Qtd. in Rodríguez Demorizi 136.
70. Qtd. in Rodríguez Demorizi 160.
71. Coopersmith 22.
72. M.E. Davis 146.
73. Hoffnung-Garskof 11.
74. M.E. Davis 146.

Chapter Three

1. Hoffnung-Garskof 11.
2. Derby 132.
3. Hoffnung-Garskof 26.
4. Derby 67.
5. Derby 68.
6. Derby 70.
7. Derby 69.
8. Derby 88.
9. Derby 102.
10. Derby 88.
11. Derby 107.
12. Crassweller 30; Derby 194.
13. Crassweller 83; Galíndez 182.
14. Hartlyn 49.
15. Hartlyn 49.
16. Aquino 92–3; Moya Pons *Dominican Republic* 359.
17. Moya Pons *Dominican Republic* 365; Hartlyn 50.
18. Derby 208.
19. Derby 197; Wucker 51.
20. Crassweller 154; Wucker 48.
21. Derby 164–6.
22. Aquino 69; Espaillat 25–6.
23. Derby 264.
24. Derby 135–9.
25. Foucault 201.
26. Aquino 69–70; Moya Pons *Dominican Republic* 376.
27. del Castillo and García Arévalo 81; Wucker 45–6.
28. Sellers 94; Jorge 76.
29. Rivera González 3:10–11.
30. Sellers 94–5.
31. Pacini Hernandez *Bachata* 73.
32. del Castillo and García Arevalo 82.
33. Manuel 102.
34. Hoffnung-Garskof 11.
35. Sellers 97.
36. Rivera González.
37. Veloz Maggiolo 83.
38. Derby 109.
39. Qtd. and translated in Crassweller 295.
40. Crassweller 298.
41. Diederich 43.
42. Derby 240.
43. Derby 257–60.

Chapter Four

1. E. Paredes interview.
2. Rodríguez.
3. Calderón interview.
4. Calderón interview.
5. Calderón interview.
6. Unless otherwise noted, all songs are listed by performer name in the List of Recordings Cited.
7. Calderón interview; Batista Matos *Bachata* 11.
8. *José Manuel Calderón.*
9. *José Manuel Calderón.*
10. *José Manuel Calderón;* Batista Matos 12.
11. Calderón interview.
12. The practice of producing bachata versions of songs from other genres has continued throughout the genre's history. For reasons of space, the author does not indicate each song that is a remake in this study.
13. Batista Matos 10.
14. *José Manuel Calderón.*
15. *José Manuel Calderón.*
16. Batista Matos.
17. Batista Matos 14; *José Manuel Calderón.*

18. Calderón interview.
19. E. Paredes interview.
20. Batista Matos 15.
21. D. Paredes interview.
22. Sánchez.
23. Batista Matos 23.
24. Although a simple, single word translation of *desengaño* is "disillusion," "disillusionment," or "eye-opener," it can carry with it the undertone of a nasty surprise, as is often the case in bachata.
25. Sánchez.
26. Paniagua interview.
27. One of the barrios, *La Ciénaga* (The Swamp), grew up underneath the capital's Duarte Bridge where it was clearly seen by anyone crossing above. This increased visibility evolved into a popular saying among residents who referred to any barrio popular as *debajo del puente*—under the bridge (Hoffnung-Garskof 41). This saying was so common that it appropriately became the title and subject of a bachata by Víctor Víctor in which the narrative voice contrasts two physical locations, beneath and above the bridge, positing them as two separate worlds. Above, people pass and look down upon those living in the shantytown below without compassion or compunction.
28. V. García interview.
29. Paniagua interview.
30. Calderón interview.
31. Pacini Hernandez *Bachata* 100.
32. Calderón interview.
33. Hoffnung-Garskof 62.
34. Hoffnung-Garskof 62.
35. Hoffnung-Garskof 62.
36. Andújar Persinal 68.
37. Love interview.
38. H. Santos interview.
39. T. García interview.
40. Silfa interview.
41. E. Paredes interview.
42. Corniel interview.
43. E. Paredes interview; *Santo Domingo Blues.*
44. T. García interview.
45. T. García interview.
46. T. García interview.
47. D. Paredes.
48. *Santo Domingo Blues.*
49. Corniel interview.
50. *Santo Domingo Blues.*
51. Paniagua interview.
52. E. Paredes interview; D. Paredes interview.
53. E. Paredes interview.
54. Silfa interview.
55. Hoffnung-Garskof 12.
56. Hoffnung-Garskof 13.
57. Derby 257–60.
58. Hoffnung-Garskof 64.
59. E. Paredes interview.
60. Silfa interview.
61. Batista Matos 19.
62. T. García interview.
63. Pacini Hernandez *Bachata* 88–91.
64. Silfa interview.

65. Pacini Hernandez *Bachata* 97.
66. Pacini Hernandez *Bachata* 97–8.
67. T. Santos interview.
68. T. García interview.
69. T. García interview.
70. Pacini Hernandez *Bachata* 92.
71. Pacini Hernandez *Bachata* 92.
72. Anderson 33.
73. Anderson 35.
74. J.M. Pérez 387.
75. R. D. Aponte interview.
76. T. García interview.
77. *Santo Domingo Blues.*
78. Batista Matos 20.
79. See also Chapter Five.
80. Wayne "Edilio Paredes."
81. Wayne "Edilio Paredes."
82. Wayne "Edilio Paredes."
83. Wayne "Edilio Paredes."
84. E. Paredes interview.
85. *The Bachata Legends.*
86. Paniagua interview.
87. Paniagua interview.
88. Paniagua interview.
89. Paniagua interview.
90. Paniagua interview.
91. Batista Matos 49.
92. Batista Matos 51.
93. Paniagua interview.

Chapter Five

1. Morgan, Hartlyn, and Espinal 8.
2. Pacini Hernandez *Bachata* 155–6.
3. Pacini Hernandez *Bachata* 155–7.
4. Aparicio 128.
5. Hoffnung-Garskof 38.
6. Krohn-Hansen 115.
7. Pacini Hernandez *Bachata* 158–61.
8. *Bachata* 161.
9. Pacini Hernandez *Bachata* 194.
10. Batista Matos 119.
11. Sergio Reyes, qtd. in Brito Ureña 208.
12. Qtd. in Brito Ureña 208.
13. Qtd. in Brito Ureña 209.
14. T. Santos interview.
15. "Sexual Double Entendre Bachata."
16. Ángel is from the province of Santiago Rodríguez in the northwestern region of the nation.
17. Ángel interview.
18. Ángel interview.
19. Ángel interview.
20. Batista Matos 55.
21. "Blas Durán."
22. Pacini Hernandez *Bachata* 200; Wayne "Sexual Doble Entendre Bachata."
23. "Blas Durán"; Pacini Hernandez *Bachata* 200–1.
24. Wayne "Sexual Double Entendre Bachata."
25. "Blas Durán."
26. Mattern 39.
27. Pacini Hernandez "La lucha sonora."
28. T. García interview.

29. T. García interview.
30. Pacini Hernandez *Bachata* 204–5; T. García interview.
31. T. García interview.
32. Pacini Hernandez *Bachata* 205.
33. Batista Matos 86–8.
34. E. Paredes interview.
35. Jiménez 29.
36. ACROARTE; T. García; Batista Matos 91.
37. del Castillo 471–3; Tejada "Víctor Víctor."
38. Batista Matos 91; del Castillo 473; T. García interview.
39. ACROARTE.
40. Pacini Hernandez *Bachata* 208.
41. Batista Matos 91.
42. E. Paredes interview.
43. T. García interview; Batista Matos 91.
44. Slobin 11.
45. T. García interview; Paniagua interview; E. Paredes interview.
46. *Bachata: Music of the People.*
47. E. Paredes interview; T. García interview.
48. Fernández interview.
49. Love interview; Santana interview.
50. Calderón interview.
51. Wayne "Frontier."
52. Wayne "Luis Vargas."
53. *Santo Domingo Blues.*
54. Batista Matos 76.
55. *Santo Domingo Blues*; Wayne "Luis Vargas."
56. Wayne "Luis Vargas."
57. This song's original title was "*Con los crespos hechos* (All Dressed Up and Nowhere to Go)" but it is commonly known as "Loco de amor" and appears under this title in greatest hits collections.
58. Pacini Hernandez *Bachata* 161.
59. *Santo Domingo Blues.*
60. Antony Santos's name is sometimes spelled Anthony. The author follows this earlier spelling of his name to help identify him from Anthony "Romeo" Santos (see Chapter Eight).
61. This rift, perhaps exacerbated by both bachateros' success, has become a part of music history. One of Vargas's hits, "*El envidioso* (The Envious One)," pokes fun at his rival, Antony Santos. The narrator proclaims a mambo war to decide who really has swing and criticizes a so-called friend who he mentored and who now copies him.
62. Kugel.
63. Pacini Hernandez *Bachata* 210.
64. Wayne "Antony Santos."
65. ACROARTE 29.
66. Sanche interview.
67. Cruz Hierro "Diez figuras."
68. ACROARTE.
69. ACROARTE 29.
70. Batista Matos 80.
71. Batista Matos 80–1.
72. Pacini Hernandez *Bachata* 30–2.
73. Cruz Hierro "10 canciones."
74. Valdez "Pedro" 314.

Chapter Six

1. Veras interview.
2. Veras interview.
3. Veras interview.
4. "Romantic Bachata."
5. Veras interview.
6. Asociación de Cronistas de Arte 28.
7. "Respuestas."
8. H. Santos interview; L. Santos interview.
9. Cruz Hierro "10 canciones."
10. "Biography."
11. Jiménez "Respuestas."
12. Jiménez "Respuestas."
13. Cruz Hierro "Diez figuras."
14. *Bachata: Music of the People.*
15. Sanche interview.
16. Sanche interview; Cruz Hierro "10 canciones."
17. "Diez figuras."
18. Polanco.
19. Sarante.
20. Polanco.
21. Tu Momento Newyorkino.
22. Birchmeier.
23. "Luis Miguel del Amargue."
24. "La alcaldía."
25. "Luis Miguel tiene."
26. Jiménez "Respuestas."
27. Gutierrez.
28. Gutierrez; The Casandra Awards were presented yearly by the Dominican Association of Arts Journalists (*Asociación de Cronistas de Arte*— ACROARTE) and *Cervecería Nacional Dominicana* (Dominican National Brewery) from 1985 to 2012. In 2013, their name was changed to Premios Soberano.
29. Jiménez "Respuestas."
30. "El Chaval lamenta"; "'Maldita residencia.'"
31. "Maldita residencia."
32. L. Santos interview; Martínez interview.
33. Martínez interview; L. Santos interview.
34. Martínez interview.
35. Martínez interview.
36. See also Chapter Nine for more on Alexandra Cabrera.
37. Jiménez "Respuestas"; Wayne "Alexandra Cabrera."
38. Jiménez "Respuestas."
39. Acosta's nickname, the diminutive form of "bull," comes from his participation in the Los Toros Band, formed by Gerardo Díaz, who was known as "El Toro" (The Bull).
40. H. Santos interview.

Chapter Seven

1. Guitérrez 4.
2. Hoffnung-Garskof 90.
3. Levitt 238.
4. Hoffnung-Garskof 135; Levitt 238.
5. Graham 45.
6. Hume 157.
7. Hume 156; Pew Research Center.

8. Verbrigghe.
9. Duany *Quisqueya* 2.
10. Hoffnung-Garskof 196.
11. Duany *Quisqueya* 33; 40.
12. Malkki 448.
13. Hoffnung-Garskof 126–8.
14. Hume 158–9.
15. Hoffnung-Garskof 172–82.
16. Hoffnung-Garskof 166–9.
17. Levitt 248.
18. Hoffnung-Garskof 170–1.
19. Hoffnung-Garskof 230.
20. Hoffnung-Garskof 119.
21. Pacini Hernandez *Oye* 90.
22. Pacini Hernandez *Oye* 91.
23. Corniel interview.
24. Santana interview.
25. Santana interview.
26. Santana interview.
27. Santana interview.
28. "Ray Santana" 25.
29. Burgos interview.
30. Burgos interview.
31. Burgos interview.
32. The title of this song is a play on words. In Spanish, *flechar* means to cause love at first sight. The title thus refers back to Burgos as El Cupido who is hunting for hearts to shoot.
33. Corniel interview.
34. Corniel interview.
35. Corniel interview.
36. Corniel interview.
37. J.M. Pérez 391.
38. J. M. Pérez 391.
39. Burgos interview.
40. *Santo Domingo Blues.*

Chapter Eight

1. L. Santos interview.
2. H. Santos "Question."
3. L. Santos in Vívelohoy.
4. Pacini Hernandez *Oye* 91.
5. H. Santos interview.
6. Pacini Hernandez *Oye* 91.
7. H. Santos interview; L. Santos interview.
8. Wayne "The New York School."
9. Burgos interview.
10. Burgos interview.
11. H. Santos "Quote"; H. Santos "Question."
12. H. Santos "Quote."
13. L. Santos interview.
14. Grosjean 51.
15. L. Santos interview.
16. Torres 76.
17. Grosjean 52–4.
18. Grosjean 54.
19. Love interview.
20. H. Santos interview.
21. H. Santos World Debut.
22. Cáceres.
23. As explained in Chapter One, *grajo* literally means underarm odor. Idiomatically, the term ref-erences urban middle and upper class views of peasants' cleanliness. When used to describe ba-chata, it emphasizes a lack of refinement.
24. *Santo Domingo Blues.*
25. H. Santos interview; L. Santos interview.
26. L. Santos interview.
27. L. Santos interview.
28. L. Santos interview.
29. L. Santos interview.
30. L. Santos interview.
31. L. Santos; Rohter "Crossing Over."
32. L. Santos interview.
33. L. Santos interview.
34. L. Santos interview; M.C. Davis.
35. M.C. Davis.
36. L. Santos interview.
37. L. Santos qtd. in M.C. Davis.
38. Rosen.
39. "Crossing Over."
40. Qtd. in Richards.
41. Aventura also produced an English version of this song under the same title, although this is a bit of a misnomer given its Spanglish lyrics that smoothly place words from one language in the syntactically correct location within a sentence predominately in the other.
42. While machismo glorifies the male as a se-ducer and conqueror, marianismo likens woman to the Virgin Mary. These constructions are treated in greater detail in Chapter Nine.
43. Graglia.
44. Romeo Santos in "Fiesta Latina."
45. Eva Longoria Parker in "Fiesta Latina."
46. Rohter "Crossing Over."
47. ACROARTE 28.
48. ACROARTE 29.
49. L. Santos in Vívelohoy.
50. Love interview.
51. Love interview.
52. Love interview.
53. Love interview.
54. Love interview.
55. Love interview.
56. Love interview.
57. Love interview.
58. Cobo "Prince Royce Enters 'Phase II.'"
59. "Prince Royce estrenó."
60. A reference to his album, *Loco de amor* (Crazy for Love).
61. "Soy un macho de hombre (I'm a macho man)" from Rodríguez's song *"Me la pusieron difícil* (They Made it Hard for Me)."
62. Rodríguez calls the woman after the names in two of his own songs: first as *"Mi morenita* (My Sweetie)," and later as "Nereyda."
63. A reference to his album and song of the same name, *Soledad* (Solitude).
64. The title of his song, *"Linda y difícil."*
65. References to his songs *"Corazón culpable* (Guilty Heart)" and *"Pena de amor* (Heartache)."
66. A reference to his song of the same name, *"La batalla* (The Battle)."
67. References to songs *"El jueguito* (The Little

Game)," "*Qué plantón* (What a Way to Stand Someone Up)," and "*Mi timidez* (My Shyness)."
68. "Biography" *Romeo*.
69. Billboard, 2007; ASCAP 2010.
70. Ortiz de Urbina and López; *Telenovelas: Love, TV and Power*.
71. World Debut.
72. H. Santos "Quote."
73. Santos and Styles.
74. Lenny Santos in Vívelohoy.
75. Qtd. in Vívelohoy.
76. Santos and Styles.
77. In 2011, Romeo announced that he had accepted a project with Will Smith's and James Lassiter's Overbrook Entertainment to produce a sitcom for ABC. The currently untitled project portrays a young Dominican-American, Romeo, who is caught between the traditions of his migrant parents and his own hopes and dreams (Cobo "Latin Singer").
78. Cobo "Prince Royce Enters 'Phase II.'"
79. Sellers 173.
80. Aparicio 108.
81. Qtd. in Aparicio 115.
82. Sellers 173.
83. Cobo "Prince Royce Enters 'Phase II.'"
84. Rohter "Crossing Over."
85. Richards; Rohter "Crossing Over"; Rohter "Romeo."
86. Qtd. in Rohter "Crossing Over."
87. Aparicio 111.
88. Qtd. in Cantor-Navas.
89. Pew Research Center.
90. Ennis, Ríos-Vargas and Albert 3.
91. Pew Research Center.
92. Rohter "Crossing Over."
93. Rohter "Romeo."
94. Rosen.
95. Kugel.
96. Rosen.
97. L. Santos interview.
98. H. Santos interview.

Chapter Nine

1. Silfa interview.
2. DaMatta 64.
3. Derby 119.
4. Derby 119.
5. Derby 119–21.
6. T. García interview.
7. T. García interview.
8. Sellers 149.
9. Aparicio 173.
10. T. García interview.
11. Alexandra Cabrera, of the highly popular duo, Monchy and Alexandra (treated in Chapter Six), has released a few singles both on the duo's albums and afterwards. These solo efforts are not as well known as her duets.
12. E.g., changing a final *o* to *a*: *maestro*, male teacher versus *maestra* female teacher; using a feminine article instead of a masculine article for professions with only one form: *un artista* versus *una artista*.
13. "Mélida Rodríguez."
14. "Mélida Rodríguez."
15. Pacini Hernandez *Bachata*.
16. "Aridia Ventura."
17. "Aridia Ventura."
18. Silfa interview.
19. Silfa interview.
20. Silfa interview.
21. Silfa interview.
22. Silfa interview.
23. Silfa interview.
24. Bello interview.
25. Bello interview.
26. Bello interview.
27. Cuesta 40.

Conclusion

1. T. García interview.
2. I. Aponte interview.
3. E. Paredes interview.
4. E. Paredes interview.
5. Veras interview.
6. H. Santos interview.
7. Veras interview.
8. D. Paredes interview.
9. Calderón interview.
10. H. Santos interview.

Illustrations /
Ilustraciones

A music store in Santo Domingo offers a broad selection of bachata. / Tienda de discos en Santo Domingo ofrece una amplia selección de bachata.

Bolero trios helped spread the popular genre across the Dominican Republic. / Los tríos ayudaron a difundir el género popular del bolero por toda la República Dominicana.

Right / A la derecha: Bachatero Gerson Corniel demonstrates singing with amargue. / El bachatero Gerson Corniel demuestra cómo se canta con amargue.

Below / Abajo: Relations between the Dominican Republic and its island neighbor on Hispaniola, Haiti, have historically been tense. / En la Española, las relaciones entre la República Dominicana y su vecino, Haití, son históricamente tensas. (*The CIA World Factbook*)

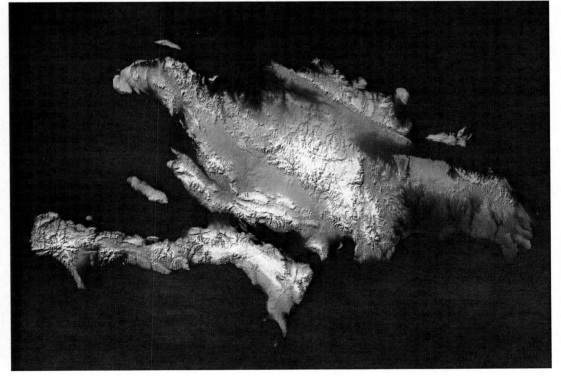

Chino Méndez and Xiomarita Pérez demonstrate the close embrace of bolero at the 3rd Conference on Music and Identity in the Caribbean, Santiago de los Caballeros, Dominican Republic, April 19, 2009. / Chino Méndez y Xiomarita Pérez demuestran el abrazo íntimo del bolero. III Congreso Música, Identidad y Cultura en el Caribe (MIC III), Santiago de los Caballeros, República Dominicana, 19 de abril, 2009.

Many Dominican car washes, such as this Santiago establishment, offer a bar and musical entertainment to clients. / Muchos carwash, como este en Santiago de los Caballeros, les ofrecen bebidas y música a sus clientes.

Dominican car washes have become popular spots to listen to music, dance, and have a drink. / Los carwash dominicanos se han convertido en lugares populares donde la gente escucha música, baila y toma tragos.

Maracas and güira souvenirs reiterate the importance of music in Dominican culture. / Las maracas y la güira como recuerdo turístico reiteran la importancia de la música en la cultura dominicana. (Cynthia J. Staley)

Left/ A la izquierda: Like the Dominican faceless doll, Dominican ethnicity has no single face. / Al igual que las muñecas sin cara, la etnicidad dominicana no tiene una sola cara. (Cynthia J. Staley) *Right / A la derecha:* Juan Pablo Duarte, founding father of the Dominican Republic. / Juan Pablo Duarte, Padre de la Patria de la República Dominicana.

Faceless dolls in a Santiago de los Caballeros souvenir store. / Muñecas sin cara en una tienda de recuerdos de Santiago de los Caballeros.

Left / A la izquierda: Merenge típico's definitive instruments: the güira, drum, and accordion. / Los instrumentos definitivos del merengue típico: la güira, la tambora y el acordeón. (Cynthia J. Staley) *Right / A la derecha:* Music, like the national flag, identifies Dominicans at home and abroad. / Tal como la bandera nacional, la música identifica a los dominicanos, tanto en el país como en el exterior.

Trujillo used merengue as early as his first campaign in 1930 when musicians such as Francisco "Ñico" Lora, depicted in this statue in front of the Monument to the Heroes of the Restoration in Santiago de los Caballeros, accompanied him on the campaign trail. / Trujillo hizo uso del merengue desde su primera campaña en 1930, cuando fue acompañado por merengueros como Francisco "Ñico" Lora, quien se ve retratado en esta estatua delante del Monumento a los Héroes de la Restauración en Santiago de los Caballeros.

The coldblooded murder of the Mirabal sisters—left to right, María Teresa, Minerva, and Patria—contributed to the growing opposition to Trujillo's dictatorship. / La muerte a sangre fría de las hermanas Mirabal—de izquierda a derecha, María Teresa, Minerva y Patria—contribuyó a la creciente oposición a la dictadura de Trujillo.

Inhabitants of lower-class barrios were early bachata's primary consumers. / Los habitantes de los barrios populares fueron los primeros consumidores de la bachata.

Bachata was a staple of the small corner stores known as colmados. / La bachata era un elemento básico de los colmados.

The author (second from left) poses with bachata legends (left to right) Julio Angel, Tony Santos, and Edilio Paredes. / La autora (la segunda a la izquierda) con los legendarios bachateros (de izquierda a derecha) Julio Ángel, Tony Santos y Edilio Paredes. (Darío Tejeda)

Luis Segura, "el Añoñaíto." (PhotoNews/Rusbert Pérez)

Luis Segura and bachata became the center of national attention in 1983 when the president of the Autonomous University of Santo Domingo forbade his bachata performance on campus. / Luis Segura y la bachata acapararon la atención de la nación en 1983 cuando el presidente de la Universidad Autónoma de Santo Domingo prohibió su presentación de bachata en la alta casa de estudio. (PhotoNews/Rusbert Pérez)

Poster announcing the international Nueva Canción festival held in the Dominican Republic in 1974. Musicians such as Luis Días, Juan Luis Guerra and Víctor Víctor, whose roots were in Nueva Canción, later experimented with the changing sound of bachata in the late 1980s and 1990s. / Un cartel que anuncia el festival internacional de Nueva Canción que tuvo lugar en la República Dominicana en 1974. Luis Días, Juan Luis Guerra, y Víctor Víctor, músicos que empezaron con la Nueva Canción, experimentaron con la evolución del sonido de la bachata a finales de los 1980 y en los 1990.

Juan Luis Guerra (left) collaborates with modern bachata star Romeo Santos in a December 22, 2012 concert held in the Olympic Stadium in Santo Domingo. Guerra's *Bachata rosa* album helped carry bachata to new audiences. / Juan Luis Guerra (a la izquierda) colabora con el bachatero moderno, Romeo Santos, en un concierto en el Estadio Olímpico (22 de diciembre, 2012, Santo Domingo). El álbum de Guerra, *Bachata Rosa*, ayudó a que la bachata tuviera nuevos públicos. (PhotoNews/Bufeo/Alberto Martínez)

Left / A la izquierda: Bachatero Joe Veras's romantic lyrics and refined arrangements influenced other bachateros both at home and abroad. / Las letras románticas y los arreglos refinados del bachatero Joe Veras influyeron a otros bachateros tanto en el país como en el exterior. (ACROARTE) *Right / A la derecha:* Antony Santos. (Imágenes Dominicanas/Reinaldo Brito)

Above, left / Arriba, a la izquierda: Joe Veras, "el Hombre de Tu Vida." (ACROARTE) *Right / A la derecha:* Frank Reyes's music depicts a variety of topics and emotions. / La música de Frank Reyes retrata una variedad de temas y sentimientos. (Rusbert Pérez)

Yóskar Sarante. (ACROARTE)

Since his debut in 1993, Raulín Rodríguez has continued to be one of the most popular bachateros. This poster announces an April 2013 concert in the Dominican Republic. / Raulín Rodríguez ha sido uno de los bachateros más populares desde su comienzo en 1993. Este cartel anuncia un concierto suyo en la República Dominicana en abril del 2013.

Another romantic newcomer of the 1990s, Zacarías Ferreira continues to rank among the most popular bachateros. This poster announces a March 2013 performance in the Dominican Republic. / Zacarías Ferreira, otra nueva estrella de los 1990, sigue siendo uno de los bachateros más populares. Este cartel anuncia una presentación suya en marzo del 2013 en la República Dominicana.

Elvis Martínez's "Así fue" was an international hit. It was the first bachata programmed on mainstream tropical radio in the United States. / El tema "Así fue" de Elvis Martínez fue un éxito internacional. Fue la primera bachata programada en las emisoras radiales de la corriente dominante de música tropical en Estados Unidos. (Jochy Fersobe)

This graffiti in Washington Heights, Upper Manhattan, New York, depicts two quintessential Dominican cultural products: baseball and music. / Este grafiti en Washington Heights, Alto Manhattan, Nueva York retrata dos productos culturales dominicanos por excelencia: el béisbol y la música.

A street vendor in Washington Heights sells Dominican *pasteles.* / Una vendedora ambulante en Washington Heights vende pasteles dominicanos.

Rafy Burgos "el Cupido" caused a stir with his 2010 hit, "Dame Cabeza." / Rafy Burgos "el Cupido" causó un escándalo con su éxito del 2010, "Dame cabeza".

Former Aventura lead singer, Romeo Santos, launched his solo career in 2011. / Romeo Santos, antiguo cantante principal del Grupo Aventura, lanzó su carrera como solista en el 2011. (PhotoNews/Bufeo/Alberto Martínez)

Aventura, with lead singer Romeo Santos, brought a new sound to bachata. / El grupo Aventura, con Romeo Santos como su cantante principal, le dio un nuevo sonido a la bachata. (Alexis Gómez)

Aventura band members (left to right) Henry Santos, Max Agende, Romeo Santos, and Lenny Santos released the first major expression of modern bachata. In this 2003 Casandra Awards ceremony, the band was recognized as the Best New Artist of the Year and the Best Bachata Performer. / Henry Santos, Max Agende, Romeo Santos y Lenny Santos (de izquierda a derecha) del Grupo Aventura, lanzaron la primera expresión importante de la bachata moderna. En los Premios Casandra del 2003, los reconocieron como Revelación del Año y Bachatero del Año. (ACROARTE)

Romeo Santos played to a sold-out crowd in the Olympic Stadium in Santo Domingo in December 2012. / Romeo Santos cantó en el Estadio Olímpico (Santo Domingo, diciembre del 2012), el cual estuvo lleno a toda capacidad. (PhotoNews/Bufeo/Alberto Martínez)

Left / A la izquierda: Toby Love. (Kike San Martin) *Right / A la derecha:* Henry Santos emphasizes that one must understand the soul of bachata to truly interpret it. / Henry Santos enfatiza la necesidad de entender el alma de la bachata para poder interpretarla de verdad. (Cameron Nielson)

Above / Arriba: **Singer-songwriter, Henry Santos. / El cantautor, Henry Santos. (Oriana Gonzalez)**

Guitarist and producer Lenny Santos was central to revolutionizing the sound of modern bachata. / Lenny Santos, guitarrista y productor, desempeñó un papel central en la revolución del sonido de la bachata moderna. (Shobiz for dpicreative)

Susana Silfa debuted in the bachata world as "Mariíta" in the early 1990s. / Susana Silfa se inició en el mundo bachatero con el nombre "Mariíta" a principios del decenio de los 1990. (EIX Photography)

Bachatero and producer Davicito Paredes. / Davicito Paredes, bachatero y productor.

Español

Para mi esposo,
P.J Vaske,
y en memoria de
Rupert,
un perro bueno y fiel

Prólogo de Darío Tejeda

Asumo que el motivo por el cual fui invitado por la profesora Julie Sellers a escribir este prólogo es por mis escritos relacionados con la bachata, partiendo de mi libro biográfico sobre Juan Luis Guerra, de 1993, donde aparecieron mis primeros textos sobre esa música dominicana, y donde detallo las conexiones del artista con ese género musical—incluso la historia de cada una de sus primeras bachatas—en el tono propio de una biografía novelada. Esta fue seguida por mi libro *La pasión danzaria*, de 2002, ensayo académico en el cual hay un capítulo especialmente dedicado al género, también publicado en forma independiente como fascículo bilingüe con el título en español *La bachata: Su origen, su historia y sus leyendas*.

En este escrito daré algunas ideas que ayuden a comprender la importancia de este libro, en el cual la autora toca los dos tópicos citados, la bachata y Juan Luis Guerra. Su obra se enmarca en lo que desde 2007, en un libro aun inconcluso, denominé *bachatología*, un concepto que utilizo para designar el hecho de pensar la bachata en el contexto de la cultura dominicana y del Caribe y sus ramificaciones alrededor del mundo, tal como su impacto en Estados Unidos y en Europa a través de las comunidades dominicanas inmigrantes en esas zonas, la primera de ellas estudiada en este texto por Sellers. El interés de la autora en la música dominicana tuvo un primer parto en el libro *Merengue & Dominican Identity: Music as National Unifier* (2004), y desde entonces ha seguido creciendo. Esta obra es la mejor prueba.

Una vez un periodista me preguntó en una entrevista a qué obedecían mis estudios de la música, pregunta entendible en un país como República Dominicana siempre dado a disfrutar las expresiones musicales casi exclusivamente como sonido, canto y baile. Mi respuesta fue precisa: obedecen al interés de pensar la música, sobrepasando así el hecho de solo oírla, cantarla o bailarla. Por esa razón empecé a hablar de *bachatología*, describiéndola como un ejercicio de pensar la bachata como fenómeno musical y cultural.

Y efectivamente, de eso se trata, de enfocar la bachata como una cultura. Yo la llamaría la cultura bachatera. Este concepto puede ser engañoso por la misma razón que se desdeñó a la bachata en sus comienzos: por responder a una forma de ser de músicos y aficionados de esa expresión musical, provenientes de las clases sociales más pobres de la sociedad dominicana, y por esa misma situación caracterizados por ser—o casi ser—iletrados (incluyendo carecer de estudios académicos de música o canto), y a menudo también negros o mulatos.

Los bachateros fueron—y son—portadores de una combinación de condiciones

155

económicas, sociales, políticas, raciales y educacionales que definieron su perfil como excluidos o marginados de los sistemas de propiedad, riqueza, poder, conocimiento, estatus y distinción, variables todas atravesados en República Dominicana por criterios clasistas y raciales. En la bachata habla el pobre, el campesino, el negro, el marginado urbano, el olvidado, en fin, el ser oprimido por las desigualdades económicas, sociales, políticas y culturales, el *"Pobre Diablo"* de Teodoro Reyes, el *"Juancito Nadie"* de Elvis Martínez.

Ese *nadie* en los campos dominicanos vestía de jornalero agrícola, de parcelero o conuquero, de peón, y en la ciudad de guardia, *guachimán* (guardián), *chopa* (sirvienta), y en el exterior de *cadenú* (*dominican yorks* que regresaban exhibiendo cadenas como adornos corporales), seres arrastrados a la indignidad (y muchas veces a la perdición social) por su condición de pobreza, incluyendo una pobre instrucción que los proyectó injustamente como "incultos". Hace ya más de medio siglo que los estudios del antropólogo estadounidense Oscar Lewis retrataron como pocos las circunstancias existenciales de ese ser sumido frecuentemente en el ocaso de la indigencia y el abandono a su suerte.

De esa múltiple condición de pobre, negro, iletrado, excluido y olvidado—es decir, *nadie*—se derivó otra aún más pesarosa: su estado de denigrado y discriminado. El bachatero fue víctima del estigma social y el prejuicio cultural, herencia de la antigua pertenencia de ese tipo de personas a la sociedad de segunda o de tercera, jerarquía de poder establecida a su vez por la "gente elegante", que hasta bien entrado el siglo XX se llamaba a sí misma la Sociedad de Primera.

De aquellos músicos autodidactas—casi sin escuela, ni educación musical ni escolar—brotaron unas letras a menudo procaces, llenas de doble sentido sexual y de simbologías fálicas, cantadas de forma tosca con un acompañamiento musical rústico, y para más, con un ritmo bailado de manera sexualmente instigadora, en la sordidez de los cabarets rurales y los suburbios urbanos. El ojo del pecado se habría posado sobre la bachata, según la mirada vigilante de los dioses de la civilización, enfrentados a esa presunta barbarie. La bachata nació marcada por un signo peyorativo, como lo evidenciaba su propio nombre. Era música arrabalera, como la exhibida en las películas del cine mexicano de los años cuarenta y cincuenta del siglo XX. Presos de miedo ante la censura social traída por los estereotipos asociados con la bachata, los propios músicos eran renuentes a aceptar el denominativo puesto por voces adversarias. Y aunque buscaban popularizar otros nombres, no pudieron cambiar el hecho de ser nombrados por la cultura dominante—el *mainstream* de la nomenclatura anglosajona.

Como Sellers subraya: "La bachata se encontró marcada por un estigma difícil de superar, ya que se asociaba primero con los migrantes rurales a la ciudad, después con los burdeles, y más tarde, con las trabajadoras domésticas de clase baja que la escuchaban mientras trabajaban". De modo que el gusto musical se convirtió en "una manera de marcar las clases", según afirma en este libro el músico Vicente García.

La barrera era fuerte. La bachata carecía de reconocimiento social. No tenía aquella cualidad de distinción social observada por Pierre Bourdieu como señal de status privilegiado, vinculado al entramado de poderes en la sociedad. Los bachateros reaccionaron ante esa condición de "nadie" mediante lo que Gramsci denominaría una lucha de posiciones, batallando por puestos de principalía en el género que le sumaran prestigio social. Dejaron atrás aquel tipo de apelativos que los sobrenombraban: el Añoñaíto, el Solterito del Sur o el Chivo sin Ley, títulos que para nada ayudaban a adquirir majestad, y adoptaron otros de mayor relieve. Mientras a José Manuel Calderón se le llamó el Padre de la Bachata, Antony Santos se convirtió en el Mayimbe de la Bachata; Luis Vargas en el Rey Supremo de la Bachata; Raulín Rodríguez en el Cacique; los del grupo Aventura—hasta su desaparición, la más destacada entre las agrupaciones bachateras de la llamada diáspora dominicana en Estados Unidos—se denominó *The Kings of Bachata* o los Reyes de la Bachata; cuando el grupo se desintegró, su líder vocal, Romeo Santos, devino en *The King of Bachata* (el Rey, ahora en singular); mientras Frank Reyes fue el Príncipe, y Linar Espinal fue El Chaval. "Debate de 4", bachata icónica de Romeo Santos analizada por Sellers, refleja esa lucha por la distinción dentro de la bachata entre cuatro de sus principales líderes.

Solo a regañadientes los bachateros asimilaron después su denominación como tales, cuando otros procesos sociales atenuaron su carga negativa y disminuyeron el grado de intolerancia y discriminación que pesaba sobre su música, como registra Sellers. La propia universidad pública le negó la entrada. Las premiaciones musicales jamás la tomaban en cuenta hasta que fue aceptada como una categoría en los Premios Casandra, los más relevantes de la isla, en el año 1995—cuando ya Juan Luis Guerra había ganado varios premios Grammy, había ocupado varias veces los primeros lugares en las listas de Billboard, y había recorrido ambas orillas del Atlántico.

Asombra que todavía existiera una paradoja tan grande en época tan reciente, en pleno período finisecular y finimilenar—como lo he llamado por tratarse también del fin de un milenio: que una música de la mayoría de la población no fuera aceptada porque no representaba a la minoría. La bachata no era marginal a la cultura del dominicano común y corriente, al pueblo llano, pero no había sido legitimada por el *mainstream*, la cultura dominante, filtrada por los medios masivos de comunicación controlados por las clases dirigentes. En *La pasión danzaria* establecí que la polarización entre elite y pueblo en la sociedad dominicana es una de las claves para entender su evolución social y cultural.

De manera similar, uno de los quid para entender la bachata es su sistema de polaridades, una de las cuales es justamente esa de elite y pueblo. El contraste arriba/abajo sirve para desvelar el imaginario del dominicano sobre propiedad, riqueza, poder, estatus y distinción, elementos todos mezclados en las nociones de clase social y racialidad; el binomio arriba/abajo dibuja en forma de imagen espacial los extremos de la estratificación social en clave funcionalista. Abajo es donde está la clase baja, arriba está la clase alta: alto/arriba, bajo/abajo. La bachata es una música de *los de abajo*. Es en ese sentido que emergió como una música de la marginalidad, como la denominó Deborah Pacini Hernandez, pionera en el estudio académico de ese genero musical, en su libro, *Bachata: A Social History of a Dominican Popular Music* (1995). Mientras esta centró su atención en la asociación de la bachata con la marginación social, en este libro Sellers se centra en su relación con la identidad dominicana.

El auge y la conversión de la bachata en una música identitaria dominicana fueron procesos paralelos y simultáneos al desarraigo de sus tierras de una alta proporción de campesinos minifundistas, convertidos en obreros agrícolas, y su paso a través de la emigración interna a la condición de proletariado urbano, o bien de marginado urbano por medio del *chiripeo*, un término usado en la isla para designar la condición de subempleado informal: alguien sin trabajo fijo y de ingresos inestables, cuya vida se basa en estrategias de supervivencia. En otras palabras, la bachata fue parte del desarrollo del capitalismo rural en la segunda mitad del siglo XX, que a través del desplazamiento de campesinos conllevó su traslado a las ciudades generando una urbanización de la pobreza. Y allí, con ellos en las márgenes de las ciudades, estaba la bachata, pasando a formar parte del nuevo imaginario urbano, primero barrial y luego incluso transnacional, como evidencia el libro de Sellers que el lector tiene ante sí.

La cultura bachatera tuvo su espacio urbano en el barrio, hábitat de los trabajadores, y su nicho especial en el *colmado*, equivalente urbano de la *pulpería* rural. Y como agentes importantes de circulación tuvo a los *guagueros* de pueblo, que transportaban de la ciudad al campo y viceversa, y los chóferes del *concho* en las ciudades grandes como Santo Domingo y Santiago de los Caballeros. El colmado suplantó como espacio de primacía musical a la gallera y la enramada, como las ciudades suplantaron en importancia a los campos.

Fue allí, en el mundo urbano, donde la bachata logró finalmente su legitimación por el *mainstream*, la mentalidad predominante, proceso que se inició en los años ochenta y cristalizó—algo aún inconcluso—en el último decenio del siglo XX. Tres jalones importantes en el trayecto hacia esa legitimidad fueron: primero, la pegada en 1983 de la bachata "Pena" de uno de los pioneros, Luis Segura, que por primera vez abrió las puertas de los centros cerveceros—que por entonces habían tomado apogeo en los barrios populares, para atender a un depauperado público que vio disminuir su capacidad de consumo, además de los *cadenuses* que bajaban del Norte a celebrar la Navidad; segundo, el surgimiento a partir de 1984, a raíz del experimental álbum *Luis Dias amargao*, grabado en casete por ese innovador artista, de la corriente denominada tecno-bachata, a la que llamé "neobachata" y a la cual se adscribieron posteriormente, y por distintas vías, Sonia Silvestre, Juan Luis Guerra y Víctor Víctor, escuela que le inyectó al género sofisticación musical y literaria, y cuyos mejores resultados se cosecharon en los años 90, siendo su cúspide discográfica *Bachata Rosa*, de Guerra; y tercero, la popularidad alcanzada por "Voy pa' llá," tema de Antony Santos que se convirtió en un verdadero *ciclón bachatero* discográfico, expresión que quiere decir que superó todos los record de los bachateros tradicionales, convirtiéndose en un fenómeno de masas.

La conversión de la bachata en música legítima ocurrió a la par con la depauperación de las capas medias en la llamada Década Perdida (así denominada por los organismos económicos de la región), la industrialización de zonas francas, el surgimiento de un nuevo estamento denominado los *dominican yorks* y su efecto de demostración—especialmente para Navidad y fin de año—que atrajeron hacia la bachata a un público más amplio, fenómeno también estudiado por la profesora Sellers. Así se pudo rebasar la ambivalencia del dominicano hacia la bachata, durante la fase de transición hacia su legitimación como identidad emergente de la nueva dominicanidad urbana y transnacional (y tendencialmente bilingüe, al menos en Estados Unidos).

Con estos cambios se puede entender que la identidad es un terreno de disputa: lo moderno pugna con lo tradicional, lo letrado con lo iletrado, lo elitista con lo popular, para quedarme en el terreno de las dicotomías propias de la cultura bachatera.

Esta está empapada de series de relaciones conflictivas. Desde la bachata se puede exponer toda una teoría sobre las ideas del dominicano acerca de la conflictividad intrínseca al ser humano: los conflictos del amor, la intriga, la infidelidad y la traición, los conflictos interiores y exteriores, las disputas entre lo masculino y lo femenino, con la particularidad—en ese caso—de que en general lo femenino se impone: la mujer suele salir victoriosa por la victimización masculina, un efecto inmanente en la bachata que se deriva de uno de sus rasgos distintivos, que es la inversión de la realidad—particularmente, de los roles de género—para convertirla en fantasía. Queda clara la herencia que el movimiento romántico legó a la bachata.

Ese legado del romanticismo quedó impregnado en la temática, las letras y el estilo interpretativo que caracterizan la cultura bachatera: cantar el desengaño, el desamor y el *amargue*, los lamentos de la opresión o la infelicidad humana con una voz temblorosa, poseída por el sentimiento, llena de tristeza y dolor—incluida una cuota de sado-masoquismo. Como el bolero y la telenovela, la balada y el tango, la bachata es un melodrama, inundado de lloros y lágrimas. La bachata es lacrimógena por naturaleza.

Detallar muchos de los elementos señalados a partir de las voces de los propios bachateros es un gran mérito del libro de Julie Sellers, que desde ya se convierte en un texto imprescindible para el conocimiento interior de esa emergente música caribeña que es la bachata.

Darío Tejeda
Santo Domingo

Darío Tejeda se graduó de licenciado en ciencias políticas y de maestría en estudios antillanos. Es miembro de la Academia de Ciencias de la República Dominicana y Director del Instituto de Estudios Caribeños (INEC). Su libro La pasión danzaria *fue galardonado con un Premio Internacional de Musicología de Casa de las Américas en 2001 (La Habana, Cuba.)*

Prefacio

Nació mi interés en la República Dominicana cuando viajé a ese país por primera vez en 1993 para trabajar en el proyecto internacional de servicio a la comunidad de mi universidad, Kansas State. Poco me imaginé en ese entonces que pasar ese verano trabajando de voluntaria en dos preescolares en un barrio marginado de Santiago de los Caballeros tendría un impacto tan importante en mi vida. Las maestras, los niños y los padres de familia nos enseñaban a diario a mis compañeros y a mí su cultura, su historia y lo que significaba ser dominicano. Ese verano fue mi primera introducción a esta cultura y este pueblo que tanto quiero, y sigo volviendo desde entonces.

Soy músico amateur y una melómana incurable, gracias a quince años de estudiar el piano, además de tocar la flauta y el píccolo en la banda escolar, y la influencia de mi abuelo, el difunto Benard Stromberg, a quien le encantaba cantar. La música siempre me ha parecido una forma profunda de comunicación, u otra lengua en sí. Tengo buen oído para los sonidos y la comunicación, y esto me condujo a estudiar los idiomas: me encantan las palabras, y sobre todo, su musicalidad. La combinación de estas dos pasiones me llevó a la música dominicana, y finalmente, a estas investigaciones. Aunque la música nacional dominicana, el merengue juguetón, me atraía más en mis años de la universidad, la bachata, nostálgica y agridulce, me llega más como adulta.

Este libro representa mis esfuerzos por escribir una historia de la bachata y describir como dicho género ha evolucionado para convertirse en un símbolo de la identidad dominicana. El lector no solo conocerá de la historia de la bachata, sino también de la historia y la cosmovisión dominicanas, y como están entretejidas tan intricadamente. Baso este estudio en mis investigaciones, mis comprensiones personales de la República Dominicana y su gente, cultura, historia, idioma y música. Además, y aún más importantes, son mis entrevistas con los músicos y productores de la bachata, las que presentan sus percepciones astutas, articuladas y conmovedoras acerca de la bachata y lo que significa ser bachatero. Mi selección para estas entrevistas estaba basada en mi capacidad de obtener sus datos, su disponibilidad, y su respuesta a mis peticiones de hablar con ellos. Es imposible incluir a cada individuo que influyó la bachata por razones de espacio. No cito las letras de las bachatas que trato por razones del derecho de autor. No obstante, escuché cuidadosamente cada una, y transcribí y estudié las letras de todas las canciones tratadas.

Este libro trata de un estudio académico; no obstante, siempre ha sido mi meta hacerlo accesible a quien le interesara la bachata. Desde un principio, mi intención fue escribir un material bilingüe para poder llevarlo a las manos de todos los que le han contribuido en el camino; a fin de cuentas, esta historia es suya. Soy intérprete certificada por los tribunales federales de Estados Unidos (inglés < > español), y yo misma traduje todo el material, a menos que se indique de otra manera.

Hasta la fecha, no se ha escrito mucho sobre la bachata, aunque la historia social del género de Deborah Pacini Hernandez fue un hito en 1995. El libro *Bachata: Historia y evolución* del periodista dominicano Carlos Batista Matos está disponible en español en la República Dominicana y presenta referencias históricas sin tratar la identidad. El fascículo de Darío Tejeda, *La bachata: Su origen, su historia y sus leyendas*, proporciona un breve panorama bilingüe de la bachata. Varios documentales han estudiado el tema de la bachata. El documental de Adam Taub, *The Duke of Bachata*, hace hincapié principalmente en la carrera del bachatero Joan Soriano. *Santo Domingo Blues* de Alex Wolfe y *Bachata: Música del Pueblo* de Giovanni Savino integran comentarios de varios bachateros. Ninguno de estos documentales trata de los lazos entre la bachata y la identidad dominicana ni contempla la bachata moderna o urbana, productos de los dominicano-americanos en Estados Unidos. Por lo tanto, este estudio presenta una comprensión más amplia de la bachata y los procesos históricos, sociales y políticos que están en juego, primero en su discriminación, y más tarde en su aceptación como símbolo de la identidad dominicana, en inglés y español.

No pudiera haber emprendido, ni mucho menos realizado, este proyecto sin la ayuda y el apoyo de un número de personas. Darío Tejeda me ayudó a hacer los contactos para las primeras entrevistas en Nueva York y me acompañó, y junto a su esposa, Dixa D'Oleo, me ofrecieron su casa durante mis estadías. Alexis Méndez también me ayudó a concretar mis entrevistas en Santo Domingo, y me acompañó por la ciudad, incluso bajo una tormenta tropical. Estos amigos me apoyaron en el transcurso de mis estudios. Agradezco la ayuda de Ray Acosta, Marti Cuevas, Mark Hason, Gilberto Vidal y Rafael Zapata, quienes me facilitaron los contactos para otras entrevistas.

Estoy agradecida con los músicos y productores que compartieron su tiempo y sus conocimientos conmigo: Julio Ángel, Mayra Bello, Rafy Burgos, José Manuel Calderón, Gerson Corniel, Vicente García, Toby Love, Elvis Martínez, Leonardo Paniagua, Davicito Paredes, Edilio Paredes, Ray Santana "el Pollito del Cibao," Henry Santos, Lenny Santos, Tony Santos, Susana Silfa y Joe Veras. Le agradezco a Henry Santos en especial por contestar mis preguntas de seguimiento, y a Joe Veras y al Pollito del Cibao por mantenerse en contacto conmigo para saber cómo va el proyecto. Reconozco además a Isidoro "Chichí" Aponte, Luis Aquino, Rubén Darío Aponte, Guillermo Cano, Crispín Fernández, Tommy García, Máximo Jiménez, Francisco Medina, Xiomarita Pérez, y a Alex Sanche por compartir sus conocimientos de sus distintos campos conmigo, y también a Máximo Jiménez y a Cynthia Staley por ayudarme a conseguir y a editar las fotografías. Una amiga, la doctora Susan Kelley, se ofreció desinteresadamente a leer mi propuesta inicial, y le agradezco sus comentarios y su apoyo moral. Alexis Méndez leyó y corrigió el texto en español con un ojo cuidadoso y articulado, y le agradezco sus comentarios.

Varios amigos me apoyaron y me animaron. Annette Starr rezaba fielmente por mí mientras viajaba y trabajaba. Carmelinda Chilelli y Rosalba Ovalle me daban ánimos constantemente. Mi concuñada, y una hermana para mí, Deisy Vaske, no solamente me apoyaba con sus palabras, sino que también me ayudó a conseguir unos artículos difíciles de encontrar. También estoy agradecida con Brettney Cole por acompañarme pacientemente por varias calles mientras buscaba yo una tienda de discos una tarde calurosa en Santiago.

La bachata trata del amor, y me siento bendecida por tener el amor y el apoyo de mi esposo, P.J Vaske. Me animó durante mis investigaciones y viajes, y ha escuchado mis opiniones sobre lo que constituye la buena bachata. Estoy especialmente agradecida con él, ya que aceptó que podríamos viajar a "la zona de Nueva York" cuando gané dos entradas para el estreno mundial del segundo álbum de Henry Santos en Sirius XM, y le agradezco el haberme acompañado. Le dedico este libro a P.J.

La bachata también trata de la pérdida, y perdí a un amigo querido, que murió de cáncer mientras yo trabajaba en este proyecto. Me refiero a mi perro fiel, Rupert, con quien pasaba muchas horas escuchando bachata, él acostado detrás de mí, mientras trabajaba. Rupert me recordaba cosas importantes, como nuestras caminatas matinales, y siempre me daba un toque ligero a la hora de comer para recordarme que tanto los perros como los escritores necesitamos un descanso. También le dedico este libro a Rupert, un amigo querido y cariñoso.

Introducción

Buscar los nexos entre la bachata y la identidad dominicana tiene mucho parecido al proceso de preguntar una dirección en la República Dominicana: todos están dispuestos a ayudar, y todos tienen su propia manera idiosincrática de contarte en donde dar la vuelta y qué señales buscar. Recuerdo particularmente la búsqueda de una casa ubicada en Villa Mella, un municipio de Santo Domingo Norte, que casi nos desesperó a mi amigo Alexis y a mí. Avanzamos en taxi por las calles empapadas de lluvia y llenas de lodo, dando tumbos en los pozos, mientras buscábamos la ferretería que figuraba como punto de referencia para llegar, y que antes nos habían dado por teléfono. Una vez que encontramos la ferretería y dimos la vuelta, descubrimos que ninguna de las calles tenía letrero. El taxista que nos llevaba, sin darse por vencido, paró y le preguntó a un grupo de motociclistas—a los que los dominicanos llaman "motoconchistas"—que estaban reunidos en el parque. Preguntó si íbamos bien, pero ellos no estaban seguros. No obstante, nos animaron a seguir adelante.

Avanzábamos, subiendo una calle, bajando otra, tocando la bocina para llamar la atención de los que estaban en las tiendas o en los portales de sus casas y motivarlos a salir en nuestra ayuda. Por fin, al acercarnos a nuestro destino, paramos en un colmado, y según la respuesta que nos dieron esta vez, parecía que estábamos en la calle que buscábamos, la cual tenía curvas y bajadas. Después de unas vueltas más, tocamos la bocina en una peluquería, y alguien salió para confirmar nuestro éxito.

—Sigan adelante hasta el colmado azul—nos explicó. Entonces doblen a la derecha y busquen una casa amarilla y grande.

—¿A cuántas calles más? —preguntó el taxista.

—No sé contarles con calles, pero busquen el colmado azul y después la casa amarilla y grande. No se van a perder.

Le dimos las gracias y seguimos adelante. Esta vez, las instrucciones eran acertadas y llegamos sin más problema.

Mis estudios de la bachata, al igual que la búsqueda de esta casa, algo difícil de encontrar, se basaron en las perspectivas de los dominicanos mismos, y seguí sus instrucciones. Mis viajes me llevaron a través de diferentes tipos de espacios y distancias, tanto geográficos, históricos, psicológicos, sociológicos y políticos, como transnacionales. Hablé con dominicanos de distintas clases sociales y con distintas experiencias. Escuché tantas opiniones diversas como voces únicas. Al final, si hay algo cierto es que algo que ha provocado tantas reacciones tan fuertes en los dos

163

extremos del espectro—desde una adoración total hasta un desprecio completo—durante toda su existencia, sin duda alguna es algo poderoso.

La música y la identidad

En el estudio del papel de la música como símbolo de la identidad, es necesario contemplar las nociones esencialistas y constructivistas de las identidades, tanto individuales como colectivas. Los esencialistas sostienen que las identidades surgen naturalmente de "una base verdadera y palpable de masas".[1] Se interpreta esta base como inherente a un pueblo y como punto de partida para entender la esencia de quien es ese pueblo. Los dominicanos, desde hace mucho tiempo, han empleado afirmaciones esenciales con respecto a la música, primero uniendo el merengue a la dominicanidad de manera inherente como un ritmo que ellos insisten que llevan en la sangre.[2] Estas mismas explicaciones también aplican para identificar la bachata como símbolo de la dominicanidad. Al describir la bachata como género dominicano, la cantante Mayra Bello observó que "dentro de mí hay bachata…. Cada uno tenemos un poquito de bachata como tenemos de merengue".[3] El bachatero Gerson Corniel reiteró este mismo argumento, el cual enfatiza la naturaleza por encima de la crianza. Este también sostiene que lleva la bachata dentro de él.[4] Los músicos, así como los aficionados a este género musical, solidifican aún más esta visión de la aparente naturalidad de la bachata, gracias a características comunes que han compartido durante su existencia: sus orígenes rurales o de clase baja, la migración, poca formación básica y la discriminación.

En contraste con tales afirmaciones esencialistas, los puntos de vista de los constructivistas proponen que los intelectuales y los que gozan de poder han de trabajar activamente para crear identidades nacionales que apoyan sus propios proyectos y planes. No existe ningún elemento central ni puro del carácter nacional, sino que las ideologías y las agendas políticas son el meollo de las identidades forjadas. No obstante, cabe recordar que "los nacionalistas no pueden, ni crean naciones *ex nihilo*. Tiene que haber un mínimo de elementos de la población seleccionada y su entorno social que favorecen las actividades y la aspiración de dichos visionarios nacionalistas".[5] Como veremos, los que han detentado el poder en la República Dominicana a través de los años contribuyeron a la creación, la propagación y la aceptación de tales elementos, tanto para mantener el poder como para hacer resaltar una identidad deseada. Estas identidades oficiales, las cuales se construyen en contraste con un Otro identificado, contribuyeron a la discriminación en contra de la bachata temprana.

La música ha jugado un papel importante en los procesos de identidades durante mucho tiempo, y "se ha usado la música por todo el mundo para expresar y ayudar a crear, disputar o disolver la identidad de grupos sociales".[6] Este arte no es solamente un reflejo de las preferencias o los gustos de un grupo, sino también un actor dentro de los procesos más amplios, tanto sociales y políticos como históricos: "la música no solo es el producto de una realidad social específica: ella también contribuye en la producción de realidades".[7] Seeger acierta a notar que "si queremos entender la música, tenemos que entender los procesos de los cuales forma parte. Si queremos entender esos procesos, nos conviene considerar la música".[8] Estas observaciones son sumamente pertinentes al contexto dominicano en donde un género musical, el merengue, ha desempeñado un papel central como símbolo de identidad dominicana. Los dominicanos abrazaron el merengue como seña de identidad reactiva durante la ocupación de los marines norteamericanos en el país (1916–1924). Más tarde, Rafael Trujillo se apropió del merengue como símbolo de la dominicanidad durante su dictadura de treinta años (1930–1961). Trujillo contrató a músicos con el fin de modernizar la versión tradicional del género y de convertirlo en una música con sonido progresivo y más apropiada a su agenda de la construcción de la nación, también usándolo para la propaganda política y la noción de su grandeza. Cuando la bachata se presentó en el escenario musical dominicano en 1962, encaraba muchos desafíos frente a la amplia pegada (popularidad) del merengue como la música nacional. Cincuenta años después, muchos dominicanos han acogido los dos géneros como símbolos de identidad. La trayectoria de la bachata, del campo a los barrios populares urbanos y más tarde, al extranjero, tanto como su viaje desde la discriminación hasta el éxito internacional, enfatizan la fluidez y la maleabilidad de ambas: la música y la identidad.

"Música de cachivache": Discriminación contra la bachata

La discriminación inicial contra la bachata surgió de la intersección del momento histórico de su origen y las raíces profundas entre la clase social y la raza. La bachata nació en el terreno cambiante tras el ajusticiamiento de Trujillo, un momento marcado para muchos por el pavor y la incertidumbre.[9] Aunque el Trujillato había sido represivo y violento, el régimen había proporcionado la estructura base de la identidad y la existencia dominicanas por tres décadas, y muchos se aferraron a las señas establecidas de identidad como si fueran anclas. La bachata se presentó en un momento poco propicio para aceptar lo nuevo, y la discriminación original contra ella surgió en parte por esta incertidumbre. Las construcciones de raza en la República Dominicana también contribuyeron al rechazo original de la bachata por parte de las clases media y alta. Durante mucho tiempo, los dominicanos aceptaron una identidad hispana que resulta de prácticas y acontecimientos históricos. Como colonia, Santo Domingo sufrió por la migración cuando muchos se fueron a colonias más rentables, y las autoridades coloniales adoptaron una definición más amplia de la categoría blanca para abarcar a los mestizos dentro del grupo gobernante. Las dos invasiones haitianas del siglo XIX reforzaron la división entre negro y blanco. No obstante, la raza no es un concepto fijo en la República Dominicana, pues está enlazada inexorablemente a la clase social. Por lo tanto, se puede aclarar la raza con cada peldaño subido de la escalera social.[10]

La antigua división entre la ciudad y el campo también contribuyó a la discriminación contra la bachata. Las clases media y alta dominicanas han mantenido opiniones contradictorias y a veces conflictivas del campesino dominicano. En algunos casos, el campesino está presentado como la representación más pura de todo lo dominicano, sobre todo en comparación con el Otro haitiano o estadounidense.[11] Desde este punto de vista, el campesino sirvió como la encarnación de una identidad criolla—la clasificación racial de indio que les permitía a los dominicanos desasociarse tanto de los haitianos y su dominio como de España y el breve regreso de la nación al dominio español (1861–1865).[12] En la práctica, sin embargo, se llegó a tratar al campesino dominicano como un cateto atrasado y sin modales que no entendía ni contribuía al progreso nacional.

El influjo grande de migrantes pobres y rurales a Santo Domingo tras el ajusticiamiento de Trujillo trajo su gusto por la música romántica de guitarra. Con frecuencia, estos campesinos adaptaban los boleros latinoamericanos populares a su propio estilo interpretativo único. Estos músicos de la clase baja, en gran parte autodidactas y sin el apoyo financiero del merengue ya atrincherado, tenían un acceso limitado a las oportunidades de grabación y producción. Estos pioneros de la bachata cantaban a partir del sufrimiento, con sentimiento y en el habla local de los barrios marginados. Sus letras dibujaban con frecuencia las realidades de la vida del barrio, las cuales iban a un público de la ciudad y del campo. En un principio, no había discriminación en contra de esta música, pero después sus críticos la presentaron como la oveja negra de la familia musical dominicana por la vinculación entre los músicos y aficionados rurales y de las clases marginadas, quienes la elite consideraba negros.

"Señora Bachata"[13]: La aceptación de la bachata

La aceptación eventual de la bachata y su recepción como símbolo de la identidad dominicana resultaron de lo que Slobin ha identificado como "la validación por la visibilidad" por la cual "un perfil más alto hace que una población local o regional considere de nuevo sus propias tradiciones".[14] La visibilidad aumentada de la bachata, más allá de sus públicos, surgió de la convergencia de varios factores. La base de sus aficionados seguía creciendo y estos escuchaban bachata en la radio o en discos tocados en lugares públicos. Algunos de estos aficionados, notablemente las mujeres jóvenes quienes se veían en la obligación de dejar sus casas en el barrio para entrar a trabajar como trabajadoras domésticas para los burgueses y la elite tocaban su música al alcance del oído de sus patrones. Así les exponían a otros a la música, sin considerar la crítica verdadera o fingida de la misma de sus patrones. Las crisis económicas continuas también contribuyeron a ampliar el alcance de la clase baja, ya que cada vez más dominicanos conocieron las realidades de vivir en la pobreza. Como nos recuerda Fiske, la música tiene que ser "sobre todo, *pertinente* a la situación social inmediata del pueblo".[15] Así, las extensiones crecientes de la pobreza crearon un grupo más amplio que llegó a relacionarse con la bachata. Luis Días observa, "cuando el miserable triunfa, triunfa la bachata, porque es la voz, es el *blues*, es la agonía, es la desesperación, es el lamento de un pueblo".[16] Además, las innovaciones a la bachata, tales como la experimentación denominada tecno bachata de Luis Días, cuyo principal catalizador fue la cantante Sonia Silvestre, y las propuestas de Víctor Víctor y Juan Luis Guerra aportaron a la penetración de nuevos públicos entre las clases media y alta.

El crecimiento rápido de la comunidad dominicana transnacional en general, y específicamente, las experiencias de los migrantes que vivían en el ambiente urbano de los barrios marginados de Nueva York, crearon nuevos públicos para la bachata.

Además de los migrantes dominicanos mismos, tanto hispanohablantes como los que no hablan español están expuestos a la bachata y muchos la han aceptado, ya que no conocen los prejuicios existentes contra el género. Una nueva generación de dominicano-americanos ha transformado el género al incluir ritmos como el *blues*, la música pop, el *rock*, y el reggaetón, además de su espanglish distintivo para crear lo que se conoce de bachata moderna. Esta versión de la bachata todavía representa lo que significa ser dominicano, pero dentro de un contexto transnacional. La bachata moderna ha llevado el género completo al mundo y también, se la ha llevado de vuelta a casa con los migrantes durante sus visitas al país. Los ingresos disponibles que tienen estos migrantes contribuyeron a la viabilidad económica de la bachata y también a su alcance dentro de la sociedad dominicana.[17]

Esta investigación

Este libro contempla la bachata dentro de su marco histórico y social. El Capítulo uno sitúa la bachata con relación a sus antecedentes musicales y otros géneros internacionales, subrayando sus orígenes humildes, sus características musicales y su paso de baile. En este capítulo también se describe y comenta el significado de la palabra "bachata" y como evolucionó. Explico los orígenes de otros nombres para la bachata, inclusos la música de cachivache, la música de guardia cobrado, y canciones de amargue. Los papeles del merengue y de la bachata como símbolos de la identidad dominicana reiteran la importancia de la música en los procesos de identidad. Las distinciones que hacen los dominicanos entre el merengue como su música de preferencia para los momentos divertidos y la bachata como su música romántica de preferencia subrayan los lazos esencialistas a estos géneros. El merengue de guitarra que tocan muchos bachateros fortalece estos lazos entre los dos géneros y también, sus conexiones con la dominicanidad.

El Capítulo dos interpreta los elementos clave de la identidad dominicana. La interpretación dominicana de pertenecer, articulada por la noción de cultura, se refleja en las geografías imaginadas de identidad, las cuales hacen hincapié en la pureza étnica y racial. Tales geografías infunden las fronteras geopolíticas con importancia. La frontera dominico-haitiana sirve de línea divisora tanto política como psicológica entre los dominicanos, quienes se consideran hispanos, católicos e hispanohablantes, y los haitianos, a quienes los dominicanos consideran negros, vuduistas y hablantes de Krèyol. Las fronteras nacionales también son significativas en las relaciones entre República Dominicana y Estados Unidos tras la ocupación norteamericana de ocho años (1916–1924). Frente a esta contravención de la frontera, los dominicanos respondieron por adoptar símbolos nacionalistas como el merengue. Este capítulo explica además los hilos históricos de la identidad racial y como está entretejida con la clase social. De la misma manera, trata de la dicotomía entre la ciudad y el campo dominicanos.

Los proyectos agresivos de construcción de la nación que Rafael Leónidas Trujillo Molina emprendió durante su dictadura de treintay un años constituyen el tema del Capítulo tres. El plan de Trujillo se enfocaba en las nociones de pertenecer y un plan de progreso moderno. Trujillo trabajó activamente para crear una identidad nacional deseada, recurriendo al hispanismo dominicano. Dada la larga historia nacional de caudillos regionales y sus sublevaciones, una imagen nacional solidificada se prestó al fortalecimiento de la posición de Trujillo y a la presentación de una imagen nacional de solidaridad. Trujillo presentó el merengue como símbolo de tal nacionalismo y como elemento esencial de la dominicanidad.

El Capítulo cuatro detalla el nacimiento de la bachata y sus primeros años en el escenario musical. Se tiene como punto de referencia para nombrar el nacimiento de lo que posteriormente se llamaría a bachata al 30 de mayo de 1962.[18] Precisamente un año después del ajusticiamiento de Trujillo, esta música aparece entre el ambiente incierto de la agitación política y de la tela social cambiante de la República Dominicana. El influjo de migrantes rurales a la capital dominicana que siguió el final de la dictadura trajo consigo los músicos autodidactas que interpretaban sus propias versiones de los boleros latinoamericanas populares de la época. La bachata no era discriminada en esa época, sino que la consideraban una música romántica de guitarra.

El Capítulo cinco estudia las tendencias y las innovaciones de la bachata después de su ola inicial. La bachata de doble sentido, que era tan popular durante los 1980 y a principios de la década de los 1990, dio lugar a las experimentaciones con la tecno bachata y los temas románticos. Estos seguían reflejando las condiciones desesperadas, tanto económicas como sociales, de muchos bachateros y sus aficionados, inclusive la participación incrementada de la mujer en la mano de obra y la diáspora dominicana. Los temas tradicionales de la bachata, tales como el amor, el engaño y el desamor, siguen figurando entre las letras más populares.

La tendencia cada vez más popular de la bachata romántica sirve como el tópico del Capítulo seis. A principios de los 1990, bachateros tales como Joe Veras empezaron a atraer a nuevos públicos al género con su bachata romántica. Sus letras cubren el espectro de enamorarse y desenamorarse, y también tratan temas sociales y otros tipos de relaciones. Sus interpretaciones aún son sinceras, pero son menos amargas en general. Este contenido variado y su acercamiento romántico seguían erosionado la discriminación contra la bachata.

El Capítulo siete contempla el papel de la bachata típica en la comunidad transnacional dominicana. Los migrantes rurales llegaron en tropel a la capital tras el ajusticiamiento de Trujillo, lo cual exacerbó una existente falta de trabajo y condujo a la miseria a cada vez más dominicanos. La dosificación de las políticas migratorias, tanto en el país como en el extranjero, alimentó la creciente migración al exterior, especialmente con destino a Nueva York. Las continuas dificultades económicas, por décadas, siguen generando la migración, así contribuyendo a una comunidad dominicana transnacional significativa. Los bachateros que viven en el exterior, tales como Rafy Burgos, Gerson Corniel y Ray Santana "el Pollito del Cibao", le entregan la bachata a un público que busca lazos con su país y un género que es la "música de desarraigo".[19]

El Capítulo ocho presenta el fenómeno transnacional de la bachata moderna y de la corriente dominante en los EE.UU. Producto de la comunidad diaspórica dominicana de Nueva York, la bachata moderna complementa el sonido tradicional de la bachata con el *blues*, el rock, la música pop, el *hip-hop* y el reggaetón. El espanglish y el cambio de código figuran como protagonistas en las letras que retratan las realidades de los dominicanos en el exterior además de los temas tradicionales de la bachata. Las tensiones y los traumas de la dislocación migratoria, la discriminación y los apuros económicos hicieron que la bachata fuera un idioma favorable para expresar la situación y las realidades de los migrantes. La bachata moderna y urbana han desempeñado un papel clave en la ampliación de la visibilidad de la bachata, y por lo tanto, su validación como una música únicamente dominicana y un símbolo de las identidades nacional y transnacional.

La participación de las mujeres bachateras en la producción del género es el tema del Capítulo nueve. La casa y la calle, dos espacios separados e inculcados con sentido de género, tradicionalmente colocan la casa como el santuario de toda mujer respetable. En contraste, la calle sirve de lugar de incertidumbre y peligro donde puede pasar lo que sea para manchar la virtud de una mujer. Ya que la bachata era una música popular de los cabarets, se asociaba con la prostitución y las mujeres de la calle, así distanciando a muchas aficionadas y mujeres músicos. De la misma manera, las construcciones sociales del machismo y del marianismo contribuyeron a estas nociones. Mientras que los machos se consideraban vencedores de muchas conquistas amorosas, la expectativa para las mujeres era que se quedaran en casa y que fueran modelos ejemplares del sufrimiento según la imagen de la Virgen. Aunque estas construcciones contribuyeron a la reducción de la participación femenina en la bachata, algunas mujeres sí se atrevieron a grabar bachata, cantando los temas comunes del género desde un punto de vista femenino.

El pulso de una nación

La música es parte íntegra de la vida cotidiana dominicana, tanto que los dominicanos hacen uso de imágenes esencialistas para describirla como un rasgo genético que pulsa por sus venas,[20] latiendo al compás de las necesidades individuales y las realidades nacionales e internacionales. Esta investigación propone tomarle el pulso a la bachata a través de sus años de historia, trazando sus lazos con los fondos históricos y sociales que afectaron tanto su rechazo como su aceptación. Una vez despreciada por las clases media y alta como "música de cachivache" o un producto de poco valor musical, tantos los dominicanos que están en el país como los en el extranjero ya la han aceptado como símbolo de identidad, para muchos, igual al merengue. Los argumentos esencialistas sostienen que los dominicanos llevan los dos géneros en la sangre y que se complementan como los dos extremos del espectro sentimental. Las construcciones dominicanas de la raza y la clase han influido la aceptación o el rechazo de los géneros musicales por mucho tiempo, y las raíces rurales y de clase baja de la bachata la marcaron como la oveja negra de la familia musical dominicana. De todos modos, los apuros económicos se hicieron una realidad diaria para un número creciente de dominicanos, así ampliando el público que escuchaba bachata. Los migrantes dominicanos al exterior adoptaron el género como representativo de sus vivencias, y una nueva generación ha dejado su huella al combinar la bachata con los sonidos del *rock*, del *blues*, de la música pop y del reggaetón para crear la bachata moderna y urbana. Más de cinco décadas después del nacimiento de la bachata, esta camina al paso de los sentimientos de los dominicanos por todo el mundo, latiendo al compás del pulso de la nación.

Uno

La contextualización de la bachata: Ponerle nombre a un género y reivindicarlo

Lo veo muy apropiado que la primera entrevista que realicé en Santo Domingo haya sido con el primer bachatero, José Manuel Calderón. "Conmigo nace el fenómeno de lo que hoy se llama bachata", recordó Calderón, aunque cuando empezó su carrera, el estilo de música que hacía él no se identificaba como algo distinto al bolero de guitarra. Calderón y otros bachateros de esa época se consideraban intérpretes de canciones románticas y por lo general, de nuevas versiones de los boleros latinoamericanos populares en aquel entonces. En el espacio disputado de la identidad musical dominicana, las clases media y alta dominicanas eran cada vez más críticas de la bachata, y los nombres que le ponían la etiquetaban como una música amarga y sin cultura, y el baile como erótico. Estos detractores eran los mismos que le pusieron originalmente el nombre denigrante de "bachata", que para ellos significaba un cachivache o algo de poco valor; más tarde, le pusieron "música de amargue", nombre que algunos de los músicos mismos adoptaron como vocablo preferido.

Los bachateros, mayormente autodidactas y de orígen rural y humilde, suelen abrazar las cualidades esencialistas de ser bachatero. Enfatizan el don innato de interpretar un sentimiento puro, transformándolo en música. No obstante, no se puede hacer caso omiso a la influencia de su ambiente social y cómo este componente figura en la formación de un músico. Aunque los críticos de la bachata se aferraban al merengue como música nacional, distanciándolo de esta, muchos de estos primeros bachateros interpretaban ambas expresiones, bachata y merengue de cuerdas, estableciendo así—desde un principio—los vínculos entre estas dos columnas de la identidad musical dominicana.

Las raíces de la bachata

La bachata es descendiente del bolero cubano, género que nació a finales del siglo XIX y que se extendió por América Latina en las siguientes décadas. Los boleristas de la región hicieron de ese género la música romántica bailable más popular en Latinoamérica en los años anteriores al nacimiento de la bachata. Un producto sincrético y único del Nuevo Mundo, y específicamente de las Antillas,[1] el bolero nació como una fusión "del bolero español, mezclado con el danzón y reforzado por el *blues*".[2] Desde sus comienzos en el Caribe, el bolero se desplazó fluidamente y sin dificultades por América Latina, gracias a sus temas universales (con frecuencia románticos), y por su base rítmica, que lo convirtieron en una música sumamente móvil y adaptable.[3] Como un género, el bolero no era solamente una música favorita en la República Dominicana, sino que también era un elemento integral de la identidad dominicana.[4]

Además de la universalidad de sus temas, las letras de los boleros también son imprecisas y con frecuencia consisten en una voz cantante de primera persona (yo) quien se dirige a una segunda persona indeterminada (tú).[5] Estos versos románticos expresaron toda la gama de emociones, desde el dolor del amor perdido hasta la declaración de un nuevo amor. Por lo tanto, el amor, elemento universal de la experiencia humana, es bastante abstracto para prestarse a la sensación de una colectividad entre los que oían boleros, y a la vez es bastante específico para inspirar un propósito individual.[6] El arqueólogo, antropólogo y autor dominicano, Marcio Veloz Maggiolo, observa que las letras de boleros forman parte de una herencia literaria que se extiende hasta la imagen de la mujer inalcanzable del amor cortés medieval hasta las novelas románticas del siglo XIX y la poesía popular del siglo XX.[7] La serenata en su función de una declaración de amor también forma parte de esta tradición, "una combinación de poesía y música ... el decir con música las verdades o mentiras del corazón".[8] De la misma manera, los boleros eran "una muleta erótica"[9] para los que se sentían inhibidos o a quienes les faltaban las palabras para declarar sus verdaderos sentimientos. Tanto los oyentes como los compositores entendían implícitamente los lazos que los unían—a aquellos les hacían falta las palabras para expresarse, y estos que cumplían el papel de una clase de Cyrano de Bergerac que hablaba por ellos.[10] Este ambiente romántico de los boleros proporciona un escenario aceptable en el que al hombre (macho) se le permite estar romántico y expresar abiertamente lo que siente, aun cuando tal expresión viene por medio de las palabras de otro.[11]

Esta falta de especificidad del bolero, además de sus temas románticos, universales y familiares, y sus situaciones predecibles facilitan la identificación individual. El que escucha siente una conexión personal con ellas a la vez que reconoce, sea de manera consciente o subconsciente, el cuerpo de oyentes que experimentan el mismo sentido de conexión. Como un "producto cultural",[12] tal sensación contribuye al sentido de comunidad y por extensión, a la formación del recuerdo colectivo, infundiendo al individuo la sensación de ser único y de su individualidad.[13]

Vanessa Knights identifica el bolero como respuesta a los cambios experimentados con la urbanización:

> Es una música para las masas ... que se han visto relegadas por las transformaciones radicales de una modernización asociada a la velocidad y fragmentariedad, es un contradiscurso a la historia oficial para las clases subalternas privadas de la representación social. Las masas urbanas no caben en las estructuras sociales tradicionales y de alguna manera la nueva cultura de masa es una respuesta a su necesidad de expresar sus formas básicas de sentir.[14]

Así, el bolero sirve tanto de espacio individual como espacio colectivo dentro del cual se puede buscar reposo de los cambios y desafíos abrumadores del mundo urbano moderno. No es casualidad que la creciente popularidad del bolero fuera paralela al advenimiento y al crecimiento de los medios masivos como parte de dicho mundo.[15]

El bolero como género no era uniforme, y sus subgéneros varían tanto en contenido como en ritmo.[16] El bolero se fusionó con otros géneros como el mambo, el son, el tango, el chachachá, la ranchera mexicana y el flamenco andaluz (en el bolero moruno), mientras atravesaba América Latina. El consumo del bolero también varía según la clase social: mientras la clase alta escuchaba las orquestas de bolero en los mejores lugares, la clase baja tal vez oyera la misma música en sitios más humildes y tocada por un trío o en una vellonera.[17] En los cabarets y los burdeles, reinaba la vellonera, y "los boleros que delataban la traición, la amargura, desamor y muerte fueron mucho más apreciados en estos centros que los típicos boleros poéticos ... o los boleros bucólicos".[18]

Los boleros llegaron sin dificultades a la República Dominicana por la radio de onda corta desde lugares como Cuba y México, y más tarde, por el cine mexicano, medio que fue exportador principal de boleros y boleristas mexicanos, entre ellos Los Panchos y Agustín Lara.[19] La edad de oro del bolero (los 1950) coincide con la del cine mexicano, época en que las películas presentaban escenas y retrataban a personajes de los cabarets y las clases bajas.[20] El acto mismo de ir al cine también se prestó al sentido de una experiencia compartida y una similitud, ya que los aficionados al cine podrían venir de muchos lugares para compartir en la historia común y las canciones que la acompañaban.[21] La vellonera, como un elemento esencial que cruzaba las líneas divisorias de la clase social, también ayudó a determinar cuáles eran las canciones populares. Además de repetir las canciones favoritas, algunos propietarios aceptaron incentivas monetarias para no tocar un disco.[22]

La bachata heredó varios elementos de la tradición del bolero. La instrumentación de los grupos más pequeños o los tríos, la centralidad de la guitarra y su forma de tocarla del bolero picado, el paradigma dialogístico entre una voz cantante de primera persona indeterminada (yo) y un destinatario igualmente indeterminado (tú), y los temas románticos del amor realizado y del amor perdido, todos se sumaron a las primeras bachatas. Así como el bolero, la bachata pronto se convertiría un producto cultural de las masas, transmitida a través de las ondas radiales, de las velloneras y las voces de los cantantes presentando en vivo en lugares pequeños. No obstante, el sentimiento subyacente de la bachata difería del bolero. Mientras la nostalgia predominaba en el bolero, la bachata expresaba la melancolía, o sea, una "*tristeza vaga, profunda, sosegada y permanente, nacida de causas físicas o morales, que hace que no encuentre quien la padece gusto ni diversión en nada*".[23] Tal como observa Juan Miguel Pérez, la melancolía no es una etapa pasajera, sino un estado persistente que, en el caso de los aficionados de la bachata, resulta de factores sociales.[24]

Las definiciones de "bachata"

La bachata[25] no se distinguía como un nuevo género cuando José Manuel Calderón grabó la que ha sido considerada la primera bachata en 1962, ni hasta los años

70. En su lugar, este estilo de música se identificaba en un contexto más amplio, llamada música de guitarra, bolero campesino y bolero de guitarra. Al principio, los bachateros, los locutores de radio y sus aficionados se referían a esta música sencillamente como bolero de guitarra.[26] Esto se debió principalmente al hecho de que el significado original de la palabra "bachata" fuera completamente otra. La palabra "bachata", que data del siglo XIX, se refería a un momento libre donde afloraba la diversión y las reuniones informales del campo, y más tarde, en los barrios marginados de la ciudad.[27] En esos lugares, los músicos tocaban instrumentos de cuerda y de percusión, la mayoría de los cuales ellos mismos habían fabricado.[28] Edilio Paredes diferencia entre una fiesta en la cual los músicos más establecidos o más conocidos tocaban para atraer a gente de la región, y una bachata—una reunión informal en la que los amigos pasaban el tiempo cantando, platicando y bailando.[29]

La creciente popularidad de la música de guitarra en los barrios populares urbanos hizo que, en los primeros años, los de la clase media llamaran a esta nueva expresión de diferentes formas: "música de guardia", porque se solía tocar en los cabarets y los burdeles frecuentados por los guardias, militares de bajo rango, y "música de cachivache" por la relativa baja calidad de sus grabaciones, la mayoría de las cuales eran sufragadas completamente por músicos que no gozaban del respaldo financiero de un sello discográfico o un agente.[30] De hecho, el nombre de "bachata", comúnmente empleado por sus detractores de la clase media, tenía la intención de servir como otro insulto. Edilio Paredes sitúa el bautizo del bolero de guitarra con el nombre de bachata en el 1969, año en el que más músicos novatos empezaron a grabar su música romántica de guitarra.[31] En ese entonces, un músico dominicano conocido se presentó en el programa de televisión popular, el *Show del mediodía*, donde compartió sus opiniones de la música, insistiendo que era de baja calidad y asociándola con los barrios populares. Para resumir, el músico insultó la música, llamándola "una bachata", o sea, algo de poco valor, una música "de campesinos, de gente que no tiene cultura, que no tiene educación".[32] Tal como sugiere el nombre del programa, este se trasmitía al mediodía, momento en que las familias se reunían en la mesa para almorzar. Como resultado, dicho programa tenía un público amplio que oyó la condenación del músico, y poco después, la clase media empezó a referirse a esta música como bachata.[33] No obstante, el término bachata pasó de identificar a una reunión informal y placentera en la boca de la clase media, y en su lugar denotaba una condenación vituperadora de la pobreza, de la falta de cultura y de una música de baja calidad: "Ya nadie ponía un disco de esos de guitarra en la casa. Se ponían en los barrios y cuando se oía la canción, decía la gente, 'Allí hay un campesino'. Eso significaba un tipo sin cultura".[34] Esta asociación con los campesinos que trabajaban en el campo más tarde fue empleada para distinguir entre la bachata tradicional y la tecno bachata y la bachata moderna y urbana al insistir en que su representación esencial siempre tenía "grajo".[35]

Muchos bachateros se resistieron a la etiqueta de bachata y buscaron otras. Por ejemplo, Leonardo Paniagua no quería aceptar el nombre de "bachata" porque se trataba de un vocablo despectivo, impuesto desde fuera a la música que él creaba: "Nunca he querido yo aceptar la palabra de 'la bachata'".[36] Edilio Paredes habló de su reacción igual de visceral con respecto a esas etiquetas denigrantes: "¡Cachivache! Me dio un coraje cuando le dijeron cachivache a mi disco. Era igual que decirle a uno que era una porquería".[37] Paniagua observó que el mismo estilo de música romántica de guitarra se producía en otros países, donde jamás se le decía bachata: "En Ecuador, en Puerto Rico, se grababa ese mismo género y no se le decía bachata. Solamente en Santo Domingo se hablaba de 'bachata.' Y esa era la misma instrumentación".[38] Por lo tanto, bachata era un término único a la República Dominicana,[39] donde no se refería tanto a un género de música, sino que comunicaba desprecio. Años después de su primera grabación en 1973, el nombre de "bachata" todavía molesta a Paniagua por sus connotaciones originales.[40] No obstante, otros llegaron a apropiarse del nombre de la bachata por un proceso de reivindicación que le confirió orgullo al vocablo. Ahora, el nombre que antes servía de insulto les ha conferido a los músicos su propio poder.

Para los bachateros, definir la bachata como género y estilo generalmente va muchos más allá de una sencilla descripción de sus compases, instrumentación y sonido. Para la mayoría, también tiene que ver con una base en el sentimiento. Para José Manuel Calderón, el Pionero de la Bachata, esta es puro sentimiento, capaz de representar no solo la amargura y el desamor—temas comunes a la bachata—sino también toda una gama de emociones, lo cual la convierte en un verdadero mensaje del pueblo: "La bachata también le canta al amor. La bachata le canta a Dios, a las madres. Le canta a la naturaleza. Porque es un mensaje que llega muy lejos al pueblo y esto es lo que la ha hecho más popular".[41] Susana Silfa describe la bachata como algo que surge desde muy dentro, algo lleno de emoción, una respuesta natural e incontrolable. Además, Silfa la define como "un grito del campesino" que canta precisamente lo que experimenta uno.[42] Para el bachatero y productor Davicito Paredes, la bachata es un tapiz de sentimientos diferentes, y todo lo que uno quisiera decirle a una persona querida sin atreverse a decírselo.[43]

El atractivo de esta música de guitarra en las zonas rurales y los barrios pobres no sorprende, dada la antigua importancia de la música y el baile en el campo,[44] además de la popularidad de su antepasado, el bolero. El bolero encontró sus partidarios entre los músicos dominicanos rurales, muchos de los cuales eran autodidactas. En las zonas rurales, la guitarra era un instrumento que se podía comprar, relativamente a buen precio, y los músicos mismos fabricaron muchos de sus instrumentos de percusión. En contraste con las orquestas de merengue más grandes, los músicos locales podían formar fácilmente un grupo de una o dos guitarras, bongó y güira. Estos músicos rurales procuraban imitar los boleros populares, aunque el tono quejumbroso y cargado de emoción con que interpretaban las canciones sería definitivamente lo que diferenció su música y condujo la bachata a tener su propio nombre. Aprendían las canciones de oído en persona, de la radio o de la vellonera, y las compartían de manera oral, tal como era común en la tradición local, y las presentaban en reuniones y eventos locales. Esta forma de consumo del bolero y su reinterpretación posterior estaba presente de manera libre, sin ser parte de ningún movimiento.[45] Tras el ajusticiamiento del dictador Rafael Trujillo en 1961, la ola enorme de migrantes rurales que llegaron a Santo Domingo trajo consigo no solo estas nuevas interpretaciones de lo que más tarde sería bachata, sino también a un nuevo público que ya consumía este estilo de música.[46]

Mientras que la bachata evolucionaba e iba tomando su propia forma y nombre como género individual, llegó a ser definida por su instrumentación básica de cinco instrumentos: requinto, segunda guitarra, bongó, güira y bajo. La guitarra ha ocupado y sigue desempeñando un papel central en la calidad expresiva de la bachata, y el cantante le pide con frecuencia que llore con o por él. Tal como explica Henry Santos, la presentación del cantante resulta de este intercambio con la guitarra: "Hay que entender ... el sentimiento, la guitarra—cómo llora, dónde llora, dónde debería de llorar.... Y cuando cantas, la guitarra, en la bachata, tiene que complementar lo que digas".[47]

Las primeras bachatas dependían de las guitarras de cuerdas de nylon, aunque los bachateros posteriores, siguiendo el modelo de Luis Vargas, reemplazaron estas con los instrumentos de cuerdas de acero y le metieron un micrófono en la boca de la guitarra. El resultado fue un sonido más fuerte y agudo. Aunque hay innovadores que han tocado bachata usando diferentes instrumentos, los bachateros describen esta combinación de cinco instrumentos como la receta para crear la esencia de la bachata.[48] Davicito Paredes enfatiza lo esencial de esta instrumentación básica: "para ser bachata, en su esencia, se necesitan esos cinco instrumentos básicos. Después de allí, tú le puedes enriquecer y fusionarla con lo que tú quieras. Pero lo básico de la bachata, tiene que tenerlo. Si no, no es bachata".[49]

Canciones de amargue

La bachata es un género que trata del amor y del sufrimiento en todas sus facetas. Un producto de la marginalidad y la pobreza, las letras bachateras reflejan con frecuencia la desilusión de los que conocen la realidad de la soledad y de vivir aprietos económicos. El músico dominicano, Crispín Fernández, sitúa este sufrimiento dentro del contexto más amplio de la historia dominicana: "Nuestro pueblo ha sufrido bastante y puede cantar su bachata al dolor".[50] El estilo baladista de bachata, con su compás de 4/4, es impactado por una letra emocional, cantada con una voz quejumbrosa que frecuentemente parece llorar de verdad. El bachatero canta al amor—y con frecuencia al amor perdido, al amor no correspondido, a la indiferencia y la angustia, y a la traición—en el lenguaje común de la vida cotidiana. Este retrata las dificultades amargas del amor y de la vida, entrelazando cada palabra y cada grito de "¡ay!" con sentimiento. El desamor con frecuencia figura como tema central de la bachata.

El sentido prevalente de amargura de la bachata contribuye a otra etiqueta para ella: música de amargue. De hecho, se dice con frecuencia que la bachata es una forma dominicana del *blues*[51]: "es totalmente un *blues*—es un *blues* dominicano".[52] El estilo interpretativo y el contenido de la bachata reflejan los del *blues* y de otros géneros que surgieron de la marginalidad, tales como la ranchera mexicana y el tango argentino.[53] El contenido de la bachata, sus orígenes dentro de los segmentos marginados de la sociedad, y el estilo interpretativo—sumamente emotivo— de los cantantes recuerdan al *blues*. Tal como observa Crispín Fernández, "La bachata es un *blues* latino y el *blues* es una canción que brota de un trato social".[54] La sinceridad con la que los bachateros cantan las dificultades de vivir en la pobreza, su sufrimiento, y el hecho de que la única opción sea la de cantar estos problemas, son elementos comunes de la bachata. La profunda desesperación expresada en la bachata también se presta a otra descripción común de su tono, "cortavenas": en su sentido figurado, significa "deprimente", mientras que en su sentido literal, se refiere a algo que te da ganas de cortarte las venas.

Algunos bachateros mismos adoptaron el nombre "música de amargue" en el decenio de los 80, cuando la bachata ya había ganado algo de terreno dentro del gusto de la clase media. De acuerdo con su atractivo recién encontrado, los músicos consideraban que este nombre era preferible, antes que acoger el que le impuso la clase media.[55] Un grupo de bachateros adoptó a propósito el término de amargue para describir su música, y como una manera de enfrentar el vocablo "bachata". Edilio Paredes, Leonardo Paniagua, Augusto Santos, Ramón Cordero e Isidro Cabrera (el Chivo sin Ley) decidieron colaborar en un show regular en un restaurante capitaleño. Reservaron el restaurante El Túnel y empezaron la serie, que originalmente se llamaba El Show de los Lunes. Poco después, Paredes oyó por casualidad a alguien referirse a él y a los otros músicos como bachateros, en un tono que expresaba un desprecio total: "Para mí, eso era como decir, 'allí están los perros.' Eso era lo que uno sentía cuando decían 'bachateros'".[56] Ofendido, Paredes reunió al grupo y se plantearon ideas para un nuevo nombre para su show que pudiera distanciarlos de la discriminación asociada con el nombre de bachata. Una de las esposas presentes sugirió el nombre de *Lunes de amargue*. Con ese nombre se quedaron.[57]

El amargue no se limita fácilmente a la definición de una sola palabra, pues tanto para los músicos como para sus aficionados, significa mucho más. De la misma manera en que la *saudade*—la esencia sentimental de la música portuguesa, el *fado*—no se traduce con una sola palabra, el amargue abarca un espectro amplio de emociones y asociaciones, incluso muchos de los mismos sentimientos de melancolía, nostalgia, pérdida, anhelo y deseo que comprenden la saudade.[58] Richard Elliot propone que la insistencia de tantos años en el carácter no traducible de la palabra "saudade" tal vez ejemplifique la creencia de que la falta de un equivalente exacto en otros idiomas "pudiera significar la imposibilidad de las condiciones para describir un aprecio de fado por uno que no hablara portugués",[59] lo cual enfatiza el carácter esencialmente portugués tanto del sentimiento de la saudade como del fado. De la misma manera, la palabra "amargue" podría servir para subrayar la singularidad tanto del sentimiento como de la bachata como únicamente dominicanos. Sin considerar las dificultades de traducción relacionadas con la saudade y el amargue, Elliot sostiene que quien domine la gramática de lo que él denomina "las gramáticas de la nostalgia"[60] puede entender estas emociones.

Tal como "el fado ... trata del anhelo de la saudade, expresando lo que está perdido y lo que tal vez nunca esté encontrado, de lo que nunca ha sido pero tal vez sea",[61] la bachata comunica varias facetas del amargue. Así, el amargue es un ingrediente esencial a la bachata, y el bachatero tiene que sentir ese sentimiento para poder interpretarlo de verdad.[62] Ambos Gerson Corniel y Rafy Burgos enfatizaron la necesidad de sentir y también de expresar el ñoño.[63] Joe Veras describió el amargue como "ese momento de tristeza, si es por un amor que perdiste, o ese momento de alegría si es por un amor que tú quieres conseguir".[64] Según Mayra Bello, "El amargue es personal. Es cuando una persona se está expresando, por ejemplo el enamoramiento, o el amor no correspondido".[65] El bachatero moderno, Henry Santos, define el amargue como "una combinación de sentimientos verdaderamente desgraciados ... y una guitarra muy triste".[66] Según Toby Love, el amargue es "esa habla profunda, esa habla que viene desde dentro".[67] El bachatero Elvis Martínez también enfatiza una selección de palabras sincera cuando los músicos les cantan a temas con los cuales puede relacionarse su público: "somos muy directos cantando ... con palabras muy llanas que se entienden".[68] No obstante, Martínez no está de acuerdo con la asociación entre la bachata y el amargue, ya que se puede tomar un trago e identificarse con cualquier canción romántica.[69] Lenny Santos cree que "no importa si tiene que ver con una muchacha que te deja o con la infidelidad, en su fondo se trata de eso: que lloras a lágrima viva. Y tiene que ver con la letra de la canción, y tiene que ver con la guitarra, la instrumentación del tema".[70]

La voz individual interpreta una canción que por metonimia representa los sentimientos de muchos, permitiendo que los oyentes se identifiquen con ella por razones individuales. Paniagua reitera este lazo entre el amargue expresado en una canción y lo que experimenta uno en su propia vida: "Si la letra me da lo que me está pasando, yo me voy a amargar".[71] Rafy Burgos observa que, "cuando tú vas a algún sitio para tomarte un trago porque te sientes un poquito triste ... tú oyes esa canción que te va diciendo exactamente lo mismo que pasó contigo".[72] Toby Love reitera tal conexión: "El concepto es lo que nos une, o sea, las penas del amargue.... Todos se identifican ... sobre todo por la literatura o el concepto cuando se trata de enamorarse o desenamorarse".[73] Según el productor y músico Davicito Paredes, uno podría amargarse si no pudiera articular con palabras sus sentimientos hacia una mujer, por ejemplo.[74] En tales casos, el amargado podría escuchar una bachata que expresara esos mismos sentimientos, o interpretarla para que la mujer la oyera. Tal como observó Paredes, "cantándolas se dicen cosas difíciles de hablar—eso es la bachata".[75] A veces, el sentimiento de amargue podría llegar tan profundo que el amargado se podría echar a llorar con la canción o aun más: "Yo conozco a personas que han abrazado la vellonera, oyendo una canción ... porque pensaban que estaban abrazando a la mujer, que estaban hablando a la mujer".[76] La bachata también puede ejercer un efecto catártico sobre sus oyentes. Tal como indica Ned Sublette, el amargue "puede ser un dolor nostálgico y melancólico que te hace sentir mejor, tal como el *blues*".[77] Rafy Burgos reitera esta opinión de que la bachata tiene el poder de convertir el sufrimiento en algo que se puede disfrutar, y así alivia la tristeza: "Entonces ya se fue la tristeza y se puso a gozar de ella".[78] Observa Lenny Santos, "No tienes que bailar la bachata todo el tiempo. También la puedes escuchar y llorar. También es curativa".[79]

El bachatero Gerson Corniel me dijo, "Dicen que para ser bachatero, hay que tener el amargue".[80] Describió el amargue como un estilo de interpretación en el que se grita melodía, y entonces se ofreció a darme una demostración para mejor ilustrarlo. Tomó su guitarra y cantó un fragmento de una canción, primero como balada y luego como bachata. Mientras cantaba con amargue, la cara, la voz y su postura reflejaban sufrimiento y puro sentimiento. La demostración de Corniel reitera los lazos que identificaron Leal y Féblot-Augustins en la saudade, los cuales "unen un elemento físico o material, el deseo, con un elemento espiritual, el pesar, y a la vez volviendo al pasado, el pesar y el recuerdo, y al futuro, el deseo y la esperanza".[81]

Bailar bachata

Aunque proviene del bolero, la manera en que se baila bachata difiere bastante de su antecedente. El ritmo más rápido de la bachata se prestó a una nueva forma de bailar que pidió prestado de ambos, el bolero y el son.[82] El bolero, el son y la bachata son bailes de pareja, pero en el caso del bolero, las parejas se abrazaban y bailaban suavemente. Este abrazo figuraba de manera central en la experiencia de bailar bolero, baile que "buscaba más que nada el enlace más profundo entre parejas".[83] En contraste, el abrazo del son es más pegado y provocativo, y hay más movimiento de caderas. El hombre hace figuras complicadas con los pies mientras baila. Estos elementos sensuales también continuaban en la bachata. Xiomarita Pérez, la Primera Directora Nacional de Folklore de la República Dominicana (2004–2012) y profesora de baile, observa que la bachata temprana empezó como un bolero, pero con algunas pequeñas contorsiones y la adición de la sensualidad del son.[84]

La bachata consiste en cuatro pasos donde el cuarto se baila de tal manera que se usa el mismo pie para el siguiente paso, así alternando entre el pie derecho y el izquierdo en cada primer paso.[85] Al principio, el paso que identificaba la bachata incluía tres pasos para adelante o hacia un lado, con un leve levantamiento del pie o un brinquito, seguidos por tres pasos para atrás o hacia el otro lado y el mismo levantamiento o brinquito. Con el tiempo, el cuarto tiempo se ha evolucionado y a veces viene marcado con un golpe ligero, y otras, con un movimiento de cadera pronunciado para marcar el tiempo.[86] No obstante, tal como observa Francisco Medina, profesor de baile y propietario de Pasos Academia de Baile en Santo Domingo, no existe una única manera de bailar bachata, y la libertad de ese cuarto paso se presta a una libertad de expresión.[87] Carlos Andújar Persinal también señala esta pausa en el cuarto tiempo como el ingrediente único que diferencia el movimiento de la bachata al de sus primos más cercanos, el bolero, el son y la salsa.[88] Medina se basa en el tratamiento de este cuarto paso para diferenciar entre "la bachata popular o callejera" con su movimiento de cadera más pronunciado, y "la bachata clásica o de salón".[89] La creciente popularidad de los lavaderos de carros—los carwash—en República Dominicana como un lugar en donde encontrarse, socializar, tomar un trago y bailar, mientras le lavan el auto o no, ha creado un nuevo espacio de innovación bachatera. En esos sitios, los bailadores han incorporado más patrones con los pies adoptados del son y del cha-cha-chá, y patrones de las manos y las vueltas, adoptados de la salsa.[90] No están limitadas las opciones que tiene el que baila bachata: "Tú vas a un sitio y tú vas a ver a cada persona bailando diferente, pero están haciéndolo en el momento con que están identificadas".[91] El bachatero, Lenny Santos, reitera esta libertad de expresión individual: "La gente siempre quiere ponerle un poco de salsa extra al mismo plato.... Con tal de que mantengas el paso de uno, dos, tres, cuatro, no importa lo que haces en medio".[92]

Según el sociólogo Tommy García, la naturaleza cada vez más innovadora del paso de la bachata establece las destrezas y las capacidades de bailar como forma de poder social y por consiguiente, sirve de reflejo de las posturas de poder adoptadas en el gobierno nacional.[93] Como resultado, el acto de bailar y de sacar a una mujer a bailar tienen su propio protocolo que recrea en miniatura tanto el paternalismo político como el machismo cultural. Para jugar su papel de galán en el mundo emergente de la bachata, un caballero le prestaba atención especial a su atuendo—ropa, zapatos y sombrero—y se empeñaba en llegar vestido de manera impecable. Tal atención al detalle tenía el fin de enfatizar que el hombre era todo un caballero, sin considerar su rango social o estado laboral. El rito detallado del baile empezaba cuando el galán se acercaba a una mesa y le pedía un baile a la dama; si venía acompañada por otros hombres, el galán les pedía su autorización para bailar con la dama.

Una vez en la pista de baile, el galán dominaba el acto de bailar. Los hombres abrazaban a su pareja de forma tradicional, en la cintura, y determinaban los pasos, la dirección y las vueltas que tomaban. Algunos demostraban sus juegos de pies al realizar figuras y pasos complicados, dando vueltas a su pareja, una práctica común al baile del son. Tal como una pelea de gallos requiere que el campeón reinante siga ganando a sus contrincantes, el baile requiere al bailador esperanzado que continúe mejorando sus pasos en un esfuerzo constante que compruebe que es el bailador más experto.[94]

Hoy día, la bachata sigue siendo un baile dominado por los hombres, aunque la postura de la pareja ha cambiado con relación del uno a la otra. En la actualidad, muchas parejas bailan agarradas de las manos, y el movimiento de sus manos se convierte en parte de la ostentación del baile, además de los juegos de pies. Ya es tan probable que las mujeres decidan cuándo y cómo dan la vuelta como sus compañeros varones. Desde este punto de vista, si la bachata temprana reflejaba el juego de poder nacional, esta evolución hacia la igualdad entre parejeas se ha vuelto más democrática a la vez que la bachata es aceptada cada vez más por la sociedad.[95]

El bachatero: ¿Nace o se hace?

Un tema interesante que surgió de mis entrevistas con los bachateros era la naturaleza esencial de ser bachatero. La mayoría de los que cantan y tocan bachata tienen muy poca o tal vez ninguna formación musical, y muchos han tenido poco acceso a los estudios formales. Tal como señala Rafy Burgos, la bachata sigue siendo "una música que no está escrita en papeles. Sale de la cabeza. Todo es de oído".[96] Claro está, las destrezas musicales de los bachateros y sus éxitos resultantes son notables, y al considerar si un bachatero nace o se hace resulta ser perspicaz para comprender el contenido y la interpretación de la bachata, tanto como su discriminación inicial y su aceptación eventual como símbolo de identidad.

Según Davicito Paredes, "el bachatero es bachatero desde que nace".[97] Aunque los músicos de otros géneros tal vez tengan la capacidad musical de cantar y tocar bachata, les falta la habilidad de interpretar sus sentimientos si no son bachateros natos.[98] De la misma manera, José Manuel Calderón opina que el bachatero nace y no se hace: "Para poder darle el *swing* ese, el *feeling* ese ... hay que sentirlo para poder transmitirlo".[99] Edilio Paredes reitera tal primacía de sentimiento: "lo primero es sentir".[100] El bachatero Elvis Martínez añade que hay que nacer con ese sentimiento: "El bachatero realmente nace.... La bachata no acepta a impostores porque realmente hay que nacer con ese sentimiento, con ese anhelo de cantar.... Hay que llevar ese romanticismo por dentro".[101] De la misma manera, Susana Silfa (Mariíta), una cantante con formación musical, cree que la bachata tiene una calidad esencial. Para Silfa, "tienes que ser muy sensible para interpretarla si no vienes del campo, de esas raíces".[102] De igual manera, Rafy Burgos enfatiza que "no todos nacen para cantar bachata". Para Burgos, un verdadero bachatero tiene que sentir y "la voz tiene que ser dulce, casi llorando" para comunicar ese sentimiento.[103] Crispín Fernández también enfatiza tal sinceridad de expresión y la relaciona con el ambiente económico y social de la miseria y la indigencia en el que nació la bachata.[104] Tal como el *blues* norteamericano surgió del sufrimiento económico y racial de los negros del Sur de los Estados Unidos, la bachata surgió entre los dominicanos pobres (también entendido como "negros")[105] en los barrios marginados habitados por los migrantes nuevos y recientes de Santo Domingo. Según Fernández, es la posición social de uno que lo convierte en músico de *blues* o en bachatero.[106]

Leonardo Paniagua, quien no tiene estudios formales, no lee música y toca completamente de oído, mantiene que o se nace con el *swing* de la bachata en la sangre o no: "Eso no se aprende; con eso se nace. Hay que nacer con ese don".[107] Según Paniagua, la música de uno nunca se pegará sin este patrimonio del *swing*, sin importar la calidad de su música o su letra. Paniagua también cita su propio caso para apoyar el carácter esencial del bachatero, ya que ningún familiar suyo había sido músico, y él no tenía ninguna ilusión de ser cantante de ningún género. Paniagua señala al Pionero de la Bachata, José Manuel Calderón, como alguien que nació para cantar bachata, y al grupo de bachata dominico-americano, Aventura, como intérpretes que llevan la bachata en la sangre.[108] Ray "el Pollito del Cibao" Santana también cree que "la música viene por la sangre" y Tony Santos describe al bachatero que toca de oído como "el músico más grande del mundo", ya que su talento viene desde dentro.[109]

Joe Veras, que tiene familiares con talento musical—su mamá cantaba y su papá tocaba acordeón—pero quien no tiene estudios formales de música, hace eco de este sentimiento, enfatizando que nació en la bachata y que es "un bachatero nato".[110] Veras, oriundo del municipio de Cevicos, describe la bachata como su propia geografía, así subrayando sus raíces y los orígenes de la música en el campo: "Yo soy de allí, de la bachata.... Soy hijo nato de la bachata".[111] El bachatero moderno Henry Santos reitera este punto de vista: "Siempre he sido orgulloso de ser bachatero, porque es algo que nací para ser, y lo digo con orgullo.... No hay nadie en mi familia que sea músico.... Nunca tomé ninguna clase de música".[112]

El bachatero Lenny Santos cree que el bachatero nace y también se hace. Por una parte, Lenny cree que nace el bachatero: "Nace porque ... naces en la República Dominicana, oyes la bachata todos los días. Tú naces con ese ritmo.... Pero nunca había bachatero en mi familia".[113] Lenny describió el esfuerzo que le costó aprender a tocar la guitarra como adolescente y la cantidad de tiempo, esfuerzo y práctica que tenía que dedicar para desarrollar sus capacidades. Por esas razones, Lenny cree que se hizo el bachatero que es hoy.[114]

En contraste, el sociólogo Tommy García, quien ha sido Director del Museo de Música Dominicana en Santo Domingo, opina que el bachatero es una figura construida por la sociedad y que la música es un fenómeno socialmente construido también. Aunque García admite que un músico tiene que tener cierto don natural para tener éxito, no ve ninguna esencia genética en el bachatero sino que el esfuerzo, la capacitación y el deseo de actuar sobre esas tendencias y habilidades naturales son lo que finalmente contribuyen a la realización del bachatero.[115]

Tales discusiones reiteran la pregunta de si las identidades son inherentes o construidas. Los que apoyan un punto de vista esencialista—el bachatero nato—interpretan el talento musical como algo innato y puro que late por el músico. Es precisamente este punto de vista que respalda la explicación común de que los dominicanos llevan el merengue y la bachata en la sangre.[116] Tal comprensión también sirve de explicación de por qué los músicos sin formación pueden escribir e interpretar música que se hace ampliamente popular. En contraste, el punto de visita constructivista contempla el ambiente más amplio del músico, inclusos los aspectos sociales, históricos y económicos. El bachatero que se hace es el producto de sus experiencias, las cuales contribuyen a su formación musical, aun si tal formación es completamente informal. Es posible que aprenda a tocar de oído o por imitar el sonido o el estilo de otro, pero adquiere y desarrolla una destreza, en contraste al hecho de nacer con esas habilidades. Además, las realidades sociales y las dificultades económicas del bachatero sirven de fundamento para su construcción, y contribuyen a su preferencia por un género que canta esas dificultades.

El debate que trata la pregunta de si un bachatero nace o se hace reitera la centralidad de la música a la identidad dominicana y opone las vivencias a la capacitación musical. Al hablar del *blues*, Julio Finn diferencia entre el que vive el *blues* y el que lo interpreta; para estos, "el *blues* no es algo que *viven*, sino algo que *hacen*—lo cual marca una diferencia enorme. Lo que diferencia al músico que vive el *blues* del que lo interpreta es su formación cultural y racial".[117] A fin de cuentas, tales diferenciaciones están ligadas a la raza y a la clase y su consideración seguirá latente entre los bachateros y sus aficionados mientras su atractivo siga creciendo a través de las fronteras entre clases sociales.

El merengue y la bachata: La música y la identidad dominicana

La distinción entre el merengue como la música preferida de los dominicanos para la diversión y la alegría y la bachata como su música preferida cuando se siente romántico o deprimido es común entre los dominicanos.[118] También sostienen que la selección musical a veces gira en torno a un cambio de estado sentimental: si uno se siente deprimido y triste, es posible escuchar merengue para levantarse el ánimo, mientras que si se siente demasiado eufórico, una bachata lo traerá de vuelta a la tierra.[119] Sea cual sea el estado sentimental, estas referencias comunes a los lazos entre las influencias de la música sobre los sentimientos hacen hincapié en una comprensión esencialista del papel que desempeñan en la vida dominicana. Para muchos, son como los describe Crispín Fernández: "Nuestros sentimientos son el merengue y la bachata. Son un complemento".[120] Mayra Bello reitera este esencialismo cuando comenta, "Dentro de mí hay bachata.... Cada uno tenemos un poquito de bachata como tenemos de merengue".[121]

Aunque hay personas que todavía no quieren nada con la bachata, Crispín Fernández cree que actualmente es la música dominicana más pegada, aun en Santiago de los Caballeros y el Cibao, la zona conocida como la cuna del merengue.[122] No obstante, Fernández entiende la bachata y el merengue como una pareja que forma un matrimonio que funciona bien, dos géneros dominicanos que se unen en armonía. El merengue, el esposo, es la música preferida por los dominicanos para la alegría, la diversión y para levantar el ánimo. La bachata, descrita por Fernández como la esposa del merengue, es la música romántica de los dominicanos—su propio bolero—y trata del amor, del perdón y de la angustia con completa sinceridad.[123]

Joe Veras, quien toca merengue también, no cree que la bachata reemplace al merengue; en contraste, considera que los dos géneros van a seguir conviviendo y serán emblemáticos para los dominicanos.[124] Susana Silfa también cree que "el merengue es realmente lo que nos identifica" como dominicanos.[125] De la misma manera, Davicito Paredes y el comunicador social Guillermo Cano[126] creen que cada género, el merengue y la bachata, ocupa su propio espacio; Cano asimila la situación a la del vallenato y de la cumbia, ya que ambos representan a Colombia. No obstante, Paredes dice que mide la popularidad al sacar su "termómetro" mientras va desde su casa a la capital. Según sus indicaciones, la temperatura nacional va subiendo por la bachata, la música que se oye tocar predominantemente por su ruta.[127]

En contraste, el promotor musical Isidoro "Chichí" Aponte cree que la bachata puede sobrepasar eventualmente el merengue, ya que el merengue ha perdido algo del terreno que ocupaba anteriormente. Según Aponte, la bachata ya está más pegada sobre el merengue mundialmente. Aponte opina que "la bachata tiene algo que no se puede evitar. Esto es algo que se entra por los pies, se sube a la cabeza, y se quiere bailar".[128] El locutor de radio Rubén Darío Aponte está de acuerdo en que más gente escucha y baila bachata que merengue.[129] Alex Sanche, propietario de una tienda de discos en Santiago, sostiene que "la bachata ha llegado adonde no ha llegado el merengue" por su romanticismo.[130] El bachatero Toby Love nota que "la bachata es la música que domina ahora".[131] Love le atribuye esta popularidad a lo fácil que es bailar bachata y a su contenido universal: "¿a quién no le gusta una canción romántica?".[132] Leonardo Paniagua cree que una parte de la crítica original y continua de la bachata resultó del miedo de los inversionistas, músicos y aficionados del merengue, al pensar que la bachata pudiera superar fácilmente el merengue, dada la base amplia de sus aficionados.[133] Un tema común entre muchos dominicanos es la percepción de la decadencia del merengue por su compás cada vez más rápido y las letras que se estiman de baja calidad, ambos al costo de la musicalidad y el significado.

El merengue de cuerdas, o sea, el merengue realizado con guitarras en lugar del acordeón, en el caso de merengue típico, o en lugar del saxofón y los instrumentos sintetizados en el caso del merengue de orquesta, ha sido un elemento básico para muchos bachateros que también tocaban merengue con sus guitarras.[134] Esta combinación de géneros es otra herencia de las orquestas que tocaban bolero y que incluían unos merengues "[p]ara que las parejas no perecieran de tanto amor abolerado".[135] Cuando empezaron a interpretar bachata, adoptaron la práctica de incluir merengue de cuerdas en su repertorio. Esto surgió de la verdadera necesidad de no perder a un público que buscaba otros lugares de reunión. El productor y bachatero Davicito Paredes explica que la inclusión del merengue de cuerdas en las presentaciones de bachata ofreció una manera de encontrar un equilibrio.[136] El merengue ofrecía un contraste alegre y juguetón a la bachata, y algunos del público solamente querían divertirse y no relacionarse con la amargura ni deprimirse por ella.[137] Tanto en las bachatas como en los merengues de cuerdas, los guitarristas bachateros y virtuosos imitaban el jaleo del merengue, realizado en el merengue típico por el acordeón y por el saxofón en el merengue de orquesta.[138] Algunos grupos de bachata incluyeron el saxofón en sus merengues, y posteriormente llegaron a involucrarlos en sus bachatas, aportándoles a estas un sonido nuevo.[139]

Eladio Romero Santos desempeñó un papel central en la evolución y la popularización del merengue de cuerdas. Romero Santos empezó a grabar bachata bolero en los primeros años de la década de los 1960. Su primer sencillo, "Por ti" de 1964, estaba muy de acuerdo con el estilo y el contenido de otras bachatas románticas de ese entonces, con una voz masculina que le echa la culpa de toda la angustia que siente a la mujer. Romero Santos y su grupo tocaba principalmente en los escenarios rurales, sobre todo en la zona del Cibao en el norte. Como resultado, su público era sobre todo rural y su música no tenía las asociaciones negativas de los cabarets y los burdeles. Estos lugares también conducían a una gama más amplia de estilos musicales, incluso el merengue de cuerdas, para responder al gusto del público.[140] Aunque Romero Santos y su banda solían tocar merengue de cuerdas, además de bachata y otras formas populares de música bailable, no había pensado en su posible atractivo comercial hasta que Edilio Paredes abrió camino cuando grabó el primer merengue de guitarra.[141] Siguiendo el ejemplo del éxito de Edilio Paredes con el merengue de guitarra, Romero Santos grabó un elepé que destacaba muchas canciones en este estilo. El tema titular, "La muñeca", tuvo mucho éxito.[142] Tal como sugiere el título, el cantante compara a su amada con una muñeca que se le perdió en la ciudad. Le ruega a sus oyentes que le devuelvan su muñeca, e insiste que él es su dueño y no piensa prestársela a nadie. A pesar del tono más dulce de este merengue de cuerdas, en contraste con el doble sentido obviamente sexual de las bachatas de más tarde, la figura de la muñeca perdida en la calle se presta a la interpretación de una mujer que dejó a su pareja y que tiene que buscar ingresos en la calle por medio de la prostitución.

Blas Durán, quien empezó con la bachata, también experimentó con el merengue de cuerdas, dándole un sonido nuevo y moderno al incluir guitarras eléctricas. La canción hito de Durán de los 80, "Consejo a las mujeres", le abrió un nuevo camino al merengue de cuerdas tanto en términos de su sonido eléctrico y moderno, como su forma de producción basada en la grabación en múltiples pistas, mejorando la calidad del sonido.[143] Una vez que el valor comercial se hizo claro, otros bachateros siguieron el ejemplo, y el merengue de cuerdas se hizo elemento común de sus grabaciones. Es posible que se identifiquen estos merengues de guitarra como bachatas solamente por el hecho de que hayan sido producidos por bachateros. De todos modos, estos merengues desempeñaron un papel importante al ayudar a que la bachata y los bachateros llegaran a un público más amplio y al reiterar los lazos entre los dos géneros.

Conclusión

El terreno controvertido de darle nombre al nuevo género de esta música romántica de guitarra y los nombres despectivos que le fueron atribuidos nos recuerdan el acto humano de ponerle apodo despectivo a alguien. Tal como observa James Valentine, el "ponerle un nombre a otros es común en los asuntos de la identidad" ya que los nombres "pueden ser impuestos a la fuerza, contra la voluntad de los destinatarios". Los nombres nos identifican, no solamente como individuos, sino también con respecto a nuestras relaciones con otros, como forma contrastiva de identificación. La habilidad de bautizar a alguien o algo con un nombre indica tener poder, pero no todos tienen un acceso igual a ese poder. De hecho, los que tienen el menor poder y por lo tanto, el menor acceso al proceso de nombrar, con frecuencia son los destinatarios de los apodos menos deseados. Tales "personas marginadas están demasiado cercanas para la comodidad y están bastante cercanas para el desprecio. Aquí el poder de la corriente principal se dispone al emplear la autoridad pericial para definir lo marginado, y por lo tanto las fronteras que abarcan a los que pertenecen completamente".[144] Así, el ponerle nombre a alguien o algo puede servir como una forma de "constreñimiento de voluntad" que limita las acciones individuales para "proteger y promocionar las creencias y las prácticas que los que están en poder consideran como representativas de la sociedad en su totalidad".[145] Por lo contrario, la reclamación de una etiqueta impuesta puede conferirles poder a los nombrados por ella. Tal apropiación derriba la intención original del vocablo y le imbuye orgullo y a veces, desafío.[146]

Tal fue el caso del proceso de dar nombre a la música romántica de guitarra que nació en Santo Domingo alrededor de 1962. Los músicos que tocaban este descendiente del bolero latinoamericano solían crear nuevas versiones de los boleros pegados, interpretándolos con un estilo cargado de sentimiento. Estos primeros intérpretes tenían que costear ellos mismos la grabación, la fabricación y la distribución de sus discos. Sin el respaldo financiero del merengue arraigado, estas grabaciones no gozaban de una producción de alta calidad, lo cual condujo a sus detractores de las clases media y alta a ponerle la etiqueta de una bachata, en alusión a algo de poco valor. El timbre quejumbroso y sollozante de la música contribuyó a su crítica como una música de amargue. Estos nombres ofensivos en efecto tenían el propósito de promocionar una imagen de dominicanidad sobre otra relacionada con una clase rural y baja. Los bachateros y sus aficionados, sin embargo, han reclamado y aceptado estos nombres como propios. La bachata y la música de amargue, antes nombres que servían como el peor insulto, desde entonces han sido inculcados con orgullo. Su carácter ofensivo original se va derribando mientras la popularidad mundial de la bachata sigue creciendo.

DOS

La interpretación de la dominicanidad

Una amiga, Belkys, me orientó ante las complejidades de definir la raza y la clase social en la República Dominicana. Ella enseñaba en un preescolar. Allí trabajaba yo como voluntaria durante el verano con otros dos estudiantes de mi universidad. Ese sábado llegó de visita para llevarnos de compras. Pasó primero por la casa de la familia anfitriona de uno de mis compañeros donde le cerraron la puerta en la cara porque provenía de Pekín, un barrio popular de Santiago de los Caballeros, y la consideraban una negra. Lloraba cuando llegó a mi casa, y aunque comprendí las palabras que usaba para contarme lo sucedido, todavía no captaba la relación intricada entre la raza y la clase social.

El sentido de pertenecer se ha articulado en la comprensión general por el concepto de la cultura. Esta interpretación "mide quién o qué le pertenece a la República Dominicana, y quién o qué le pertenece a los Estados Unidos o a Haití, los dos 'otros' de la construcción de la nación dominicana".[1] Esta interpretación de la cultura se unió a la herencia española de los dominicanos como fuente del refinamiento, aunque originalmente, no había ningún vínculo racial. Para los primeros años del siglo XX, la cultura se refería igualmente a la raza y a las señas de identidad nacionales de la dominicanidad, las cuales mantenían sus raíces hispanas, y más tarde, marcaba diferencias entre las clases sociales.[2]

Esta forma de diferenciar contribuyó a la práctica de definirse, o como individuo o como grupo, por medio de un contraste con el Otro. Como construcción social, el Otro puede ser abstracto o concreto, interior o exterior, un individuo o un grupo, cerca o lejos. A veces, el Otro es notablemente semejante: "seres vinculados conmigo en todo en un plan cultural, moral e histórico".[3] En otros casos, los que conforman el Otro son tan notablemente diferentes que identificarse con ellos es imposible, pues son "cantidades desconocidas, intrusos cuyas lengua y costumbres no entiendo, tan ajenos que en los casos más extremos vacilo en admitir que le pertenecen a la misma especie que yo".[4] Frente a esta otra entidad, juzgamos su valor y su proximidad, y finalmente, elegimos entre abrazarlo o rechazarlo. Fueron estas mismas formas de aceptar o rechazar a otros como parte o representantes del grupo que influyeron en la discriminación original en contra de la bachata.

Las geografías imaginadas

La República Dominicana y Haití, dos naciones destinadas a compartir la misma isla, tienen una historia conflictiva. Las autoridades coloniales españolas despoblaron la región occidental de la isla durante el siglo XVII para tratar de ponerle un alto al contrabando lucrativo que pasaba por allí. Poco después, los colonos franceses de una isla cercana, La Tortuga, empezaron a llegar a la antigua región de contrabando, y para finales de los 1600, los hacendados de habla francesa habían establecido sus haciendas en esa zona. La frontera entre las dos regiones era una construcción nebulosa. Los francoparlantes eran más numerosos que los de habla española, lo que llevó a España a renunciar eventualmente a su jurisdicción sobre la isla en 1795.

Los hispanohablantes del este mantenían una paz tenue con Saint-Domingue donde había bastante mestizaje. Aunque la esclavitud fue abolida y los mulatos eran iguales a los blancos bajo la ley,[5] los blancos discriminaban a los negros y mulatos. La esclavitud de Santo Domingo produjo relaciones inquietas entre las dos regiones, y en 1801, Toussaint L'Ouverture dirigió sus fuerzas del occidente hacia una invasión a Santo Domingo. Una vez que se apoderó de la capital, Toussaint abolió la esclavitud y tomó pasos para unificar la isla, política y económicamente. Estas políticas no entraron plenamente en vigencia, ya que los franceses derrotaron a Toussaint en 1802.[6]

Es revelador que los habitantes de la parte oriental de la isla preferían ser gobernados por un poder europeo en lugar de un gobierno criollo dirigido por un negro. Aproximadamente el setenta y cinco por ciento de los habitantes de Santo Domingo eran negros libres o mulatos, agricultores de subsistencia y se consideraban criollos, ya que no eran esclavos, y por extensión, no eran negros.[7] Tal autoidentificación refleja la construcción de la raza en la Republica Dominicana como algo que no depende únicamente del fenotipo. Tal como observa Candelario, en el siglo XVIII, "el ser blanco ... era un estado explícitamente logrado (y posible de lograr) con connotaciones del privilegio social, político y económico, y el ser negro indicaba lo extranjero, la subordinación socioeconómica y la inferioridad".[8] La manera en que los dominicanos entendían el mundo incluía la antigua práctica de una definición más amplia de ser blanco, y como resultado, era indeseable aceptar ser dominados por los que se consideraban negros.[9]

Estas tensiones seguían aumentando tras la declaración de la independencia haitiana en 1804 como la primera república negra del mundo, y tras una segunda invasión haitiana (1822–1844). Durante este periodo, el más largo de dominio haitiano, el presidente Jean Pierre Boyer abolió la esclavitud por toda La Española y usó los ingresos de las tierras orientales para ayudar a rembolsarles a los franceses por los territorios tomados durante la revolución.[10] Boyer alienó a los habitantes del lado oriental en lo cultural al poner límites con respecto al tiempo dedicado a celebraciones religiosas y al prohibir el deporte nacional, la riña de gallos.[11] La memoria colectiva dominicana recuerda esta segunda ocupación como violenta, represiva y denigrante. Desde este punto en adelante, "los recuerdos nacionales de todo lo haitiano se basaban en los veintidós años de la ocupación haitiana".[12] La fecha en que los dominicanos ganaron su independencia de Haití (el 27 de febrero, 1844) señaló un punto divisivo en su nacionalismo. Aunque no sería esta la última vez que los dominicanos se ganaron su independencia, reconocen esta fecha como su Día de Independencia.

Dada esta historia conflictiva, no sorprende que la identidad dominicana haya sido parcialmente contrastada con Haití al otro lado de la frontera geopolítica. Sarah Radcliffe y Sallie Westwood asocian este concepto del Otro con "las geografías de la identidad", o sea, "el sentido de pertenecer y las subjetividades que están constituidas en (y que también pueden constituir) diferentes espacios y sitios sociales".[13] Tal como Anderson acierta al notar, "una nación es imaginada con *límites* porque hasta la más grande de ellas ... tiene fronteras finitas, aun si sean elásticas, más allá de las cuales hay otras naciones".[14] De la misma manera, las fronteras cumplen una función importante en las geografías imaginadas, ya que "refuerzan las nociones de pureza y similitud dentro del territorio, y de las diferencias y la impureza fuera del territorio".[15] Por lo tanto, las geografías funcionan como "anclas simbólicas de identidad" al unir las identidades con "un sentido de pertenecer a un territorio específico".[16] Este vínculo entre uno y un lugar fortalece y refuerza las fronteras:

> Las comunidades con fronteras fijas no solo privilegian sus diferencias sino que también suelen desarrollar una intolerancia y una sospecha hacia la adopción de las prácticas del otro, e intentan distinguir las prácticas que comparten de una manera u otra. Así, las comunidades con fronteras fijas disponen las diferencias entre sí.[17]

Los dominicanos entienden la dominicanidad en contraste con la etnicidad haitiana en términos de la raza, el idioma y la religión. Mientras que los dominicanos se consideran hispanos (blancos), hispanohablantes y católicos, ven a los haitianos como negros, hablantes del krèyol y vuduistas. Estas dos identidades opositoras se refuerzan por medio de estereotipos y fronteras flexibles. Sander Gilman observa que tales estereotipos

> perpetúan un sentido necesario de diferencia entre el 'Yo' y el 'objeto', el cual se convierte en el 'Otro'. Ya que no existe ninguna línea verdadera entre el Yo y el Otro, es necesario trazar una línea imaginaria; y para que la ilusión de una diferencia absoluta entre el Yo y el Otro nunca se preocupe por nada, esta línea es tan dinámica en su capacidad de cambiarse como el Yo mismo.[18]

Imaginamos las fronteras como protectivas e impenetrables, y así solidifican el vínculo percibido entre "'la raza y el lugar'".[19] La identificación racial y cultural de los dominicanos con una identidad predominantemente hispana le infunde a la frontera dominico-haitiana un significado aún más importante: sirve como una barrera imaginada, y así retiene lo dominicano y le prohíbe la entrada a lo que no lo es.

La frontera dominico-haitiana ha sido una fuente de preocupación para los dominicanos durante mucho tiempo, situación muy parecida a esa en que la frontera entre EE.UU. y México recibe cada vez más atención. Las historias oficiales y los esfuerzos nacionalistas han aumentado la preocupación por la intrusión haitiana a tierras dominicanas como una invasión silenciosa. Cuestiones laborales han contribuido a tal sentido de invasión desde las primeras décadas de los 1900 cuando los productores de azúcar primero buscaron una mano de obra barata en Haití. Desde entonces, los haitianos siguen migrando a la República Dominicana en busca de trabajo y aceptan trabajos que los dominicanos consideran poco dignos para ellos. Cuando hay una baja económica, se les echa la culpa a los haitianos, convirtiéndolos en un chivo expiatorio conveniente.[20] Las "generaciones de la difamación oficial de los haitianos"[21] ayudaron a crear lazos de identidad entre los dominicanos, basados en la comprensión de quiénes no son.

Esta misma comprensión de pureza dentro de las fronteras es igual de importante para comprender la construcción del Otro estadounidense, primero durante los ocho años de la ocupación por los marines (1916–1924). La ocupación fue el resultado de ambos factores, económicos y políticos, incluyendo el creciente endeudamiento dominicano con poderes extranjeros, entre ellos Alemania, y la continua inestabilidad política dominicana. Las fuerzas de la ocupación disolvieron el gabinete dominicano y destinaron los ingresos anteriores del Contralor de Aduanas para el uso del gobierno y proyectos de obras públicas para mejor unificar el país. Varias medidas económicas otorgaron incentivos a las compañías azucareras norteamericanas para facilitar su expansión en una época en que subió vertiginosamente el precio del azúcar. Crecieron ciudades bulliciosas donde antes solo había pueblos. La fuerza y la represión también eran elementos comunes de la ocupación. Las fuerzas norteamericanas censuraron la prensa, desarmaron a la población, y formaron y capacitaron a la Guardia Nacional Dominicana para sofocar las sublevaciones regionales, una vez concluida la ocupación.

La ocupación norteamericana fue una afrenta mordaz para la soberanía dominicana, y los nacionalistas respondieron por volver a aceptar un significado esencial de la dominicanidad. En parte, tal representación incluía la imagen idealizada del campesino dominicano como la esencia misma de una identidad dominicana hispana.[22] Se veía al campesino como inocente y puro, "listo y honrado, pero engañado por los yanquis astutos y rapaces".[23] Los dominicanos se habían alejado del hispanismo y sus asociaciones con España durante la anexión (1861–1865), pero las acogieron de nuevo durante la intervención norteamericana.[24] La resistencia cultural a la ocupación se oponía a la intrusión de la cultura norteamericana (considerada grosera) y glorificaba todo lo dominicano.

A pesar de estos sentimientos nacionalistas tan fuertes, la mirada dominicana hacia fuera cambió de una vez por todas desde Europa a Estados Unidos en esa época. Antes de la ocupación, los dominicanos demostraban una preferencia por productos europeos[25]; no obstante, los productos estadounidenses entraban al país para el consumo local y de los marines durante la ocupación. Esa ocupación de ocho años "dejó un gusto muy marcado por el consumo de artículos … norteamericanos".[26] El béisbol reemplazó a las riñas de gallos como el deporte nacional dominicano, y el español dominicano adoptó numerosos préstamos lingüísticos del inglés.[27] El abismo cada vez más amplio entre la gran mayoría de dominicanos de la clase baja y la elite fue otra consecuencia. Se especificaron más y más las distinciones de clase, ya que la elite perdió su poder político, y la clase alta se refugió en un elitismo cultural que hacía hincapié en su capacidad de consumir productos de alta calidad.[28]

La raza y la identidad

Aproximadamente medio millón de indígenas, los taínos, vivían en la isla que llamaban Quisqueya cuando llegó Cristóbal Colón en 1492. Esta población se disminuyó rápidamente, ya que los taínos fueron víctimas de las enfermedades europeas y las condiciones duras del trabajo forzoso. Los colonos españoles empezaron a importar a los esclavos africanos en el decenio de 1530, y estos trabajaban en las minas y los campos.[29] En ese entonces, se fueron muchos colonos rumbo a México y varias colonias sudamericanas, atraídos por el descubrimiento de plata en estas tierras. Esta migración sobrepasaba la llegada de esclavos, y para 1546, los esclavos eran más numerosos que sus amos por un ratio de 2.5 a 1.[30]

Aunque el mestizaje racial había sido común en Santo Domingo, los colonos no lo reconocían abiertamente. Esto sucedió en parte por la práctica de reconocer a gente mestiza como española (entiéndase blanca) que las autoridades coloniales empezaron con el motivo de aumentar el número oficial de ciudadanos ante la disminución de su población europea.[31] Esta práctica colonial de aceptar a las personas mestizas como hispanas (blancas) señaló el comienzo de un sistema lingüístico intricado para identificar la raza en la República Dominicana. La asociación de todo lo malo con Haití distanció aún más a los dominicanos de su herencia africana. Tal como observa Frank Moya Pons, los dominicanos "habían llegado a creer que solo eran negros los haitianos".[32] Aunque los dominicanos reconocen actualmente el mestizaje, la importancia que les atribuyen a las tres etnicidades presentes en la dominicanidad—la española, la indígena y la africana—se imagina de forma distinta. Dentro de esta pirámide, consideran su herencia europea como la base amplia e influyente, mientras que la influencia africana es mínima. La herencia de los taínos—quienes fueron diezmados en los primeros años de la Colonia—ofrecieron la solución ideal al reconocimiento del mestizaje sin reconocer la negritud, pues los taínos "representaban una categoría que simbolizaba ambos, lo que no es blanco y lo que no es negro".[33] La dominicanidad se convirtió en la mezcla de una identidad racial indígena y una identidad cultura hispana,[34] una autoidentificación que evoca raíces que datan de antes de las invasiones extranjeras e imperialistas de Haití y Estados Unidos.

Aunque las influencias y contribuciones africanas se han minimizado oficialmente o han sido desacreditadas por la historia, no son ignoradas por completo. Ginetta Candelario se refiere a un chiste común entre dominicanos que dice que la octava maravilla del mundo sería un dominicano blanco.[35] En el título de su estudio, Candelario recuerda otro dicho dominicano, "Tenemos el negro detrás de las orejas".[36]

Este dicho reitera una crítica tratada en el poema de Juan Antonio Alix, "El negro tras de la oreja" (1883). En este poema, la voz poética se burla de los dominicanos que insisten en una identidad hispana y critica su falta de juicio por trata de pasar por blancos:

> *Como hoy la preocupación*
> *A más de una gente abruma,*
> *Emplearé mi débil pluma*
> *para darle una lección;*
> *Pues esto en nuestra Nación*
> *Ni buen resultado deja,*
> *Eso era en la España vieja*
> *Según desde chico escucho*
> *Pero hoy abunda mucho*
> *"El negro tras de la oreja".*[37]

Tal como sostiene la voz poética, la herencia africana de muchos dominicanos siempre está "detrás de la cara de la identidad nacional dominicana y de los cuerpos individuales".[38]

Los dominicanos han empleado durante mucho tiempo una cuidadosa selección de palabras para definir más precisamente la raza en la República Dominicana, borrando las fronteras entre razas. Ya para 1549 existían categorías raciales específicamente definidas en Santo Domingo, así dividiendo a los habitantes entre siete grupos diferentes: los negros (los esclavos africanos o sus descendientes); los blancos (los españoles o sus descendientes); los mulatos (hijos de un padre negro y otro blanco); los mestizos (hijos de un padre indígena y otro blanco); los tercerones (hijos de un mulato y un blanco); los cuarterones (hijos de un tercerón y un blanco); y los grifos (los hijos de un indígena y un negro).[39] Esta tendencia de especificar y diferenciar ha continuado a través de la historia dominicana, y el idioma contribuye a la articulación de los variables sutiles de la raza. En el siglo XIX, los dominicanos de tez morena adoptaron la práctica de llamarse "blancos de la tierra".[40] En los 1920, el vocablo "indio" empezó a usarse como identificador inofensivo de la gente de color; este mismo vocablo, modificado por numerosos descriptores para diferenciar, llegó a enfatizar el sentido de pertenecer durante la dictadura de treinta años de Rafael L. Trujillo.[41] Como ha observado el poeta y ensayista Blas Jiménez, aun los dominicanos que querían identificarse como negros en sus documentos oficiales fueron registrados bajo uno de los grupos de indios, tal como indio oscuro.[42]

La identificación racial dominicana es muy específica y de igual manera es indeterminada. Un adorno y recuerdo popular, la muñeca sin cara dominicana, ejemplifica de manera concreta esta tendencia de incluir y excluir a la vez. Estas muñecas de cerámica tienen flores o canastas y llevan vestidos largos de falda amplia, algunos de estilo folklórico y otros más europeos y coloniales. Los dominicanos explican que la característica definitiva de las muñecas, o sea, su falta de rasgos faciales, indica la esencia de la dominicanidad, pues tal como las muñecas, el dominicano es una mezcla de tres etnicidades y no tiene una sola cara.[43] Es notable que la tez de las muñecas sea de matiz bronce, matiz que recuerda una identidad indígena. Sin considerar si se las llevan como recuerdo o sirven para adornar una casa dominicana, las muñecas sin cara son un recordatorio sutil de lo que es la dominicanidad.

Los dominicanos siguen empleando un conjunto de vocablos intricados pero específicos para identificar un espectro amplio de diferenciaciones raciales. En su estudio de principios de los 1970, Daysi Josefina Guzmán contempló el vocabulario que emplearon los residentes de Santiago para definir la raza y las características raciales, incluyendo el tipo de cabello; el color de la piel, el pelo y los ojos; y rasgos faciales y corporales.[44] Entre los entrevistados, Guzmán halló que los participantes pudieron identificar quince categorías de texturas de cabello y nueve colores del pelo. También identificaron seis tipos de talle, diez de rasgos faciales, y cinco de tonos o matices raciales.

Es interesante observar que la característica que más categorías tenía—la textura de cabello—sigue siendo el factor determinante principal de la raza entre los dominicanos, "seguido por los rasgos faciales, el color de la piel, y por último, la ascendencia".[45] El susodicho poema de Juan Antonio Alix también enfatiza el papel comprometedor del pelo.[46] El "pelo bueno"—el pelo suave, liso y caucásico—y el "pelo malo"—el pelo crespo, tosco y negroide—residen en los dos extremos de una lista larga de categorías de textura de pelo.[47] El estudio etnográfico de Ginetta Candelario se enfoca en un salón de belleza dominicano en Washington Heights (Alto Manhattan, Nueva York) y reitera cómo esta comprensión del pelo como significante de la raza se realiza diariamente sobre los cuerpos de las dominicanas que se alisan y cambian su cabello para encarnar una identidad nacional imaginada (según la terminología de Anderson). Tal insistencia en el pelo como rasgo que señala la raza es tan ambigua como importante, ya que el pelo crespo o rizado puede alisarse, y el color del pelo también puede cambiarse.[48]

La raza también está vinculada a la clase social, convirtiéndola en una categoría cambiante que se puede lograr. El vínculo entre la clase y la raza es indivisible y las dos se apoyan recíprocamente.[49] En la medida que uno mejora su clase, puede blanquearse la raza; de semejante manera, si uno pierde su posición social, su raza puede oscurecerse como consecuencia.[50] Este vínculo entre la raza y la clase social realza las divisiones entre clases; tal como ha señalado Lauren Derby, la raza está tan entretejida con la clase social que sirve como su indicador principal.[51] A la inversa, la clase social puede más que la raza en ciertos casos, por ejemplo, en el caso de los dominicanos morenos con estudios y un trabajo de oficina.[52]

La relación entre la raza y la clase va de la mano con la cultura, concepto que los dominicanos emplean comúnmente para diferenciar entre las clases sociales: los que son refinados y los que no. Aunque "la raza puede basarse en una metáfora del parentesco por sangre ... fundamentalmente se logra en parte por la clase social y en parte por el estilo y los modales".[53] Por esta razón, "los dominicanos de clase media y pobre suelen expresar sus identidades en términos que equivalen la raza a la cultura, en lugar de términos que equivalen la raza a una comunidad social que se determina por el color [de la piel]".[54] La cultura une a la gente de diferentes fenotipos bajo un perfil más amplio compuesto de elementos que remontan a la Colonia y su interpretación más contemporánea como seña de clase social, y por extensión de la raza.[55]

El campesino dominicano

La oposición entre la ciudad y el campo es una tradición duradera del pensamiento y de la política dominicanos. Esta división se basa en la falta de unidad geográfica que contribuyó a las lealtades regionales profundas y feroces. Este regionalismo se prestó a la continua inestabilidad y el conflicto políticos tras la independencia de Haití. La falta de una infraestructura interna separaba los centros poblados del país, tanto en lo geográfico como en lo político. Sin un sentido de identidad nacional, se solidificaron las identidades regionales en torno a los caudillos locales que formaron sus propios ejércitos de campesinos. Este modelo dominó la política dominicana durante la última mitad del siglo XIX y los primeros años del siglo XX, y la participación del campesino en estos ejércitos convenció a los nacionalistas liberales que el campesino era el obstáculo principal para cumplir su meta de crear una nación centralizada, democrática y formada.[56]

Los nacionalistas representaban y entendían a los campesinos de maneras contrastantes. Por un lado, se les pintaba como bárbaros y sin cultura, y por otra, de portadores de los elementos esenciales de la dominicanidad. Los campesinos eran mayormente independientes y vivían de la tierra hasta el siglo XIX. Los nacionalistas señalaron la conexión del campesino con la tierra como símbolo de su pureza, y ese arraigo a la tierra como la esencia de todo lo dominicano. Esta visión colocó al campesino en una posición entre el esclavo negro haitiano y el conquistador europeo de España.[57] Los nacionalistas veían cada vez más al campesino como la esencia de una identidad hispana dominicana frente a la intervención estadounidense.[58]

A pesar de los lazos que lo unían a la tierra, sin duda alguna el campesino era pobre. No se trataba de los grandes hacendados, sino de los agricultores de subsistencia que se las arreglaban por cultivar lo suficiente para sobrevivir y por cazar lo que fuera disponible.[59] Esta manera de supervivencia le era completamente ajena a la gente de la ciudad, y su estilo de vida, arraigado durante años en la tradición, no pertenecía a ningún modelo de progreso y modernidad. Esta visión del campesino condujo a políticas migratorias estrictas cuyo objetivo fue mantenerlo alejado de las ciudades y guardarlo en el campo. Después del ciclón San Zenón de septiembre del 1930, fueron aprobadas leyes con el fin de controlar la entrada de migrantes rurales a los centros urbanos; quedaron vigentes dichas leyes durante muchos años después de esa tragedia.[60] En 1953, se decretó como ilegal el traslado de los campesinos a las áreas urbanas sin primero obtener la autorización de las autoridades locales.[61] Por lo tanto, la mayoría de los dominicanos todavía vivían en el campo en el momento en que Rafael L. Trujillo empezó su plan para modernizar la nación durante los treinta y un años de su dictadura.

El merengue y la identidad dominicana

Varios eventos históricos contribuyeron al ascenso del merengue como música nacional dominicana; de la misma manera, esos mismos eventos condujeron a la construcción de una identidad racial flexible entre los dominicanos. Los orígenes exactos del merengue se desconocen, y otras naciones caribeñas también sostienen que son el lugar de su nacimiento. Una leyenda temprana contó que el primer merengue fue creado y presentado tras la batalla de Talanquera, cuando los dominicanos derrotaron a los haitianos. Según cuentan, el abanderado pusilánime dominicano corrió de la batalla, llevándose el pabellón nacional. Esa noche, las tropas dominicanas conmemoraron tanto su victoria como la cobardía del abanderado en el primer merengue.[62] Esta leyenda no es confirmada, pero concretiza los vínculos entre la música nacional, el merengue, y la independencia nacional,[63] y reitera los lazos esencialistas de los dominicanos con el género como su música nacional.

La primera referencia por escrito sobre el merengue ocurrió cuando los intelectuales dominicanos emprendieron una campaña literaria apasionada en su contra, con la publicación de una serie de artículos que lo condenaron. Esta crítica retrata el merengue como inculto e inapropiado para una sociedad refinada, y lo ataca como instigador de la mala conducta entre los que lo bailaban. Otros también empezaron sus ataques en contra del merengue porque temían que se hiciera más popular que el baile nacional de esa época, la tumba.[64] El autor Manuel de Jesús Galván clama contra el merengue en su poema, "Queja de la tumba contra el merengue". En este poema, la tumba lamenta que el merengue la haya obligado a exiliarse y acusa a los dominicanos de darle la espalda para servir a Satanás en su lugar.[65] El movimiento de las caderas del merengue y la manera en que se bailaba pegado también fueron una fuente de preocupación. La tumba de Galván demanda una respuesta: "¿Dó está el pudor, dó la moral?", y también insiste que los hombres contemplen cómo se sentirían si pensaran que su hermana o su hija fuera tan "ágil de caderas".[66] Aunque esta forma de bailar afligía a los que estaban preocupados por su decencia, también la condenaron por asociar el movimiento de caderas con la música africana. Su independencia reciente de Haití contribuyó a un rechazo de todo lo asociado con la república negra. Un debate tan acalorado demuestra el papel destacado que desempeña la música en la cultura dominicana y los procesos de identidad. Para los críticos del merengue, la tumba, de influencia europea, era mejor representante de la dominicanidad que el merengue.

La campaña apasionada en contra del merengue es indicio de los seguidores que iba ganando en la República Dominicana, sobre todo entre los campesinos. Este público no era insignificante, ya que unos 425,000 de la población total de 435,000— el noventa y ocho por ciento—vivían en las zonas rurales.[67] Las tradiciones culturales de origen africano eran más fuertes en el campo, y la música y el baile eran prácticas culturales y sociales importantes entre los campesinos.

Aunque la instrumentación del merengue variaba por región, comúnmente incluía instrumentos de cuerda, una tambora y un güiro, este último fabricado de una calabaza. Se pretendía que estos instrumentos reflejaban las tres etnicidades de la dominicanidad: los instrumentos de cuerda eran de origen español, la tambora es común a la música africana, y se le atribuía el güiro a los taínos.[68] El acordeón de una fila, importado de Alemania, reemplazó los instrumentos de cuerda en los 1870. Entonces, los intelectuales emprendieron otra campaña literaria en contra del merengue, encabezada por el antiguo presidente Ulises Francisco Espaillat. Este condenó el merengue por sus influencias negativas sobre los que lo escuchaban, y sostenía que "afectaba demasiado el sistema nervioso, y que dejaba *el achaque de no poder dominar la imaginación*".[69] El acordeón se hizo el chivo expiatorio para los detractores del merengue ya que alegaban que había sacado a los supuestos instrumentos típicos como el tres, el cuatro y el seis. Es posible que tal antipatía surja del hecho de que el sonido agudo del acordeón acentuara los aspectos rítmicos del merengue, y por lo tanto, sus vínculos con las influencias africanas. En "El cuatro y el acordeón" de Juan Antonio Alix, el cuatro acusa el acordeón de tener un atractivo pasajero y profetiza que le sucederá algo peor en el futuro, "si otra cosa mejoi viene".[70] Hoy en día, la décima de Alix parece profética, dadas las diatribas del siglo XX en contra de la bachata.

El merengue en todas sus variantes regionales seguía acumulando un público, a pesar de las diatribas literarias de los intelectuales. En el Cibao, el merengue cibaeño solidificaba su forma en la víspera de la ocupación norteamericana. Esta invasión del siglo XX sirvió como ímpetu para que los dominicanos buscaran un elemento cultural que los definiera y que pudieran abrazar frente a este nuevo Otro extranjero. Los nacionalistas aceptaron el merengue y sus variantes como forma simbólica de resistencia. Específicamente, promovieron el variante cibaeño del merengue como símbolo nacional de la cultura dominicana, en contraste con los géneros estadounidenses populares entre la elite antes de la ocupación. Un grupo de compositores trabajaron los géneros tradicionales, tales como el merengue, y modificaron su versión rural para que apelara al gusto de la clase alta.[71] Al escoger el merengue, estos nacionalistas le abrieron el camino al género para que participara en la unificación y el fortalecimiento de un sentido de identidad nacional.

Es importante observar que los dominicanos adoptaron una forma musical criolla como la base de su resistencia musical a la ocupación estadounidense.[72] Las formas de la cultura popular, tales como el merengue, les han servido a los nacionalistas dominicanos a través de los años, pues idealizan las formas culturales folklóricas y tradicionales como la esencia de la dominicanidad.[73] La selección del merengue como una herramienta para enfatizar una identidad hispánica opositora a los invasores norteamericanos "representa un tipo de reinterpretación de *hispanidad* como una identidad criolla".[74] Además, la importancia del baile como una costumbre social de la cultura dominicana ofreció otro punto de contraste: la capacidad de los dominicanos de bailar bien el merengue en contraste con los esfuerzos poco coordinados de los norteamericanos. Así, el baile les inculcó a los dominicanos un sentido de dominio individual sobre el cuerpo y también sobre su música.

Conclusión

La interpretación de la dominicanidad revela una construcción compleja de la identidad, construcción que tiene fronteras fluidas como otras rígidas. Por otra parte, las categorías raciales infundidas desde la Colonia, con el objetivo de ampliar el alcance del grupo hispano, fueron imprecisas. Se solapan la raza y la nacionalidad, pues la nacionalidad haitiana ha llegado a ser el equivalente de la negritud, mientras que la dominicanidad consta de su propia categoría única que enfatiza el mestizaje sin especificidades. A pesar de las diferencias raciales detalladas, la raza no es una construcción fija sino una que se puede cambiar, por sus vínculos con la clase social. Los nacionalistas entendían al campesino como el portador esencial de todo lo dominicano cuando convenía, o como el obstáculo sin cultura a la modernización y al progreso. Esta misma tendencia a la imprecisión se prestó a la aceptación del merengue entre grupos diversos de dominicanos durante la ocupación norteamericana. En contraste, las fronteras nacionales son rígidas. La herencia de tratar de trazar límites estrictos en donde no había—o por lo menos, en donde había uno bastante ambiguo— continuaría aun después de la desocupación norteamericana en 1924. Para 1930, Rafael L. Trujillo, un caudillo dominicano moderno, se aprovecharía de las antiguas prácticas de identificación para solidificar un sentido de identidad nacional, y por medio de la misma, su propio poder.

TRES

La dictadura y
la construcción nacional:
La Era de Trujillo

"En este lugar fue donde mataron a Trujillo", me dijo Alexis mientras volvíamos de una entrevista y pasábamos en taxi delante del Monumento Héroes del 30 de Mayo. Di un vistazo rápido al monumento que se deshacía en la lejanía. Ya habían pasado cincuenta años desde esa noche decisiva cuando ajusticiaron al dictador, pero aún es imposible olvidar su influencia.

Durante la dictadura de treinta y un años de Rafael Leonidas Trujillo Molina, se consolidó una identidad nacional en torno a las raíces hispanas y a una agresiva modernización. La construcción nacional según la visión de Trujillo se fundó en los conceptos de cultura y progreso. Como parte del proyecto nacionalista de Trujillo, la cultura enfatizaba el hispanismo dominicano, en parte como contraste con el Otro haitiano. El concepto del progreso se originó como parte del lenguaje liberal del siglo XIX y se trata de "una idea del cambio histórico: a través de los años, las cosas se mejoran.... El progreso se trata de cómo las cosas deberían de funcionar".[1] Trujillo apeló a esta comprensión del progreso constante para modernizar y urbanizar el país; de la misma manera, el progreso se hizo análogo a la mejoría social, y por extensión, al blanqueamiento.[2] Trujillo, un arribista quien también vino de orígenes humildes, estableció un nuevo orden social en el que la clase (y por lo tanto, la raza), podía lograrse y se hizo la encarnación de ambos, la cultura y el progreso.[3] Estos dos conceptos se reflejaron durante el Trujillato en aspectos clave que tuvieron efectos duraderos en el nacimiento, el crecimiento y la recepción de la bachata.

La ascensión de Trujillo

Rafael L. Trujillo, un hombre sin estudios que anteriormente fue telegrafista, subió rápidamente por los rangos de la Guardia Nacional desde informante a oficial en poco tiempo. Encabezaba la Policía Nacional (anteriormente la Guardia Nacional) cuando los Estados Unidos desocupó el país en 1924. Trujillo apoyaba públicamente a Horacio Vásquez mientras que en privado, preparaba al ejército dominicano para que le fuera fiel a él. Cuando Vázquez se enfermó antes de las elecciones de 1930,

Trujillo planeó y organizó un golpe con Rafael Estrella Ureña. Luego, Trujillo postuló su candidatura para la presidencia en las elecciones de mayo de 1930 y las ganó, según los informes, con el cuarenta y cinco por ciento del voto. Trujillo hizo uso de la intimidación y la violencia para ganar, según la tradición caudillista; las amenazas y el temor a la violencia serían corrientes subyacentes durante los treinta años del régimen de Trujillo.

Solamente unas semanas después de que Trujillo asumió el poder, el ciclón San Zenón arrasó la capital y devastó el país en septiembre de 1930. Este desastre natural contribuyó inadvertidamente a su consolidación de poder y también se prestó a su estrategia de modernización. Trujillo salió de la destrucción como un jefe de estado sólido y digno de confianza en ese momento de necesidad,[4] lo cual le ganó el favor de algunos de sus antiguos adversarios. El apetito voraz del ciclón había destruido mucho de la capital, ofreciéndole a Trujillo la oportunidad de hacer borrón y cuenta nueva, y de diseñar la capital moderna que deseaba.

El ciclón San Zenón también fue significativo por su destrucción repentina de las fronteras físicas que antes separaban a los barrios de clase baja de los dominicanos burgueses y elites. Antes del ciclón, los barrios populares literalmente estaban fuera de la vista; después, estaban abiertamente expuestos, y sus habitantes se mezclaban con los de los vecindarios de las clases media y alta en los espacios públicos. Para muchos de estos, "el borrado de las señas por las cuales se representaban las identidades sociales de la ciudad fue tanto una parte del terror del evento como fueron las muertes y la devastación de propiedades".[5] Apoyaron el plan de Trujillo para volver a construir la capital como un centro urbano moderno porque así se restablecerían esas fronteras físicas. Este énfasis en la urbanización y la modernización estableció el progreso como algo deseable, y pintó el campo y al campesino como su polo opuesto.[6] Ambos, los campesinos y los pobres de las urbes, llegaron a ser vistos como impedimentos al progreso, una traba sobre la cual urgía prevalecer.[7]

Los esfuerzos de reconstrucción después del ciclón intensificaron el contraste entre la ciudad y el campo. Los que habían llegado a la capital cuando se disolvieron los terrenos comunitarios, o porque buscaban ayuda tras el ciclón, reconstruyeron sus viviendas, convirtiéndolas en ranchitos.[8] Los diseñadores urbanos de Trujillo también subrayaban los vínculos entre las viviendas desvencijadas, la pobreza y la bajeza moral.[9] Los ranchitos aguantaron lo más recio del desdén de las clases altas porque introdujeron de manera tan concreta lo rural en la ciudad.[10] El abismo que se percibía entre lo rural y lo urbano mantenía viva una larga tradición de las imágenes conflictivas del campesino dominicano como alguien sin cultura por una parte, y como el depositario de la dominicanidad por otra. Después del ciclón San Zenón, el gobierno aprobó medidas legales para obligar al campesino a que se quedara en el campo y para prohibir su migración a la ciudad.[11]

Trujillo seguía proyectando la imagen de ser el protector de la nación dominicana después del ciclón. Trabajaba activamente para solidificar su imagen como la presencia inquebrantable de la cual dependía el progreso. Esta percepción se concretizó por su forma de vestir impecable, la cual incluía un uniforme militar cubierto con medallas y reconocimientos,[12] muchos de los cuales fueron creados únicamente para otorgárselos al dictador. Los numerosos títulos otorgados a Trujillo también reiteran su centralidad en todas las facetas de la vida dominicana.[13] Desde temprano se reconoció a

Trujillo como "el Benefactor de la Patria" (1932), y dos años después, se le otorgó un doctorado *honoris causa*, sin considerar su falta casi completa de estudios formales. Fue reconocido como el Padre de la Patria Nueva en 1955, título que enfatiza la creencia comúnmente difundida de que Trujillo de verdad había formado una nueva nación y una nueva identidad.[14]

Como observa Hartlyn, el régimen de Trujillo no se basaba en ninguna ideología política concreta; en su lugar, estaba basado en el precedente de los caudillos de gobernar para fines de riqueza y poder personales.[15] Trujillo se aprovechaba de la tradición caudillista de mantener lazos y relaciones por lealtades personales, y por explotar la nación como si fuera su industria privada para enriquecerse. El gobierno dominicano gozaba de las arcas de la nación, pues Trujillo creaba monopolios de numerosas industrias, tales como el azúcar, el arroz el ganado, la sal y hasta los zapatos.[16] La economía estaba tan entretejida con la vida política nacional que era sinónimo de Trujillo mismo. En el momento en que fue asesinado, Trujillo controlaba aproximadamente el 80 por ciento de la industria, sus empresas empleaban al 45 por ciento de la mano de obra, y el estado empleaba a otro 15 por ciento.[17] El crecimiento y el desarrollo industrial le forraron el riñón a Trujillo y también iban de la mano con el programa de modernización y progreso del gobierno.

Forjar una identidad dominicana

La identidad forjada activamente por Trujillo unió a los dominicanos por medio de un sentido de pertenecer al nivel nacional por primera vez. Las lealtades y las identidades regionales habían contribuido históricamente a una continua inestabilidad política. Trujillo se aprovechó de las nociones de pertenecer—o sea, la cultura—para sembrar intencionadamente un sentido de identidad nacional como otra herramienta para mantenerse en el poder. Trujillo apeló astutamente a la identidad hispana que se había articulado durante la historia, intensificando así el sentido de pertenecer de los dominicanos porque contraponía agresivamente dicha identidad al haitiano como el Otro. Trujillo exacerbó la imagen profundamente arraigada de Haití y sus ciudadanos como la raíz de todos los problemas nacionales. Su antihaitianismo, sin embargo, es irónico, pues su abuela materna era haitiana y se rumoreaba que él mismo recurría a la poderes ocultos.[18] No obstante, Trujillo expresaba abiertamente su tendencia a lo hispánico y escondía todo lazo con Haití en la misma manera que trataba de aligerar su cutis con maquillaje en polvo compacto, práctica que tenía durante toda la dictadura.[19]

En los años tempranos del régimen, el espacio contestado de la frontera fue el escenario en donde se realizó esta supuesta diferencia. Trujillo aprobó la masacre de los ciudadanos haitianos que se encontraban en tierras dominicanas fronterizas en octubre de 1937, y ordenó a los soldados dominicanos que usaran machetes para realizar el acto para que pareciera el resultado de una sublevación de los campesinos.[20] El ataque horrendo fue blanco de la indignación internacional; al nivel nacional, el régimen lo presentó como acto justificado frente a la incursión haitiana en tierras dominicanas, realizando así la costumbre medieval española de la limpieza de sangre en el contexto del Nuevo Mundo.

Trujillo también solidificó el sentido de compromiso al régimen a cambio de regalos y nombramientos oficiales,[21] y de extender los lazos familiares a través del compadrazgo. Se hizo padrino de numerosos niños dominicanos, inclusos los de los niveles más bajos de la sociedad.[22] Tales prácticas crearon un sentido de vinculación en los beneficiados, el cual les impidió actuar en su contra.[23] Los nombramientos a puestos oficiales del gobierno o del ejército también les proporcionaban a los dominicanos más pobres la oportunidad de subir la escala social, y por extensión, les dio acceso al mecanismo de blanquearse por medio del privilegio social. Trujillo también aprovechó la otra cara de la moneda de esta práctica, el temor a ser excluido, ya que los funcionarios públicos temían todo defecto percibido o acusación que pudiera quitarles su puesto. De la misma manera, los ciudadanos dominicanos se preocupaban por ser denunciados públicamente en el Foro Público, columna del periódico *El Caribe*. Estos chismes cortos y escritos criticaban a los individuos tanto por comisión como por omisión, ya que no alabar suficientemente al dictador y el régimen era suficiente para etiquetar a uno de antipatriótico.[24]

Las consecuencias de caer en desgracia con Trujillo variaban entre el ostracismo social al peligro físico. Trujillo estableció la amenaza, el temor y la brutalidad como la base subyacente de su poder. Dependía de un grupo de matones organizados, La 42, y una red elaborada de espías, el Servicio de Inteligencia Militar (SIM), quienes reportaban, amenazaban y castigaban. Juntos, las amenazas verdaderas e imaginadas produjeron un sentido dominante de terror que refleja el modelo que propone Bentham para la prisión ideal, el Panóptico. Este diseño hace hincapié en el papel del guardia/observador que vigila desde un lugar aislado de los presos en una torre donde él mismo no puede ser visto. El observador tiene la ventaja de saber las acciones de cada preso a la vez que ellos nunca saben si de hecho está presente para verlos. Esta falta de certidumbre resulta en el efecto del Panóptico, ya que produce

un estado de visibilidad consciente y permanente que asegura la función automática de poder.... [L]a vigilancia es permanente en su efecto, aun si es suspendida en su comisión.... El poder debería de ser visible pero no verificable ... el preso no ha de saber nunca si lo ven en un momento dado; pero siempre tiene que estar seguro de que es posible que así sea.[25]

Trujillo también entretejió una serie de claves simbólicas para acceder en la participación en la Nueva Patria. Retocó las características geográficas de la nación, nombrando Ciudad Trujillo a la capital, y cambiando el nombre de la montaña más alta del Caribe, el Pico Duarte, al de Pico Trujillo. Los lemas, la poesía y las canciones reiteraron la presencia de Trujillo y literalmente lo pusieron a flor de labio de todos los dominicanos.[26] Cada casa mostraba un retrato del dictador y el lema "Dios y Trujillo" en un lugar destacado.

El merengue resultó ser una de las herramientas más penetrantes y poderosas de Trujillo para la represión y la construcción de una identidad. Se ha ofrecido un número de razones por la obsesión de Trujillo con el merengue, que varían desde fines propagandísticos a antagonizar a la elite o aun una preferencia musical personal del dictador.[27] De hecho, Trujillo se enfocó en el merengue para fortalecer un sentido de identidad entre los dominicanos y para controlar y replicar el régimen en un nivel íntimo y cotidiano.[28] Trujillo hizo uso del potencial del merengue desde su primera campaña cuando viajaban conjuntos de merengue con él para tocar "Se acabó la bulla", merengue que celebraba su acenso y el haberle puesto fin a las sublevaciones constantes de los caudillos.[29] En su selección del merengue recurrió a sus conocimientos de primera mano del uso del mismo como símbolo nacionalista de resistencia durante la ocupación, y también de la historia del merengue como manera de documentar los acontecimientos históricos y actuales.[30]

En la misma manera en que renovó la capital tras el ciclón, Trujillo buscaba convertir el merengue "en un símbolo del poder y de la modernidad de su régimen".[31] El dictador contrató a Luis Alberti y su grupo como su conjunto personal, y este músico reconocido le hizo varios cambios significativos al merengue para reflejar la nueva imagen del progreso, y para que le fuera más apetecible a la elite dominicana. Estos cambios a la instrumentación—se reemplazaron a la guitarra y al acordeón con el saxófono, el clarinete o la trompeta—y la inclusión del paseo para que las parejas pudieran pavonearse en la pista de baile en su mejor atuendo, resultaron en una fisura entre este merengue y el merengue típico tradicional.[32] Mientras este seguía siendo popular entre los campesinos y las clases bajas, el merengue de orquesta fue la forma preferida de la elite. Los dos géneros se representaban como esencialmente dominicanos, y el merengue fue proclamado el baile oficial.[33] Tal cooptación de una música popular hace resaltar la elección intencional de la misma:

> el hecho de que los nacionalistas elites hagan uso de la idea de la cultura popular para representar la identidad nacional no significa que siempre acepten y celebren las costumbres culturales verdaderas de los pobres dominicanos. En su lugar, significa que los intelectuales nacionalistas tanto de la izquierda como de la derecha con frecuencia consideran que las costumbres populares que les gustan son verdaderamente dominicanas.[34]

Los cambios hechos al merengue de orquesta son un reflejo acertado del dictador mismo: "un baile del campo con elementos africanos cubiertos con maquillaje más ligero".[35] Los compositores produjeron merengues en honor a Trujillo y todos sus actos y atributos en profusión,[36] así sirviendo como una fuente constante de propaganda sobre su presencia y grandeza.

Los medios masivos favorecieron la penetración del merengue, así prestándole a Trujillo infinitamente más posibilidades de control que las que tenían los caudillos del siglo XIX. La censura determinaba lo que se podía transmitir y consumir, y el hermano del dictador, José "Petán" Arismendi Trujillo, fundó su propia emisora de radio, La Voz del Yuna, en 1942.[37] Petán incursionó también en la televisión y la grabación, y por todos lados transmitió sus propias preferencias musicales y las noticias sancionadas por el estado.

Los últimos años

En 1955, la República Dominicana fue la sede de la Feria de la paz y la confraternidad del mundo libre en honor a los 25 años de Trujillo en el poder. El país se convirtió en el escenario sobre el que Trujillo podría representarse como el benefactor supremo, el que le trajo la paz, la prosperidad y el progreso a la nación isleña.[38] El discurso del dictador en la dedicación de la feria reitera el papel que desempeñó en la construcción de la dominicanidad desde su ascensión al poder en 1930, pues reitera sus esfuerzos por fijar las fronteras nacionales y fortalecer una identidad nacional.[39]

A pesar de tales proclamaciones grandiosas de progreso y prosperidad, la feria de 1955 no generó los ingresos anticipados para compensar los proyectos de construcción realizados para ella, por lo que el país ya no gozaría del mismo grado de estabilidad económica bajo el régimen.[40] Otros acontecimientos contribuyeron a un creciente descontento, tales como la desaparición (alegadamente aprobada por el gobierno) de Jesús Galíndez por haber escrito su tesis doctoral sobre el régimen, y el asesinato a sangre fría de las tres hermanas Mirabal quienes participaron en las actividades de la oposición. Aunque varios grupos contemplaban el derrocamiento del gobierno, uno, formado principalmente por hombres de la clase alta, eventualmente logró reunir armas y el respaldo de la CIA. Estos no aceptaban ninguna ideología política en particular, sino que los lazos del compadrazgo los unían y se vieron obligados a actuar por asuntos personales pendientes y una preocupación por más violencia en el futuro.[41] Aun cuando perdieron el apoyo estadounidense, los confabuladores siguieron adelante con su plan. Tendieron una emboscada y ajusticiaron al dictador la noche del 30 de mayo, 1961, mientras realizaba su viaje semanal a su pueblo natal.

Conclusión

La Era de Trujillo fue violenta y represiva. De todos modos, Trujillo se había constituido en una parte tan importante de la vida cotidiana que muchos dominicanos se sentían a la deriva cuando cayó el régimen. El final del régimen de Trujillo representó mucho más que un cambio de liderazgo; en su lugar, señaló el final de toda una forma de vivir, pensar y ser que había cambiado muy poco durante los últimos treinta años. Como resultado, "[e]l final de la era de Trujillo también provocó un tremendo terror popular sobre el futuro que para muchos, rayaba en lo apocalíptico".[42] El aferrarse a las antiguas anclas de identidad les proporcionaba un punto de certidumbre a esos dominicanos aprehensivos ante un futuro incierto.

Trujillo solidificó un sentido de dominicanidad, y redactó las comprensiones entretejidas de la clase y la raza por el lente del progreso y de la cultura. Trujillo difundió las señas de ser blanco a los dominicanos de la clase baja repartiendo puestos oficiales y regalos, sirviendo él mismo como ejemplo del asenso social; les confería la creencia que ellos también podrían transformar su raza, a la vez que mejoraban su nivel social.[43] Frente a estos cambios abruptos, muchos dominicanos se aferraron a las señas de identidad que Trujillo les otorgó, inclusive el merengue como su música nacional. El respaldo del merengue y su afianzamiento en la mentalidad nacional dominicana le concedía ciertos privilegios durante años, aun a costo de la popularidad creciente de la música de guitarra que más tarde se conocería como la bachata.

CUATRO

Los albores de la bachata

El bachatero Edilio Paredes recuerda la primera bachata que se grabó, "Condena", interpretada por José Manuel Calderón: "en 1962 se hizo la primera grabación de lo que hoy se llama bachata. Entonces se llamaba 'bolero de guitarra'. Todo el mundo le llamaba así. En ese tiempo no le llamaban bachata".[1] Irónicamente—o tal vez, poéticamente—Calderón estrenó lo que más tarde se reconocería como el primer sencillo de la bachata, el 30 de mayo de 1962—justo un año después del día de la muerte de Trujillo. Mirar hacia atrás nos permite con claridad poder ver que la bachata se remonta a este tema, grabado en aquellos días. En una entrevista para el *Listín Diario* relacionada con la conmemoración del 50 aniversario de la bachata, Calderón notó esta fecha significativa y observó que no era casualidad que el nacimiento de la bachata coincidiera con la nueva era tras el ajusticiamiento de Rafael L. Trujillo, ya que la bachata ayudó a aligerar la carga de esos tiempos difíciles.[2]

Los primeros bachateros

José Manuel Calderón, el Pionero de la Bachata, nació el 9 de agosto de 1941 en San Pedro de Macorís. Tras una breve estadía en la capital cuando tenía 10 años, su familia se estableció en Santo Domingo en 1954. La mamá de Calderón, quien tocaba la guitarra, fue su primera influencia musical. Recordó él, "Mi mamá entonces me compra una guitarra y cuando mi papá llegaba, esa guitarra se guardaba para que él no la viera".[3] El papá de Calderón tenía mala opinión de los músicos y este no supo la verdad hasta que las canciones de Calderón ya se escuchaban en la radio y la gente ya empezaba a hablar de ellas. Afortunadamente, su papá lo apoyó y hasta lo felicitó.[4]

En su juventud, Calderón trabajaba de mensajero en Santo Domingo, y se dedicaba a la música como actividad aparte. Formó el Trío los Juveniles, con Andrés Rodríguez en la primera guitarra y Luis Pimentel en la segunda; además de cantar, Calderón tocaba la tercera guitarra. Juntos, el grupo empezó a aprender sobre la marcha: tocaban entre sí y para fiestas locales y serenatas.[5] Cuando decidieron grabar el disco de prueba "¿Qué será de mí?",[6] el trío, además de una marimba, un bongó y unas maracas, alquiló tiempo en la emisora, La Voz del Trópico. Es irónico que Radhamés Aracena, cuyo nombre llegaría a ser sinónimo de la bachata, haya desanimado al joven Calderón, pues en ese entonces le veía muy poco futuro a su estilo de música.[7]

Afortunadamente, Calderón no le prestó atención y perseveró. Dos amigos locutores de Calderón, César Bobadilla Rivera y Marco Antonio Rojas, conocido como "Papá Rojita", se encargaron de que al disco de prueba se le diera tiempo en antena, y pronto el público empezó a pedir la canción de Calderón.[8] Estos locutores le sugirieron que grabara el sencillo de nuevo en los modernos estudios de Radio Televisión Dominicana. Aunque no estaba seguro de que le permitiera usar las instalaciones, Calderón preguntó y pudo alquilar el espacio y los equipos. Esta vez los músicos cambiaron la marimba por un bajo y las maracas por una güira.[9]

Calderón siguió los consejos de Atala Blandino, propietaria del Salón Mozart, y pagó la impresión de los primeros 100 discos en los Estados Unidos. Cuando llegaron los discos, Calderón distribuyó la mitad en las emisoras de radio y vendió la otra mitad él mismo por dos pesos cada uno.[10] Calderón dirigió todo aspecto de este esfuerzo musical: "yo era el productor, el vendedor, el relacionador público, era todo porque ... eso era un invento".[11] Este estreno incluía dos versiones nuevas o "fusilamientos" de canciones: el bolero popular, "¿Qué será de mí?", escrito por Bienvenido Fabián con el título original, "Condena",[12] y al lado B, un bolero waltz, "Borracho de amor". Las canciones tenían un nuevo sabor en la voz del trío de Calderón, y a la medida que seguía ganando tiempo en antena, "¿Qué será de mí?" llegó a altos niveles de popularidad.[13] Pronto, Calderón llegó a vender todo ese primer lote de discos, y envió hacer más.[14]

Las ventas continuaban y Calderón empezó a trabajar en otro disco. Su segunda producción incluyó dos composiciones suyas, "Lágrimas de sangre" y "Muchachita linda".[15] Los títulos de otras canciones suyas en los próximos años (1962–1964) hacen resaltar el tono que los críticos de la bachata después identificaron como un matiz amargo: "Quema esas cartas", "Te perdono", "Serpiente humana", "Vano empeño", y "Llanto a la luna".[16] La popularidad de las canciones de Calderón seguía creciendo y en 1963, firmó con el sello Kubaney. En ese entonces, los contactos y un viaje a Puerto Rico ayudó a extender el entusiasmo por la música de Calderón en el extranjero.[17]

Pronto, otros músicos siguieron el ejemplo de Calderón, atraídos por el nuevo sonido: "Se fueron sumando porque fue un contagio".[18] En ese entonces, la bachata todavía era considerada bolero de guitarra o música romántica de guitarra, y "en ese tiempo no estaba discriminada".[19] Rafael Encarnación se estrenó en octubre de 1963, cantando de una manera parecida, llena de lloros y emoción. El disco de Encarnación incluía dos temas de su propia autoría, "Muero contigo" y "Pena de hombre". Aquellos tenían la temática distintiva de la bachata: el abandono, el desamor, y frente a todo, el amor eterno. Rafael Encarnación, un estudiante universitario de orígenes humildes, le ofrecía una nueva posibilidad a la bachata. Tommy García recuerda que Encarnación se vestía formalmente, con traje y corbata, un *look* que recordaba la tradición bolerista. Encarnación murió trágicamente en un accidente de tránsito en marzo de 1964, después de grabar solamente once temas, todos de su autoría.[20]

La grabación de estreno de Inocencio Cruz en 1964, "Amorcito de mi alma", continuó en la misma vena de interpretación afligida. Acentuado por gritos de "¡Ay, ay, ay, ay, ay!", la letra promete el amor eterno. El segundo éxito de Cruz, "Mal pago", fue una nueva versión del bolero "Amor gitano" cuya letra incorporaba imágenes cada vez más vívidas del dolor y del sufrimiento. En esta canción se retrata la amargura del narrador al descubrir que su amada le ha sido infiel. Después de reprobarle el mal pago que le dio a cambio de su amor eterno, el narrador le suplica que le corte las venas, pues la vida no significa nada sin ella.

Bernardo Ortiz también sacó una bachata romántica popular en 1964, "Dos rosas". La letra dulce de este tema une la bachata con la emoción de manera inextricable, pues presenta las dos rosas como una canción en sí. Por todo el tema, las rosas hablan por el narrador, expresando su amor y su adoración, y suplicándole a su amada que no le defraude. Ya que el título y el contenido de esta canción se enfocan específicamente en dos rosas en lugar de una sola, queda implicado un mensaje secundario: "Te amo". Los sentimientos expresados en "Dos rosas" bien podrían ser el contenido que tendrían en mente los que dicen que la bachata sirve como una manera de comunicar los sentimientos que uno no se atreve a decir por miedo al rechazo. El productor y músico, Davicito Paredes, nota que "cantándolas se dicen cosas difíciles de hablar. Eso es la bachata".[21]

Las canciones de Rafael Alcántara, más tarde conocido como Raffo el Soñador, figuraban entre las más tristes de esta primera oleada de bachateros. Desde el comienzo, las bachatas de Raffo proyectaban cierto fatalismo que reflejaba las dificultades y los golpes debilitantes que recibió de la vida. Como niño, Raffo era limpiabotas; como adulto, perdió a su esposa y a su hijo en un accidente de tránsito en Nueva York.[22] Aunque Batista Matos insiste en que las canciones de Raffo son más bien boleros rítmicos,[23] se parecen a otras bachatas tempranas en cuanto a la amargura y los sentimientos que expresan. En "No me hablen de ella", la voz narrativa les pide a los oyentes—probablemente un grupo de amigos—que no le hablen de su amor perdido, pues prefiere llorar tranquilo. "El soñador" se enfoca en el tema común de la bachata, el desengaño.[24] En esta bachata, el cantante contrasta sus sueños amorosos y felicidad con el vacío y la soledad que siente cuando el destino le roba inesperadamente a su amor. Las letras de Raffo el Soñador eran verdaderas, surgidas de sus vivencias. Tal como revela el título de una canción, había sufrido una "Cadena de tragedias". Para finales de su vida, Rafael Alcántara vagabundeaba al azar por las calles de Santo Domingo; en 1985, a la edad de los 41 años, se suicidó.[25]

La bachata temprana: Producción y consumo

Aunque esta música de guitarra sentimental tenía bastantes seguidores, no gozaba del apoyo popular de las clases media y alta ni tampoco del respaldo financiero recibido por la arraigada música nacional, el merengue. Este había gozado del respaldo oficial del estado dominicano durante las tres décadas del Trujillato y tenía público en todo el país y una larga historia con los sellos discográficos. El merengue atravesó las fronteras de la clase social, la edad y el género por sus dos estilos diferentes: el merengue típico y el merengue de orquesta. Además, el merengue tenía el respaldo de inversionistas. Una parte de la crítica y la discriminación originales de la bachata surgió de los que tenían intereses económicos en el merengue. Cuando se dieron cuenta de que la bachata tenía un público importante entre las masas, "los que tenían las grandes inversiones en el merengue hablaban fuerte de la bachata para que se parara, para que no siguiera".[26]

La bachata estaba asociada con los habitantes de los barrios populares y los campesinos que se habían migrado a ellos.[27] Estos eran sus principales consumidores. Tal como observa el músico Vicente García, el gusto musical se convirtió en "una manera de marcar las clases".[28] La clase media consideraba que la bachata era atrasada, ordinaria y carente de valor. Las presentaciones en vivo de la bachata solían realizarse en espacios pequeños, tales como fiestas locales o en los bares. También se relegaban los discos a un ambiente limitado que incluía las velloneras de los cabarets, los burdeles y los colmados. Aunque a la bachata se le impidió la entrada a los lugres de gran escala donde estaba el merengue, esta tenía una base de aficionados importante. Los bachateros atendieron los gustos de su público por la música de guitarra, y muchas veces presentaron sus nuevas versiones de los boleros y las baladas populares.[29]

Según la descripción de Calderón, la producción de la bachata temprana era de carácter muy personal,[30] en gran parte porque a las disqueras no les interesaba. Sin el equipo, los consejos, o el respaldo económico de un sello, los bachateros eran responsables de cada aspecto de la grabación, la promoción, la distribución y la venta. Ya que les faltaba el respaldo profesional, la música era producida, presentada y distribuida completamente dentro del sector informal. Los bachateros se costeaban todo, lo cual afectó a su vez la calidad de los discos. Los músicos tenían que alquilar tiempo y espacio en un estudio de grabación, donde grababan en una sola pista. Por eso, las nuevas tomas eran caras. Ya que los músicos pagaban por su tiempo en el estudio, solían sacar sencillos y rara vez grabaron un elepé. No se les solía pagar regalías a los bachateros, como las que recibían los merengueros, y sus pagos solían ser pequeñas y de una sola vez.[31]

Los bachateros también tenían la responsabilidad de distribuir sus discos ellos mismos, vendiéndolos en la calle o llevándolos a las velloneras. En esos años, la venta promedio de las velloneras era de 7000 a 8000 discos.[32] La familia Trujillo había contribuido inadvertidamente a esas ventas para las velloneras, ya que el hermano del dictador, José "Petán" Arismendi Trujillo, importó las velloneras en los 1950. Petán las colocó en los colmados y sacó provecho cobrando el 50 por ciento de las ganancias.[33]

La vida en los barrios giraba con frecuencia alrededor de los colmados donde los residentes locales compraban comida y artículos del hogar y compartían noticias y chismes. La cercanía del colmado además de la necesidad de comprar lo justo para arreglárselas por un tiempo lo convirtió en el centro de intercambio social y comercial del barrio.[34] Los colmaderos entendían la situación difícil de sus clientes, y les vendían con frecuencia solamente la cantidad del producto que hacía falta por unos cheles.[35] De todos modos, el colmado era mucho más que un negocio, pues también era el centro social de un barrio, un lugar para compartir noticias, pasarla bien, conocerse y saber de los otros miembros de la comunidad.[36] Ya que eran un centro para congregarse y para la socialización económica, los colmados se convirtieron en el distribuidor principal del nuevo sonido de la bachata que se tocaba en el fondo para los clientes y todos los que estaban lo suficientemente cerca.

Aun antes de que esta música romántica de guitarra tuviera su propio nombre, tenía sus propios seguidores entre los residentes de los barrios populares y los arrabales urbanos. También era un elemento básico de los bares, cabarets y burdeles de dichos barrios, lugares todos que alejaban aún más a la bachata de las clases media y alta: "antes, la gente la criticaba porque era una música de los bares".[37] Además de los guardias a quienes les refería uno de sus nombres, la bachata era popular entre muchos habitantes de los barrios pobres, cuyas realidades duras y cuyas desilusiones se retrataban con frecuencia en sus letras. Estas asociaciones con la clase baja contribuyeron a su discriminación "porque venía muy de abajo".[38]

Por esta base de popularidad, la bachata siempre estaba presente en las habitaciones de las trabajadoras domésticas en las casas más acomodadas de las clases media y alta. Estas jóvenes, que dejaron su casa para buscar trabajo en las casas de la clase media, llevaban su música con ellas. Estas jóvenes influyeron, pues su "casi condición para trabajar a gusto era tener un radio ... en la cocina. Entonces, en todas las casas de clase media, los oficios se hacían oyendo la música de los marginados".[39] Por todo el país, los quehaceres domésticos se realizaban con una pista sonora de la música de las clases bajas. La familia oía esta música en la radio, mientras sus empleadas domésticas la escuchaban. Susana Silfa recuerda que de niña, "Yo iba a un sitio detrás de la casa y allí me ponía a fantasear, a cantar.... La habitación de servicio domestico estaba cerca de allí y yo escuchaba Radio Guarachita".[40]

La clase media dominicana, sin embargo, criticaba esta música y a los músicos como atrasados y de mal gusto. La bachata se encontró marcada por un estigma difícil de superar, ya que se asociaba primero con los migrantes rurales a la ciudad, después con los burdeles, y más tarde, con las trabajadoras domésticas de clase baja que la escuchaban mientras trabajaban. Si un dominicano de la clase media la tocaba lo suficientemente cerca como para que la oyeran los demás, bien podría ser acusado de ser un campesino. Edilio Paredes recuerda que le decían, "'Esa es una música ... de campesinos, de gente que no tiene cultura, que no tiene educación'".[41] De la misma manera, Gerson Corniel cuenta que otros le decían, "'Ah, tú eres campesino, tocas guitarra'".[42] Eso no quiere decir que no hubiera aficionados de la bachata entre las clases media y alta, sino que eran aficionados secretos que escuchaban la música donde no la podían oír los demás[43] y "de manera clandestina".[44]

El estilo de bailar bachata—las parejas abrazadas y las luces bajas, tal como se bailaba el bolero—también contribuía al rechazo y a la condena de la clase media. En ese entonces, era posible que una mujer dudara de bailar un bolero a menos que su pareja fuera su prometido o su esposo, ya que hacerlo prácticamente servía como "una declaración de amor".[45] Dada tal reacción en el caso del bolero, la respuesta aún más fuerte en el caso de la bachata no sorprende, sobre todo considerando sus asociaciones con los burdeles de Santo Domingo.[46]

En aquel entonces, los bachateros también corrían el riesgo del menosprecio público de los críticos de su música.[47] El bachatero Eladio Romero Santos recuerda vívidamente que le dijeron "comesopa", referencia al alimento básico que podía permitirse un músico sin recursos, y también "pasacantando", una valoración de las actividades de uno como algo sin futuro.[48] De semejante manera, Gerson Corniel recuerda que le calificaron de "mediocre" porque cantaba bachata.[49] Luis Segura recuerda que tenía que ocultar su guitarra cuando caminaba por la calle para evitar las burlas de los demás.[50] A Leonardo Paniagua le insultaron como "dañadiscos" porque su primera grabación fue una adaptación—o lo que de manera despectiva se entiende como "fusilamiento"—de una balada popular. Esto era visto por los detractores de la bachata como dañar una buena canción.[51] Edilio Paredes relata que le echaron tanto huevos como insultos mientras se presentaba, y su hijo, Davicito Paredes, compartió una anécdota que le contó otro bachatero a quien le pidieron que se bajara del transporte público cuando los otros pasajeros se enteraron de que era bachatero.[52] Los términos despectivos que se empleaban para referirse al bolero de guitarra eran iguales de ofensivos. Edilio Paredes admitió que dejó de grabar por un tiempo después de oír una referencia a su disco como un cachivache, o sea, algo sin valor.[53] La hermana de Susana Silfa le comentó, "que qué bueno que me había cambiado el nombre porque así no tenía que decir que era mi hermana".[54]

Estas discriminaciones y estos reproches agresivos se hacían oír, y se basaban en mucho más que las preferencias musicales. Tal reacción visceral puede atribuírsele, en parte, al grado en que la identidad musical nacional dominicana estaba arraigada en el merengue. Como ya se ha visto, los dominicanos se sentían a la deriva cuando se les derrumbó el mundo tal y como lo conocían bajo Trujillo. Estas opiniones fuertes sobre la preferencia musical y cuál género debería de considerarse la música nacional ya tenían una historia larga en la República Dominicana, como revelan las ardientes campañas literarias del siglo XIX contra la posibilidad del merengue de reemplazar a la tumba. No es sorprendente que muchos se aferraran al merengue como símbolo de su identidad hispana, dada la incertidumbre de la política dominicana a principios del decenio de 1960, y más tarde, las situaciones económicas y sociales.

La campaña apasionada en contra de la bachata también surge de cuestiones de la raza y la clase. La cultura como forma de medir el pertenecer tenía raíces profundas. Aunque originalmente se asociaba la cultura con todo lo hispano, a través del tiempo, llegó a ser una seña de la clase social y un mecanismo para distinguir entre las clases sociales.[55] De la misma manera, los dominicanos de las clases baja y media solían emplear el concepto de la cultura como seña de la comunidad racial, en lugar de entender la raza como algo determinada por fenotipo o el color de la piel.[56] Trujillo se había aprovechado de este sentido de pertenecer para encarnar el mito del ascenso social[57] (y por lo tanto, el blanqueamiento), posibilidad que algunos tal vez vieran amenazada por la llegada de una música rural y de la clase baja, que consideraban negra.

Se podía reconocer fácilmente la cultura en los que tenían buenas costumbres, y de la misma manera, faltaba por completo en los que no las tenían. Los espacios distintos de la nación, o aun dentro de un barrio en particular, podrían edificar las buenas costumbres y la cultura o ser completamente lo opuesto: un lugar de perdición.[58] Estos eran los mismísimos lugares en donde se tocaba bachata. Tal distinción contribuía a las divisiones de la identidad basadas no solamente en cuestiones de clase y raza, sino también en la noción de la decencia. Decirle "una bachata" al bolero de guitarra significaba un insulto, y el mensaje que se deseaba comunicar era que se trataba de una música de los campesinos y música sin cultura.[59] La mala pronunciación de palabras o la dicción inarticulada de los músicos rurales también avivaron el desdén por la bachata de las clases media y alta: "la dicción, la pronunciación de las palabras no eran correctas. Entonces, a una persona estudiada le molestaba oír una canción grabada, mal hablada".[60] Por sus críticas fuertes de la bachata, los dominicanos de dichas clases se definían al mantener firmemente quiénes no eran: de la clase baja, negros y sin cultura. El proceso de identificación era todo lo contrario para los nuevos migrantes a Santo Domingo. Los seguidores de la bachata, de los sectores pobres de la sociedad tanto en los lugares rurales como urbanos, se veían reflejados en las canciones y las vidas de los bachateros. Para estos, el bachatero "era el espejo que devolvía el rostro de las aflicciones del amor, las caras de la miseria, y el valor de la vida".[61]

Radio Guarachita

A pesar de que rechazó inicialmente la bachata y se negó a incluirla en su programación radial, el locutor y productor Radhamés Aracena tenía un buen sentido de negocios y de la promoción, lo cual lo llevó a pensarlo de nuevo. Aracena se dio cuenta del público masivo que escuchaba este género cada vez más popular. Tommy García enfatiza la relación mutua entre Aracena y la nueva música: "¿Qué es lo que la ... [la bachata] ... hace popular? La visión de este tipo comerciante que se da cuenta que con una nueva emisora es más fácil competir, teniendo para él el nuevo público masivo que poblaba la ciudad".[62]

Hasta los discos mal producidos de la bachata se vendían bien, y Aracena optó por aprovechar la amplia base de consumidores y las preferencias musicales actuales. En 1964, instaló su equipo de segunda mano y estrenó su nueva emisora para tocar solamente música popular—hasta que el gobierno le ordenó que por lo menos identificara la emisora—para estimular el interés y la expectativa del público. La emisora de Aracena empezó a emitir oficialmente en marzo de 1965, pero sufrió un revés cuando estalló la guerra civil ese mismo año, por la cual dejó de transmitir. Cuando Radio Guarachita empezó a transmitir de nuevo en 1966, Aracena desechó su modelo anterior y en su lugar, se dedicó a la música de guitarra dominicana y su creciente público.[63] Radio Guarachita se convirtió en "la primera emisora y la única en ese entonces que tocaba el género de la bachata".[64]

Aracena también grababa a los bachateros, además de tocar la música de guitarra en Radio Guarachita. Participaba en todas las etapas de la grabación y la distribución de su sello, Discos la Guarachita, para lograr lo que él consideraba un buen producto. El mismo les hacía audiciones a los posibles bachateros y grababa las canciones que le gustaban. Más tarde, hacía una transcripción de las letras de esas canciones y corregía los errores de gramática, quitándoles todo vínculo lingüístico que pudiera delatar la clase social u origen regional del cantante.[65] Entonces le requería que aprendiera el tema corregido antes de grabarla para el mercado. Así, la música a la producción de Aracena resultó ser más accesible al público diverso de diferentes regiones del país a la vez que conservaba el estilo y el sentimiento típicos de la bachata.[66] Radio Guarachita resultó ser una empresa certera. Aracena era un astuto hombre de negocios, y su emisora solamente incluía a esos bachateros de quienes él mismo era productor, y solamente a esas canciones para las cuales tenía derecho de distribución. El bachatero Tony Santos reconoce el talento de Aracena para los negocios: "No dejo de reconocer que él tenía un negocio. Porque él buscaba a los cantantes, o sea, si uno le llevaba un disco, no lo iba a poner. Había que grabarle a él".[67] Esta mayor visibilidad creó efectivamente una demanda, y Aracena sacó provecho al ofrecerla.

Radio Guarachita no solamente tocaba bachata, también se arraigó en todos los aspectos de la vida de su público. Por una parte, Aracena reconoció a estos nuevos migrantes como un público viable, lo cual les prestó una presencia en un ambiente en donde eran marginados. Además, Radio Guarachita llegó muy pronto a ser el vínculo, tanto concreto como simbólico, entre los migrantes a las ciudades y los que se quedaron en el campo. Aracena promocionaba y facilitaba la interacción entre los oyentes y la emisora con la instalación de un teléfono en la cabina. Los radioyentes llamaban para pedir una canción, o para transmitirles un mensaje a sus amigos o familiares por radio. Estos mensajes, llamados "servicios públicos", eran especialmente importantes porque mantenían los vínculos en una época en que los servicios telefónicos y de correo eran muy limitados o poco fiables en la República Dominicana.[68] Estos mensajes solían ser de carácter personal y específico, e iban desde la notificación que daba cuenta del retorno de un migrante que iba a visitar en cierta fecha y que la familia debería de encontrarse con él en un lugar dado, hasta los esfuerzos del campesino recién llegado para encontrar a un familiar en Santo Domingo.[69] El programa de saludos del domingo era también muy popular y cumplía una función semejante, pues se trataba de enviar saludos.[70] Además de esta interacción por teléfono, Radio Guarachita les abrió las puertas a sus oyentes. Se le permitió al público venir a la emisora y ver las transmisiones desde la cabina del DJ, la cual estaba elevada para ver mejor.[71]

En su conjunto, este estilo de programación ayudó a concretizar un sentido de unidad entre los oyentes, y cumplía una función semejante a la de un "producto cultural"[72] que une a los individuos para vincular sus acciones y crear conciencia de que otros consumen el mismísimo producto. Anderson describe tal consumo como una "ceremonia en masa":

> Se realiza en una privacidad silenciosa, en la guarida del cráneo. Sin embargo, cada comulgante está muy consciente de que la ceremonia que realiza es replicada simultáneamente por miles (o por millones) de otros de cuya existencia está seguro, aunque no tiene la más mínima idea de su identidad. Además, la ceremonia se repite sin cesar a través de todo el año del calendario. ¿Qué imagen más vívida de la ... comunidad imaginada se podría imaginar?[73]

Por lo tanto, escuchar bachata "resulta una operación a la vez social e individual".[74]

Radio Guarachita ayudó a difundir la popularidad de la bachata rápida y efectivamente[75] y también se prestó al sentido de pertenecer a la vez que aliviaba el sentido alienante del anonimato de la vida urbana: "fue su vínculo a todo lo que dejaron".[76] De la misma manera, la emisora se prestó a un sentido de comunidad entre los oyentes de diferentes lugares geográficos al unir a oyentes urbanos y rurales que escuchaban la misma música y los mismos mensajes por toda la nación. Radio Guarachita transformó a su público, creando consumidores de música y productores de sus propias vivencias por medio de sus mecanismos de unir la ciudad y el campo y de ofrecerle a un público creciente su música preferida. De esta manera, le ofrecía una voz a una población que se encontraba silenciada en muchas maneras.

El reconocimiento de un nuevo género

Aunque la bachata no fue reconocida como un género distinto hasta los 1970, cada vez más desarrollaba su propio estilo en los 1960, ya que los artistas seguían produciendo su música romántica, infundiéndoles a sus canciones su propio estilo. Este fue el caso particular de los temas de Luis Segura, "el Añoñaíto". Este apodo se refería al estilo interpretativo de Segura, pues a los que no eran aficionados les parecía el llanto de un ñoño. Segura se consideraba un cantante romántico y para él, su estilo sencillamente le servía para expresarse, ya que "cantaba con delicadeza".[77]

Como muchos de los bachateros que le precedieron, Luis Segura nació en el campo (en Mao) y más tarde se trasladó a Santo Domingo. Un músico autodidacta, Segura seguía el modelo de los tríos y los cantantes de boleros tan populares en ese entonces a quienes trataba de imitar.[78] Estas influencias tempranas se quedaron con Segura durante toda su carrera, y todavía es un cantante de bachata romántica o bachata boleros. La primera grabación de Segura, "Cariñito de mi vida" (1964), enfatiza el sufrimiento del cantante y la culpa de la mujer de negarle su amor. Segura fue todo un éxito por su estilo emotivo de cantar y las letras sentimentales de este y otros temas posteriores.[79]

El cantante y guitarrista, Edilio Paredes, grabó con Luis Segura por primera vez como parte de la producción temprana de la bachata. Edilio Paredes, quien nació en un campo cerca de San Francisco de Macorís en 1945, tenía solamente cuatro años cuando conoció un instrumento de cuerdas, el tres, en un colmado. Este músico autodidacta se fue para Santo Domingo a los 13 años y empezó a trabajar en la disquera del músico y cantante, Cuco Valoy,[80] quien también producía y grababa a los artistas con su propio sello, y Paredes empezó a tocar la guitarra para dichas producciones. Poco después, Paredes empezó a grabar para Rhadamés Aracena, primero tocando la primera guitarra para muchos de los nombres más importantes del sello Guarachita, y también grababa sus propias canciones.[81]

El estilo único de tocar de Edilio Paredes resultó influir en la evolución de ambos, la bachata y el merengue de cuerdas. Paredes imitaba ingeniosamente con su guitarra el sonido del acordeón del merengue, así acelerando el tempo y marcando más el ritmo para que fuera más bailable.[82] Las figuras intrincadas y prestadas del merengue, interpretadas por la voz de la guitarra, le prestó un nuevo sonido a la bachata en las manos hábiles de Paredes, lo cual la distanció aún más del bolero.[83] Edilio Paredes también ayudó a abrirle el paso a la bachata a un público más diverso. Paredes, además de los reconocidos bachateros Augusto Santos, Leonardo Paniagua, Ramón Cordero, e Isidro Cabrera "el Chivo sin Ley", lanzaron el show, *Lunes de amargue*.[84] La forma y el lugar de estos shows atrajeron a un público compuesto de diferentes clases sociales. Ayudaron a presentarle la bachata a una base más amplia de consumidores y a erosionar el estigma asociada con ella.[85]

Leonardo Paniagua Alberto, quien grabó unos 800 temas de bachata romántica, cuenta que comenzó su carrera por casualidad.[86] Paniagua, quien nació el 5 de agosto de 1950 en Las Yayas, La Vega, empezó a trabajar como mensajero para el Instituto Nacional de Aguas Potables (INAPA) por un sueldo de 58 pesos y 80 centavos.[87] Una tarde de 1973, Paniagua fue por un corte de pelo cuando el peluquero, Danilo Rodríguez, lo invitó a quedarse para un ensayo musical esa tarde. Cuando el grupo ya había ensayado, Rodríguez invitó a Paniagua a cantar. Este cantó la única canción que sabía, la popular "Amada amante". Rodríguez se quedó impresionado y le pidió a Paniagua que lo acompañara al estudio de Rhadamés Aracena donde tenía una cita para grabar al día siguiente.[88]

Ese día, Rodríguez tuvo que pedirle permiso a Aracena para que Paniagua pudiera estar presente en el estudio. Aracena consintió, pero con una advertencia: "Rhadamés me permitió que yo entrara, que me sentara en una mesita, pero que no respirara cuando estaba grabando".[89] Paniagua se quedó inmóvil durante la grabación, y al final, Rodríguez le pidió a Aracena que escuchara a Paniagua cantar. Otra vez, aceptó Aracena, y Paniagua cantó "Amada amante", tema original de Roberto Carlos, acompañado por el grupo de Rodríguez. Paniagua no lo sabía, pero Aracena había dejado prendida la grabadora. Impresionado, Aracena le pidió que cantara otro tema, y a Paniagua no le quedó de otra que admitir que ya había cantado el único que sabía. Se ofreció a cantar "Amada amante" otra vez, pero a Aracena le gustaba su primer esfuerzo, e insistió en que Paniagua cantara algo más. Paniagua sostuvo que no sabía ninguna canción más, pero Aracena mantenía firmemente que le faltaba una canción para el lado B. Según Paniagua, "nos quedamos y dan las tres de la mañana. El no nos saca, tiene la llave. Y digo yo, 'Bueno, yo he oído una canción'.... Se llamaba 'Insaciable'. ... [Dijo Rhadamés].... 'Yo la tengo en disco, yo le voy a copiar'. Entonces puso en el pedestal la letra y la grabé, leyendo".[90]

El tema romántico, "Amada amante", que canta de la belleza de un amor desinteresado, fue un éxito inmediato. Paniagua seguía grabando en este estilo romántico, y siguió a su primer éxito con otro, "Un beso y una flor" (1973), una adaptación de una balada del cantante de pop español Nino Bravo. Paniagua tuvo muchos éxitos en los siguientes años, tanto que lo invitaron a participar en el programa televisivo, el *Show del mediodía*, conducido por Yaqui Núñez del Risco. A pesar de su éxito, Paniagua no gozó de ingresos significativos en ese entonces por una combinación de factores, incluyendo el que el merengue dominaba el mercado musical, y la producción y la distribución de la bachata dentro del sector informal.[91]

La popularidad de Paniagua subió vertiginosamente en 1979 con su adaptación del éxito del conjunto sueco, ABBA, "Chiquitita". Este tema llegó a nuevos niveles de popularidad nacionales e internacionales, y gracias a él, Paniagua fue nominado por el premio El Dorado como el Cantante del Año.[92] Varios amigos dominicanos compartieron conmigo una anécdota basada en un juego de palabras relacionado con el título de esta canción. Según cuentan, un aficionado escuchaba este éxito de Paniagua en una vellonera y le gustaba tanto que insistió en voz fuerte, "¡Pónganme Chiquitita hasta que crezca!". Fue tanto el éxito de este tema que las emisoras que anteriormente no habían tocado bachata lo colocaban. A pesar de tanta popularidad, la bachata como género seguía siendo señalada como una música de la clase baja y de poco valor artístico, y fue criticada por lo mismo. "Era discriminada en el país, la bachata. Incluir una canción con esa entonación era como malo para la sociedad".[93]

Conclusión

La bachata nació en una encrucijada de la historia dominicana. Cargada en la ola de migrantes rurales a la capital, las primeras bachatas comúnmente fueron adaptaciones en guitarra de los boleros latinoamericanos populares, versiones interpretadas principalmente por músicos autodidactas. La bachata no era discriminada en esos primeros años, aunque su público principal estaba constituido por la clase baja rural y urbana. Más tarde, mientras crecía su presencia con el influjo continuo de migrantes rurales a la ciudad y con el alcance de Radio Guarachita, la bachata se iba convirtiendo, cada vez más, en el blanco de la crítica y el desprecio de las clases media y alta. Los primeros intérpretes de esta música romántica de guitarra no gozaban de un acceso igual a las oportunidades de grabación, pues se encontraban en la sombra de la música nacional, el merengue. Esta falta de acceso fue reflejada en la calidad de sus grabaciones, lo cual contribuía a las críticas de las mismas.

Las construcciones duraderas de la raza y la clase también servían de trasfondo a la discriminación contra la bachata, y estas subrayaban las tensiones continuas entre las zonas rurales y urbanas. Muchos de los campesinos que acudían en masa a la capital de las regiones sureñas eran morenos, y por lo tanto, se les consideraban atrasados y pobres. Estos campesinos no tenían lugar en la vista esencialista del campesino dominicano como la esencia más pura de la dominicanidad. Los vínculos entre la raza y la clase social pintaban de negros a los músicos de clase pobre que tocaban y grababan bachata. La palabra "bachata" originalmente representaba un insulto de las clases media y alta urbanas que reflejaba su opinión de que no tenía ningún valor artístico.

El terreno inseguro de la vida después del ajusticiamiento de Trujillo también contribuyó al rechazo temprano de la bachata. Frente a la incertidumbre de ese entonces, muchos dominicanos se aferraban a las anclas de identidad proporcionadas por el plan de construcción nacional de Trujillo, entre ellas la música nacional, el merengue. Los debates sobre la bachata y los insultos ofensivos dirigidos tanto a ella como a sus intérpretes reiteran la tradición de entender las identidades musicales como inquebrantables. Tal como los críticos del merengue lo condenaron cuando amenazaba y eventualmente reemplazó a la tumba, los detractores de la bachata se fueron a la ofensiva contra este nuevo género cada vez más popular. Aceptar la bachata en esa época habría sido el equivalente de reconocer abiertamente la negritud y una contribución valiosa por parte de los pobres rurales y urbanos. Los críticos de la bachata apoyaban una herencia de progreso y modernización, y consideraban que el campesino y el pobre eran obstáculos. En vez de hacer caso omiso a la música nacional que se les había impuesto, la burguesía y la elite dominicanas optaron por tratar de mantener el estatus quo.

CINCO

Las muchas caras de la bachata: Desde la zona roja a la bachata rosa

Mis compañeros y yo habíamos visto al mismo limpiabotas, Eduardo, todos los días mientras caminábamos a casa desde el preescolar en Santiago donde trabajábamos ese verano. Cuando por fin aceptó que no queríamos que nos limpiara los zapatos de tenis, nos hizo otras preguntas: ¿De dónde éramos? ¿Cómo era aquel lugar? ¿Qué hacíamos en la República Dominicana? Cuando le dijimos el nombre de la escuelita en dónde hacíamos de voluntarios, comprendió: "¡Ah, sí! Iba a comer allí cuando era niño".

Al contemplarlo ahora, el comentario de Eduardo le presta una cara personal al trasfondo constante de necesidad y desempleo que seguía en la República Dominicana bajo diferentes mandatos. A través de los años, las crisis económicas han llevado a cada vez más dominicanos a la clase baja. Las tasas de pobreza siguen altas, y más del 40 por ciento del pueblo vive bajo la línea de pobreza.[1] Estas crisis también se prestaron al crecimiento de la comunidad transnacional dominicana debido a la siguiente migración de un número significante de personas al exterior. Como resultado, cada vez más dominicanos en el país y en el exterior conocieron las condiciones, el sufrimiento y el anhelo por los tiempos pasados que retrata la bachata. Aunque la bachata de doble sentido era popular en los 1980 y a principios de los 1990, unas letras más suaves y románticas además de innovaciones a la instrumentación y la interpretación lírica ayudaron a la bachata a conquistar nuevos seguidores.

Cantando el *blues*

La economía se iba empeorando a finales de los 70 y principios de los 80, lo cual motivó a más mujeres rurales a trasladarse a las ciudades y obligó a más mujeres a trabajar fuera de la casa. Ellas solían encontrar trabajo más fácilmente que los hombres ya que se les pagaba un sueldo menor. Su participación en el lugar de trabajo público afectaba la familia dominicana tradicional y las costumbres matrimoniales, y su solvencia financiera significaba que no tenían que depender de un hombre.[2] Las uniones consensuales se hicieron más comunes y les dieron más oportunidades de tomar decisiones por la pareja o familia.[3] La participación de la mujer en el mundo laboral las convirtió esencialmente en "mujeres de la calle ya que gozaban de un mayor acceso a ... los espacios públicos".[4] El gobierno no dudó en echarles la culpa de las altas tasas de nacimiento a nivel nacional a las relaciones consensuales de las residentes femeninas de los barrios—y muchas de dichas relaciones ocurrían en serie—y también a la falta de los hombres de reconocer a sus hijos.[5] Este cambio de papeles también contradecía una comprensión duradera y machista, o sea, "una noción de lo que significaba ser un buen hombre ... [que acepta] ... que el hombre tiene que ser buen padre, mantener a su mujer ... y a sus hijos".[6] Ahora, muchas mujeres eran económicamente independientes y mantenían a los hombres que se encontraban a la deriva en esta nueva realidad.

La bachata andaba al paso de este cambio. Las letras retrataban cada vez más a los hombres que buscaban consuelo fuera de la casa y el núcleo familiar, al fondo de una botella o en las conquistas de una noche en los burdeles.[7] Las letras también representaban las conversaciones entre amigos—hombres—que se compadecían en un bar. El estudio de Pacini Hernandez de las letras de bachatas muestra que la mayoría de los hablantes de las primeras bachatas se dirigía a una segunda persona que escuchaba; en contraste, las letras de los 1980 solían hablar de una mujer indirectamente con la tercera persona.[8] Las letras y el tono de la bachata eran tan amargos que sus detractores le decían "música de amargue".

Luis Segura figuraba de manera destacada en la historia de la bachata de 1983. Ese año, sacó su disco, *Pena*, con su estilo único de interpretación que imitaba el llanto. El tema titular, en el cual el narrador lamenta la falta de comprensión por parte de su amada, marcó el primer éxito de la bachata a gran escala dentro de la corriente dominante. De repente, la bachata se encontraba en primer plano y de manera positiva. Tal fue el interés repentino en el género, más allá de la clase pobre, que produjo algo parecido a su propia fiebre de bachata.[9]

Luis Segura y la bachata acapararon la atención de la nación en 1983 cuando los estudiantes de la Universidad Autónoma de Santo Domingo (UASD) lo invitaron a tocar, y el rector Joaquín Bidó Medina prohibió las presentaciones de bachata,[10] decisión que recordaba los ataques decimonónicos contra la decencia del merengue. El escándalo resultó ser una crítica del presidente y de la universidad por haber perdido el contacto con el pueblo dominicano y especialmente, con el gran porcentaje de estudiantes de la UASD que venían del campo.[11] Sergio Reyes, escribiendo para *Fuero* (la publicación de la Asociación de los Empleados Universitarios), mantenía que tales gustos individuales y culturales "se llevan dentro, como la sangre misma".[12] Según opinaba Reyes, el mensaje de la bachata era poco profundo, pero sostenía que "nunca debemos negar su valor cultural y popular, pues sería como negarnos a nosotros mismos".[13] El escándalo de la UASD enfocó la atención nacional en la bachata y las cuestiones de identificación musical.

La bachata de doble sentido

Las letras de las bachatas de los 1970 y 1980 se hicieron cada vez más picantes. Mientras bachateros tales como José Manuel Calderón, Luis Segura y Leonardo Paniagua continuaban grabando su bachata romántica, había otros que empezaron a incluir doble sentidos muy sugestivos y poco disimulados en sus bachatas de cabaret. Tony Santos, el bachatero más popular del doble sentido de los 80, se fue del campo para Santo Domingo a los 18 años, soñando con ser un cantante romántico. Santos recuerda con mucha emoción la oportunidad de grabar que le dio Marino Pérez en 1977. Un domingo por la tarde, Santos se acercó a Pérez y le explicó que le gustaba cantar. Pérez le dijo que viniera al día siguiente a cantarle, oferta que casi le parecía increíble: "¡Yo estaba temblando porque alguien quería grabarme!".[14] Santos admitió que no tenía con que pagar una grabación, pero Pérez insistió, y una vez que lo oyó cantar, le pidió otro tema.

Después de este comienzo fortuito en 1977, Santos fue el más popular de los bachateros de doble sentido del siguiente decenio, empleando juegos de palabras cargados de sentido sexual y pasos teatrales y sugestivos cuando bailaba en el escenario. Santos, junto con Julio Ángel y Blas Durán, eran los favoritos de este estilo de bachata, convirtiéndolo en una opción lucrativa. Una de las canciones más conocidas de Tony Santos, "Mamá me lo contó", trataba de un juego de palabras cuidadosamente construido con insinuaciones sexuales, pues cuando se ligan las palabras del título, significa algo completamente distinto.[15] A pesar de las críticas de esta bachata, a la cual algunos la etiquetaban diplomáticamente de "bachata de doble sentido" o "bachata del cabaret" y otros de "obscena", el éxito de Santos de 1986, "Amarilis, échame agua", comprobó que este estilo de bachata sí vendía. En este tema, el cantante le ruega a Amarilis que lo empape con agua para quitarle el calor, un eufemismo por tener relaciones. Aparte de toda protesta por la indecencia, esta canción le cosechó a Santos tiempo al aire en las emisoras de radio de la corriente dominante, y también en la televisión.

Julio Ángel es otro ejemplo de un cantante del campo[16] que tuvo éxito con el doble sentido de la bachata de cabaret. A Ángel, quien recuerda haber pasado hambre más de una vez cuando era niño, le cautivaba la música que oía en la radio y en vivo tocada por tríos. Recuerda una de las primeras bachata boleros que oyó, "Tinieblas" de Raffo el Soñador.[17] Ángel compró su primera guitarra por 11 pesos con la mayoría del dinero que ganó al salir premiado una quiniela. Aunque le dio a su mamá 2 pesos de esas ganancias imprevistas, no le admitió cómo los llegó a tener, ni cómo había comprado una guitarra; dijo que alguien se la prestó. Unos días después, su mamá insistía en que le devolviera la guitarra a su dueño legítimo. Ángel se daba una caminata y se detenía todo el tiempo posible antes de volver a casa. Una vez allí, le dijo a su mamá que el dueño de la guitarra le dijo que se quedara con ella un tiempo más. Estaba feliz de la vida: "Y me quedé con mi guitarra vieja. Ni sabía afinarla, ni nada más".[18]

Eventualmente, Ángel decidió probar su suerte en la capital. Llegó a Santo Domingo con solamente una idea vaga de cómo localizar a un tío que vivía allí. La situación de este tío no era mucho mejor, y le dijo a Ángel que tendría que irse y le prestó los 4 pesos para el boleto de guagua. Afortunadamente, Ángel encontró un trabajo y se quedó. Durante ese tiempo, escuchaba a Radio Guarachita y le daba por cantar. Con el tiempo, Ángel ahorró bastante dinero para grabar su primer disco en 1971.[19] Seguía grabando después, y su éxito de 1983, "El salón", es otro ejemplo vívido de los dobles sentidos poco sutiles de este estilo de bachata. Esta canción depende mucho de la rima y las semejanzas entre palabras, tales como la semejanza entre "peine" y "pene", por ejemplo. El título y el ambiente de la canción es el salón, el cual rima con "pajón", o sea, el vello púbico de la mujer. Esta asociación llevó a muchos a referirse a la canción por otro título, "El pajón".

El cantante Blas Durán llegó a ser conocido por sus bachatas de doble sentido y también sus merengues de cuerda, pero empezó su carrera cantando las bachatas bolero románticas. Su estreno de 1970, "Clavelito". presentó una comparación dulce entre la boca de la amada y un clavel rojo. Los temas subsiguientes de Durán de los 70 y los primeros años de los 80 reflejaban las realidades sociales cambiantes. La voz masculina de "Equivocada", por ejemplo, presenta un punto de vista machista, pues tiene muchas amantes, pero no ama a ninguna; además enfatiza que la mujer se equivoca a creer que le rompió el corazón. Ya que había pocas oportunidades disponibles a la bachata porque el merengue dominaba el mercado, Durán empezó a dedicarse al género más lucrativo (el merengue) a principios de los 70. Durán cantó para varios grupos y cantantes diferentes, incluyendo los merengueros más populares como Johnny Ventura y Joseíto Mateo.[20]

Durán continuaba grabando su propia bachata de cabaret también. "El huevero" retrata a un hombre que no puede encontrar trabajo y por lo tanto, tiene que vender huevos, modismo para referirse a los testículos. Se invierten los papeles y el cantante tiene que darle de comer a su amante hambrienta que no quiere nada más que huevos que sean grandes y duros. Su tema de 1986, "La arepa", se basa en el mismo tema de un vendedor ambulante, en este caso, de arepas. El narrador de este merengue de cuerdas llama a su vecina para que venga por un pedazo de arepa; después, le advierte que no la manosee demasiado, pues teme no poder venderla después. Además de la popularidad de estas letras de doble sentidos abiertos y sexuales, estos temas también presentaban las realidades sociales de los hombres que buscaban trabajo desesperadamente.

El sonido cambiante de la bachata

A mediados de los 80, Blas Durán empezó a experimentar con su sonido y su estilo. Su bachata de cabaret de 1986, "El motorcito", fue la primera que hacía uso de una primera guitarra eléctrica que tocaba líneas repetitivas a un ritmo acelerado.[21] El narrador explica que se compró un motor porque no tenía carro. Las insinuaciones económicas de esta revelación son claras: no puede costearse más que un motor. Este medio de transporte, no obstante, es aceptable y apropiado para la mujer de su vida, ya que siempre le gusta que deje prendido su motor, pues le gusta montarlo.

"Consejo a las mujeres" de Blas Durán fue un hito, pues se llevaron sus innovaciones a la bachata también. Lo más notable de este merengue de cuerdas fue una instrumentación innovadora que incluía una guitarra eléctrica y la güira (típica del merengue) en lugar de las maracas comúnmente usadas en la bachata.[22] El grabar en múltiples pistas mejoró la calidad de la producción y del sonido.[23] "Consejo a las mujeres" también fue un éxito por sus atrevidas referencias de doble sentido. Este tema se metió en el lenguaje cotidiano por sus primeras palabras, un grito a las mujeres para llamarles la atención: "¡Mujeres hembras!". Se pegó la frase como un segundo título de este merengue que "transcendió todos los sectores de la sociedad dominicana".[24] Durán le integró estas mismas innovaciones a su bachata, y su "éxito se prestó a que la popularidad de la bachata llegara a tal nivel que a los medios de la corriente principal no les quedaba de otra que aceptarla".[25] El estilo de Durán estableció la base sobre la cual una nueva generación de bachateros podría construir sus carreras.

La tecno bachata

La influencia de la Nueva Canción

Varios músicos dominicanos que influyeron en la bachata de principios de los 90 tienen sus raíces en la Nueva Canción, un movimiento que tuvo sus orígenes en la región del Cono Sur de Sudamérica a finales de los 50 y principios de los 60 con un interés renovado en la música folklórica. Los estudiantes de la clase media fusionaron varios géneros con la música y los instrumentos folklóricos tradicionales, llevados a las ciudades por los migrantes indígenas y rurales que buscaban mejores condiciones económicas y sociales. Las letras desafiaban los problemas políticos y sociales por América Latina, y por lo tanto, la Nueva Canción "tenía un proyecto dual de recuperar las raíces y de la crítica social".[26] Por toda la región, servía como un lente por el cual examinarlo todo, desde las tradiciones hasta las condiciones actuales sociales, políticas y culturales, y una vía de cambio.

El grupo Convite, un grupo de académicos, músicos y folkloristas activos en la política, abrazó la Nueva Canción y su premisa del cambio social por la música en la República Dominicana. Tal como sucedió en otras partes de Latinoamérica, la vuelta a las formas folklóricas y el uso de las mismas como la base de su experimentación ocupó un lugar central en la misión de Convite. En términos musicales, Convite se oponía particularmente a la comercialización de la cultura popular y a la manera en que los intereses económicos deformaron el carácter de la música. Por lo tanto, los miembros de Convite participaban en investigaciones y trabajo de campo para descubrir las raíces de las formas musicales folklóricas y tradicionales con el fin de preservarlas, experimentar y educar al público en general.[27]

Yo quiero andar

Luis Días, compositor y músico, fue miembro de Convite y el movimiento Nueva Canción dominicano. Sus experimentos musicales incluían la mezcla de elementos de la música folklórica dominicana con géneros tales como el jazz, el *rock* y el *blues*. Días grababa poco, y en su lugar dedicaba su tiempo a componer y explorar las fusiones musicales durante los 70 y los 80.[28] Tal como los otros bachateros, Días reconocía las posibilidades que tenía la guitarra al imitar el papel del saxofón en el merengue. Tommy García, quien conocía a Días, cuenta que una vez descubrió a este estudiando y practicando un manual del método del saxofón. Cuando lo presionó, Días explicó que primero tenía que entender la técnica del saxofón para poder hacer lo mismo en su guitarra.[29]

La exploración musical de Días incursionó en la bachata, e introdujo sus elementos musicales y líricos a varias composiciones de ese entonces que se presentaron sin grabarlas.[30] Días aceptó las calles y la forma de vida de los que escuchaban bachata y se mudó a un burdel para vivir en carne propia ese ambiente de la bachata de cabaret.[31] Estos conocimientos por vivencias, además de sus estudios musicales, colocaron a Días en una posición única para poder cambiar de manera significativa la trayectoria de la bachata. En 1988, el productor Cholo Brenes se acercó a Días con la idea de colaborar con la popular cantante de baladas, Sonia Silvestre, en una producción. Días aceptó, con tal de que fuera una producción de bachata.[32] Se trataba de un proyecto atrevido, ya que la discriminación en contra de la bachata por parte de las clases media y alta todavía era prevalente. No obstante, Brenes y Silvestre aceptaron y empezaron a trabajar con el músico, Manuel Tejada, en el elepé *Yo quiero andar* (1989), disco que incluía cinco bachatas. Además de las mejores opciones de grabación que tenían disponibles estos artistas, era única la instrumentación del álbum ya que fue completamente producida por sintetizadores. Este sonido electrónico único inspiró a sus creadores que le pusieran un nuevo nombre: tecno bachata o tecno amargue.[33]

En contraste con el sonido de esta tecno bachata, sus letras se parecían mucho a las de la bachata bolero cantada por casi treinta años. La canción titular, "Yo quiero andar", expresa el deseo de la mujer de dejar a su amante y viajar a un lugar en donde no la pueda encontrar, pegar o abusar. "Andresito Reyna" relata como las adicciones al juego y al alcohol del personaje titular conducen a su muerte. "Mi guachimán" cuenta los peligros enfrentados por la mujer a quien le gusta salir y pasarla bien cuando los hombres malintencionados se aprovechan de ella. La colaboración de estos tres, Días, Silvestre y Tejada, marcó la primera oportunidad para que la bachata llegara a un público más amplio que atravesaba las divisiones sociales y de clase. Sin duda alguna, la bachata ya era muy popular y tenía muchos seguidores,[34] y los esfuerzos y las innovaciones de estos músicos se prestaron a que la bachata se difundiera entre un público más amplio.

Por este papel importante que jugó en la historia de la bachata, *Yo quiero andar* fue incluida en la lista de los Cien discos esenciales, compilado por la Asociación de Cronistas de Arte de República Dominicana (ACROARTE) en 2013. Esta lista tiene el fin de "identificar aquellos álbumes que abrieron el camino para el surgimiento de nuevos estilos, los cuales por su calidad, con el tiempo alcanzaron categoría de clásicos".[35] Ciertamente, no se debería de subestimar la importancia de esta colaboración, ya que contribuyó a la erosión de los estereotipos sociales asociados con la bachata.

Juan Luis Guerra

En 1990, Juan Luis Guerra publicó su álbum, *Bachata rosa*, título que distanciaba a su bachata rosada de la de las zonas rojas. Guerra, quien participó en el movimiento dominicano Nueva Canción, estudió música en Berklee College of Music en Boston.

Mientras sus primeras composiciones reflejan más bien una influencia pop, volvió a los ritmos caribeños para crear un merengue de orquesta refinado. Guerra usó una técnica semejante con la bachata para componer temas suaves, dulces, y definitivamente color de rosa, de la misma manera en que había creado un merengue de orquesta muy refinado.

A pesar de su nombre, *Bachata rosa* incluye solamente cuatro bachatas. Sus títulos—"Como abeja al panal", "Estrellitas y duendes", "Bachata rosa", y "Burbujas de amor", contrastan con el hilo amargo que entreteje la bachata tradicional. Los temas son de verdad románticos; por ejemplo, un hombre le ruega a una mujer que lo acepte en "Como abeja al panal", y el cantante de "Estrellitas y duendes" lamenta la salida de su amante, admite sus celos, y mantiene que no puede vivir sin ella. Aunque existen estas similitudes con los temas bachateros en la superficie, las letras poéticas de Guerra no revelan ninguna franqueza ni crudeza. En el mundo de Guerra, las heridas causadas por la separación son temporales y existe la posibilidad de superarlas en "Como abeja al panal". De la misma manera, la voz cantante de "Burbujas de amor" es impaciente y le ruega a su amante que se quede para pasar juntos una noche más. Aunque el cantante de "Estrellitas y duendes" insiste que va a morir sin su amada, no le pide que le corte las venas, como lo hizo Inocencio Cruz en "Mal pago". En su lugar, este amante herido jura seguir vivo en su recuerdo como un aguacero, una tormenta compuesta de los duendes y las estrellas del título. Tal como indica su nombre, "Bachata rosa" es la bachata más dulce del disco, una expresión de amor declarado por medio de tropos y figuras poéticas delicados.

Las bachatas de Guerra todavía hacían uso del doble sentido, pero su calidad poética alisó bastante el filo. El narrador de "Burbujas de amor", por ejemplo, desea ser un pez para poder tocar la pecera de la mujer con su nariz y soplar burbujas de amor. Aunque son claros los doble sentidos sexuales—la nariz del pez es un símbolo fálico que penetra el mundo cerrado de la pecera—son ciertamente expresados en matices de rosado y no de rojo. El mundo de la bachata de Guerra es refinado y desinfectado—el ambiente de agua mineral de "Bachata rosa" y no el interior sórdido de un bar de mala muerte, un burdel de la zona roja o el fondo de una botella.

Aunque Luis Días y Sonia Silvestre le habían presentado la bachata a un público nacional más grande con su tecno amargue, el disco *Bachata rosa* de Juan Luis Guerra le trajo el género a un público global.[36] *Bachata rosa* logró precisamente lo que intentaba hacer: se vendió internacionalmente, lo cual convirtió al disco en todo un éxito y le ganó a Guerra un premio Grammy en la categoría tropical latino, en la edición de 1991.

Víctor Víctor

Las raíces del cantautor Víctor Víctor también se remontan a la Nueva Canción. Desde un principio, la música de Víctor Víctor tenía fuertes vínculos con el contexto social, así que no sorprende que sus intereses lo hayan llevado a la bachata. Este cantautor, que tuvo estudios formales de la música, adoptó varias influencias musicales, incluyendo las caribeñas, tales como bolero, son y bachata, y otras, tales como el *rock* y la música brasileña.[37] Víctor Víctor ya trabajaba con bachata antes de publicar su álbum del 1990, *Inspiraciones*, con su bachata "Mesita de noche".[38] Esta canción incorpora los temas comunes de la bachata, el amor y una separación inminente; las letras, aunque sinceras, no son de carácter cortavenas. El narrador de esta canción pinta la imagen del amor de la mujer como su norte, una luz que deja prendida en su mesita de noche. Más tarde, extiende un paralelo entre esta lámpara en la mesita de noche y su amor como una luz que brilla desde el centro de su corazón. Además de sus imágenes líricas e interpretación vocal suavizada, la instrumentación sintetizada de "Mesita de noche" reemplazó el sonido más agudo de la guitarra punteada y la infundió una calidad más suave de balada. Esta aproximación a la bachata resultó todo un éxito que cruzó las líneas sociales y nacionales. Ayudó a presentarle el género a un público más amplio, convirtiéndolo en uno de los álbumes más importantes desde el 1950.[39]

La bachata de Víctor Víctor atrajo aún más la atención nacional en diciembre de 1993 cuando organizó dos conciertos, "De bachata en bachata", e incluía a Sonia Silvestre, Luis Segura, y la nueva estrella, Raulín Rodríguez, además del mismo Víctor Víctor. Estos conciertos tuvieron lugar en Santo Domingo y Santiago de los Caballeros (la segunda ciudad de la nación) e incluyeron ambas, bachatas populares a través de los años y sus bachatas del momento, así uniendo la vieja escuela con la nueva. Estos conciertos también les expusieron el estilo tradicional que se había presentado por tres décadas a los que fueron a disfrutar de la tecno bachata. Víctor Víctor expresó su respeto para sus predecesores en el género y los señala como su inspiración.[40] Sigue grabando bachata, además de otros géneros, aunque ninguna de sus producciones de bachata posteriores ha igualado el éxito de "Mesita de noche".[41]

¿Qué hay en un nombre?

Muchos identifican a estos músicos que no eran bachateros tradicionales, y sobre todo a Juan Luis Guerra y su *Bachata rosa*, como los que hicieron agradable la bachata para un nuevo público. De hecho, esta visión pasa por alto la base importante de aficionados que ya tenía la bachata entre sus seguidores originales, y también el hecho de que creciera esa base con la popularidad de otros bachateros jóvenes como Antony Santos y Luis Vargas,[42] tal como veremos a continuación. Además, el trabajo de Víctor Víctor con la bachata más el éxito de *Yo quiero andar* ya habían establecido las posibilidades de la bachata entre los de la clase media.[43] De todos modos, la popularidad de los temas de estos artistas le dio a la bachata una publicidad nacional e internacional y contribuyó a su "validez por visibilidad".[44]

Por sus letras poéticas y su estilo más suave, algunos bachateros no consideran que Juan Luis Guerra o aun Luis Días, Sonia Silvestre o Víctor Víctor pertenezcan a su filas.[45] No crecieron en el ambiente social de la clase baja, y tenían oportunidades de estudios y capacitación musical, desconocidas por los bachateros. Víctor Víctor y Guerra han continuado grabando bachata a través de los años; pero el mismo Guerra reitera que no es bachatero, sino alguien que experimentó con el género.[46] Para muchos de los que siempre han conocido, tocado y escuchado bachata, Guerra y su gerente, Bienvenido Rodríguez, entraron en la bachata en mucho de la misma manera que lo hizo Rhadamés Aracena originalmente: como una incursión de negocios.[47]

Este debate refleja otra pregunta importante: ¿qué nombre ponerle a este estilo de bachata? Sin duda alguna, estos artistas modificaron de manera importante la bachata; de hecho, se podría comparar a las experimentaciones de Luis Alberti cuando este modificó varios elementos del merengue típico para que le fuera más apetecible a un público urbano.[48] Aunque Días, Silvestre y Tejada le pusieron "tecno bachata" o "tecno amargue" a su creación, ya no se usa este nombre pues se suele agrupar toda la bachata bajo la etiqueta más amplia y sencilla de "bachata". Hay otros que se refieren a toda la tecno bachata con el epígrafe de bachata rosa, por el álbum de Guerra.[49] Para el Pionero de la Bachata, José Manuel Calderón, la música de Guerra tiene sus raíces en la bachata, y no se puede entender en su contexto sin mirar hacia atrás a la larga serie de bachateros que lo precedió, como el Pionero mismo.[50]

Los bachateros de la zona fronteriza

Tres músicos de la zona fronteriza del noroeste también desarrollaban sus propios sonido y estilo a la vez que se evolucionaba la tecno bachata. Estos bachateros— Luis Vargas, Antony Santos y Raulín Rodríguez—continuaban con lo que empezó Blas Durán con sus innovaciones en la guitarra eléctrica. También le integraron patrones innovadores prestados del merengue, y también el mambo, una sección instrumental.[51] Esto llevó a la bachata a nuevos oyentes, y más tarde, inspiraron a nuevas generaciones de bachateros, tanto en el país como en el exterior.

Luis Vargas

Luis Vargas continuó con la tradición de Blas Durán, la bachata de doble sentido y un sonido más moderno. Las grabaciones de Vargas de los 80 no tuvieron mucho éxito, e incluyen más merengues de cuerdas que bachatas. No sorprende su enfoque original en el merengue, dada la popularidad del merengue típico en la zona fronteriza donde nació Vargas.[52] De todos modos, la bachata también figuró en la formación de Vargas, y desde muy joven escuchaba esa música de guitarra: José Manuel Calderón, Luis Segura y Paniagua.[53] Inspirado por el sonido de la guitarra eléctrica del grupo de Blas Durán, Vargas reemplazó las cuerdas de nylon en sus guitarras con otras de acero, y le metió un micrófono en la boca para lograr un timbre más agudo; también incluyó definitivamente la güira, y les dio a otros instrumentos—el requinto, el bongó y el bajo—un papel más importante y rítmico.[54]

El merengue de guitarra de Vargas le llamó la atención al público a finales de los 80, con su tema popular, "La maravilla".[55] Su sonido diferenciaba su música del merengue de guitarra anterior, y también del merengue de orquesta y el típico. Sus letras también llevaron la tradición de doble sentido a nuevas alturas. Los doble sentidos sexuales seguían vendiendo y su merengue de 1990, "El tomate", fue todo un éxito, a pesar de sus insinuaciones abiertas, las cuales comparaban el aparato sexual femenino con un tomate por un énfasis rítmico en la primera sílaba de la palabra "tomate". Una rápida repetición en el primer y el tercer pulso de la canción en esencia rindió la palabra "toto", la jerga de vulva. Estas innovaciones también estaban presentes en las bachatas del disco del mismo nombre. En la bachata de Vargas, esta nueva aproximación incluía temas más rítmicos, y patrones y un tempo acelerado heredados del merengue.[56] Vargas trajo esta innovación musical a la bachata con su estilo tradicional de interpretación vocal sentimental.

El gusto por el doble sentido empezó a menguar frente a la censura y la crítica. Como respuesta, Luis Vargas emprendió otro camino con su nuevo estilo de bachata y en su disco, *Loco de amor* (1994). Las bachatas de esta grabación volvieron a las raíces del género en ambos, temas e interpretación. Con una voz que irradiaba sentimiento, Vargas canta al desamor, al abandono, y a la amargura de estar solo. Esta fórmula combinaba los ritmos bailables de Vargas, su sonido innovador, y los temas tradicionales de la bachata, lo que resultó ser una combinación exitosa.

Las letras de Luis Vargas tratan una amplia selección de temas. El amor es un constante, tal como en "Simplemente te amo". El narrador de esta canción supera las dudas que tienen los demás del futuro que espera su amada a su lado. Aunque no tiene nada que ofrecerle que tenga un valor monetario, ella es su tesoro. Tal como sugiere el título, el narrador de "Loco de amor"[57] está trastornado por una mujer. Pasa tanto tiempo en su barrio que los vecinos temen que vaya reconociendo el terreno para cometer un robo. Enumera todo lo que va a hacer para enamorarla, y espera que un médico le diagnostique con mal de amores y que se la recete como remedio. En algunos casos, se trata de un amor imposible. El narrador de "Carta final" lamenta que la suerte no lo haya permitido conocer a la mujer de sus sueños antes. Aunque ella ya está con otro, piensa jugar su última carta, o sea, sus sentimientos, y no duda en ganarle a su rival. De la misma manera, la voz narrativa de "No puedo vivir sin ti" se enamora de una mujer que no es libre. Aunque declara con una voz sollozante que no puede vivir sin ella, no lucha por su amor.

La indiferencia y el sufrimiento también figuran como temas comunes en las bachatas de Vargas, y asumen diferentes formas. La voz narrativa de "Veneno" sufre durante años a manos de una mujer cruel y la describe como el veneno mismo. En "Volvió el dolor", la voz narrativa sufría hasta que le llegó el amor. Luego, volvió su dolor cuando su amada lo traicionó. El narrador de esta bachata opta por lo noble, pues la perdona y le dice que haga lo mismo si su nuevo amor la traiciona. El narrador de "Yo mismo la vi" cae desde lo alto del amor hasta las profundidades de la desesperación cuando su amada le es infiel. Para este, lo peor de su infidelidad no es que alguien se lo haya comentado, sino que él mismo fue testigo ocular.

Vargas reitera los vínculos entre el desamor, el tomar y el bar en varios temas. En "La mesa del rincón", la voz narrativa se sienta solo en dicha mesa, ahogando sus penas con el ron. Aunque la mesa misma se la recuerda, piensa seguir tomando en ella. El coro se alterna entre los comentarios del narrador y las respuestas de los coristas, así presentando la tradición de la bachata de los hombres que comparten y cantan de sus problemas sentimentales en el bar.[58] "Dos hombres bebiendo" es un dúo con el merenguero estrella Sergio Vargas, y retrata la camaradería masculina. Cuando uno trata de meterse en la borrachera de tres días de su amigo, este le explica que lo traicionó su mujer y que no busca consejos sino más licor. Su amigo está de acuerdo y decide unirse a la borrachera. Una vidente le revela un destino de traición y de alcoholismo al narrador de "Yo no muero en mi cama", destino que acepta sin parpadear. Le informa que va a morir tomando, y les dice a sus amigos que conmemoren su muerte con licor.

Luis Vargas, conocido como "el Rey Supremo de la Bachata", fue entre los primeros que demostraron que la bachata podría ser lucrativa,[59] y todavía es uno de los bachateros favoritos de los aficionados a la bachata. No obstante, Vargas recuerda los tiempos difíciles. Tal como notó en el documental del 2004, *Santo Domingo Blues*, "Qué bueno ser bachatero ahora ... pero *ahora*. En aquel tiempo no era muy bueno".

Antony Santos[60]

Antony Santos, "el Mayimbe de la Bachata", es también producto de la zona fronteriza. Santos empezó su carrera tocando güira en la agrupación de Vargas, pero la dejó cuando se pelearon, y sacó su propio disco en 1992.[61] De las bachatas en este disco, "Voy pa' allá" fue la más conocida. Esta canción llegó a ser famosa por una vía indirecta cuando el grupo femenino de merengue, las Chicas del Can, ayudó a lanzarla hacia la popularidad en las emisoras de radio de la corriente dominante.[62] Esta versión, que incluía ambas, una sección de bachata y otra de merengue, le dio visibilidad a la canción y a sus orígenes como bachata. Los aficionados de esta fusión bachata/merengue buscaron la versión original, y subieron las ventas de Santos.[63]

El tema de Antony Santos, "Voy pa' allá", seguía la tradición bachatera en cuanto a su letra y su estilo interpretativo: la voz del cantante está llena de tristeza y sentimiento, y jura buscar al amor de su vida a pesar de las circunstancias adversas. No obstante, fueron las innovaciones musicales de Santos las que le dieron gran popularidad a esta canción, convirtiéndola en un tema fundamental para la historia de la bachata. Este creó un sonido rítmico, distinto y agudo en su guitarra al tocarla con un toque de pulgar y un movimiento hacia abajo, y frecuentemente incorporaba los patrones y figuras del merengue; también incluyó el mambo del merengue, un interludio instrumental marcado por la improvisación.[64] Estas innovaciones resultaron ser algo muy bailable, y la bachata empezó a ganar terreno dentro de los sectores que antes la rechazaban.[65]

Antony Santos sigue sacando su bachata con éxito, y se queda entre los primeros nombres de los bachateros.[66] A través de los años, Santos ha interpretado temas comunes e innovadores de la bachata con su sonido único. Por ejemplo, el narrador de "Qué plantón" sufre la pena de que siempre lo deje plantado su amada indiferente. Decide emborracharse y amenaza con matarse si no es correspondido. En "Lloro" la voz narrativa relata su sufrimiento y su abandono en tonos sollozantes y quejumbrosos. En contraste, el narrador de "Vete y aléjate de mí" decide terminar una relación prohibida con una mujer que jugó con él, pues prefiere sentir dolor por un tiempito para que su historia tenga mejor final. De la misma manera, el narrador de "Yo quiero" trata en vano de olvidarse de la mujer que amaba. Santos interpreta este tema de un amor sin reservaciones en un estilo más suave pero aún lleno de sentimiento.

Las bachatas de Antony Santos frecuentemente retratan el amor con un giro inesperado. Por ejemplo, el narrador de "Corazón culpable" declara que no quería enamorarse y le echa toda la culpa a su corazón caprichoso. El amor pende de un hilo en "Por mi timidez". El narrador tímido teme perder a la mujer que amaba desde niño. Frente al matrimonio inminente de ella, jura luchar por ganarse su amor a todo costo. "Ay de mí, ay de ti" representa un diálogo entre una voz masculina y otra femenina. Esta sostiene que el narrador no ha sabido amarla ni valorarla, y él trata de convencerla de que no permita que se muera su amor. El tema "Creíste" retrata a un narrador que le presume un nuevo amor a su antigua amada. Le recuerda a su ex que ella pensaba que jamás sobreviviría después de que rompieron, y le explica cómo su nuevo amor le borró todo lo que ella le hizo. Este sencillo del 2013 nos ofrece un buen ejemplo de cómo Antony Santos sigue siendo líder de la innovación bachatera. Mezcla la instrumentación tradicional del género con instrumentos electrónicos, un tempo optimista, y progresiones de acordes entre las secciones del tema. Esta receta exitosa le cosechó a Santos el Premio Soberano por la Bachata del Año del 2013.

Antony Santos se encuentra actualmente entre los bachateros más populares tanto en República Dominicana como en el exterior.[67] La Asociación de Cronistas de Arte de la República Dominicana (ACROARTE) reconoció el papel fundamental que jugó Santos al ayudar a eliminar la discriminación en contra de la bachata al incluir su primer álbum, *La chupadera*, en su lista de Cien discos esenciales entre 1950 y 2010.[68] En específico, ACROARTE hizo hincapié en el álbum de Santos en una muestra de diez álbumes y observó que canciones tales como "Voy pa' allá" se prestaron a que el género "empiece a romper la barrera del rechazo en algunos sectores".[69] Su estilo e innovaciones le inspiraron a otros músicos, incluyendo a muchos bachateros modernos en el extranjero, tal como veremos en el Capítulo ocho.

Raulín Rodríguez

El bachatero Raulín Rodríguez empezó como cantante con Antony Santos, poco después de que este dejara la agrupación de Vargas. Rodríguez dejó sus estudios porque era demasiado lejos y caro asistir a la secundaria en otra comunidad; no obstante, aprendió lo básico de la guitarra.[70] En 1992, Rodríguez—el Cacique del Amargue—formó su propia agrupación y lanzó su carrera como solista. Poco después, el tema de su autoría, "Qué dolor", con su letra dulce que lamenta las acciones del cantante hacia un amor perdido y cantado en una voz suavizada pero aún acongojada, se hizo todo un éxito y cruzó las divisiones de clase social.[71] Las letras inocentes y románticas de Raulín Rodríguez, además de su sonido moderno, su vestimenta profesional, y su apoyo gerencial hizo apetecible la bachata para muchos que anteriormente la despreciaban.[72] Esto le dio a Rodríguez acceso a lugares más grandes, tiempo al aire en la radio FM y en la tele—oportunidades todas que anteriormente no les habían sido disponibles a los bachateros.

El éxito de Rodríguez no se limita únicamente a su apariencia o apoyo gerencial. Más bien ha seguido tratando los temas tradicionales de la bachata del amor y del amor perdido con letras innovadoras, su voz tierna y un ritmo bailable. El mensaje de "Mi morenita" es sencillo y repetitivo: el narrador le recuerda a su amada lo mucho que la amaba e insiste que jamás la olvidará. La letra de "Medicina de amor", una de sus canciones más conocidas, varía más. Este hablante sufre de cáncer del amor porque lo dejó la mujer que ama, y le ruega que vuelva para sanarlo. El narrador de "Mujer infiel" sufre por una mujer traicionera. Le advierte que un día la tratarán igual y comprenderá cómo siente él. En "Ay hombre", la voz narrativa se dirige a su cañaguate y le pide que llene el camino de su amada con sus flores. Este hablante reconoce que le mintió a su amada y que está en su derecho de dejarlo. De todos modos, no puede olvidarla y espera que oiga su canción y comprenda su angustia.

Rodríguez también canta a los diferentes matices del amor. La voz narrativa de "Me la pusieron difícil" piensa casarse con la mujer que ama, cueste lo que cueste. Revela que su familia lo considera caprichoso y mujeriego, y sufre por su oposición.

No obstante, está empeñado en comprobarles que la hará feliz, y finalmente, se escapan juntos. En contraste, la voz narrativa de "Culpable" le ruega a su amada que no se sienta culpable por su relación con él, ya que le pertenece a otro que no la ama y le es infiel. Le dice que le dé una oportunidad y que se deje amar. El éxito de Rodríguez de 2013, "Esta noche", es una declaración tierna de amor. El narrador ya no puede dominar su pasión por la mujer que ama y le promete una noche inolvidable para los dos.

Raulín Rodríguez sigue siendo uno de los bachateros más populares tanto en el país como en el exterior. En este momento, "Esta noche" figura entre las diez canciones más sonadas en la República Dominicana.[73] Aunque los estilos y los sonidos han cambiado desde que estrenó Rodríguez en el 1993, sigue iniciando la moda en su apariencia de momento y sus temas y sonidos de bachata.

Conclusión

A medida que se iba empeorando la economía dominicana, la bachata continuaba representando las realidades de un grupo creciente de aficionados, tanto en el país como entre los dominicanos que migraron al extranjero. La bachata de doble sentido, tan popular en los 80 y los 90, fue seguida por la tecno bachata, e innovaciones al sonido, estilo y contenido lírico. Pedro Antonio Valdez, autor de la novela *Bachata del ángel caído*, observa que la bachata de esa época era producto común entre "la gente de los barrios y campos, o sea en la mayoría de la gente dominicana ... no se trataba de una expresión marginal, sino de una muestra estética del ser colectivo de nuestro país".[74] Los aficionados de la bachata incrementaron por el creciente número de dominicanos que conocían las realidades retratadas en la bachata además de los nuevos públicos atraídos por sus innovaciones.

Seis

La bachata romántica

Cuando le pedí al bachatero romántico, Joe Veras, que me definiera el amargue, me explicó que "toda canción tiene un amargue",[1] o sea, un toque de sentimiento. Veras diferenció entre el "amargue de ayer y el amargue de hoy" y describió aquel como más "cortavenas".[2] Según Veras, quien ha sido uno de los primeros bachateros que escribió, sacó y presentó una bachata más romántica, el amargue aún está presente en su bachata—"pero es más poético".[3]

Así como Joe Veras, varios bachateros llegaron a la escena musical en los 90, un momento en que el género hacía avances importantes en el gusto de las clases media y alta. En su mayoría, estos músicos representaban las mismas características que sus predecesores: venían del campo o la clase baja, eran mayormente autodidactas, y frecuentemente tenían poco acceso a los estudios formales. La bachata que producían, sin embargo, era en su mayoría romántica, y se enfocaba en las diferentes facetas del amor y del desamor. Tal como observa David C. Wayne, es evidente la influencia de la balada en este estilo de bachata romántica, considerando en especial el que unos bachateros incluyeran baladas en sus discos.[4] El contenido y las imágenes continuaban evolucionando, y es posible encontrar a narradores masculinos que le desean lo mejor a su ex, admiten su miedo de enamorarse, se jactan de superar la pena con un nuevo amor, o admiten que cometieron un error. La profundidad lírica, una textura musical más suave, y una forma de cantar más templada de estos bachateros que estrenaron en los 90 y el nuevo milenio, ayudaron a erosionar los prejuicios en contra de la bachata e incrementar su difusión en las principales emisoras.

Joe Veras

Joe Veras fue uno de los primeros que se dio la vuelta hacia el romanticismo cuando publicó su primer álbum, *Con amor*, en 1993. De niño, Veras escuchaba ambos, merengue y bachata, y sigue tocando y grabando los dos; no obstante, describe la bachata como el género que siempre ha ocupado el enfoque central de su vida.[5] Sus letras, muchas de las cuales escribe él mismo, se alinean con el romanticismo de bachateros como Luis Segura, aunque tiene una voz más suave y menos afligida. Los temas estándar de la bachata, el despecho y el desamor, también están presentes en las bachatas de *Con amor*, pero las letras y el estilo interpretativo de Veras los tratan con más nostalgia romántica que sollozos. El tema "Te necesito", por ejemplo, recuerda la música *doo-wop* de los 50, y su letra incluye el recurso repetitivo y rítmico, *dua*. En esta canción, la voz masculina alimenta sus recuerdos del lugar del primer beso compartido con su amor, aunque ya no sabe dónde está. De la misma manera, la voz de "Sonámbulo" no puede dormir porque no deja de recordar a la mujer que amaba, por mucho que quisiera olvidarla. En lugar de ahogar sus penas, promete seguir buscándola hasta encontrarla.

A través de los años, las bachatas de Veras siguen representando las muchas facetas del amor. El tema filosófico, "En el amor", contempla ambos, los sentimientos de enamorarse y desenamorarse. Esta bachata le recuerda a su público que todos hemos tenido nuestra propia historia de amor y podemos relacionarnos con el tema. "Chiquilla Chiquita" presenta a un narrador enamorado que siente el calor de las llamas del amor y anhela ver a su amada. "Por tu amor" trata del amor no correspondido, y el narrador sostiene que hará lo que sea—desde los quehaceres domésticos hasta darle unas vacaciones extravagantes—por su amor. El hablante de "Pido auxilio" también sufre del amor no correspondido y pide socorro porque muere.

Los murmullos de los demás también pueden influir en el amor. En "El hombre de tu vida", el narrador le pide a su enamorada que no escuche las mentiras de otros sobre su supuesta actitud de Don Juan y sus juergas. Le recuerda que es el hombre con que ella siempre ha soñado. En contraste, la voz narrativa de "El cuchicheo" reconoce que ha escuchado como quien oye llover los rumores de la infidelidad de la mujer que ama. De hecho, sostiene que lo que más le duele no es su infidelidad sino las murmuraciones—el cuchicheo—de los demás. El hablante de "Cartas del verano" deduce de las insinuaciones de los demás que la mujer que ama ya no lo quiere. Ahora que sabe la verdad, se encuentra solo en su pueblo, todavía enamorado de ella.

Varias de las bachatas de Veras contrastan la belleza interior y exterior. En "Tu belleza interior", el narrador enfatiza que se enamoró de la belleza interior de la mujer que ama. En contraste, la voz masculina de "Cirugía en el alma" critica la obsesión de la mujer con su apariencia física. Mantiene que le hace falta una cirugía en el alma para que cambie de opinión y para ganarse de nuevo su amor. Su tema clásico y encantador, "El molde", une la belleza interior y la exterior por medio de la noción de romper el molde con el que la hicieron. Este narrador enumera las características físicas y la calidad angelical y divina de su amada e insiste que su creador rompió el molde que usó para formarla para que no hubiera ninguna imitación.

Las bachatas de Veras también contemplan la otra cara de la moneda, o sea, el desamor y la pena. El narrador de "Inténtalo tú" se encuentra incapaz de olvidar a su amada, y está convencido de que ella tampoco logrará olvidarlo. En "Duele", la voz narrativa se queja del trato que le hizo su amada y observa que a muchos animales los tratan mejor. Enfatiza lo mucho que sufre y le advierte que ella sabrá cómo se siente algún día. En contraste, el narrador de "Sobreviviré" está confiado de que va a olvidar a su antiguo amor. Enumera todo lo que él y otros ya han superado—incluyendo que su papá sobrevivió el Trujillato—y jura olvidarla, aun si eso significa que tiene que aprender a amar otra vez. El tema "Te solté" retrata la alegría casi eufórica del narrador al encontrarse libre de la mujer que lo hacía sufrir. Ahora, ya no la quiere y piensa vivir por él mismo.

El lugar de Joe Veras entre los grandes de la bachata es incuestionable y, empleando el vocablo comúnmente pronunciado en sus canciones para describir su bachata, "inconfundible". Su álbum *Carta de verano* figura entre los 100 álbumes publicados desde 1950[6] y reconocidos por la Asociación de Cronistas de Arte como esenciales. El periodista Máximo Jiménez, ex-presidente de ACROARTE y quien encabezó la comisión evaluadora de dicho listado, observa que, "Joe Veras no podía quedarse fuera de esta lista y *Carta de verano* es, sin duda, el disco que mejor define su estilo: canciones románticas, arreglos muy bien logrados y un cancionero que logró dimensionar su carrera dentro y fuera de RD. Con este álbum, Veras hace sus aportes para que los bachateros de su generación lo tomaran en cuenta como referencia importante dentro del género".[7] Sus letras románticas y su estilo refinado también inspiraron a nuevas generaciones de bachateros.[8] Las bachatas de Veras siguen entre las más sonadas en la radio[9] y están incluidas en los álbumes de compilación de las mejores bachatas del año.

Frank Reyes

Frank Reyes, "el Príncipe de la Bachata", es uno de los bachateros más exitosos entre los que optaron por el romanticismo y una gama más amplia de temas a principios de los 90. Tal como hicieron muchos otros bachateros, Reyes dejó su vida en el campo por la de Santo Domingo a los doce años, donde trabajaba en lugares diferentes antes de poner su propio colmado, en el que eventualmente conoció al productor Juan Genao, quien le grabó su primer álbum, *Tú serás mi reina*, en 1991.[10] Las canciones de Reyes en este y sus álbumes posteriores subieron rápidamente los peldaños de la popularidad. Se posicionó de manera definitiva en el mundo de la bachata con *Cuando se quiere se puede* en el 2004, álbum que le cosechó cuatro Premios Casandra en el 2005.[11] Reyes todavía es uno de los bachateros más populares[12] y "que más temas ha pegado".[13]

Las bachatas de Reyes abarcan toda una gama de sentimientos y temas. "Se fue mi amor bonito", uno de sus primeros éxitos, revela una visión menos dramática del amor y del amor perdido. El narrador de este tema relata la historia de un amor no correspondido y del abandono. Es evidente su tristeza ante la partida de su amada, pero el tono y la selección de palabras en general son menos cortavenas. Esta voz narrativa no le guarda rencor y le desea lo mejor, pues dejarla ir se convierte en su propia manera de amarla. Este mismo tema de un amor no correspondido se va desde un nivel personal hasta otro global en "A quien tú quieres no te quiere". Aunque el narrador comparte su propia historia de amor y abandono, contempla su sufrimiento dentro del misterio universal de por qué queremos a los que no nos quieren. "Princesa" retrata la historia tierna de un amor colegial que ya se maduró. Ya un hombre hecho y derecho, el narrador se encuentra asombrado por su belleza y le pide que sea su reina.

El desamor y las relaciones conflictivas aún son temas populares en la bachata de Reyes, aunque las intrigas son más complejas que las de las primeras bachatas. "Cuando se quiere se puede" combina un dicho aparentemente motivador con la incapacidad del hablante de olvidar a la mujer que ama. "Tú eres ajena" trata una doble traición por parte de la mujer. Este narrador se entera demasiado tarde de que se enamoró de una mujer que ya está con otro. Aunque la ama y se siente engañado, observa sabiamente que ella podría engañarlo a él también y renuncia a la relación. "El alcohol" retrata el alcoholismo del narrador como el culpable de destruir la relación. Le suplica a la mujer que lo perdone por las cosas duras que le dijo, e insiste en que hablaba el alcohol. La bachata romántica de Reyes también revela que a veces es mejor terminar una relación. En "Nada de nada", la voz narrativa explica como sufría cuando lo dejó su amor. Ahora, ya no la quiere, y ella decidió demasiado tarde que se equivocó. Su éxito, "24 horas", también retrata a un hombre que está listo para ponerle fin a una relación corrosiva. Este narrador le dice a su antigua amada que siga su propio camino, y le da a su propio corazón el plazo de veinticuatro horas para olvidarla.

La música de Reyes también aborda las realidades de la comunidad transnacional dominicana. El tema "Extraño mi pueblo" enfatiza la soledad de estar separado de la patria y la familia por querer crear una mejor vida para los niños. Las promesas de volver un día, cantadas con vibrato, resonaban con muchos migrantes dominicanos y de otros países que han vivido en carne propia esta misma situación; de hecho, la universalidad de este tema le sirvió de inspiración a Reyes.[14] Aunque su canción, "Amor a distancia", no menciona específicamente la diáspora, su situación básica— olvidar a una persona amada que uno dejó atrás—es común para algunos migrantes. El propietario de Alex Music en Santiago, Alex Sanche, señala la pertinencia del tema del amor a larga distancia, además de la interpretación agridulce de Reyes, como los ingredientes que hicieron que "Amor a distancia" fuera una de las bachatas más pegadas de 2012–2013. Mientras escuchábamos esta canción en su tienda, observó él, "Esta canción es muy buena. Tiene melodía, tiene letra. Es una bachata de alguien que vivió afuera, esa es la distancia ... y terminaron".[15]

Además de un contenido más variado, Reyes también ha experimentado con el sonido de la bachata. A principios del nuevo milenio, emprendió un proyecto ambicioso: la bachata de orquesta. Su "Bachata de Gala", concierto del 2002 en el Hotel Jaragua de Santo Domingo, fue todo un éxito de taquilla. Este evento histórico en que una orquesta completa tocó bachata es indicativo de la creciente aceptación de la bachata y su popularidad entre un blanco de público más amplio. Las bachatas de Frank Reyes siguen encabezando las listas de las canciones más sonadas,[16] y Cruz Hierro lo señala como uno de las diez figuras influyentes de los primeros 50 años de la bachata.[17]

Yóskar Sarante

Yóskar Sarante nació en 1970 y creció en Villas Agrícolas, un barrio capitaleño. Trabajaba de limpiabotas cuando era niño, y como joven, en la construcción.[18] Cantó en varias agrupaciones de merengue antes de emprender su carrera como solista de bachata en 1994.[19] Durante varios años, seguía trabajando en la construcción para ganarse la vida antes de que pegara su tema, "La noche", en el 1999.[20] Su voz y su interpretación emotivas contribuyeron a su éxito continuo, no solamente en República Dominicana, sino también en Europa, los Estados Unidos y mundialmente.

La bachata de Sarante trata una variedad de temas románticos que canta en un vibrato claro y trémulo. Su susodicho éxito, "La noche", gira en torno a una serie de antítesis que contrastan la noche, cuando el narrador recuerda a su amada y sueña con sus momentos felices, con el día, cuando todo está claro y recuerda su ira a su partida. La articulación de "la noche" además del acompañamiento de guitarra le prestan un tono misterioso a la canción, así enfatizando el contraste entre lo que cree el narrador en la oscuridad y la dura realidad a la luz del día. "No tengo suerte en el amor" presenta una introspección pensativa que pinta el amor como una fuerza incontrolable y contrasta lo bonito del amor con el dolor que le puede traer. Aunque este narrador sufre del amor no correspondido, espera encontrar el verdadero amor algún día. La voz narrativa de "He tenido que llorar" también reconoce que el amor va de la mano del dolor. Acepta que tiene que llorar, pues aún ama y extraña a su amada, y no puede olvidarla. "Llora alma mía" trata de una conversación entre el narrador y su alma. Sufre y llora por la soledad y su incapacidad de cambiar las cosas, y le ruega a su alma que lo libre de su adiós venenoso. "Guitarra" se trata de un apóstrofe a la guitarra en que el narrador le pide que hable por él para convencer a su amada de que vuelva. Esta letra reitera el vínculo entre el cantante, el sentimiento y el instrumento, vínculo que se articula con frecuencia cuando un cantante le pide a la guitarra que llore por él.

Yóskar Sarante se considera esencialmente un romántico, y relaciona el contenido de sus temas con el predecesor de la bachata, el bolero. Según él, siempre habrá un espacio para las canciones de amor, mientras exista el amor.[21] Sigue pegando bachatas con su fórmula romántica, tanto en su país como en el exterior.

Luis Miguel del Amargue

Luis Miguel del Amargue entró en el ámbito bachatero con su primer álbum en 1994. Es irónico que haya gozado de un primer éxito en Europa, y especialmente en España, antes de pegar en su patria y en los Estados Unidos.[22] Su romanticismo envuelve los temas bachateros tradicionales en imágenes más tiernas. Por ejemplo, la soledad está personificada en "Se acabó lo bonito" y se burla de la voz que lamenta el pasar de todo lo bonito de su amor. En contraste con las primeras bachatas, este narrador no le echa la culpa a nadie por esta creciente indiferencia. "Abrázame amor" retrata a una mujer que piensa irse para seguir sus propios sueños y a un narrador que no piensa detenerla. De todos modos, este le suplica que lo abrace y que le haga el amor una última vez. El hablante de "De rodillas" enfatiza su verdadero arrepentimiento por engañar a su amor y le suplica de rodillas que lo perdone. De la misma manera, el narrador de "Teléfono ocupado" admite que cometió un error. Insiste que no es más que un teléfono ocupado sin su amor. "Sal de mi vida" presenta un paradigma opuesto: este narrador reprende a su amada por trastocar su vida, primero con su amor, y luego con su engaño.

Luis Miguel del Amargue sigue cosechando éxitos internacionales por su voz dulce, sus letras románticas y su interpretación. Su trayectoria es indicio de los crecientes y distintos mercados que disfrutan la bachata por todo el mundo. Luis Miguel ha protagonizado conciertos y festivales europeos, tales como el Festival Latinoamericano en Milán y El Gran Bachatazo en Madrid, los dos en el 2008.[23] Lo reconocieron por su desempeño en el género en el *Dominican Heritage Festival* (el Festival de la

Herencia Dominicana, Nuevo Jersey) en el 2012.[24] Además, fue nombrado el Bachatero del Año en su patria.[25]

Zacarías Ferreira

Zacarías Ferreira, otra nueva estrella de los 90, continuó con estas tendencias románticas, y extendió el alcance del romanticismo por la profundidad de sus letras y arreglos.[26] Creció en el campo del Cibao, pero en contraste con la gran mayoría de los bachateros que le precedieron, Ferreira sí estudió música formalmente en el Conservatorio Nacional de Santo Domingo antes de unirse a la orquesta de la empresa Brugal.[27] Su apodo, "la Voz de la Ternura", es una descripción acertada de su estilo de interpretación. Ferreira publicó su primer disco como solista, *Me liberé*, en 1997, y fue galardonado con un Premio Casandra.[28] Su disco de 2000, *El triste*, afirmó su lugar entre los bachateros románticos del nuevo milenio, lugar que ha mantenido con sus éxitos posteriores.

Aunque las bachatas de Ferreira siguen tratando los distintos aspectos del amor y del desamor, con frecuencia se encuentra que la voz narrativa masculina se siente indecisa con respecto al amor, y/o que le desea a un antiguo amor lo mejor después de que terminan. Por ejemplo, el narrador de "No hay mal que por bien no venga" contrasta su amor puro con la falta de sinceridad por parte de la mujer. Aunque ella no sabía valorar sus sentimientos, todavía le desea lo mejor y espera que sea feliz. "La avispa" también retrata a un narrador comprensivo que le desea bien a una mujer cruel. El narrador de "Es tan difícil" reitera que no puede olvidar a su antiguo amor. Son inútiles sus esfuerzos por olvidarla, pero admite que no está seguro de quién tiene la culpa por su amor fracasado. "Quédate conmigo" presenta una separación inminente. No obstante, aún queda un rayito de esperanza, pues la voz narrativa le suplica a su amada que le diga que no piensa irse, o que va a volver—aun si, a fin de cuentas, no es verdad.

Las relaciones amorosas son multifacéticas en la bachata de Ferreira. El narrador de "Me ilusioné" describe el flechazo que se le dio y el amor que siente. Le ruega a la mujer que ama que le dé una oportunidad que le alivie el sufrimiento que padece y que lo mata poco a poco. En "Me sobran las palabras", la voz narrativa celebra el amor que siente crecer dentro de él. La letra directa y sin adornos de este tema extiende un paralelo con su título, y la interpretación romántica de Ferreira hace hincapié en que efectivamente, no es necesario un exceso de palabras para expresar el amor. El amor no correspondido es la base de "Dime que faltó". El narrador no le culpa a su antiguo amor el haberlo dejado, sino que reconoce que ella tiene el derecho de ser libre y hacer lo que quiera. Así, su pregunta sirve de un adiós. Esta bachata romántica contrasta con los temas anteriores que les recriminaban a las mujeres y que las presentaban como propiedad del hombre.

En otras canciones, el narrador toma una decisión deliberada de rechazar el amor. "Como amigo sí, pero como amor no" presenta a un narrador que insiste que está mejor como el amigo de una mujer. Cree que va a conocer el amor un día, pero a la vez, admite que tiene miedo de enarmonarse en este momento. De la misma manera, "Un buen amigo que un mal amor" contempla la pregunta: ¿cuál es mejor, una buena amistad, o una relación romántica que termina mal? El narrador se refiere a los sabios consejos de otros que ya han sufrido por tal error, y opta por la libertad de la amistad en lugar de estar encarcelado en una mala relación.

La popularidad de Ferreira no se ha disminuido desde que sacó su primera canción. Su álbum, *Dime que faltó* (2007), estableció su papel de bachatero romántico y su sonido individual. Este álbum figura entre los 100 discos esenciales identificados por ACROARTE, ya que no solamente pegó entre los aficionados de Ferreira, sino que la crítica lo acogió también.[29] Su variedad lírica y su interpretación romántica siguen atrayendo a públicos por todo el mundo, tanto en persona como en la radio.

El Chaval de la Bachata

Linar Espinal, El Chaval de la Bachata, es producto del barrio santiaguense, Pekín. Su interés por la bachata se desarrolló al escuchar a Blas Durán. El Chaval publicó su primer álbum como solista en 1997, después de haber grabado dos álbumes con otras agrupaciones. Desde ese entonces, interpreta bachatas que tratan una gran variedad de temas en su voz única y un poco ronca.

La bachata de El Chaval trata de todo un espectro de temas románticos. Su versión bachatera de "No molestar" (2011) presenta la súplica del narrador para que su amada se aleje con él a un lugar en donde nadie los interrumpa. Varios temas del cantante son observaciones de la naturaleza humana y las relaciones. En "¿Dónde están esos amigos?", el narrador explica cómo lo abandonaron sus supuestos amigos y las mujeres que amaba cuando se desintegró su estabilidad financiera. La voz narrativa de "Por el maldito dinero" también lamenta los males del dinero. Este le echa la culpa de haber perdido a su amada a su falta de dinero. En "El golpe avisa", el narrador le advierte a su público que preste atención para evitar una catástrofe en la vida y en el amor, aunque es posible que tenga que aprenderlo a base de cometer errores. "Maldita residencia" refleja los sentimientos de un hombre que se queda en su país mientras su esposa emigra a Nueva York con sus hijos. Además de la separación familiar, esta canción pinta las otras realidades de muchos migrantes: ella puede migrar porque la patrocina un familiar, o sea, su mamá, y él no puede seguir la por no tener una visa. Se queda aún más insatisfecho por las posibilidades disponibles de comunicarse con su familia—una que otra llamada de teléfono o alguna interacción por el Facebook— y le suplica que no lo olvide allá en Nueva York. Esta canción fue inspirada por lo que vivía un amigo del músico, y pegó durante su primer mes de difusión en las emisoras, convirtiéndose en un himno para muchos.[30]

El Chaval es popular tanto en el país como en el exterior por la variedad lírica y su sonido individual. Ha realizado muchas giras por Europa, no solo por España, sino también por países no hispanohablantes, tales como Francia, Italia, Alemania y Holanda.[31] Los temas que retrata son pertinentes a públicos mundiales que pueden relacionarse con las situaciones representadas en ellos. Su tema "¿Dónde están esos amigos?" le ganó un Casandra como la Bachata del Año y un Premio ASCAP (Sociedad Americana de Compositores, Autores y Productores) en el 2009.

Elvis Martínez

La bachata se disparó en las emisoras en Estados Unidos en 1998 con Elsido "Elvis" Martínez, "el Camarón / el Jefe". Oriundo de San Francisco de Macorís, Martínez creció en el seno de una familia musical y participaba en agrupaciones locales antes de formar la suya. En 1998, su canción "Así fue" fue la primera bachata programada en las emisoras radiales de la corriente dominante de música tropical en Estados Unidos.[32] Martínez describe la pegada tan amplia del tema como "un escándalo internacional", y el guitarrista Lenny Santos quien tocaba en la canción, señala su pegada como el momento decisivo de la bachata en su entrada en la programación radial dominante.[33] "Así fue" entreteje los dos temas del amor y del amor perdido. En esta canción, la voz masculina le explica a su antiguo amor que ya la olvidó y encontró un nuevo amor. Tanto el contenido del tema como la interpretación tierna de Martínez hicieron que la canción le fuera accesible a un público diverso, y abrió el camino para otros.

Las bachatas de Martínez retratan una selección diversa de temas. El amor romántico sigue como tema común, pero desde múltiples puntos de vista. Por ejemplo, la voz narrativa de "Yo te voy a amar" declara sus sentimientos y promesas de amor eterno con imágenes clásicas: para él, la mujer es su aliento, alma, presente y futuro. En contraste, el narrador de "Así te amo" se enfrenta a los estereotipos asociados con su vestimenta urbana (pantalones jeans y aretes), mal vista por los padres de su amada. Enfatiza las diferencias entre el mundo exterior y el interior en donde residen sus sentimientos, los cuales son más poderosos que la apariencia. En otros temas, la voz narrativa declara su amor y prueba el terreno de una nueva relación. El narrador de "La luz de mis ojos" subraya sus sentimientos y le pide a su amada que le revele los suyos. De igual manera, la voz de "Dime" expresa su amor sin rodeos e insiste en que la mujer le diga por qué esconde su amor por él. Dos bachatas de Martínez representan una iniciación en el arte de amar. Su éxito del 2001, "Maestra", retrata a un joven que le suplica a una mujer mayor que le enseñe el arte de amar. "Profesor" hace una referencia intertextual y juguetona al contenido de la otra canción, y ahora, el joven es perito—un profesor—en el amor, y le ofrece a una jovencita enseñarle todo lo que sabe.

Las bachatas de Martínez dibujan el desamor tanto tradicional como innovadoramente. En "Tú sabes bien", la voz narrativa insiste que no podrá seguir si su amada lo deja. Emplea imágenes tradicionales de lágrimas, una sensación de vacío, y soledad para hacer hincapié en su desesperación. En contraste, el enojo es el sentimiento predominante de "Amada mía", pues el narrador maldice a una mujer infiel por engañarlo con su mejor amigo, y también se culpa por su propia ceguera ante sus acciones. "Ambición" pinta a una mujer ambiciosa que prefirió lo material al amor sincero. "Yo no nací para amar" intensifica los temas de la indiferencia y la soledad. El narrador de esta canción describe como veía a todos sus amigos enamorarse sin poder encontrar el amor él mismo.

Dos de las bachatas de Martínez contemplan los temas de estar lejos de un ser querido durante las Navidades y la soledad resultante. "Esta Navidad" y "Triste Navidad" subrayan la distancia, la separación y la soledad. Aunque no se dice específicamente que una parte vive en el extranjero, por este énfasis en la separación, además de la tendencia de muchos migrantes dominicanos de volver al país para las Navidades, la migración es un marco verosímil para estas canciones.

El tema "Juancito Nadie" presenta a un personaje único, o sea, el palomo. Este niño marginado narra un día común en su vida, el cual incluye vender flores en la calle y husmear de vez en cuando el cemento para escaparse de su dura realidad. Los videojuegos y los superhéroes no figuran en la realidad de este niño, pero perder una comida y los golpes del novio de su mamá, sí. La figura de Juancito Nadie, un niño de ocho años con las vivencias de alguien de ochenta, recuerda a los oyentes que su realidad será la realidad futura del país. A fin de cuentas, este niño del barrio popular no puede ignorarse, igual que la bachata.

Además de la variedad temática de su bachata, Martínez varía su presentación según su público:

> Yo no puedo hacer música para tan solo un público. La bachata que disfruta la República Dominicana es una bachata calurosa, una bachata bailable…. En otros mercados, les gustan las bachatas románticas, suavecitas, calladitas…. En Europa, ya hay que hacer música con un poquito de tecno…. Hay que cantar y hacer arreglos para diferentes mercados.[34]

Martínez también reitera la importancia de la evolución del género. Martínez se interesó originalmente en la bachata por lo que oía durante los 90, y señala los cincuenta años de su historia para encontrar sus influencias en él y también el futuro del género:

> Esas personas como Calderón, Luis Segura, como Paniagua, todos esos exponentes … Antony Santos, Luis Vargas, Raulín, entre otros … ellos hicieron también un trabajo extraordinario. Pero si se quedan allí, yo estoy cien por ciento seguro que la bachata no sigue creciendo…. Tiene que haber relevos para que sigan los géneros creciendo. Si no existen los relevos, puedo asegurarte que el género se va a estancar en este lugar en donde está.[35]

Martínez ha experimentado con una instrumentación variada y con mezclar otros géneros, tales como el techno, el *hip-hop* y el cha-cha-cha, por este proceso natural de cambio. El sonido, el contenido y el estilo interpretativo tierno de Martínez se juntan para contribuirle a su pegada internacional.

Monchy y Alexandra[36]

El romanticismo de principios del nuevo milenio encontró una voz popular en el dúo mezclado de Monchy y Alexandra; estos figuraban de manera importante en la aceptación de la bachata más allá de la República Dominicana. Monchy (Ramón Rijo) y Alexandra Cabrera estrenaron con su éxito de 1999, "Hoja en blanco", una versión en bachata de un vallenato colombiano popular que narra el cuento de dos amantes cuyas vidas van por rumbos distintos. Este y sus temas subsiguientes fueron éxitos internacionales y ayudaron a llevar la bachata mucho más allá de las fronteras dominicanas.[37] Aunque algunos criticaban su música, diciendo que se parecía más a la balada que a la bachata, los temas centrales de esta siguieron la tradición del amargue, pero presentados desde el punto de vista de una voz masculina y otra femenina en diálogo. Así, las situaciones se retratan como las dos caras de la misma moneda. Por ejemplo, los narradores de "Dos locos" declaran que tienen que estar locos por estar con otros cuando aún se aman. En contraste con este argumento, la pareja de

"Te quiero igual que ayer" admite que todavía se aman tanto como antes, y encuentran el perdón y la armonía al cantar juntos. De la misma manera, la pareja de "No es una novela" jura defender su amor de los de pensamientos negativos que tratan de escribir su historia de amor por ellos. El amor prohibido también es tema en las canciones del dúo, tal como es el caso de la pareja de "Perdidos", pues tienen que verse a escondidas y perderse en su propio mundo de amor.

Las bachatas románticas de Monchy y Alexandra rápidamente lograron una pegada internacional, y otros siguieron su ejemplo. Su álbum del 2002, *Confesiones*, se convirtió en un punto de referencia "de la mejor bachata que se produjo en la década de los 2000".[38] El dúo se disolvió en el 2009; no obstante, impactaron la producción y la acogida de la bachata de manera importante con sus letras románticas, sus canciones a dúo, y sus fusiones de otros sonidos y ritmos con la bachata.

Héctor Acosta "El Torito"

Héctor Acosta "El Torito"[39] empezó su carrera cantando merengue con la agrupación popular Los Toros Band en 1990. Fue su cantante principal por 15 años antes de emprender su carrera como solista de merengue y bachata. Las bachatas de Acosta siguen la tradición temática de amor y del amor perdido, temas retratados con imágenes refinadas. Por ejemplo, el narrador de "Tu primera vez" describe el acto sexual con la imagen eufemística de un barco que ancla en el cuerpo femenino. Sus relaciones no son un acto de pasión desenfrenado sino una decisión consciente y basada en el amor verdadero. "Primavera azul" presenta a un narrador que sufre del amor no correspondido; no obstante, su dolor es atenuado por las imágenes del amor como una luz que le guía y una primavera idílica que le promete a la mujer que ama. Las imágenes naturales hacen que el sufrimiento sea menos inaguantable en "Perdóname la vida". La unidad de la naturaleza recuerda al narrador su propia soledad, pues ve el abrazo que comparten la orilla del mar y el beso que le dan los pájaros al cielo después de escampar. El pasar del día no le trae ningún alivio, y le suplica a su amada que le perdone la vida.

La culpa y pedir perdón son temas comunes en las bachatas de Acosta. En "Sin perdón", el narrador admite sus errores y busca perdón. Su amada le sermonea acerca del amor y del perdón, y aunque lo perdona, ya no se confía en él. La voz narrativa de "Me duele la cabeza" también reconoce que se equivocó al mentirle, engañar y dejar a su amada. Ahora, sufre los dolores físicos de su malestar sentimental. En "No soy un hombre malo", el narrador reconoce su infidelidad, pero mantiene que no merece la indiferencia de su amada y que ella será responsable por su muerte si lo deja.

Aunque varios merengueros han grabado bachata, pocos tuvieron el éxito que ha tenido Acosta en aceptarse como bachatero. Aunque este sigue grabando ambos, merengue y bachata como solista, más de un dominicano me informó, "ya es bachatero". De hecho, el bachatero Henry Santos señaló a Acosta como un ejemplo de un bachatero nato: "Héctor Acosta, El Torito—nació bachatero. Hacía merengue, pero cuando lo oí, me dije, este tipo parece bachatero.... Su voz, su sentimiento, su forma de cantar ... suena como un bachatero.... Entonces empezó a hacer bachata, y ya ves hasta dónde lo llevó".[40] Acosta fue reconocido con el Gran Soberano en el 2013, el galardón máximo de los Premios Soberano.

Conclusión

La bachata romántica de los 90 y del nuevo milenio sigue retratando las diferentes perspectivas del amor y del desamor, aunque ahora con una letra más suave y desde múltiples puntos de vista. Los bachateros ampliaron su contenido y contemplan las relaciones humanas en general, los temas sociales, y lo que significa ser parte de una comunidad transnacional. Los arreglos más complejos y las fusiones musicales acompañaron este acercamiento sentimental. Un contenido amplio y una interpretación más suave se prestaron a la creciente popularidad de la bachata y así, ayudaron a socavar su discriminación. El alcance de la bachata había llegado tan lejos para el 2003 que la Orquesta Sinfónica Nacional la tocó en una presentación especial, *Bachata sinfónica,* bajo la dirección de William Liviano. El trabajo de estos bachateros románticos sirvió como punto de partida para una nueva generación de bachateros en la comunidad transnacional dominicana en el exterior.

SIETE

La comunidad dominicana transnacional y la bachata típica

Un amigo, Darío, y yo le habíamos comprado un majarete a un vendedor ambulante en Washington Heights, Alto Manhattan, una tarde fría de diciembre. Mientras disfrutábamos de su dulce sabor, llevaba con mis pies el ritmo de una bachata que tocaban en un negocio que había cerca. Temblaba por el frío mientras miraba a mi alrededor, y me parecía que lo único que diferenciaba la escena de una calle en la República Dominicana era el frío glacial y la amenaza de nieve. Allí mismo, en medio de dicha escena, que tanto me recordaba el país, entendí concretamente lo que significa ser parte de una comunidad transnacional.

La migración dominicana hacia el exterior

Durante la Era de Trujillo, la migración dominicana hacia el exterior fue selectiva, pero las tendencias migratorias cambiaron de manera importante tras su muerte. Los Estados Unidos, y específicamente la ciudad de Nueva York, se convirtieron en el destino principal de los dominicanos. La inmigración incrementó con la agitación política tras la caída de Trujillo y cambios a la política migratoria norteamericana. La Ley de Inmigración y Nacionalidad Hart-Celler (1965) abolió el sistema de cuotas a base de la nacionalidad que había sido vigente desde los 1920, pero dispuso además que los inmigrantes latinoamericanos presentaran pruebas para demostrar que cumplían una necesidad laboral.[1] Los dominicanos continuaban inmigrando en números sin precedente por exenciones otorgadas a los parientes cercanos de los migrantes ya establecidos. Dichas exenciones establecieron la base para que las redes de parentesco fueran un elemento clave de la migración dominicana.[2] Aproximadamente el 75 por ciento de los migrantes eran de las zonas urbanas de la República Dominicana durante esos primeros años,[3] y la mayoría de los dominicanos que migraban a Nueva York en los 1960 y los 1970 eran de la clase media baja y trabajadora.[4] La población dominicana en Nueva York creció por más del 400 por ciento durante esa época.[5] En los 90, el número de dominicanos en los Estados Unidos subió vertiginosamente de 348,000 a 695,000, y otra vez entre 2000 y 2004, cuando vivían apro-

ximadamente un millón de dominicanos en los EE.UU.[6] En la actualidad, los dominicanos constituyen el cuarto grupo más grande de hispanos en los EE.UU.; solamente
los mexicanos, puertorriqueños y los cubanos están por encima.[7] Aunque Nueva York
todavía es el destino principal en los EE.UU., también hay comunidades dominicanas
importantes en Nuevo Jersey, Massachusetts y la Florida. Puerto Rico es otro destino
migratorio común, y sobre todo para los que inmigran ilegalmente por cruzar el Canal
de Mona en yola.[8]

Los inmigrantes dominicanos a los Estados Unidos mantienen fuertes vínculos
con su patria a la vez que se integran a la vida de este país. Por lo tanto, los dominicanos ejemplifican las características comunes del transnacionalismo con su "flujo
constante de gente en ambas direcciones, un sentido dual de identidad, compromisos
ambivalentes con dos naciones, y una red extendida de lazos de parentesco y amistad
que cruzan las fronteras políticas".[9] El vivir simultáneamente con un pie en dos mundos distintos se ha prestado a un sentido flexible de identidad entre estos migrantes.
Estas dos realidades son igual de importantes, pues los migrantes dominicanos "se
incorporan simultáneamente a dos comunidades nacionales ... los vínculos con la
patria eran parte del proceso de hacerse neoyorquinos, y el proceso de hacerse neoyorquinos ayudaba a constituir los vínculos con la patria".[10] Las operaciones económicas, y especialmente las remesas, los bienes raíces, e inversiones en pequeños negocios
dentro de la República Dominicana, y los dólares gastados en visitas al país ayudan
a fortalecer estos vínculos transnacionales.

La doble participación de los dominicanos en dos mundos se presenta ante una
distinción sicológica y verbal entre dos lugares que se solapan. Muchos migrantes
dejaron la isla originalmente con la intención de quedarse solo un tiempo en los Estados Unidos para volver eventualmente a su país para siempre. Aunque no suele ser
el caso, los lazos afectivos de los migrantes con su patria siguen fuertes y son reite-
rados por el lenguaje que emplean para describir su país y la nación anfitriona;
contrastan los EE.UU.—"aquí" o "este país"—con "allá" o "mi país".[11] Tales vínculos
nostálgicos con la patria siguen fuertes, aun entre los dominicano-americanos nacidos
en los Estados Unidos, y así revelan la manera en que "[l]as diásporas siempre dejan
las huellas de un recuerdo colectivo de otro lugar y otro momento, y crean nuevos
mapas de deseo y cariño".[12]

Soñar con y hacer visitas al país refuerza los lazos íntimos con la patria. La
Oficina de Turismo en Nueva York contribuyó a esta tendencia de volver con sus
anuncios comerciales animando las visitas navideñas. Se imaginaban y se representaban todos los aspectos de la industria turística con imágenes de lo que es considerado
típicamente dominicano, imágenes que servían como un imán para tocarles la fibra
sensible a los migrantes nostálgicos.[13] Numerosas agencias de viajes de propietarios
dominicanos en los EE.UU. facilitan los viajes de los migrantes al país. Estas ofrecen
vuelos económicos al país, y así incrementan la frecuencia con que los dominicanos
vuelven.[14]

Los lazos con el país se concretizan en los vecindarios dominicanos en EE.UU.,
tales como Washington Heights y el Bronx. Allí, los colmados, restaurantes y vende-
dores ofrecen productos, comida y artículos típicos dominicanos, y se oyen merengue
y bachata en las calles, negocios y casas. Los inmigrantes también se actualizan
con los periódicos y los medios dominicanos disponibles. Desde un principio, los

dominicanos en el extranjero crearon un intercambio intricado con los periódicos nacionales. No solamente leían los periódicos recién salidos de la imprenta cada mañana, sino que les contribuían como escritores. Tal como ha señalado Hoffnung-Garskof, las representaciones enviadas al país por los migrantes dominicanos para la prensa dejaron fuera muchas de las verdaderas dificultades a que se enfrentaban, y en su lugar enfatizaban las oportunidades y los ejemplos de éxito.[15] Los migrantes se hicieron autores y protagonistas de sus propios cuentos de éxito en los Estados Unidos, e hicieron realidad esos mismos cuentos cuando volvían al país con regalos, llevando una apariencia exterior de su progreso. Regalarles obsequios a los amigos y familiares afirmaba no solamente el éxito sino los continuos vínculos con la patria.[16] Desafortunadamente, el éxito no es común para muchos migrantes dominicanos, cuya situación económica no ha mejorado mucho en los EE.UU. Aunque muchos migrantes todavía viven bajo la línea de pobreza, sus compatriotas siguen dejando la isla en búsqueda de una vida mejor.

Las leyes dominicanas fomentan los vínculos políticos con el país. En 1996, la nueva constitución les otorgó el derecho a retener todos los derechos de la ciudadanía dominicana a todos los dominicanos que se hicieran ciudadanos de otro país. La constitución les permite todos los beneficios de la ciudadanía dominicana a los hijos de padres dominicanos que nacen en otros países.[17] En el 1997, el Congreso Nacional Dominicano aceptó permitir a los dominicanos que viven en el extranjero postularse como candidatos y votar en las elecciones presidenciales, decisión que ha estimulado todavía más participación en la política nacional.

A pesar de estos lazos, algunos en el país creen que los inmigrantes no tienen cultura, o sea, que no son dominicanos auténticos. Distinguen a los migrantes con los vocablos despectivos, "Dominican York" o "domínican". Estos se refieren a los que pierden su cultura (y por lo tanto, su capacidad de pertenecer) por ser inundados por la cultura norteamericana.[18] Se desarrolló la descripción del "dominicano ausente" para referirse a esos migrantes que no habían perdido su cultura o su dominicanidad esencial. Otros desdeñaban las remesas y los regalos que les eran tan importantes a muchos, usando otra palabra despectiva, "cadenú", una referencia a las cadenas que usaban muchos migrantes que volvían. Este vocablo "se refería específicamente a los artefactos culturales, o a los símbolos del poder del consumidor ... y más ampliamente aún a las pretensiones inspiradas en el extranjero de los dominicanos sin una verdadera cultura".[19]

A los migrantes dominicanos hacia los EE.UU. se les incluyen con frecuencia en el grupo general de personas de color, o se les identifica equivocadamente como puertorriqueños, ya que hablan español. Aunque los migrantes dominicanos tienen que enfrentarse a muchos de los mismos desafíos que estos grupos, no suelen alinearse con ellos.[20] Los migrantes dominicanos se alejaron de otros grupos minoritarios, y el idioma y la música se convirtieron en herramientas comunes para señalar estas líneas divisorias. Primero el merengue, y luego la bachata, sirvieron como señas musicales de identidad para los dominicanos, y los diferenciaban de otros grupos. A la vez, los ayudaban a enfrentarse a las ansiedades traumáticas de la migración al reforzar los lazos nacionalistas con el país. El creciente número de migrantes de la clase obrera que vinieron a Nuevo York en los 80 aumentó de manera significativa el número de seguidores que ya conocían la bachata, y así creció su público en el extranjero.

Los inmigrantes no solamente importaban estos géneros de la isla, sino que hicieron sus propias producciones de estos dos géneros dominicanos por excelencia, incorporando los ritmos y las vivencias de sus propias realidades. La bachata, con su tradición del sufrimiento, apelaba especialmente a los migrantes dominicanos en Nueva York:

> Si las asociaciones de la bachata con la clase baja anteriormente la hicieron odiosa a quien ambicionaba formar parte de la clase media, en Nueva York, donde los inmigrantes de diversos orígenes sociales compartían las experiencias semejantes de las penurias económicas y del desplazamiento social, tales presiones sociales empezaron a perder terreno ante el deseo poderoso de los inmigrantes por los sonidos más 'auténticos' del país.[21]

El repertorio sentimental de la bachata expresaba todas las perspectivas del sufrimiento y del anhelo, y atrajo como imán a los dominicanos en el exterior, especialmente a las mujeres.[22]

La bachata y la comunidad transnacional

La presencia de la gran comunidad transnacional dominicana en los EE.UU. les ofrece nuevas oportunidades a los bachateros tradicionales que viven allá. Estos presentan su música y los temas de otros en escenarios que varían entre fiestas de cumpleaños a bares y conciertos. Sus ingresos difieren por evento y varían desde una suma fija a cobrar por entrada.[23] El potencial de un tema depende también del mercado, pues "Si no pega allá [en República Dominicana], puede pegar aquí [en EE.UU.] Es local".[24] Esta sección retrata a tres bachateros radicados en Nueva York que siguen tocando y sacando la bachata tradicional en el exterior.

Ray Santana, "el Pollito del Cibao", nació en Dajabón en 1967. Su historia refleja los temas comunes a otros bachateros: su familia trabajaba la tierra, y desde los siete u ocho años, manejaba la finca de arroz. Recuerda escuchar a los grandes bachateros, tales como Eladio Romero Santos y Luis Segura, lo cual le hizo sentir curiosidad por la música. Empezó a tocar en las fiestas y los eventos locales en Dajabón, y después, se fue a Santiago, luego a la capital, y finalmente, a Nueva York, donde lleva más de una década. Ahora, toca en Nueva York, Boston, y adónde lo llamen.[25]

Pollito ha visto estallar el número de agrupaciones de bachata durante el tiempo que vive en EE.UU.: "Ahora hay más grupos de bachata que sitios para tocar".[26] A pesar de que crece el número de bachateros, la bachata ha sido un negocio lucrativo para Pollito: "Ya tengo unos cuántos años viviendo de la música, de la bachata.... Gracias a Dios pude comprarle su casa a mi mamá por la bachata".[27] Pollito fue galardonado como el Artista Bachatero del Año (Premios Too Much), y lo nominaron para Los Premios Latinos en el 2010.[28]

Rafy Burgos "el Cupido" es de una familia rural y humilde. Creció escuchando bachata con su familia: "A mi familia siempre le gustaba la bachata, siempre la escuchábamos".[29] También observó que no tenía acceso al merengue por falta del respaldo económico: "Tenía apenas lo suficiente para comprarme una guitarra. El merengue viene con muchos instrumentos caros. Solo los podían comprar aquellos muchachos cuyos papás decían, 'toma y cómprate un instrumento'. Yo no tenía ese apoyo".[30] Burgos se mudó a la casa de su madrina en San Francisco de Macorís cuando era adolescente para poder asistir a la secundaria. Trabajaba en una tiendita de día y estudiaba de noche, y en medio, se juntaba con un amigo que tenía una agrupación para cantar como corista.[31]

En 1997, Burgos se unió a la agrupación Tropical, y se fue en gira con ellos al exterior. Llegó a los EE.UU. en 1998 para presentarse, y se quedó para dedicarse a su carrera como solista. Publicó su primer álbum, *Flechando corazones*,[32] en 1999. Su segundo álbum, *Con el corazón flechado*, incluye una adaptación popular del merengue de Sandy Reyes, "Enamorar", de los 1980. Gracias en parte a este tema, nominaron a Burgos para un Premio Lo Nuestro como Revelación del Año en el 2003.

El bachatero y productor Gerson Corniel, oriundo de Salcedo, es de una familia rural que trabajaba la tierra. A los doce años, Corniel se fue para Santiago con su familia donde su papá puso un negocio. Corniel describió a su papá, un acordeonista, y a su tío como sus primeros ejemplos musicales. Su mamá apoyaba sus inclinaciones a la música desde joven y le fabricaba instrumentos.[33] Corniel dejó la escuela a los 15 años para trabajar y dedicarle más tiempo a la música. Se fue de Santiago para la capital y seguía tocando con diferentes agrupaciones, subiendo poco a poco: "Me fui escalando. Empecé tocando segunda guitarra, y después primera guitarra".[34]

Corniel recuerda cómo la bachata era discriminada y la etiquetaban como una música de la clase baja. Esos insultos de sus detractores no influyeron en Corniel: "No me sentía mal; me gozaba mi bachata ... porque eso era lo que tenía dentro de mí. Me sentía orgulloso de ser músico".[35] También recuerda los desafíos de grabar bachata sin poder acceder a los mejores estudios: "Ya es bien fácil para grabar. Antes, era todo el mundo metido en un cuarto con un solo micrófono".[36]

Las canciones de estos artistas siguen la tradición bachatera de pintar los diferentes matices del amor y del sufrimiento. En "Ante una flor" de Gerson Corniel, la voz narrativa reconoce que tiene que dejar libre a su amada y que volverá si su amor es verdadero. Mientras tanto, le promete amarla y no olvidarla jamás. El narrador de "Enamorar" de Rafy Burgos se niega a renunciar a la mujer que ama, sin importar cuánto se resista ella. Este narrador le ofrece el corazón y le suplica que le ponga fin a su sufrimiento por corresponderle.

El desamor todavía es un tema importante también. El narrador de "Corazón enamorado" del Pollito del Cibao sostiene que es su corazón, y no él, quien sigue enamorado. Su corazón caprichoso se niega a olvidar a su amada, aunque está con otro, y pronuncia su nombre en cada latido. "Ella no me quiere" de Gerson Corniel relata la decisión del narrador de irse en lugar de seguir sufriendo por un amor no correspondido. En "Romeo y Julieta: La historia", Rafy Burgos le da una vuelta a la historia de Romeo y Julieta. Este narrador lamenta la desilusión de los románticos por todo el mundo cuando descubren que el amor de esa pareja legendaria no es eterno.

El éxito de Burgos del 2010, "Dame cabeza", vuelve a la tradición del doble sentido de la bachata. Esta canción gira en torno al doble sentido en su título, pues puede significar "pensar en algo", o literalmente, "dar cabeza". En esta bachata, el narrador admite que se enamoró una vez y sufrió por la infidelidad de su novia. Ahora, no busca una relación seria, y le dice "dame cabeza" a la mujer con quien habla, interprétese como se quiera.

"La travesía" del Pollito del Cibao entreteje el amor, el abandono y la inmigración. El narrador de este tema le suplica a su amada que lo lleve adondequiera que vaya. Más tarde, observa que nadie está conforme en su tierra ni contento con su suerte. Por fin revela que su amada era ambiciosa e inconforme con lo que él podía darle, así que trató de migrarse a Puerto Rico en una yola y murió en la travesía. Este narrador jura vivir bien para poder estar con ella en el cielo un día. Esta bachata cuenta una historia que recuerda muchos aspectos de la experiencia dominicana: el amor, la separación, la ambición, o la esperanza de un futuro mejor que se logra al inmigrar, cueste lo que cueste, a veces.

Conclusión

Las restricciones migratorias menos estrictas y una continua inestabilidad tanto económica como política contribuyeron al incremento de la emigración dominicana. A la vez, las redes de parentesco y los vínculos a la patria reforzaban la dominicanidad. "La bachata es una música de desarraigo",[37] y le dio voz a la experiencia de aprender a vivir, trabajar, amar y soñar en un mundo nuevo y en un entorno desconocido. Muchos de los inmigrantes se enfrentaban a las mismas condiciones sociales que conocieron los que se mudaron a las grandes ciudades de República Dominicana después del ajusticiamiento de Trujillo: los trabajos mal pagados, la pobreza, la discriminación—condiciones todas que son exageradas por el sentido de no estar en su elemento, "producto de la disonancia cognitiva insuperable e irrevocable de vivir donde *'yo no sé vivir'*".[38]

Los bachateros en Nueva York le entregan la bachata a un público creciente que busca vínculos con el país o que otras veces, solamente quiere divertirse. Tal como observó Rafy Burgos, "La música es un idioma internacional",[39] y la popularidad de la bachata cruza fronteras de clase, nacionales y lingüísticas y habla por sí misma. Los ingresos disponibles de los migrantes facilitaron su acceso al consumo musical, lo cual también aumentó la posibilidad de la bachata de lograr una viabilidad comercial. La posición social de la bachata se mejoraba a la par de la de los migrantes. Estos tocaban bachata en sus autos nuevos cuando volvían de visita al país, llamándoles la atención a las clases media y alta y así ayudando a la bachata a ganarse más seguidores y un mejor estatus en el país.[40]

La bachata norteamericana y la bachata moderna de la corriente dominante

La calle en donde se encontraba la dirección que me dieron estaba oscura y desierta cuando nos dejó allí el taxi a mi esposo y a mí, a eso de las diez de la noche. Percibí el sonido de sirenas en la lejanía, y también el del pulso inconfundible de la bachata latiendo en el aire tranquilo de la noche. Momentos después, el productor y bachatero Lenny Santos me explicó que ese ambiente le era integral a la bachata moderna, forma a la que él mismo ayudó a dar vida, y que sigue tocando y produciendo: "Nací y crecí en el Bronx, de hecho, a unas dos o tres cuadras de aquí. Ahora vivo en el norte del estado … [de Nueva York] … pero tengo mi estudio aquí, porque aquí me surgen todas las ideas … todo viene de aquí. No puedo hacer música en frente de los venados y las ardillas. Necesito oír las sirenas y el ruido".[1]

En tal ambiente, la bachata se ha evolucionado para expresar las realidades de estas nuevas generaciones de dominicano-americanos. Es una fusión de idiomas— las letras son una interacción del español y el inglés—y de influencias musicales como el *blues*, pop, *rock* y reggaetón que la complementan. Más tarde, los músicos enfatizaron "las progresiones del *R&B* y los efectos de sonido infundidos por el *R&B*" juntos al "ritmo marcado por un bombo durante toda la bachata"[2] para hacerla urbana. La pegada internacional de la bachata moderna y urbana ayudó a transmitir el género por todo el mundo.[3] La bachata moderna y de la corriente dominante es representativa de lo que significa ser dominicano dentro de un entorno transnacional y también influyó en un revaloración del género en su contexto tradicional.

La bachata en la diáspora

Aunque los hijos suelen rechazar la música de sus padres como algo pasado de moda, los jóvenes dominicano-americanos escuchaban cada vez más la bachata.[4] Con frecuencia eran aficionados en secreto, tal como sucedía en la República Dominicana. El bachatero moderno Henry Santos, que se graduó en una secundaria estadounidense en 1996, recuerda, "Uno veía a mis amigos de la secundaria escuchando bachata, pero a escondidas. Se escondían…. Aun en mi casa, recuerdo que mi papá me decía, 'En mi casa no se escucha bachata'".[5] Estos jóvenes dominicano-americanos aceptaban cada vez más la bachata como una música simbólica de sus raíces étnicas durante los 90,[6] escuchando y coleccionando las grabaciones de bachateros tales como Antony Santos, Luis Vargas, Joe Veras y Frank Reyes.[7]

Estos jóvenes aficionados no solo eran consumidores de la música sino que se hicieron bachateros también, y en sus manos y voces, transformaron la bachata típica con las influencias musicales y lingüísticas que los rodeaban para darle vida a la bachata moderna. Aunque estos músicos no eran de familias privilegiadas en el contexto norteamericano, sí tenían acceso a oportunidades que no tenían los bachateros en República Dominicana,[8] incluyendo ventajas lingüísticas que ayudaron a llevar a la bachata a un mercado más amplio: "nacieron y crecieron en Estados Unidos. Hablan inglés, conocen muchas más palabras cultas que esos muchachos del campo que no saben".[9] En sus manos, "la bachata tiene muda de piel.... Pero con la consciencia de lo que es la bachata original".[10] Su bachata se basaba en su comprensión y su interpretación de la esencia musical del género.[11] Henry Santos afirma, "Para hacer la bachata moderna, hay que conocer el alma de la bachata tradicional".[12]

Para estos inmigrantes, la vida también era una mezcla de idiomas, y el espanglish en las letras de la bachata moderna, más que un esfuerzo de mercadotecnia, es una realidad cotidiana. Lenny Santos describe esta mezcla de español e inglés como representativa de quiénes son: "queremos mostrarle a la gente que somos los dos. Somos americanos y latinos. Y queremos mostrarles de dónde somos, cómo nos criaron, nuestra cultura. Ya sabes, yo hablo espanglish".[13] Lenny reitera que tal cambio de código—"el uso alternado de dos idiomas"[14]—depende del destinatario: "Ya que tú hablas español también, sencillamente intercambio el español y el inglés.... Así es que lo hacemos con la música".[15]

Tal como sucede en la literatura, el cambio de códigos en la música "representa una realidad en la que hay segmentos de la población que viven entre culturas e idiomas".[16] Estos cambios no son el resultado de un uso descuidado del idioma, sino que reflejan las realidades de gente bilingüe que cambia de un idioma a otro para encontrar una palabra o frase que mejor exprese un pensamiento o concepto.[17] Tal como observa Grosjean, el cambio de códigos "también se usa como una estrategia social o de comunicación, para demostrar la participación en la conversación ... [y] ... para señalar la identidad del grupo".[18] El inglés es el idioma principal o de base para muchos de estos migrantes de segunda y tercera generación, mientras que el español es su segundo idioma. El bachatero Toby Love observa:

> Supongo que así nos criaron—hablamos español con nuestras familias, y en las calles con nuestros amigos, hablamos más inglés.... Ya tú sabes, muchos de mis amigos latinos no hablan el español con soltura, así que tengo que hablar inglés.... Quería devolverle la música a mi gente, de dónde soy.... Así es como hablamos normalmente.[19]

El cantautor Henry Santos describe el uso del espanglish como el resultado de las calidades rítmicas y melódicas de las palabras. Según él, el colocar las palabras con cierta melodía es "como un rompecabezas ... la melodía me dice ciertas cosas.... Y si está en inglés o español, verdaderamente no me puedo sentar y decirte, 'Te voy a escribir una canción en inglés ahora'. Porque así no funciona.... Nace por sí misma".[20] El unir las palabras al ritmo de la melodía es un proceso natural y orgánico que no se puede forzar.[21]

Todas estas innovaciones llegaron con su propia dosis de crítica y discriminación de los puristas. Algunos aficionados y músicos criticaban a los bachateros modernos por haber dañado su música con la inclusión del inglés, otros instrumentos, y diferentes géneros,[22] tal como hicieron los aficionados del bolero con las primeras bachatas. Otros la pensaban demasiado refinada y decían que le faltaba "grajo".[23] De todas maneras, la bachata moderna atrajo rápidamente a un grupo grande y fiel de seguidores entre los jóvenes dominicano-americanos y dominicanos, y también entre los públicos al nivel mundial. La creciente popularidad internacional de la bachata dio la vuelta para llegar a la República Dominicana por rutas transnacionales, y el poder del consumidor y las prácticas de consumo de los migrantes ayudarían a darle un empujoncito a la bachata para que terminara al frente del ámbito musical internacional.[24]

Aventura

Los cuatro miembros del grupo Aventura ofrecieron la primera expresión importante de la bachata moderna. Se proclamaron los *"Kings of Bachata"* (Reyes de la Bachata) o "K.O.B." y le dieron un nuevo sonido y una nueva cara a la bachata que son únicas a la experiencia de los migrantes dominicanos y sus hijos en Nueva York. Tal como muchos de sus aficionados, el cantante principal, Anthony "Romeo" Santos, el guitarrista y arreglista Lenny Santos, y el bajista Max "Mikey" Santos (Max Agende) nacieron en el Bronx; el cantautor Henry Santos nació en Moca, República Dominicana y migró a Nueva York a los trece años. Como adolescentes, eran aficionados de los innovadores de la bachata, Antony Santos y Luis Vargas, y de los bachateros románticos, tales como Joe Veras y Raulín Rodríguez.[25] Recuerda Lenny Santos, "La bachata empezó a gustarme después de oír a Antony Santos y a Luis Vargas tomar por asalto toda de la zona de Nueva York y a la comunidad dominicana. Ya esos otros hicieron su trabajo—gente como Paniagua y Luis Segura. Pero aquí, la gente estaba señalada, y todavía no formaba parte de la corriente principal".[26] El distanciamiento famoso entre Antony Santos y Luis Vargas le atrajo más atención a la bachata tanto en el país como en el exterior. Mientras Lenny escuchaba cada vez más bachata, la guitarra le llamó más la atención, y se preguntaba cómo los bachateros le sacan esos sonidos a su instrumento.[27]

Lenny empezó a ver videos de su ídolo, Antony Santos, incluyendo los videos personales de sus parientes que asistían a conciertos cuando visitaban la República Dominicana. Asombrado por el sonido de la guitarra, Lenny se compró una guitarra por veinticinco dólares en una farmacia local, y le pidió a su primo que le enseñara a tocarla. Lenny practicaba los tres acordes que le enseñó su primo y los tocaba mirando los videos y discos de Antony Santos, y también los de otros géneros tales como el *rock* y el *heavy metal*; siempre se esforzaba en imitar lo que veía en esos videos. En la medida que se desarrollaban sus capacidades, su deseo de presentarse en público seguía creciendo. Cuando aún estudiaba en la secundaria, formó su primer grupo, Sueños, con su hermano Max en el bajo, otro primo como cantante principal, y varios amigos que tocaban el bongó, la güira, el piano y la batería. En ese entonces, el grupo era un pasatiempo para Lenny, importante, pero no le parecía una posible profesión.[28]

El grupo practicaba en un club social puertorriqueño y tocaba frente a los negocios locales con una caja en el suelo para recibir cualquier dinero que dejaran los que pasaban por allí. Un día, el pianista de Lenny le habló de la posibilidad de incluir a un nuevo cantante en el grupo. Lenny recuerda que insistía ese amigo, "'Siempre está cantando. O sea, canta como un pájaro.... Tiene una voz dulce.... Es que suena tan único'".[29] Así que Lenny invitó al cantante, Anthony "Romeo" Santos, a practicar con el grupo, pero primero, Romeo lo visitó en su apartamento en el Bronx. Los dos compararon a sus bachateros favoritos en la escalera antes de que Romeo le ofreciera una muestra al cantar un tema de Antony Santos. "Estaba asombrado", recuerda Lenny. "Y con ese eco que te da un pasillo, estaba como, ¡guau! Este tipo suena fenomenal. Este muchacho es impresionante!".[30] Y así se unió Romeo a la agrupación.

El grupo dio su primera presentación en el club social donde practicaban. El evento era informal, sin publicidad ni un orden específico de canciones, y los dos cantantes principales se turnaban. Poco después, el primo de Lenny dejó el grupo, dejando a Romeo como el único cantante principal; el primo de Romeo, Henry Santos, se unió como cantante también. El grupo se cambió al nombre de "Los Tinellers", una pronunciación dominicana de la palabra inglesa *teenagers*, o "adolescentes". Tocaban bachatas conocidas en los eventos locales. Con el pasar del tiempo, empezaron a ensayar los temas compuestos por ellos mismos, y eventualmente, grabaron su primer álbum, *Trampa de amor*. Aunque no llegó lejos el álbum, eventualmente les abrió la puerta cuando Romeo se lo tocó al productor, Julio César. Este reconoció su talento, firmó un contrato con ellos, y cambió su nombre al grupo Aventura para representar la atracción nueva y fresca de un grupo de bachata compuesto por jóvenes dominicano-americanos. En 1999, Aventura sacó su álbum, *Generation Next,* el cual incluía nuevas versiones de varios de los temas de su primer álbum.

La música de Aventura refleja sus experiencias de crecer rodeados por múltiples idiomas, culturas y ritmos en el Bronx. Para los integrantes del grupo, la vida siempre era un *collage* de diferentes sonidos que los rodeaban en casa y en la calle.[31] Lenny Santos cita la presencia constante de la música en su vida como su motivación: "Me metí en la música porque por todas partes, solo se oía música. Sales, y oyes a la gente con la música subida en los autos ... *hip-hop*, *R&B*, música *rock*.... Pero en casa, oía música de merengue y bachata. Era una mezcla".[32]

Aventura aporta estos sonidos innovadores a su bachata, la cual se inspira mucho en los arreglos de Lenny Santos: "La primera persona que de verdad le metió sonidos a la bachata y que tenía el valor de cambiarlo todo, en términos de implementar los efectos de guitarra, y del *hip-hop* y *R&B*, fui yo—Lenny".[33] Lenny señala al bachatero Antony Santos como su influencia principal al crear el sonido nítido de punteo en las cuerdas, por bajarlas y tocarlas con el toque del pulgar.[34] Con este punto de partida, Lenny experimentó para crear su propio sonido al incluir la guitarra eléctrica, el pedal wah-wah (efecto que imita la voz humana) y el trémolo.[35] Lenny identifica los sonidos nuevos e innovadores, la instrumentación y los temas de su bachata moderna como los elementos que realmente la separan de la bachata típica: "Usamos más armonías... . Hay más *R&B* y *rock*. Usamos más instrumentos—sintetizadores y cuerdas—y ritmos en la bachata.... Somos los primeros que incluimos canciones sociales y temas actuales".[36]

Además de sus innovaciones musicales y líricas, Aventura mostraba una cara contemporánea y joven de la bachata sin perder nada del sentimiento tan importante para el género. La portada de su primer disco, *Generation Next* (1999), declara que el grupo representa "La nueva generación de la bachata", mostrándolos en jeans, con Romeo llevando una camisa blanca de manga larga desabrochada y Lenny, Henry y Max en camisetas blancas sin mangas. Este *look* se contrasta con las portadas de los primeros discos de bachata que mostraba a los bachateros como Rafael Encarnación en traje y corbata. El atuendo de Aventura, tanto en sus portadas como en el escenario, refleja ese *look* contemporáneo, con su vestimenta común de jeans, camisetas, sudaderas con capucha, cachuchas de béisbol con la visera plana o gorros, sacos informales, y chalecos. Cuando el grupo se vistió con traje y corbata para de portada de *K.O.B. Live* (2006), fue para enfatizar su imagen como líderes del último grito juvenil. Esta portada en blanco y negro mostraba al grupo con el corte de pelo *mop-top*, trajes de la época de los Beatles, y corbatas delgadas, lo cual enfatizaba su papel de ídolos. El sabor neoyorquino de la bachata de Aventura también se reitera con las portadas que hacen resaltar un trasfondo urbano y los edificios de Nueva York recortados contra el horizonte.

Para algunos aficionados puristas de la bachata, la instrumentación en los temas de Aventura, además se sus letras en espanglish y la inclusión de otros géneros como *R&B* y *hip-hop*, le ganaron la crítica y las quejas de que el grupo "'arruinaba nuestra música'".[37] Los de Aventura ni siquiera se inmutaron cuando les dijeron que no eran más que una *boy band* de la bachata, o sea un versión dominicana del grupo norteamericano N'Sync.[38] Siguieron adelante con su estilo innovador, y el título de su segundo disco, *We Broke the Rules,* es uno que responde a los que decían que Aventura había estropeado o desvalorado la bachata.

El *look* y el sonido de Aventura resonó con una generación joven de los consumidores dominicanos y dominicano-americanos, y también con un público latino más amplio y otro mundial. Tal como señala Larry Rohter, "Según el censo del 2010, la población hispana de los Estados Unidos asciende a más de 50 millones, lo cual los hace el grupo minoritario más grande de la nación. De los que tienen 18 años o menos … más del 90 por ciento nacieron en este país, y muchos son bilingües y biculturales".[39] Tal conexión con un mundo multicultural y multilingüe es esencial para la popularidad de Aventura en el contexto dominicano-americano. Leila Cobo de Billboard explica la atracción de Aventura por medio de un paralelo con la estrella tejano-americana, Selena Quintanilla, "'quien era de Tejas y le hablaba a la gente que se parecía a ella…. Romeo atrae a un público que se parecía a él y que no veía a otra gente como ellos en el escenario'".[40] Los temas comunes de la bachata—el amor perdido, la penuria, el sufrimiento, y el deseo de algo mejor—sazonados con los temas y las realidades del siglo XXI, resuenan con los hispanohablantes de diferentes orígenes. Cuando se toca por medio de las experiencias dominicano-americanas, el sonido único de Aventura apela a los migrantes en general.

Aun con las innovaciones instrumentales y la mezcla de idiomas y géneros, el estilo sentimental de larga tradición bachatera además de los temas del amor, pena y desilusión también están presentes en la música de Aventura. Por ejemplo, la voz narrativa de "Cuándo volverás"[41] canta de su abandono inmerecido, y se pregunta lastimeramente en dónde se encontrará su amor y cuándo volverá. De la misma manera, el narrador de "Por un segundo" lamenta su amor perdido, y describe su romance como un cuento de hadas en el cual él tiene el papel estelar del rey, y su amada juega el papel de una princesa. El hablante de "Dile al amor" conversa con Cupido y lo critica por no dar en el blanco con sus flechas encantadas. "Ella y yo" retrata la doble traición de la mujer y un amigo. En este reggaetón con Don Omar, un hombre tiene que enfrentarse a la realización amarga de que su mujer le fue infiel con su amigo. Antes de que se revele la verdad, el esposo disculpa las acciones adulteras de su amigo y le recuerda que vale la pena luchar por el amor, sobre todo si el esposo de su amante ya no la quiere. El esposo se retracta cuando la verdad sale a la luz. Así, esta canción presenta un doble estándar del machismo: seducir a múltiples mujeres es aceptable con tal de que no se trate de la mujer de uno.

El amor figura como tema central en otras canciones de Aventura. En "Un beso", el narrador relata como Cupido dio en el blanco con su flecha con un beso de su amada. De la misma manera, el poder redentor del amor es el enfoque principal de "Princesita". La voz narrativa admite que antes era un sinvergüenza que iba de flor en flor. Ahora, frente al amor purificador de la mujer, jura dejar esa vida atrás para crear un futuro a su lado. El amor del narrador se ha vuelto una obsesión en la bachata del mismo título, "Obsesión". Ya no tiene amigos y perdió el sentido de la realidad, y aunque insiste que lo que siente es amor, de la misma manera la mujer asegura que se trata de una obsesión.

Aventura también canta de las situaciones que reiteran los papeles sociales propios de cada género, tales como el machismo y el marianismo.[42] Su merengue, "Mujeriego". presenta los elementos centrales del machismo. La voz narrativa de este es la del conquistador por excelencia que admite que sale con dos mujeres a la vez. Se dirige a un grupo de oyentes masculinos y se perdona sus acciones al declarar que es mujeriego por haber nacido hombre, y sobre todo, por ser hombre dominicano. Insiste que Dios le dio esta característica, y se disculpa al insistir que no le miente a ninguna de las mujeres que seduce. Cuando sus oyentes lo reprochan, justifica sus acciones al indicarles que no es el único que tiene más de una mujer, y sigue con una lista de culpables.

Aventura abrió nuevos caminos al tratar temas sociales en su bachata. "No lo perdona Dios" relata la situación contemporánea de una mujer que tiene la libertad de optar por abortar a un hijo concebido fuera del matrimonio y en la pobreza; a la vez, subraya los papeles tradicionales de la familia y la importancia aún más amplia del papel de madre de la mujer. En esta canción, el narrador critica severamente a su pareja por decidir abortar, aunque ya no están juntos. Su selección de palabras la describe de ignorante, sin corazón e insensible. Declara que su antiguo amor mató a un inocente quien, como lo esperan muchos padres dominicanos, pudiera haber crecido para ser pelotero o bachatero; por toda la canción, enfatiza su pérdida y la oportunidad de ser padre que perdió. Pone en tela de juicio sus razones por abortar, las que dice ser excusas: su arrepentimiento por su amor fracasado y su deseo de no traer a un niño al mundo en la pobreza. Por lo tanto, "No lo perdona Dios", aunque presenta una situación contemporánea, refuerza los papeles y valores sociales tradicionales de ambos, hombres y mujeres.

"Amor de madre" apoya la construcción de la mujer como una madre que sufre y lo aguanta todo por el bien de su familia. En esta canción, una madre soltera se encuentra en apuros económicos. Descubre que no es suficiente el bienestar social, y se mete en la prostitución—su única opción, según la canción—para mantener a su hijo. Los esfuerzos de la madre de asegurarse de que nunca le falte nada a su hijo sirven para consentirlo: manejo un auto nuevo y ropa de la marca Armani. La madre tiene telarañas en los ojos con respecto a las acciones de su hijo, quien eventualmente está encarcelado por asesinato. En esta canción, se disculpan las acciones de la madre por su amor de madre, a la vez que se critica al hijo el no haber reconocido el cariño y el sacrificio de su mamá a tiempo. Juntas, estas representaciones refuerzan los valores tradicionales y propios de cada género.

En contraste, "Hermanita" critica la violencia doméstica. En esta canción, la voz masculina trata de hacerle ver a su hermana la realidad de su situación. La selección de palabras es directa y honesta, retratando ambos, el abuso físico y el emocional de la mujer golpeada. El culpable se retrata como un monstruo, una rata y un perro—un borracho cruel a quien no le importa nada su pareja ni sus hijos. A pesar de este ambiente violento, este tema aún reafirma los valores familiares, pues el narrador recuerda a su hermana que son familia y se ofrece para poner en su lugar al hombre abusivo.

El tema de la mujer sirena que lleva al hombre por mal camino es central en "Su veneno" y "Peligro". En "Su veneno", la voz masculina acusa a su amada de envenenarlo con sus besos y de quitarle su sano juicio y su sentido común. Ya no controla sus acciones ni sus decisiones y es incapaz de resistirse a su atractivo venenoso. En "Peligro", la mujer infiel es descrita como una serpiente peligrosa, una diabla vestida de mujer. Ella engaña al narrador inocente para aprovecharse de sus sentimientos y su dinero.

El Grupo Aventura fue muy exitoso al hacerle llegar la bachata a un público más amplio de la corriente dominante que incluye a anglohablantes. En septiembre de 2007, el grupo hizo historia al ser el primer grupo de bachata que tocó en Madison Square Garden.[43] Dos años después, Aventura logró otra primicia para la bachata cuando fueron invitados a presentar "Su veneno" ante el Presidente de EE.UU. y la Señora Obama en el concierto "Fiesta Latina", parte de una serie de presentaciones en la Casa Blanca norteamericana (*In Performance at the White House*). Aventura hizo resaltar sus raíces dominicanas—"Queremos compartir nuestra cultura dominicana con ustedes"—y su crianza en el Bronx—"¡Ya llegó el Bronx!".[44] Un producto único de la experiencia dominicano-americana, Aventura cumplió con la meta del programa Fiesta Latina: "celebrar el lugar de la música latina en el tapiz rico y lleno de colores que es la cultura norteamericana".[45]

En la actualidad, Aventura ha tomado lo que se ha llamado una "pausa".[46] Los cuatro integrantes siguieron sus propios caminos después de sacar su álbum, *The Last* (*El último*) (2009), el cual identificó ACROARTE como uno de los 100 esenciales[47] y que describió como "el mejor álbum de su transcendental discografía".[48] Estos artistas cambiaron por siempre el mundo de la bachata: "Fuimos los que innovamos la bachata moderna. Hicimos que la gente del mundo escuchara este ritmo que se llama bachata.... Se la enseñamos al mundo.... Ampliamos el mercado y lo abrimos".[49] El Grupo Aventura se disolvió, pero sus fundadores siguen influyendo en la bachata, como veremos a continuación.

Toby Love

Octavio Rivera, cuyo nombre artístico es Toby Love, nació en el Bronx, de padres puertorriqueños. Love es de una familia musical y describe el ambiente familiar como uno en donde "siempre había música, sea Navidad o un cumpleaños.... Así somos como familia".[50] Love empezó a tocar varios instrumentos de percusión antes de su estreno como cantante como un candelero en una producción musical de *La bella y la bestia* a los nueve años.[51] El papá de Love tenía un grupo de merengue, y Love lo acompañaba a sus presentaciones, tocando el bongó y la güira cuando era niño. Más tarde, Love cantaba y tocaba güira en su propio grupo de merengue.[52]

Empezó su carrera formal a los 16 años como cantante con Aventura, antes de que lanzara su propia carrera como solista en el 2006. Admite que la primera música que le gustó era el *R&B*, y también la música pop de Michael Jackson, aunque su familia escuchaba una variedad de géneros. Para Love, la bachata le significaba una respuesta dominicana al ritmo y amargue que tanto le gustaba, y cuando su amigo, Max Agende, lo invitó a ser parte del grupo, se unió sin firmar ningún contracto, cumpliendo los deseos de sus papás.

La bachata de Love combina el *rock* suave, el *R&B* y el *hip-hop* con la bachata y lo interpreta todo con su voz tierna. Love enfatiza que quería diferenciarse de Aventura con algo nuevo, así que cuando grabó un sencillo con el rapero Pitbull, le dio el nombre de "crunkchata".[53] Love describe su estilo como uno "más callejero" que el de la bachata tradicional y moderna.[54] Según Love, él empleó por primera vez el vocablo "urbano" en una entrevista para describir las fusiones con la bachata. Se pegó el nombre y ahora, se usa con frecuencia para referirse a toda la bachata moderna.[55]

La bachata de Toby Love contiene muchos de los temas comunes del amargue, mientras que con su apodo—"la Voz de la Juventud"—y su atuendo de última moda reitera una conexión con una nueva generación de consumidores de bachata. El desamor sigue como tema común, pero Toby Love lo canta en inglés y español. El narrador de "Lejos" condena a la mujer como una seductora cruel que lo hechizó y se aprovechó de él. Ahora, le dice que se ahorre sus lagrimitas de cocodrilo y que se vaya lejos. En contraste, el hablante de "Tengo un amor" sigue la tradición bachatera y del bolero de hablarle directamente a la mujer para quejarse de su abandono. El narrador de "Llorar lloviendo" también sufre del amor perdido. Revela que los hombres a veces necesitan llorar, por muy machos que parezcan. No obstante, pide que le caiga un aguacero para esconder la prueba de sus lágrimas, para que no sepa nadie que tiene el corazón roto. De esta manera, "Llorar lloviendo" sirve como un espacio seguro donde es socialmente aceptable que llore un hombre—o sea, una canción de bachata—y a la vez reitera que los machos esconden sus sentimientos.

El amor y la posibilidad de amar también son temas en la bachata moderna de Love. Su versión de *"I Just Can't Stop Lovin' You"*—"Todo mi amor eres tú"—del 2013 celebra los atributos de la mujer y el amor que comparte el narrador con ella. Aunque la voz narrativa de "Nueva York" perdió su corazón en alguna parte del mundo, aún abriga la esperanza de que encuentre a su amada otra vez en Nueva York—el lugar en donde se cumplen los sueños y se juntan todos los caminos. De la misma manera, el hablante de "Y volveré" tiene la esperanza de que amanezca un nuevo día que le ponga fin al sufrimiento de la pareja y un nuevo mañana a su amor.

La incertidumbre del amor es el tema central de otras bachatas de Love. "Casi, casi" retrata a un hombre cuya timidez le impide declararse. Este narrador no sufre del amor perdido sino del amor aún no realizado. En "Te parece poco", el cantante tampoco está seguro, aunque en este caso, surge su confusión de la aparente falta de aprecio de su amor por parte de la mujer. Enumera todo lo que ha hecho por ella, acciones que ella considera insignificantes.

Ahora, Love es uno de los nombres más importantes de la bachata moderna, pero admite que los aficionados de la bachata tradicional no aceptaban sus experimentos: "En el principio, los dominicanos tradicionales no aceptaban mucho lo que hacía, o sea toda la fusión del *hip-hop*, *R&B*, con la bachata.... Pero los jóvenes lo aceptaban".[56] De todas maneras, no se queja Love de la crítica:

> Siempre habrá crítica, pero sin la crítica, pues eso significa que no haces bien tu trabajo....
> Cuando empezamos algo diferente en este género, fue difícil de romper esos límites. Y ahora, la gente lo acepta por todo el mundo. Es verdaderamente increíble porque he estado desde el principio, la transición, hasta adónde ha llegado la bachata.[57]

Xtreme

El dúo de la bachata Xtreme estaba formado por los dominicano-americanos Danny D y Steve Styles, ambos nacidos en los EE.UU. Este grupo también salió en el 2004 y gozó de varios éxitos antes de disolverse en el 2011. Xtreme complementó la bachata con *hip-hop* y *R&B*, además de las interpretaciones sentimentales de los temas tradicionales de la bachata. En "Te extraño", por ejemplo, el narrador le habla directamente a la mujer de sus lágrimas y su sufrimiento, aunque lo ha dejado y ya no está presente en persona. Reitera su sufrimiento con imágenes de quemarse, del dolor y de la soledad. El desamor también es el tema principal de su colaboración con la actriz y cantante Adrienne Bailon en "No me digas que no". Esta canción presenta al dúo como una sola voz narrativa que conversa con su amada, pidiéndole que le explique por qué piensa irse. La voz femenina enumera sus transgresiones y niega amarlo. Entonces, cambia el enfoque y el narrador habla de su amada con la tercera persona, reiterando que lo deja a pesar de sus esfuerzos por reparar sus acciones.

Su canción "Shorty, shorty" representa la mezcla más fluida entre la bachata y el *hip-hop*. Este tema, cuyo título incluye un vocablo del *hip-hop* de referirse a una mujer bonita como *"shorty"* (bajita), depende mucho del cambio de códigos mientras el narrador relata la historia de sus esfuerzos por encontrar a la mujer que lo dejó. En toda la canción, le habla directamente a la mujer y le explica que sufre de insomnio y que muere sin ella. Tales imágenes de sufrimiento se entremezclan con las expresiones de la belleza de la mujer en español e inglés. Esta combinación fue un éxito, y "Shorty Shorty" subió al puesto número uno en la categoría de Sencillo Latino de la revista Billboard.

Xtreme también aportó su propio *look* a la bachata con sus caras jóvenes (ambos Danny D y Steve Styles nacieron en 1985), sus trenzas *cornrow*, los pantalones flojos y el accesorio común de Steve Styles, una banda para la cabeza. Los pasos de baile del dúo en sus videos musicales hicieron hincapié en este *look*. Por ejemplo, en "Te extraño", llevan jeans flojos, zapatos de tenis y camisetas blancos, y chaquetas de cuero negras. Presentan un número coreografiado de *hip-hop* durante el mambo, que hace resaltar sus pasos.

Xtreme señaló otra primicia para la bachata al participar en una serie de la televisión *reality* de ocho episodios para la cadena de cable en español, Mun2. Tal como sugiere el nombre del programa, *On the Verge* (*A punto*), se trataba que el grupo estaba a punto de llegar al éxito total, o de no llegar a ninguna parte. Tal como otros programas parecidos, este subrayaba los conflictos entre los dos cantantes al seguir su vida diaria y sus carreras musicales, tanto en el Bronx como de gira. Aunque Xtreme se disolvió, su sonido y su *look* aportaron mucho a la creciente popularidad de la bachata entre un público global.

Prince Royce

Prince Royce (nombre artístico de Geoffrey Royce Rojas) irrumpió en el mundo del arte en 2010 como solista con su bachata moderna, un cover en espanglish de la canción clásica de Ben E. King (1961), "*Stand by Me*". Nacido en el Bronx de padres migrantes dominicanos, las experiencias de Royce se asemejan a las de otros bachateros modernos y urbanos, pues creció con un pie en la música, el idioma y la cultura de dos mundos. Royce concretizó esta realidad con su versión de "Stand By Me", pues este mezcla de forma bilingüe la bachata y un clásico norteamericano. Siguió este primer éxito con otros de su álbum de estreno del 2010, y este llegó a ser el álbum latino de mayor venta en 2011; Royce ganó el premio Billboard como el Mejor Artista Latino Nuevo del 2011.[58] En su segundo disco, *Phase II* (2012), Royce mezcla otros sonidos y estilos con su bachata, tal como el de la música mexicana de mariachi en "Incondicional"; en otras canciones, abandona por completo la bachata para tomar la música pop y tempos bailables más rápidos. En el preludio ("Prelude"), la artista, La Bruja, habla al compás de tambores afrocubanos, narrando cómo Prince Royce llegó del Bronx a ser una estrella y cómo es un representante orgulloso de la dominicanidad. Royce también ha experimentado con otras fusiones con el grupo rockero mexicano Maná en "El verdadero amor perdona", con el salsero Luis Enrique en "Sabes", y con la cantante mexicana Thalía en "Te perdiste mi amor".

Con su voz enternecedora, su cara de niño, y su elegante forma de vestir—con frecuencia lleva sombrero—Prince Royce retrata la sinceridad cuando interpreta los temas románticos y tradicionales de la bachata en sus canciones del siglo XXI, muchas de las cuales son escritas por él mismo. En su éxito "Corazón sin cara", por ejemplo, el narrador reprende a la mujer que ama por preocuparse por su apariencia física y le recuerda que el verdadero amor es ciego. De la misma manera, el narrador de "Tú y yo" recuerda a su novia que son el uno para la otra, y le suplica que no les haga caso a las mentiras de sus amigas con respecto a su supuesta infidelidad. Tal como sugiere el título de "Incondicional", el narrador declara su amor incondicional. Mantiene que su amor es verdadero y desinteresado, y siempre va a luchar por él. De la misma manera, "Las cosas pequeñas" ensalza la belleza de los pequeños detalles, como un abrazo, un beso, o una mirada, que juntos constituyen el amor.

Prince Royce también canta al amor perdido. En "El amor que perdimos", el hablante se pone nostálgico por su antiguo amor. De la misma manera, "La última carta" se presenta como la última carta que le escribe el narrador a su esposa en un último esfuerzo por su perdón. La voz narrativa de "Mi habitación" está solo en su cuarto donde lamenta su amor perdido y su traición, mientras que reconoce su culpa de haber lastimado a su amada en "Te me vas". El narrador de "Memorias" recuerda cada aspecto de un antiguo amor. El timbre de esta canción, que se parece tanto a la música pop como a la bachata, hace que el desamor casi parece insensible.

La música de Prince Royce también tiene su dosis de machismo. En "Su hombre soy yo", el narrador recuerda a su novia que le pertenece a él. La reprende y le dice que lo respete. El tema pop/*rock* bailable, "Rock the Pants" (principalmente en inglés) es una declaración machista y urbana del dominio masculino a que hace referencia el narrador, asegurando que él es quien lleva los pantalones en la relación. En esta canción, el hombre declara que está harto de las preguntas de la mujer y piensa comportarse de tal manera que sus peores sospechas se hagan realidad. La reprende por no darle suficiente espacio, y se va para el club. Tal como un gallo que se pavonea, piensa volver locas a las mujeres en el club con sus movimientos hábiles en la pista de baile.

Prince Royce sigue siendo uno de los bachateros modernos más pegados. Su *look* y sonido le han cosechado nominaciones y premios, entre ellos, los Premios Billboard, Premios Lo Nuestro, Premios Juventud y los Latin Grammy. Los Premios Billboard de la Música Latina lo reconocieron como el Compositor del Año en el 2012, y se convirtió en el más joven en ganar este galardón a los 22 años.[59] Sus dos álbumes han llegado al número uno en las listas norteamericanas Latin y Tropical de Billboard. Fue el entrenador de voz para la participante ganadora, Paola Guanche, en La Voz Kids.

Romeo Santos

El antiguo cantante principal de Aventura, Romeo Santos, fue el primero de la agrupación en sacar un álbum como solista en el 2011, *Fórmula Vol. 1*. Este disco incluye la voz inconfundible de Romeo cantando sus bachatas características en espanglish, además de varios temas pop y *rock*, y varios músicos invitados: Usher, Lil Wayne, Mario Domm, la rapera La Mala Rodríguez, y el guitarrista flamenco Tomatito. El álbum tiene como marco dos escenas, el "Intro" y el "Outro" (juego de palabras que se refiere a una salida), que explican que la fórmula musical de Romeo es única y que se enfrentan a sus críticos. Por todo el material, Romeo sigue refiriéndose como el *King* (el Rey, pero ahora en forma singular) de la Bachata.

Las bachatas de Romeo tratan los temas comunes: el amor, el sufrimiento y el desamor. Su primer sencillo como solista, "You", celebra el amor y su poder para cambiar a un antiguo mujeriego a un hombre de una sola mujer. "Promise", a dúo con Usher, mezcla inglés y español por encima de una base de bachata. Esta canción retrata al narrador como un prisionero, condenado y atrapado en el cuerpo de la mujer. Aunque se trata de un dúo, la acción se plantea desde la perspectiva de un solo hombre. Por sus letras bilingües (Romeo canta en español y Usher en inglés), esta canción a dúo puede entenderse como una sola persona que se expresa en dos idiomas. "Mi santa" presenta el amor como si fuera una religión. En esta canción, el narrador le rinde culto a la mujer y promete comprobarle su amor ante desafíos, peligros y hazañas valientes. El tema depende mucho del simbolismo y del lenguaje religiosos, por ejemplo, oraciones, prender velas, ayunos y el sacramento del bautismo. En contraste con una santa, la mujer se pinta de diabla en "La diabla". Aunque el narrador reconoce que se arriesgó voluntariamente, esta mujer fatal es más lista que el hombre inocente y le gana en el juego del amor. "Soberbio" también hace uso de las imágenes de los cuentos de hadas, pues un rico se encuentra abandonado y solo, y en su castillo no tiene a su princesa.

El tema más interesante del disco es "Debate de 4", la colaboración de Romeo con Luis Vargas, Raulín Rodríguez y Antony Santos, que pinta un enfrentamiento entre los cuatro bachateros que quieren ganarse el amor de una mujer. Cada uno reitera sus virtudes individuales, enfatizando su papel dentro del mundo de la bachata: Romeo, el *King* (rey); Luis Vargas, el Rey Supremo de la Bachata; Raulín Rodríguez, el Cacique; y Antony Santos, el Mayimbe. En el coro, enumeran las armas que traen al debate, armas todas que simbolizan la bachata y su papel de música romántica: rosas, una guitarra y una botella de alcohol. Los argumentos de cada cantante reiteran sus propias calidades como bachatero y su lugar dentro del género. También incorporan numerosas referencias intertextuales a sus propios temas. Romeo canta en espanglish y se retrata como el *King of Bachata* infeliz que sufre. Luis Vargas está loco de amor,[60] pero es sincero, e insiste que todavía hay una chispa entre él y la bachata. Raulín Rodríguez enfatiza que es un macho de hombre[61] y apela directamente a la mujer/bachata,[62] e insiste que ya no quiere nada con la soledad.[63] Antony Santos describe a la mujer bachata como "linda y difícil",[64] y admite que su corazón es culpable y que sufre por ella.[65] No obstante, está seguro de ganar la batalla.[66] Santos le dice a la mujer bachata que deje su jueguito y que no lo deje plantado, aun por su timidez.[67] Aunque "Debate de 4" es, a primera vista, un enfrentamiento entre cuatro hombres que se compiten por la misma mujer, esta canción también puede entenderse en otro nivel en que cada uno de los cuatro bachateros busca dominar la bachata. Al final, aún no se sabe quién ganó. La bachata no escoge a ninguno de ellos, y se puede inferir que los necesita a todos para sentirse completa.

Romeo ha sido nominado para los Premios Billboard de la Música Latina, Billboard, Juventud, Lo Nuestro, y Soberano por su talento como cantante, compositor y productor. Ganó el Premio de la Sociedad Americana de Compositores Autores y Editores (ASCAP por sus siglas en inglés) por la Canción Tropical del Año y otro en el mercado norteamericano de pop en el 2006, siendo así el primer hispano que gana un premio ASCAP en dicho mercado.[68] Lo reconocieron como el Compositor del Año,[69] y su tema, "You", le cosechó un premio ASCAP por la Canción Tropical del Año en el 2012.

Henry Santos

El cantautor Henry Santos, antiguo integrante de Aventura, también ha sacado dos álbumes como solista, el primero, *Introducing*, en el 2011, que tiene solo bachata, y el segundo, *My Way*, en el 2013, que incluye un merengue y música bailable. Las canciones de Santos, muchas de las cuales escribió él mismo, hacen resaltar la sensibilidad de su estilo de interpretación. La primera canción que sacó, "Poquito a poquito", trata de la petición del narrador de que su amada le abra poquito a poquito su corazón. Además de facilitar la rima, el uso abundante del diminutivo comunica la misma ternura que se oye en la voz de Santos. "Dame una sonrisa" pinta una situación semejante, pues el narrador por fin se sobrepone a su timidez y se declara. Le pide que le dé una sonrisa y que no demore al enamorarse de él.

Henry Santos también canta los temas ampliamente probados de la bachata, el desamor y el desprecio. "Por nada" pone en tela de juicio la conveniencia de seguir con una relación cuando los dos se lastiman sin razón alguna. A pesar de sus palabras y actos dolorosos, el narrador admite que todavía la ama y que no la puede olvidar. En "Mi adicción", la voz narrativa describe a su amada y su amor como una adicción insuperable. Aunque le da un alivio pasajero, al final será su perdición.

En contraste con el sufrimiento de estos temas, el narrador de "Deja de llorar (Mi desprecio)" es el que inicia la ruptura. Esta canción sigue un relato breve, "*Flippin' Channels*", en el que el narrador hace zapping y se oyen fragmentos de anuncios y un breve pronóstico de tiempo que sitúa la acción plenamente en Nueva York. Termina con una escena de telenovela en español en que un personaje rompe con una mujer sollozante, y se niega a dejarse convencer por sus lágrimas de remordimiento. "Deja de llorar" se basa en esta escena, y la voz narrativa, igual que el personaje de la telenovela, le dice a su antiguo amor que no llore y que se olvide de él. La telenovela esta entretejida de manera intertextual por la canción, pues los personajes aparecen con cortos diálogos, lo cual enfatiza el papel de los dos géneros dentro del paradigma romántico cultural de los latinoamericanos. Esta interacción entre expresiones culturales, sin embargo, se presta a diferentes interpretaciones, ya que el amor verdadero siempre triunfa en el género de la telenovela, y hay un final feliz.[70] Así, está presente la posibilidad de reconciliarse, pues nunca se sabe lo que puede pasar—tal como el pronóstico del tiempo en "Flippin' Channels" predice un día sin lluvias pero les advierte a los televidentes que lleven paraguas, por si acaso.

La denuncia más fuerte y más moderna del tema tradicional de infidelidad en el primer álbum de Henry es "*Gotcha*", o sea, "te caché". En este caso, el narrador revela que ya va un tiempo que sabe de la infidelidad de su novia. Aunque estaba ciego al engaño en un principio, pone cámaras para comprobar si son verdaderas sus sospechas, y estas le sirven de otros ojos que pueden ver con más claridad que los suyos. Se enfrenta a su novia con las pruebas que la muestran con las manos en la masa y le anuncia que también subió los videos a YouTube. Aunque la inclusión de videocámaras y de YouTube sitúa la canción en el siglo XXI, sus temas forman parte de una larga tradición bachatera de cantar el desengaño, el desamor y el amargue.

El segundo álbum que grabó Henry Santos como solista, *My Way* (A mi manera) (2013), contempla los temas comunes de la bachata dentro de un amplio marco cultural. En "Mi poesía", el narrador define a su amada como la musa de ambas, su música y su poesía. Se clava en sus pensamientos, tal como una canción popular se pega en la mente, y le inspira a que realice grandes hazañas valientes, como cruzar descalzo el desierto. Piensa constantemente en ella y por lo tanto está inquieto. Según la tradición del amor cortés, el amor es un culto gobernado por Cupido; también es una enfermedad y ella, su único remedio. La voz narrativa de "Vuelve conmigo" también está enfermo de amor. Admite que se equivocó, lamenta sus acciones y pide perdón. Le pide a su amada que vuelva para salvarlo de la muerte que lo espera sin su amor. Cuando ya no encuentra palabras, el narrador busca un intermedio en la guitarra y le pide que llore por él. La instrumentación punteada de la guitarra imita las lágrimas. Al final, la voz narrativa pide perdón en ambos, español e inglés. "No sé vivir sin ti" es un dúo con el músico tejano Bobby Pulido, y también presenta el amor como enfermedad y locura. Este narrador lamenta su abandono y le dice a su ex que es el único remedio que puede curarlo. Se vuelve loco y sostiene que muere lentamente sin ella. "Preso en tu cárcel" nos recuerda la novela sentimental española medieval, *Cárcel de amor*. Mientras el preso enamorado de este *best seller* de 1492 se deja morir por el amor no correspondido, la bachata de Santos retrata a un narrador que se deja cautivar voluntariamente por el amor de su amada, y lo hace con el mayor agrado. Está enfermo de amor y locamente enamorado de su carcelera, y aunque no pensaba enamorarse, jura que se enamoraría de ella de nuevo. Este narrador está tan enamorado de ella que no teme casarse y convertirse en su preso de por vida.

Otros temas del álbum forman parte de tradiciones musicales. "Tango a la diva" se refiere a la telenovela como un marco para entender los recovecos del amor. Esta canción mezcla la bachata y el tango, otro género originalmente de la clase baja, para retratar a una mujer cruel y de besos venenosos. Es la protagonista de la telenovela personal del narrador, y también de su desgracia. La selección de palabras hace hincapié en un ambiente teatral en el que las apariencias engañan y la mujer, por su engaño, es merecedora de la misma canción que le canta el narrador: un tango. El título de "Bésame siempre" nos recuerda al bolero clásico "Bésame mucho". Este expresa la idea de vivir el momento con muchos besos y alargarlo como si los dos amantes pasaran su última noche juntos. La bachata de Santos, "Bésame siempre", enfatiza que el beso que propone el narrador es de por siempre; no obstante, es un solo beso—un beso profundo que pasará a la historia para ganarle el corazón a su amada. El amor es una religión que le inspira al narrador a dejar atrás su timidez y jugarlo todo por ella. En contraste, la bachata urbana, "*My Way*", se enfoca por completo en el momento vivido. Este tema sirve como la invitación íntima, personal y apasionada que el narrador le da a su amada, y cuenta con detalles todo lo que hará para que su experiencia sea inolvidable. El coro de esta bachata, que llegó al puesto número uno en el listado Billboard de temas tropicales de mayor difusión, nos da un excelente ejemplo del cambio de códigos, y el narrador cambia sin esfuerzo entre el inglés y el español para convencerle a ella que lo deje demostrarle su amor. "Amor y dinero" le da una vuelta al tema bachatero común de sufrir por el dinero. En esta canción, un narrador rico se pregunta si la mujer que ama se quedaría con él si fuera pobre. Emplea imágenes de cuentos de hadas, tales como un castillo y la Cenicienta, pero observa que su princesa llevaba ropa de marca y manejaba un Mercedes. Las contemplaciones hipotéticas de este narrador acerca de los motivos interesados de su amada lo convencen que un amor falso no es ningún amor.

Henry Santos también ha destacado la presencia de la bachata con otras actividades artísticas. Fue el director musical de la película dominicana, *La soga*. En el 2012, ganó la competencia, *Mira quién baila*, del canal televisivo, Univisión. Santos fue el primer dominicano que participó en la competencia, y jamás lo nominaron para eliminarlo, lo cual es testimonio no solo de sus destrezas de baile sino también del grado en que se congenia con su público.

Las letras refinadas de las bachatas de Henry Santos dibujan el panorama variado del amor en todas sus dimensiones. Aunque dice que solamente el 20 por ciento de sus letras se basan en sus vivencias,[71] Henry interpreta las melodías sólidas de sus bachatas con sinceridad. Para Henry, su bachata es el resultado de un proceso intricado y una combinación de elementos, especialmente "el alma" de la bachata tradicional. Lo explica así: "No es tan fácil como tomar y combinar una música, porque hay una química tácita que nace.… Hay que entender el sentimiento, de dónde viene para comprender la bachata".[72]

Vena

Lenny Santos, productor y guitarrista, y su hermano Max Agende se han unido con Steve Styles, el antiguo cantante principal de Xtreme, para formar el grupo Vena, un conjunto que Jon Caramanica describe como un "supergrupo dominicano". La agrupación toma su nombre de la visión elemental de que los dominicanos llevan la bachata en la sangre[73]: "Vena básicamente es la música corriendo por nuestras venas".[74] A pesar de sus éxitos con Xtreme y Aventura, Styles, Santos y Agende enfatizan que su agrupación, Vena, es una empresa nueva—un mundo nuevo, como mantienen en sus canciones—y que su meta consiste en siempre mejorarse. Dice Styles, "Comenzando de nuevo, otra vez … una nueva era, un nuevo grupo, un nuevo mundo".[75]

Los cuatro sencillos de Vena hasta la fecha tienen un timbre que complementa el contenido sentimental y el ritmo tradicional de la bachata con otros géneros y el espanglish. Su primera canción, "Señora", retrata a un narrador que se encuentra incapaz de olvidar a la mujer que amaba, aunque reconoce que la culpa la tiene él de que se haya ido. El hablante de "Por Mentiras" también reconoce su responsabilidad por las mentiras que hicieron fracasar su relación. Al reflexionar, se rompe la cabeza pensando en lo que pudo haber sido y le suplica a su amada que vuelva. En contraste, la voz narrativa de "Ya no" es la víctima del desprecio, la indiferencia y la falta de sinceridad de la mujer. No entiende cómo le pudo haber sido infiel, ya que él sí siempre le fue fiel. Siendo el esclavo de ella, se declara libre y le pone fin a la relación dañina.

El tema "Sangre de mis venas" emplea imágenes elementales para presentar a la amada como una parte vital del narrador. Ella lo completa, y su amor sabrá resistir toda prueba, hasta los chismes. También se puede interpretar esta canción desde otro ángulo, como un comentario sobre la bachata misma. Tal como la novia del narrador es la sangre de sus venas, la bachata corre por las venas de estos bachateros. La pareja de esta canción no le hace caso a los que quisieran destruir su amor, tal como los aficionados y bachateros tampoco les hicieron caso a los críticos de la bachata.

Steve Styles, el cantante principal de Vena, cree que "es importante que … la bachata salga del corazón",[76] y la música de esta agrupación le da voz a una miríada de emociones. Los temas de Vena—el amor, el amor perdido y el sufrimiento—sirven como un vínculo entre su música y la tradición bachatera a la vez que su sonido innovador y fresco los diferencia. Vena se empeña en darles a sus aficionados una experiencia divertida y única en sus presentaciones en vivo. Ya tienen un público fiel antes de publicar su primer álbum. Hay clubes de aficionados en varios países, y las Vena Mamis—mujeres aficionadas—los apoyan incondicionalmente. Este comienzo prometedor indica buenas posibilidades de que sean la "súper agrupación" que pretenden ser.

La posibilidad *crossover* de la bachata

Muchos están convencidos de que Romeo Santos será la cara misma de la bachata *crossover*, o sea, que tendrá éxito en el mercado de la corriente dominante de la música en inglés (e.g., Richards; Rohter "Crossing Over"; Rohter "Romeo"). Se basan sus razones en la experiencia de Romeo como el cantante principal del grupo Aventura, el éxito que ha logrado con su primer disco como solista, y un futuro programa de televisión.[77] Prince Royce, con su *look* del chico sencillo, su imagen elegante, y su cover bilingüe y de bachata de "Stand By Me", también es un excelente candidato para tomar ese paso.[78] Efectivamente, los bachateros y los grupos de bachata moderna y urbana, como Aventura, Prince Royce, Toby Love y Xtreme, aportaron mucho a la difusión de la bachata en otros países hispanohablantes, más allá del Caribe. Ahora, la bachata forma parte del sonido popular de los discos en muchos lugares de Europa, Centroamérica y Sudamérica. El efecto secundario lamentable de esta popularidad es que muchos desconocen la bachata fuera de esas formas moderna y urbana.

Estos músicos a quienes les ponen "*crossover*" son los que tenían éxito en el mercado de lengua española antes de entrar en el mercado de lengua inglesa con canciones para un blanco de público anglohablante. El vocablo *crossover*, sin embargo, conlleva ciertas expectativas y valoraciones. Aunque la palabra implica un movimiento horizontal entre géneros musicales, culturas, lenguas y consumidores, movimiento por el que una música latina "simplemente cambió de carril para entrar en la corriente dominante norteamericana", este vocablo efectivamente conlleva un orden jerárquico.[79]

Varios cantantes latinos empezaron con éxito sus carreras como músicos *crossover* en los primero años del milenio. Ricky Martin estalló en la escena musical del mundo de habla inglesa en mayo del 1999 con su famoso éxito, "Livin' la Vida Loca". Este sencillo incluía una fusión de *rock*, ritmos latinos y el espanglish, además de la imagen de Martin, bailando con mucho movimiento de cadera, que recordaba a Elvis Presley en el escenario. Aunque había sido reconocido internacionalmente por sus discos en español, el disco en inglés que Martin sacó el 11 de mayo de 1999 lo convirtió en uno de los músicos más populares de ese verano. Creció su popularidad a tal grado que pocas semanas después, su foto adornaba la portada de la revista *Time*.

De semejante manera, la rockera colombiana Shakira hizo el *crossover* al mercado de habla inglesa con su disco de 2001, *Laundry Service*. Para Shakira, hacer el *crossover* significaba más que cambiar de idioma, pues también incluyó un cambio de *look*. La Shakira rubia y seductora que adorna su primer disco en inglés era opuesta a como se veía a la de la portada de su primer disco en español, *Pies descalzos* (1996), donde lleva el pelo castaño y liso, o la de *Dónde están los ladrones* (1998), donde lleva trenzas sencillas y una camisa de manga larga. Esta transformación de Shakira revela claramente que no solamente se blanquea el idioma de la música *crossover*, sino tal vez su apariencia también.

Examinar a los músicos *crossover* que más éxito han tenido en la industria musical de habla inglesa revela que han sido en su mayoría "músicos blancos, con estudios, y de las clases media y alta",[80] como, por ejemplo, Gloria Estefan, Juan Luis Guerra, Ricky Martin, Shakira y Enrique Iglesias. Tal como observó acertadamente Willie

Colón, "'las músicas negras solamente fueron aceptadas cuando venían disfrazadas de blanco'".[81] Este proceso de aceptación, que recuerda el proceso semejante por el cual pasaron el rap y el *hip-hop*, lo describo como un proceso de filtración por medio del cual la música es blanqueada a través del tiempo para crear un producto que más atrae a nuevos públicos del grupo dominante.[82]

Los bachateros modernos y urbanos podrían ser la mismísima imagen de los que logran atraer los gustos musicales norteamericanos, por su tez más clara, su papel de cantantes ídolos que cantan dulcemente en espanglish y sus fusiones musicales. Royce ya ha incluido canciones completas o principalmente en inglés en sus dos discos, y se rumorea que trabaja con el sello Atlantic para sacar un disco en puro inglés.[83] Romeo, sin embargo, sostiene estar decidido en hacer el *crossover* como él quiere, o sea, con bachata y en español.[84] En contraste con los artistas que cambiaron completamente o casi por completo al inglés y al pop o *rock* para su *crossover*, Romeo se ha quedado casi completamente con la bachata y un espanglish en el que predomina el español.[85] Romeo desafía la noción que plantea al *crossover* como cosa de dirección única: "'Nunca me gustaba el vocablo *crossover*, o por lo menos la definición de él que tiene todo el mundo, o sea, que tú grabas un disco en inglés, y ese es un *crossover*.... Pensaba que si iba yo a hacer el *crossover*, ¿por qué no lo hace también el público de habla inglesa, por qué no hacia mi mundo?'".[86]

Por lo tanto la demanda por la música *crossover* de los artistas latinos no debería de interpretarse equivocadamente como una demanda solamente de los anglohablantes monolingües. Tal como observa Frances Aparicio, "un nuevo y emergente público hispano, 'imbuido cada vez más de la cultura anglo y animado por sus propias aspiraciones políticas y económicas', ha hecho posible el *crossover*, y no ha sido el resultado 'de una atracción a un público nuevo y principalmente anglohablante'".[87] El productor Sergio George reitera,

> Sean mexicano-americanos, puertorriqueños, dominicanos, ya no les importa de donde viene la música.... Estos son jóvenes hispanos de la cuarta generación, son norteamericanos. La mayoría nació y creció aquí. Así que quieren estar a la moda; pero todavía quieren retener su cultura, con el idioma [español].[88]

El éxito supuestamente *crossover* de la bachata, entonces, tal vez a la larga sea unido a la cara verdadera del demográfico norteamericano en que los hispanos son el grupo minoritario más grande.[89] Los primeros diez años del nuevo milenio señalaron un aumento importante de latinos en los Estados Unidos con un cambio de crecimiento de 43 por ciento.[90] Los hispanos constituyen además el grupo minoritario más joven del país, pues cada uno de cuatro recién nacidos en los Estados Unidos es hispano, tal como lo es cada uno de cinco colegiales.[91] Aunque el estilo, el sonido y la apariencia de Romeo y de Prince Royce tal vez atraigan a un público de habla inglesa, el público que los ayudará en el *crossover* bien podría ser hispano.

Para los anglohablantes, el propuesto *crossover* de la bachata se contempla desde el lente hegemónico de la corriente dominante, o sea, el pop en inglés. Se describe a Romeo como una cantidad "poca conocida"[92] más allá del mercado de habla española, y "un secreto escondido en plena vista".[93] Los escritores de habla inglesa pintan la bachata como "una balada dominicana sensual ... una música pueblerina de dudosa reputación ... una música folklórica del Caribe"[94] que tiene "letras verdes ... y que se toca en fiestas y bares-cabarets de mala muerte", música tocada por músicos que visten "atuendos chillones".[95] En contraste, se describen a los bachateros modernos y urbanos como los que refinaron el género por mezclarlo "con *R&B*, *hip-hop* y una actitud propia de las grandes ciudades ... [que] ... ha creado un estilo arrogante, distinto de Nueva York".[96] De la misma manera, Cantor-Navas le atribuye el crédito a "los ídolos de Aventura ... quienes convirtieron a la bachata con su sonido dominicano del barrio en una música de los jóvenes pan-latinos". De igual manera, el carácter urbano (entiéndase negro) de esta creación dominicano-americana tiene que filtrarse también. Castor-Navas reconoce al antiguo productor de Prince Royce, Sergio George, por haber transformado a Royce, "un bachatero del underground que llevaba gorra de béisbol ... [en] ... un intérprete bien vestido". Estas representaciones subrayan la mirada colonial inherente a las consideraciones de las músicas y los músicos denominados "*crossover*" y que los ven como algo que no existe o que es inferior hasta que pasen por el filtro de la música en inglés de la corriente dominante norteamericana.

Conclusión

La importante comunidad dominicana transnacional ayudó a crecer nuevos públicos de la bachata. Este género, que frecuentemente trata de las vivencias de la gente que vive en las urbes, es emblemático a las experiencias de muchos dominicanos que han vivido en el exterior, a la vez que una nueva generación de dominicano-americanos interpreta la bachata por el lente de sus propias realidades. Su sonido moderno, que mezcla la bachata con *R&B*, *rock*, pop y hasta reggaetón, hace el cambio de códigos entre español e inglés. Esta generación de dominicano-americanos ha adoptado la bachata moderna como una música representativa de lo que significa ser dominicano dentro de la comunidad transnacional. Esta combinación única refleja las realidades tanto musicales como lingüísticas de este grupo, a la vez que todavía confirma la herencia musical de los dominicanos en el país.

En "Mi niña cambió" de Aventura, la voz narrativa observa que bien dice el dicho que Nueva York te puede cambiar, hasta la piel. Esta canción se entiende, por una parte, como la crítica del narrador de su novia, ya que esta se cree superior a los de su país porque habla inglés y conoce Europa. El narrador reconoce que ha progresado, tal como se entiende el progreso en República Dominicana; no obstante, lamenta que haya olvidado tanto a él como sus raíces. Por otra parte, esta canción y este dicho reiteran el papel desempeñado por la bachata moderna en la aprobación general de la bachata y cómo simboliza la dominicanidad. Los migrantes abrazaron la bachata porque les era pertinente en su situación como una expresión de la dominicanidad dentro del contexto de la migración. Trajeron la música de vuelta al país, además de los símbolos de la movilidad social a los cuales tenían acceso, así desvinculando la bachata de la clase baja. Los vínculos entre la clase y la raza también se reflejan en este proceso: la mejor posición social de la bachata equivale a su blanqueamiento gradual, lo cual mejoró su creciente atracción.

Lenny Santos describe este fenómeno como una fuerza incontrolable: "Fue imposible pararla. A fin de cuentas, lo que importa es lo que le gusta a la gente. Si hay millones que dicen, 'No, esto es lo que quiero oír', tendrás que seguir con lo que dicen. No intentes controlarlo—¡esa cultura dominicana te va a buscar!".[97] Henry Santos articuló cómo la bachata se validó en el país por su visibilidad internacional: "Es un poco triste que así tiene que ser. Tiene que ser aceptada por el mundo antes de que sea completamente aceptada. Nos odiaron.... Entonces conseguimos la fama internacional, por todo el mundo, y ahora nos aman".[98] Las innovaciones de la bachata moderna de la corriente dominante y la bachata norteamericana llevaron la bachata por todo el mundo, y su pegada internacional ayudó a validar la bachata en el país.

NUEVE

Las bachateras

Una vista retrospectiva de la bachata revela la poca participación femenina en la industria bachatera. Cuando le pregunté a la cantante Susana Silfa el por qué, me explicó, "Para una mujer, ocupar un puesto en este género ... no ha sido difícil, todavía *es* difícil".[1] Esta tendencia refleja el cruce de varios factores, incluyendo las expectativas sociales para los dos géneros, los sitios en donde se producía y se consumía la bachata, y las tendencias de la empresa musical dominicana.

La delimitación duradera entre la casa y la calle tiene raíces profundas en América Latina. Estos dos espacios contrastivos se oponen y son propios de cada género. La familia es el centro de la casa, la cual representa la domesticidad y un lugar controlado de descanso del mundo de afuera. Es un espacio organizado en el que cada familiar desempeña su propio papel. Aquí, la familia como una unidad colectiva tiene precedencia sobre el individuo, y se mantiene el orden. En contraste, la calle es el espacio del individuo. Los papeles no son tan obvios con una ojeada, y ya que cada persona vigila sus intereses, siempre existe la posibilidad de "engaño, mentiras y picardía".[2]

La distinción casa/calle importa particularmente cuando se aplica a los papeles femeninos. En la casa, un espacio femenino, la mujer está segura y protegida de todos los posibles peligros y amenazas. Allí, las niñas respetan a sus padres cuando son pequeñas, y cuando son esposas, crían a sus hijos y cumplen con las necesidades de sus maridos. En la calle, no obstante, las mujeres están sin protección y expuestas a un sinfín de peligros siniestros. Las mujeres de la calle, tal como sugiere el nombre, no son las mujeres puras y domesticadas de la casa.

Estos dos ámbitos son análogos a las construcciones sociales del machismo y el marianismo, los cuales definen el comportamiento aceptable y esperado de los dos géneros. El macho es la imagen del conquistador original que conquista y domina, no solo a su mujer y a sus hijos, sino también a otras mujeres. Le preocupa salvar las apariencias y mantener su imagen de macho, cueste lo que cueste, pues nunca revela lo que siente y siempre demuestra e impone un sentido de masculinidad. El marianismo, con referencia a la Virgen María, postula que la mujer ideal tiene que ser pura, humilde y pasiva. Su vocación más importante es ser madre, y tiene que sacrificarse constantemente, soportando toda la mala conducta del hombre. Tiene que ser resignada y preparada para aguantarlo todo, pues la vida es un martirio.

La diferenciación entre la casa y la calle se hizo aún más pronunciada en la República Dominicana durante el Trujillato. Trujillo, el máximo caudillo, enfatizaba su masculinidad, y por lo tanto, su control machista del país, por propagar una construcción oficial de los géneros que representaba la femineidad como "ornamental, barroca y piadosa".[3] Este ideal contrastaba con la propia imagen machista de Trujillo, tal como fue representada por las numerosas medallas en sus uniformes, sus conquistas y seducciones incontables de mujeres, y los merengues que lo alababan. Lauren Derby también señala la representación intencional por parte del estado de la virilidad de Trujillo por medio de la construcción de un obelisco grande para conmemorar el primer aniversario del cambio del nombre de la capital a Ciudad Trujillo. El obelisco, descrito por Derby como "un gran símbolo fálico del dominio fecundo y promiscuo de Trujillo",[4] fue un recordatorio tanto visual como sicológico del caudillo y su dominio férreo. La visión oficial de la femineidad difundida bajo Trujillo resonó con las mujeres dominicanas de las clases media y alta, en parte porque también contrastaba con la imagen de la mujer norteamericana moderna cuya independencia, según creían, le había quitado el instinto sexual femenino y le había hecho demasiado individualizada y descarada.[5]

La imagen oficial de la mujer difundida bajo Trujillo fue inaccesible para muchas mujeres rurales y urbanas de la clase baja, especialmente con los cambios de la demografía después del ajusticiamiento de Trujillo. Como ya se ha visto, la llegada de migrantes a la capital llevó a más mujeres a la población activa laboral de la nación. Estas mujeres no gozaban del lujo de quedarse dentro de las paredes seguras de la casa, sino que tenían que salir al mundo de afuera para ganarse la vida. Aunque no todas eran literalmente mujeres de la calle, algunas sí trabajaban de prostitutas en los cabarets en donde se consumía la bachata. Este vínculo entre la bachata y los burdeles dejó una mancha duradera en la música, y con frecuencia resultaba en que se supusiera que cada mujer que escuchaba bachata por extensión era prostituta.[6] Desde los burdeles y los bares, la bachata iba llegando a las casas de la clase media, a través de las trabajadoras domésticas de clase baja que entraron a trabajar en ellas. Esto unió la bachata aún más con la clase baja y con las mujeres que tenían que trabajar fuera de la casa para sobrevivir.[7]

También se consideraba que el ser músico no fue un oficio apropiado para las mujeres, y muchos hasta creían que a las mujeres sencillamente les faltaba la capacidad de tocar bien los instrumentos.[8] Entre los pobres rurales y urbanos, la formación musical se realizaba informalmente, fuera de la casa, o sea, en la calle. Los músicos aprendieron los unos de los otros informalmente y por experiencia directa, muchas veces en los mismos lugares en donde se tocaba y se consumía la música.[9] En el caso de la bachata, esto significaba tener acceso a sitios tales como los bares y burdeles. Además, era difícil que una mujer tuviera y dirigiera su propio grupo en el contexto machista de la producción musical dominicana.[10] Es posible que la manera en que se bailaba bachata contribuyera a los estereotipos de las mujeres que la consumían y la bailaban. Aunque también el merengue se bailaba pegado, el brinquito o movimiento de cadera en el cuarto tiempo de la bachata al bailar pegado le ganó mucha crítica de sus detractores.

Juntas, estas construcciones y prácticas sociales son de larga tradición y alejaron de manera preventiva a muchas mujeres de la industria musical. De hecho, aun después de cincuenta años de historia, ha habido pocas exponentes de bachata.[11] Las pocas mujeres que participan en la bachata también han aportado más confusión a su identificación. Para unos, decirles "bachatera" conlleva connotaciones negativas, pues asocia a las mujeres con el desdén y el estigma originales que acompañaban la palabra "bachata". Para otros, un exponente femenino de bachata es algo tan novedoso en una profesión dominada por hombres, que la asocian a la misma categoría de nomenclatura que se aplica a profesiones como las fuerzas de orden público, las tareas de extinción de fuegos, y las fuerzas militares. En estos campos, los nuevos vocablos en español no siguen las reglas comunes para indicar el género; en su lugar, se incluye la palabra "mujer", por ejemplo: mujer policía; mujer bombero; mujer soldado. En el caso de la bachata, sería una "mujer bachatero". En su totalidad, esta indeterminación con que tratan a las mujeres exponentes de bachata subraya su lugar ambiguo dentro del mundo de la bachata.

Mélida "la Sufrida"

Aunque los hombres dominaban en los primeros años de la bachata, una mujer también figuraba entre la primera oleada de grabaciones. Esta, Mélida Rodríguez, pronto les llamó la atención a los aficionados y a los que criticaban la bachata con los temas y letras crudas de sus canciones. Rodríguez compuso muchas de sus bachatas, las cuales recuerdan los temas tratados por Blanca Iris Villafañe, una cantante puertorriqueña de boleros de guitarra muy popular: el desamor, el desengaño y el sufrimiento, todos desde el punto de vista del bar.[12]

Mélida Rodríguez, apodada "la Sufrida" por el título de una de sus canciones, presentaba abiertamente muchas de las mismas realidades de las mujeres de la clase marginada. La voz narrativa de "La sufrida" desafía abiertamente las expectativas burguesas para las mujeres. Insiste que no le importa el que los demás piensen que es mala, pues es feliz. Esta declaración enfatiza el abismo entre las expectativas para los hombres y para las mujeres con respecto a la fidelidad sexual, y así, resulta una declaración atrevida que desafía las construcciones sociales del marianismo y del machismo.

Muchas de las canciones de Rodríguez tienen lugar en o se refieren a los bares y a tomar, y así representan abiertamente a una voz femenina que se burla de las convenciones de la clase media y sus construcciones del decoro social. En "Bebiendo y llorando", la voz narrativa se pone a beber para aliviar su pena. Les dice a los demás que no se metan, y observa que si toma, lo hace con su propio dinero. Esta última declaración reitera el grado más alto de libertad económica de la mujer e insinúa la condición de muchos hombres de ese entonces que migraron a la ciudad buscando trabajo, no lo encontraron, y tenían que depender de lo que una mujer les proporcionaba. En contraste, la voz narrativa de "Me quiero emborrachar" declara que tiene un buen hombre, pero aún quiere emborracharse para conocer sus opciones.

El amor también figura como tema en la música de Rodríguez, aunque se trata de un amor que tiene que defenderse de los chismes. La voz femenina de "No importa, vida" declara audazmente que no importa que los demás digan que es malo su amado, ni lo que opinan de su relación. Su amor los hace feliz a los dos, y daría la vida por él. En contraste, la voz femenina de "Incredulidad" tiene que defenderse frente a las acusaciones de los demás para convencerle al hombre que ama de su honestidad. Estas dos canciones reiteran el poder y la influencia de lo que dicen los demás, o sea, una preocupación siempre presente por la opinión pública o el qué dirán.

Tanto el desamor como el amargue figuran en las letras de Rodríguez. La voz femenina de "Él me mintió" repite las palabras del título en sollozos mientras cuenta la traición del hombre que amaba. Concluye la canción con un breve interludio hablado en el que la narradora insiste que jamás lo perdonará, aun si vuelve. La canción termina con la repetición de "él me mintió", entrelazada con los sonidos de sollozos en el trasfondo. De la misma manera, la voz narrativa de "Cobardía" exige una explicación por la traición y el abandono del hombre. Mantiene que es cobarde ya que no responde por sus acciones.

Algunas de las canciones de Rodríguez le dan un giro al desamor, pues la voz narrativa no solo cuenta su dolor y sufrimiento, sino que también asume una postura de poder al negarse a ser la víctima y al calificar las acciones del hombre como inapropiadas. Los títulos y las letras de estos temas van al grano y no le permite al hombre defenderse ni justificar sus acciones. En "Mal hombre", la voz narrativa acusa a su antiguo amor de engañarla con una prostituta, observando que no debería de sorprenderse por eso, ya que es hombre. Dice además que no quiere que esté y prefiere olvidarlo para no equivocarse más. De semejante manera, la narradora de "Traicionero" no tiene pelos en la lengua al acusar al hombre de traicionar su amor. De todos modos, insiste que él no crea que vaya a morir de pena, pues va a encontrar un nuevo amor. La voz narrativa de "Lo peor de la vida" describe al hombre como un ingrato, y le recuerda que ella le dio todo lo que tiene. Es lo peor que le ha pasado, y mantiene que ya le da igual si se va.

La narradora de "La ley" combina varias de las características únicas de la bachata de Rodríguez. Aunque no se dice directamente, se entiende que la acción tiene lugar en un bar donde la voz femenina declara que va a cantar mientras espere que vuelva el hombre traicionero que amaba. Se impone al declarar que él no puede vivir sin sus besos y sostiene que no le dará ni un solo beso, aun si se lo ruega. El coro reitera que va a castigarlo para que no juegue con ella, ya que ella es la ley. En total, las letras de la canción lo pintan claro: la narradora es todo menos una víctima de la pena.

A pesar de que eran populares las canciones de Rodríguez, no volvió a grabar después de estos éxitos iniciales. Se mudó de la capital y lejos de la industria incipiente de la bachata, lo cual también contribuyó a su falta de participación. Siguió cantando de vez en cuando hasta su muerte prematura de un infarto en 1975.[13]

Aridia Ventura

En 1975, Aridia Ventura sacó su primera grabación, así convirtiéndose en la segunda mujer que dejó su huella en el mundo de la bachata a nivel nacional.[14] Esta primera producción fue poco exitosa, pero su segunda, "En la misma tumba", fue todo un éxito. Esta canción, un vals al estilo de una ranchera mexicana e interpretada con la misma emoción con que se interpretaba la bachata de los hombres, proclamó el amor eterno de la cantante y compara al amado con un ángel enviado por Dios. Solamente la muerte los puede separar, pues así de grande es su amor, y su último deseo es estar enterrada con él en la misma tumba. Estos temas resonaban entre los aficionados de la bachata, y el éxito de Ventura con "En la misma tumba" también le llamó la atención al locutor y productor de bachata, Rhadamés Aracena, que firmó un contrato con ella.

Aridia Ventura seguía grabando hasta los 80. Se presentaba regularmente en el Cibao y también participaba con frecuencia en los shows *Lunes de amargue* de Edilio Paredes. Durante su carrera, Ventura continuaba sacando canciones que retrataban las situaciones únicas de la mujer, haciendo resaltar su sufrimiento y también su enojo frente a la traición. Sus letras fuertes le ganaron el apodo de "La verduga", ya que la voz femenina de sus canciones tenía poca merced con el hombre infiel que ella dibujaba.[15] Ventura aceptó el apodo, y se refiere a este en la canción "Vengo con el garrote". En esta, la narradora declara que ha llegado la verduga con su garrote, y dice que está lista para darle golpes al hombre perverso de su vida. Luego explica cómo ha sufrido a manos de este hombre, quien gasta todo el dinero de la pareja en el alcohol. Termina por declarar que piensa empezar a tomar, igual que él, ya que tiene los mismos derechos.

Las letras de Ventura no andan con rodeos al enfrentarse a los hombres con papeles diferentes. En una de sus canciones más conocidas, "No eres varón", la cantante le informa a su antiguo amante que ya no lo quiere ni piensa llorar por él. Admite que sufrió mucho cuando la abandonó, pero ahora se niega a perdonarlo y le dice que se vaya. En "La hija abandonada", la cantante condena a su padre por dejar a su mamá sin fundamento, lo cual la lleva a su muerte prematura. Aunque la figura materna trabajaba para mantener a su familia, el padre "canalla" no cumplió su papel protectivo.

Ventura seguía grabando y presentando como exponente favorita hasta los 80. Unos problemas de salud limitaron su participación en la época en que la bachata iba evolucionando y alejándose del sonido tradicional de Ventura.[16] No obstante, no se puede negar su lugar como pionera de la bachata y un baluarte del género. Sus letras cubren toda la gama de los temas bachateros, y les dan una voz femenina al retratarlos desde la perspectiva de la mujer.

Mariíta

A principios de los 1990, Susana Silfa entró en el mundo de la bachata como Mariíta. Silfa, quien es de una familia capitaleña de clase media y estudió formalmente la música y la voz en el Conservatorio Nacional, tomó ese nombre artístico porque este le parecía más auténtico al campo dominicano donde nació la bachata.[17] Silfa admite que no estaba segura cuando se le sugirió la posibilidad de cantar bachata, puesto que no tenía las mismas raíces que la mayoría de los bachateros y su público. No obstante, Silfa recuerda haber escuchado bachata de niña en Radio Guarachita. Siempre había soñado con ser cantante e iba a una parte alejada de la casa donde se imaginaba cantando en un escenario. Allá estaba lo suficientemente cerca para oír la bachata en la radio de las trabajadoras domésticas, pues la música se desbordaba de sus habitaciones. Recuerda que su canción favorita a los cuatro años era "Dos rosas" de Bernardo Ortiz.[18]

Silfa creció rodeada por la bachata, aunque no pertenecía a la clase social comúnmente asociada con esta. Como resultado, pudo infundirle todos los sentimientos expresados en la bachata a su propia música como Mariíta. Silfa, quien tomó como modelo a la estrella de la música tejana, Selena Quintallana, quería abrazar un género que consideraba auténticamente dominicano y abrirlo a nuevos públicos, utilizando sus propios estudios formales y vivencias para buscar "los otros colores de la bachata".[19] El disco de Mariíta, *Bachata amargue*, incluía los temas probados de la bachata (el amor, el desamor, el abandono y el amor prohibido) y los interpretaba según el estilo sentimental tradicional. Aunque las letras de las bachatas de Mariíta no son tan desoladas como las de Mélida Rodríguez, ni tan hirientes como las de Aridia Ventura, estas presentan una imagen de los temas comunes a la bachata por el lente único del punto de vista femenino. En "El que ríe último ríe mejor", Mariíta reprocha a su amante por su traición y le recuerda que es valiente y sabe aguantarse, aun si él ríe ahora por su sufrimiento. En contraste, Mariíta describe su relación en "Amor de novela" como un amor duradero de cuento de hadas. En "Lo buscaré", Mariíta jura buscar por todas partes al hombre que la dejó y seducirlo otra vez cuando lo encuentre.

La canción titular del disco, "Bachata amargue", sirve como una explicación retrospectiva de cómo llegó Mariíta a cantar bachata. Empieza con una serie de cadencias vocales que hacen resaltar la destreza y las habilidades de la artista capacitada tras el nombre aparentemente rural. Las letras explican como la cantante nacida en República Dominicana buscaba cómo conectarse con su pueblo por una música que animaría a que todos cantaran con ella. Mariíta enfatiza que lleva la bachata en la sangre, y es por eso que llegó a cantarla al final. Tanto en el sonido como en el contexto, "Bachata amargue" subraya el carácter único de Mariíta como bachatera, pues es una cantante formada de la clase media, y aun así siente un lazo esencial con la bachata.

Silfa admite que ser bachatera representaba sus propios desafíos en un género machista y en una industria dominada por los hombres.[20] Además del estigma que se le atribuía a los locales comunes del consumo y de la producción de la bachata, las letras de algunas canciones recriminaban a las mujeres, a veces de forma violenta. La bachata de doble sentido también era popular cuando Silfa empezó su reinado como Mariíta, "la Reina del Amague". Silfa aceptó el desafío y encontró la manera de adaptarse a la moda también. Su merengue "El pullaíto" era muy popular. Este proclamó un nuevo baile con el mismo nombre que era tan popular que se bailaba por la noche en donde fuera. Mariíta dice que "El pullaíto" es suyo y anima a todos los hombres a que lo bailen, diciéndoles que lo bailen tal cual les indica, y así, los domina. Para Silfa, este merengue de doble sentido sirvió como respuesta al gusto de ese entonces, y su popularidad revela que las mujeres podían hacer exitosamente esta misma clase de música juguetona.[21]

Las tendencias machistas de la bachata le representaban un desafío a Silfa, pero nunca un obstáculo. Silfa recuerda particularmente cómo la condenó un periodista por cantar bachata en un artículo, y luego la alabó en otro cuando tuvo éxito. Admite que oyó decir de ella cosas desagradables y peyorativas cuando se presentaba en algunos lugares.[22] Como Mariíta, Silfa cantó con la gran cantante de la bachata, Aridia Ventura, y otros músicos destacados del género, entre ellos Paniagua, Luis Segura y Raulín Rodríguez. Por razones personales, no siguió trabajando con la bachata, aunque ha sacado unas bachatas bajo su propio nombre, las cuales describe más como tecno bachatas.

Mayra Bello

Al igual que Susana Silfa, Mayra Bello no estaba segura de cantar bachata al principio por la discriminación en su contra. Nacida en 1964, Bello creció oyendo que la bachata era de gente de otra clase—la música del populacho y el género de preferencia de prostitutas y guardias. Bello recuerda que su mamá era firme en que nadie tocara bachata en su casa, aunque era común oírla en la calle. Bello se alejó de la bachata al principio, y escuchaba en su lugar la balada y el bolero. Aunque la música le interesaba a Bello desde niña y cantaba en el coro eclesiástico, terminó sus estudios universitarios antes de lanzar su carrera musical. Bello cantó con el grupo de merengue Los Toros Band, y más tarde, con la estrella femenina de merengue Milly Quezada, además de otras estrellas internacionales.[23]

Cuando el mánager de Bello le sugirió que considerara la posibilidad de grabar bachata, no estaba segura al principio por su educación. Recuerda la opinión machista y muy negativa que se tenía de las representantes femeninas de la bachata, opinión que cerró las puertas del género a las mujeres. De todos modos, reconoció que le atraía el sonido de la guitarra en la bachata. Aunque dudaba en un principio, Bello reconoció la autenticidad de la bachata como una música popular de su patria: "Dentro de mí hay bachata. Es muy de nosotros".[24]

Las letras de Bello tratan la gama de las diferentes facetas del amor y del desamor y las retrata desde el punto de vista femenino. En "La infiel", que incluye a la estrella de merengue Milly Quezada, la voz narrativa le admite a su mejor amiga que tuvo amoríos con el esposo de esta. Aunque le ruega a su amiga que se compadezca de ella y que salven la amistad, la otra se niega a oírla. De semejante manera, la narradora de "El hombre casi perfecto" se encuentra enamorada de un hombre que tiene todas las características que pudiera desear salvo una: está casado. El desamor es el tema central de "Pero me acuerdo de ti". En esta canción, la voz femenina reconoce repetidas veces que ha superado un amor malsano. Aunque parece que todo le va bien, todo se deshace al instante cuando recuerda su antiguo amor. El amor verdadero también figura en el repertorio de Bello. Aunque los personajes de "Sé que volverás" (a dúo con Nacho Bianco) están separados, los dos reiteran que creen que estarán juntos otra vez. De la misma manera, la voz femenina de "Contigo" está segura de su amor y desea pasar cada momento de su vida con el hombre que ama.

Bello describe el sonido de su música como "diferente" y señala a Juan Luis Guerra como influyente en llevar la bachata por otro camino y hacer posible que otros lo siguieran. La instrumentación de la bachata de Bello es más compleja que la de los cinco instrumentos originales, lo cual la coloca más en línea con el tecno amargue de Guerra. Tal como admite Bello, "Yo no me puedo presentar en un sitio con dos tipos tocando una guitarra y un requinto, un bongó y una güira. La mía necesita una guitarra acústica, una batería…. Tal vez no voy a tener un violín, pero voy a tener un piano sintetizador con ese sonido".[25] Por lo tanto, la bachata de Bello combina el sonido del tecno amargue con los temas probados de la bachata cantados en voz de mujer.

Leslie Grace

Leslie Grace Martínez hizo historia en Billboard en octubre de 2012 cuando su bachata urbana bilingüe, "*Will U Still Love Me Tomorrow*", una adaptación de la canción clásica de las Shirelles de 1960, llegó al puesto número uno en el listado de temas latinos de mayor difusión. A los diecisiete años con nueve meses de edad, Leslie Grace se hizo la cantante femenina más joven en ocupar ese puesto codiciado. Su adaptación de esta canción clásica es apropiada en muchos niveles, sobre todo una historia compartida de colegialas que tuvieron éxito en la industria musical (las Shirelles fueron el primer grupo de mujeres que llegó al puesto número uno) y su posibilidad de influir a otras cantantes. Su interpretación de esta letra clásica—la narradora le pregunta a su amado si todavía la querrá la mañana después—capta los sentimientos tradicionales de la bachata en su interpretación bilingüe.

Su álbum, *Leslie Grace* (2013), es su primer álbum secular tras haber empezado con la música cristiana.[26] Este incluye una mezcla de bachata urbana, música pop, *R&B* y temas bailables. Su instrumentación es sintetizada, y en muchos casos, la guitarra, instrumento tan central en la bachata típica y la moderna, juega un papel menos destacado. Su bachata refleja la fuerte influencia del *R&B*. Sus letras no son complejas pero siguen la tradición lírica de la bachata. *"Day 1"*, tema que también llegó al número uno en la lista tropical de Billboard, trata del amor a primera vista. El amor de la narradora parece sacado de un cuento de hadas, pues se enamoró de su amado el primer día que lo vio. Su adaptación bilingüe del tema de las Ronettes del 1963, *"Be My Baby"*, también describe el amor a primera vista. Esta narradora promete amar y serle fiel a su amado, si él la acepta. El amor también tiene que enfrentar las críticas. En "Hoy", la voz narrativa reafirma que confía en su amado cuando otros lo acusan. Su amor es más grande que sus dudas, y reitera que cree en él.

Leslie Grace también le canta al desamor, pero es un desamor de carácter mucho menos cortavenas que él de la bachata típica. La narradora de "Odio no odiarte" no puede olvidar a su antiguo amor. Aunque quisiera odiarlo y seguir con su vida, no puede. "Peligroso amor" hace uso de varias antítesis para describir la atracción de un amor que no tiene futuro. Aunque la narradora sabe que tiene todas las de perder, no puede evitar la atracción del amor. La voz narrativa de "No me arrepiento" le canta al desamor casi exclusivamente en inglés. Critica a su novio por no hablar de sus sentimientos, pero insiste que no se arrepienta de nada.

"A mi manera" es el tema que más se desvía de la tradición lírica de la bachata. La voz narrativa de este tema es la de una joven que está harta de que los otros le digan cómo vivir. Insiste que tiene edad para escoger su propio camino. Por lo tanto, esta narradora va a vivir su vida según sus planes y a su manera.

Leslie Grace se encuentra en la posición única de ser la primera bachatera urbana a quien han promocionado agresivamente. Sus bachatas, sacadas en los Estados Unidos, podrían ayudar a derrumbar las barreras a las que se enfrentan las bachateras, ya que a nivel mundial, entre los públicos bilingües e hispanohablantes, se desconoce la tradición de discriminación en contra de la bachata. No obstante, es demasiado temprano para saber cuál será el impacto de su bachata.

Conclusión

Las opiniones duraderas de los espacios sociales y los papeles apropiados para hombres y mujeres han impactado el acceso femenino a la participación en la producción de bachata. Los dos espacios opositores y definidos por género, la casa y la calle, enfatizan la pureza y la inviolabilidad de la casa como contraste con el peligro y la exposición de la calle. La mujer que tiene que trabajar fuera de la casa para ganarse la vida por extensión es sospechosa de ser una verdadera mujer de la calle. Las tempranas asociaciones de la bachata con la clase baja en general, y específicamente con los cabarets, la mancharon y la hicieron inaceptable, tanto como música para disfrutar como género para producir. Además, las mujeres no tenían acceso a la capacitación musical informal que les era disponible a los hombres fuera de la casa por los sitios en donde ocurría esta formación.

Las primeras bachateras, tales como Mélida Rodríguez y Aridia Ventura, asimilaron los temas y los sonidos comunes de la bachata, contándolos desde el punto de vista de la mujer. Más tarde, las bachateras formadas, tales como Susana Silfa y Mayra Bello, usaron esos mismos temas con el sonido único de los 1990 y principios del siglo XXI. Leslie Grace ha lanzado su carrera en la bachata urbana desde los Estados Unidos, por lo que es posible que les abra las puertas del género a más bachateras. A pesar de la creciente popularidad de la bachata, el acceso femenino a la industria musical en general, y específicamente a la bachata, ha sido más limitado que el de los hombres. De todos modos, como nos recuerdan las bachateras incluidas en este capítulo, el amor y el desamor son igual de conmovedores, tanto en las voces masculinas como en las femeninas.

Conclusión

La mesa en donde estaba sentada con mi amigo Alexis y otros clientes habituales que llegaban cada domingo por la noche a la Parada 9 estaba rodeada por música. Cerca de nosotros, una pareja que hacía juego con sus pantalones blancos y camisas y accesorios verdes lima bailaba en el espacio minúsculo al lado de nuestra mesa. El dueño del local circulaba entre las mesas con hielo, agitando hábilmente las manos mientras les echaba hielo a los vasos bajo el aire sofocante de la noche. Algunos cantaban las letras de los temas que se escuchaban como si fueran viejos amigos, y otro marcaba el ritmo con una güira. Afuera, un señor vestido de diablo cojuelo, muy fuera de temporada, pasaba bajo una lluvia constante de agosto.

Cuando la conversación llegó al tema de mis investigaciones, todos los presentes tenían su granito de arena que aportar al conjunto creciente de ideas y comprensiones de la bachata que iba recogiendo. Este patrón lo había notado cuando mencionaba mis razones por estar en la República Dominicana, el Bronx y Washington Heights. Desde los taxistas hasta los desconocidos por completo en negocios locales y el dueño de la pensión donde me hospedaba—todos estaban listos y dispuestos a compartir sus opiniones y vivencias conmigo. Algunos recordaban que antes les costaba cinco centavos tocar una bachata en la vellonera del colmado, antes de que subieran el precio a diez. Otros describían a los personajes locales que se presentaban en un colmado y que llevaban un rollo de monedas para tocar una canción favorita repetidas veces, generando el disgusto de los demás oyentes. Muchos pronunciaban los nombres de los bachateros y los títulos de bachatas como si fueran viejos amigos, y contaban las historias y anécdotas recopiladas durante las primeras cinco décadas de su existencia.

Los dominicanos están dispuestos a hablar de sus preferencias e historias musicales con la misma intensidad y la misma solemnidad que tienen para tratar las cuestiones políticas. Esta deferencia con la que tratan la música como un elemento crucial de la vida cotidiana reitera su papel central en la identidad dominicana a través de la historia nacional. Los intelectuales del siglo XIX atacaron con indignación al merengue cuando este amenazaba el papel de la tumba como el baile nacional de ese entonces. Más tarde, la creciente presencia del acordeón en el merengue cayó bajo el fuego de los intelectuales cuando amenazaba con reemplazar a los instrumentos de cuerda considerados autóctonos. Los nacionalistas dominicanos abrazaron el merengue criollo como símbolo de su resistencia cultural durante la ocupación norteamericana, para abandonarlo después. El potencial de la música de unir las distintas identidades dominicanas es innegable, y el dictador Rafael Trujillo sacó provecho de esas posibilidades cuando lo hizo la música nacional y comisionó la creación de una versión refinada del mismo, el merengue de orquesta. Muchas composiciones propagandísticas alabaron su grandeza y ayudaron a concretizar un sentido de identidad nacional.

La bachata nació en los años después de las tres décadas de dictadura, tiempo en que se impuso el merengue como la música nacional. Por esta razón, se consideraba un desafío al estatus quo en un momento en que tantos elementos de la vida ya habían sido desarraigados y derribados. Los primeros detractores de la bachata la menospreciaban por sus orígenes rurales y de clase baja, y por asociación, por las implicaciones raciales de esas raíces. Sus críticos y los que tenían un interés monetario en el merengue le pusieron nombres despectivos a la música de guitarra romántica con el fin de limitarla a un espacio marginado. Esta imposición del poder por asignar tales nombres relegó la producción de la bachata al sector informal, y sus representaciones a los lugares pequeños. No obstante, los bachateros y sus aficionados reivindicaron como suyos estos nombres impuestos de "bachata" y "amargue", socavando así la intención ofensiva original. Aunque el dominio del merengue de la industria musical le cerró muchas puertas a la bachata, los aficionados de esta, provenientes de las clases rurales y bajas urbanas, consumían la música por discos producidos económicamente, como oyentes fieles de Radio Guarachita, y en los colmados, bares y cabarets. Juntos, estos factores contribuyeron a la discriminación que recaía sobre la bachata por años que la retrataba como una música no refinada de la clase baja y de baja calidad.

De todos modos, tal como Tommy García acierta a notar, "Los ritmos no se pueden imponer desde el poder", y la bachata fue escogida libremente.[1] Los bachateros y los del mundo de la música suelen describir la creciente popularidad de la bachata como algo imparable y, en muchas maneras, inevitable. El promotor Isidro "Chichí" Aponte la identifica como un atractivo inevitable.[2] Edilio Paredes les atribuye el éxito de la bachata a los mensajes e historias que relata, y los sentimientos que comunica.[3] Para Paredes, la bachata era como un río que nace en la montaña y crece mientras fluye hacia el mar—"pero en el comienzo, es un chorrito de agua".[4] Joe Veras también compara la bachata con las fuerzas naturales y la describe como "un ciclón tan fuerte que no hubo nada que lo detuviera".[5]

La visibilidad de la bachata seguía ampliándose a la vez que crecía su número de aficionados a la par con la pobreza de gran alcance durante repetidos bajones económicos. Las modificaciones hechas al contenido y al sonido de la bachata a través de los años—la tecno bachata, las innovaciones instrumentales de figuras como Blas Durán, Luis Vargas, Antony Santos, letras más románticas y variadas, y eventualmente, el nuevo sonido de la bachata moderna—también atrajeron a más seguidores. Los migrantes dominicanos, cuyas experiencias de dificultades económicas y la alienación se parecían más a la bachata que el merengue de ritmos cada vez más rápidos, abrazaron el género, ya que reflejaba sus realidades. Estos mismos migrantes fomentaron aún más el alcance de la bachata cuando la trajeron de vuelta a la República Dominicana por vías transnacionales, en sus visitas al país y sus lazos con los amigos y familiares. La bachata moderna entró internacionalmente en primer plano, y su popularidad global le abrió puertas a todo el género. La mayor visibilidad de la bachata, además del mejorado estado social (y por extensión, racial) de los migrantes poco a poco ayudó a borrar la antigua discriminación. Tal como observa Henry Santos, "A veces ... pues, algo que nace en el propio país de uno, ellos son verdaderamente los últimos en apoyarlo. Son los últimos—hasta que atraiga la acogida internacional".[6]

La bachata se presta a un estudio único de cómo evolucionan los géneros musicales para representar las identidades nacionales, y de cómo los gustos individuales y colectivos llegan a aceptar nuevos ritmos y géneros como símbolos de ellos. La ascensión de la bachata a la posición sagrada de identificador nacional es especialmente significativa frente a la posición duradera del merengue al centro de la identidad musical dominicana y por su apoyo oficial durante el Trujillato. Ahora, la bachata está a la par del merengue y forma un segundo baluarte musical de la identidad dominicana que es representativo de la dominicanidad entre los que viven en el país y en el exterior.

Los bachateros no dudan en reiterar estos lazos con la dominicanidad. Para Joe Veras, la bachata y el merengue aportan a la dominicanidad y al orgullo de la patria, y señala los dos, además del béisbol, como reconocible a nivel internacional como algo dominicano.[7] Davicito Paredes hace eco de este punto de vista, y expresa su orgullo en el sentido de propiedad colectiva nacional del género.[8] José Manuel Calderón, el primerísimo bachatero, cree que el crecimiento de la bachata y su aceptación residen en el apoyo y el respaldo de los muchos seguidores que representaban la mayoría, a pesar de que no hacían tanto ruido como sus detractores.[9] La capacidad de los aficionados de la bachata de relacionarse con ella ha ayudado a convertirla en un mecanismo de identificación a una escala tan grande al nivel mundial.

Desde la época de su nacimiento entre las clases bajas y urbanas de Santo Domingo en 1962, la bachata ha latido junto con el corazón del pueblo dominicano, aun cuando las clases media y alta la criticaban con vehemencia y la condenaron como un género ordinaria y carente de valor musical. Ahora, la bachata se ha extendido lejos por los gustos de los migrantes dominicanos y ha logrado establecerse internacionalmente. "La bachata habla por sí sola", sostiene Henry Santos. "Ha llegado, es poderosa, y va a seguir creciendo. Habla por sí sola".[10] Hoy, la bachata se oye tanto en el país como entre los dominicanos ausentes, en un CD en un colmado, en vivo, o en la radio local o satelital. Le encante o no, en el país o en el exterior, la bachata ha sido y es una parte integral de la experiencia dominicana—una medida acertada del pulso de la nación dominicana.

Notas

Introducción

1. Smith 107.
2. Sellers 2.
3. Bello entrevista.
4. Corniel entrevista.
5. Smith 108.
6. Seeger 451.
7. J. M. Pérez 386.
8. Seeger 459.
9. Derby 240.
10. Derby 185; Candelario 26.
11. Hoffnung-Garskof 1.
12. Candelario 59.
13. El álbum, *Señora Bachata* (2009), es una colaboración entre los grandes de la bachata, José Manuel Calderón, Blas Durán, Leonardo Paniagua, Ramón Cordero, Ramón Torres y Luis Segura. En el tema titular, se personifica a la bachata, y esta relata su trayectoria desde una música discriminada de los bares a ser una señora decorosa a quien admiran los que antes la criticaban.
14. Slobin 11.
15. Fiske 25.
16. Días 407.
17. *Santo Domingo Blues*.
18. En esta fecha, José Manuel Calderón estrenó lo que más tarde se reconocería como el primer sencillo de la bachata.
19. J. M. Pérez 391.
20. Sellers 2.

Capítulo uno

1. Veloz Maggiolo 19.
2. Zavala 190.
3. Knights 8–9; Veloz Maggiolo 70–1.
4. Veloz Maggiolo 15.
5. Knights 11; Veloz Maggiolo 70.
6. Zavala 192.
7. Veloz Maggiolo 26–9.
8. Veloz Maggiolo 30.
9. Veloz Maggiolo 73.
10. Veloz Maggiolo 71.
11. Knights 12.
12. Anderson 33.
13. Knights 5.
14. Knights 5.
15. Knights 3, 7; Delgado Malagón 219.
16. Veloz Maggiolo 167.
17. Veloz Maggiolo 137.
18. Veloz Maggiolo 138.
19. Calderón entrevista; T. García entrevista.
20. Veloz Maggiolo 121.
21. Veloz Maggiolo 133.
22. Veloz Maggiolo 129.
23. J. M. Pérez 390.
24. J. M. Pérez 390–1.
25. Aunque no se considera que este estilo del bolero de guitarra fuera su propio género hasta los años 1970, la autora se refiere a ella como "bachata" para facilitar su identificación.
26. E. Paredes entrevista.
27. T. García entrevista; E. Paredes entrevista; Tejeda *La pasión* 129–30.
28. Corniel entrevista; T. García entrevista; Batista Matos; Pacini Hernandez *Bachata*.
29. E. Paredes entrevista.
30. Calderón entrevista.
31. E. Paredes entrevista.
32. E. Paredes entrevista.
33. E. Paredes entrevista.
34. E. Paredes entrevista.
35. H. Santos entrevista; Cáceres.
36. Paniagua entrevista.
37. E. Paredes entrevista.
38. Paniagua entrevista.
39. Love entrevista.
40. Paniagua entrevista.
41. Calderón entrevista.
42. Silfa entrevista.
43. D. Paredes entrevista.
44. Veloz Maggiolo 22.
45. T. García entrevista.
46. T. García entrevista.
47. H. Santos entrevista.
48. Burgos; Paniagua; Santana.
49. D. Paredes entrevista.
50. Fernández entrevista.
51. *Santo Domingo Blues*.
52. H. Santos entrevista.
53. Burgos entrevista.
54. Fernández entrevista.
55. E. Paredes entrevista.

56. E. Paredes entrevista.
57. E. Paredes entrevista.
58. Gray; Leal y Féblot-Augustins; Van Vleck.
59. Elliott 29.
60. Elliott 30.
61. Gray 107.
62. Corniel entrevista; Burgos entrevista.
63. Corniel entrevista; Burgos entrevista.
64. Veras entrevista.
65. Bello entrevista.
66. H. Santos entrevista.
67. Love entrevista.
68. Martínez entrevista.
69. Martínez entrevista.
70. L. Santos entrevista.
71. Paniagua entrevista.
72. Burgos entrevista.
73. Love entrevista.
74. D. Paredes entrevista.
75. D. Paredes entrevista.
76. D. Paredes entrevista.
77. Citado en *Bachata Roja: Amor y amargue.*
78. Bugos entrevista.
79. L. Santos entrevista.
80. Corniel entrevista.
81. Leal y Féblot-Augustins 181.
82. Veloz Maggiolo 189.
83. Veloz Maggiolo 189.
84. X. Pérez entrevista.
85. Medina entrevista.
86. Santana entrevista.
87. Medina entrevista.
88. Andújar Persinal 72.
89. Medina entrevista.
90. X. Pérez entrevista.
91. X. Pérez entrevista.
92. L. Santos entrevista.
93. T. García entrevista.
94. T. García entrevista.
95. T. García entrevista.
96. Burgos entrevista.
97. D. Paredes entrevista.
98. Aunque varios músicos de otros géneros han experimentado con la bachata, pocos se han cambiado completamente o de manera igual a tocarla. La excepción más notable es el merenguero Héctor Acosta "El Torito", a quién más de un dominicano describió de la siguiente manera: "ya es un bachatero".
99. Calderón entrevista.
100. E. Paredes entrevista.
101. Martínez entrevista.
102. Silfa entrevista.
103. Burgos entrevista.
104. Fernández entrevista.
105. Candelario 26.
106. Fernández entrevista.
107. Paniagua entrevista.
108. Paniagua entrevista.
109. Santana entrevista; T. Santos entrevista.
110. Veras entrevista.
111. Veras entrevista.
112. H. Santos entrevista.
113. L. Santos entrevista.
114. L. Santos entrevista.
115. T. García entrevista.
116. Sellers 2.
117. Citado en Adelt *Blues Music* vii.
118. Batista Matos 16.
119. Fernández entrevista.
120. Fernández entrevista.
121. Bello entrevista.
122. Fernández entrevista.
123. Fernández entrevista.
124. Veras entrevista.
125. Silfa entrevista.
126. D. Paredes entrevista; Cano entrevista.
127. D. Paredes entrevista.
128. I. Aponte entrevista.
129. R. D. Aponte entrevista.
130. Sanche entrevista.
131. Love entrevista.
132. Love entrevista.
133. Paniagua entrevista.
134. Paniagua entrevista.
135. del Castillo 296.
136. D. Paredes entrevista.
137. D. Paredes entrevista.
138. Fernández entrevista; T. García entrevista.
139. Méndez entrevista.
140. "Eladio Romero Santos".
141. D. Paredes entrevista.
142. "Eladio Romero Santos".
143. Wayne "Sexual Double Entendre Bachata".
144. Valentine.
145. Allen 166.
146. Valentine.

Capítulo dos

1. Hoffnung-Garskof 11.
2. Hoffnung-Garskof 12.
3. Todorov 3.
4. Todorov 3.
5. Moya Pons *Dominican Republic* 95.
6. Moya Pons *Dominican Republic* 107–8.
7. Candelario 99.
8. Candelario 5.
9. Moya Pons *Dominican Republic* 109.
10. Wucker 38–9.
11. Balaguer 15.
12. Crassweller 149.
13. Radcliffe y Westwood 27.
14. Anderson 7.
15. Radcliffe y Westwood 23.
16. Radcliffe y Westwood 22; 16.
17. Duara 169.
18. Gilman 18.
19. Radcliffe y Westwood 33.
20. Derby 18.
21. Torres-Saillant "Tribulations" 1104.
22. Hoffnung-Garskof 24.
23. Derby 35.
24. Derby 57.
25. Derby 35–6.
26. Moya Pons "Modernización" 222.

27. Moya Pons *Dominican Republic* 338.
28. Derby 37.
29. Derby 12–13.
30. Moya Pons *Dominican Republic* 40.
31. Wucker 75.
32. "Modernización" 245.
33. Torres-Saillant "Tribulations" 1104.
34. Derby 2.
35. Candelario 29.
36. Candelario 1.
37. Alix 15–17.
38. Derby 2.
39. Guzmán 4–5.
40. Wucker 33.
41. Derby 200.
42. *Mirrors of the Heart.*
43. *Sábado Gigante.*
44. Guzmán 6.
45. Candelario 223.
46. Alix 16.
47. *Mirrors of the Heart.*
48. Candelario 223.
49. Derby 185.
50. Candelario 26.
51. Derby 150.
52. Derby 202.
53. Derby 159.
54. Hoffnung-Garskof 13.
55. Hoffnung-Garskoff 12; 21–3.
56. Hoffnung-Garskof 18–19.
57. Torres-Saillant "Tribulations" 1104.
58. Hoffnung-Garskof 23.
59. Hoffnung-Garskof 17.
60. Derby 107.
61. Hofnung-Garskof 29.
62. Henríquez Ureña 147; Arzeno 127.
63. Sellers 64.
64. Tejeda *La pasión* 38.
65. Galván, citado en Rodríguez Demorizi 114.
66. Citado en Rodríguez Demorizi 115.
67. Moya Pons "Modernización" 213.
68. De hecho, no hay pruebas que apoyen las raíces indígenas del güiro, y se cree que tanto este como su equivalente de metal de años después, la güira, son de origen dominicano o puertorriqueño.
69. Citado en Rodríguez Demorizi 136.
70. Citado en Rodríguez Demorizi 160.
71. Coopersmith 22.
72. M.E. Davis 146.
73. Hoffnung-Garskof 11.
74. M.E. Davis 146.

Capítulo tres

1. Hoffnung-Garskof 11.
2. Derby 132.
3. Hoffnung-Garskof 26.
4. Derby 67.
5. Derby 68.
6. Derby 70.
7. Derby 69.
8. Derby 88.
9. Derby 102.

10. Derby 88.
11. Derby 107.
12. Crassweller 30; Derby 194.
13. Crassweller 83; Galíndez 182.
14. Hartlyn 49.
15. Hartlyn 49.
16. Aquino 92–3; Moya Pons *Dominican Republic* 359.
17. Moya Pons *Dominican Republic* 365; Hartlyn 50.
18. Derby 208.
19. Derby 197; Wucker 51.
20. Crassweller 154; Wucker 48.
21. Derby 164–66.
22. Aquino 69; Espaillat 25–6.
23. Derby 264.
24. Derby 135–9.
25. Foucault 201.
26. Aquino 69–70; Moya Pons *Dominican Republic* 376.
27. del Castillo y García Arévalo 81; Wucker 45–6.
28. Sellers 94; Jorge 76.
29. Rivera González 3:10–11.
30. Sellers 94–5.
31. Pacini Hernandez *Bachata* 73.
32. del Castillo y García Arevalo 82.
33. Manuel 102.
34. Hoffnung-Garskof 11.
35. Sellers 97.
36. Rivera González.
37. Veloz Maggiolo 83.
38. Derby 109.
39. Crassweller 295.
40. Crassweller 298.
41. Diederich 43.
42. Derby 240.
43. Derby 257–60.

Capítulo cuatro

1. E. Paredes entrevista.
2. Rodríguez.
3. Calderón entrevista.
4. Calderón entrevista.
5. Calderón entrevista.
6. A menos que se indique de otra forma, todas las canciones aparecen en la lista de grabaciones citadas bajo el nombre del artista.
7. Calderón entrevista; Batista Matos 11.
8. *José Manuel Calderón.*
9. *José Manuel Calderón.*
10. *José Manuel Calderón;* Batista Matos 12.
11. Calderón entrevista.
12. Esta práctica de publicar una versión en bachata de temas de otros géneros ha continuado durante toda la historia del género. La autora no señala cada tema sacada en bachata que pertenecía originalmetne a otro género por razones de espacio.
13. Batista Matos 10.
14. *José Manuel Calderón.*
15. *José Manuel Calderón.*

16. Batista Matos.
17. Batista Matos 14; *José Manuel Calderón.*
18. Calderón entrevista.
19. E. Paredes entrevista.
20. Batista Matos 15.
21. D. Paredes entrevista.
22. Sánchez.
23. Batista Matos 23.
24. El desengaño no solo es una revelación de la verdad que le quita la venda de los ojos a uno, sino que también puede constituir un aprendizaje por vivencias amargas.
25. Sánchez.
26. Paniagua entrevista.
27. Uno de los barrios, La Ciénaga, creció debajo del Puente Duarte en la capital donde quien cruzara el puente podía verlo. Su mayor visibilidad se prestó a un dicho popular entre los residentes que se referían a todos los barrios populares como "debajo del puente" (Hoffnung-Garskof 41). Este dicho era tan común que llegó a ser el título y el tema de una bachata de Víctor Víctor en la que la voz narrativa contrasta dos lugares físicos, debajo del puente y arriba del puente, como dos mundos separados. Arriba, la gente pasa y mira hacia abajo a los que viven en los arrabales sin compasión ni reparo.
28. V. García entrevista.
29. Paniagua entrevista.
30. Calderón entrevista.
31. Pacini Hernandez *Bachata* 100.
32. Calderón entrevista.
33. Hoffnung-Garskof 62.
34. Hoffnung-Garskof 62.
35. Hoffnung-Garskof 62.
36. Andújar Persinal 68.
37. Love entrevista.
38. H. Santos entrevista.
39. T. García entrevista.
40. Silfa entrevista.
41. E. Paredes entrevista.
42. Corniel entrevista.
43. E. Paredes entrevista; *Santo Domingo Blues.*
44. T. García entrevista.
45. T. García entrevista.
46. T. García entrevista.
47. D. Paredes.
48. *Santo Domingo Blues.*
49. Corniel entrevista.
50. *Santo Domingo Blues.*
51. Paniagua entrevista.
52. E. Paredes entrevista; D. Paredes entrevista.
53. E. Paredes entrevista.
54. Silfa entrevista.
55. Hoffnung-Garskof 12.
56. Hoffnung-Garskof 13.
57. Derby 257–60.
58. Hoffnung-Garskof 64.
59. E. Paredes entrevista.
60. Silfa entrevista.
61. Batista Matos 19.
62. T. García entrevista.
63. Pacini Hernandez *Bachata* 88–91.
64. Silfa entrevista.
65. Pacini Hernandez *Bachata* 97.
66. Pacini Hernandez *Bachata* 97–8.
67. T. Santos entrevista.
68. T. García entrevista.
69. T. García entrevista.
70. Pacini Hernandez *Bachata* 92.
71. Pacini Hernandez *Bachata* 92.
72. Anderson 33.
73. Anderson 35.
74. J.M. Pérez 387.
75. R. D. Aponte entrevista.
76. T. García entrevista.
77. *Santo Domingo Blues.*
78. Batista Matos 20.
79. Véase también el Capítulo cinco.
80. Wayne "Edilio Paredes".
81. Wayne "Edilio Pareces".
82. Wayne "Edilio Paredes".
83. Wayne "Edilio Paredes".
84. E. Paredes entrevista.
85. *The Bachata Legends.*
86. Paniagua entrevista.
87. Paniagua entrevista.
88. Paniagua entrevista.
89. Paniagua entrevista.
90. Paniagua entrevista.
91. Batista Matos 49.
92. Batista Matos 51.
93. Paniagua entrevista.

Capítulo cinco

1. Morgan, Hartlyn, y Espinal 8.
2. Pacini Hernandez *Bachata* 155–6.
3. Pacini Hernandez *Bachata* 155–7.
4. Aparicio 128.
5. Hoffnung-Garskof 38.
6. Krohn-Hansen 115.
7. Pacini Hernandez *Bachata* 158–61.
8. *Bachata* 161.
9. Pacini Hernandez *Bachata* 194.
10. Batista Matos 119.
11. Sergio Reyes, citado en Brito Ureña 208.
12. Citado en Brito Ureña 208.
13. Citado en Brito Ureña 209.
14. T. Santos entrevista.
15. "Sexual Double Entendre Bachata".
16. Ángel es de Santiago Rodríguez.
17. Ángel entrevista.
18. Ángel entrevista.
19. Ángel entrevista.
20. Batista Matos 55.
21. "Blas Durán".
22. Pacini Hernandez *Bachata* 200; Wayne "Sexual Doble Entendre Bachata".
23. "Blas Durán"; Pacini Hernandez *Bachata* 200–1.
24. Wayne "Sexual Double Entendre Bachata".
25. "Blas Durán".
26. Mattern 39.
27. Pacini Hernandez "La lucha sonora".
28. T. García entrevista.
29. T. García entrevista.

30. Pacini Hernandez *Bachata* 204–5; T. García entrevista.
31. T. García entrevista.
32. Pacini Hernandez *Bachata* 205.
33. Batista Matos 86–8.
34. E. Paredes entrevista.
35. Jiménez 29.
36. ACROARTE; T. García; Batista Matos 91.
37. del Castillo 471–3; Tejada "Víctor Víctor".
38. Batista Matos 91; del Castillo 473; T. García entrevista.
39. ACROARTE.
40. Pacini Hernandez *Bachata* 208.
41. Batista Matos 91.
42. E. Paredes entrevista.
43. T. García entrevista; Batista Matos 91.
44. Slobin 11.
45. T. García entrevista; Paniagua entrevista; E. Paredes entrevista.
46. *Bachata: Music of the People.*
47. E. Paredes entrevista; T. García entrevista.
48. Fernández entrevista.
49. Love entrevista; Santana entrevista.
50. Calderón entrevista.
51. Wayne "Frontier".
52. Wayne "Luis Vargas".
53. *Santo Domingo Blues.*
54. Batista Matos 76.
55. *Santo Domingo Blues*; Wayne "Luis Vargas".
56. Wayne "Luis Vargas".
57. El título original de este tema era "Con los crespos hechos", aunque se lo conoce mejor como "Loco de amor" y se incluye en las colecciones de éxitos bajo el mismo.
58. Pacini Hernandez *Bachata* 161.
59. *Santo Domingo Blues.*
60. A veces se escribe "Antony Santos" con "h". La autora lo escribe sin "h" para diferenciarlo de Anthony "Romeo" Santos (véase el Capítulo ocho).
61. El distanciamiento, tal vez exacerbado por el éxito de los dos, ya se ha hecho parte de la historia musical. Uno de los éxitos de Vargas, "El envidioso", se burla de su rival, Antony Santos. El narrador declara una guerra de mambo para decidir quién tiene el swing y critica a un supuesto amigo a quién se le enseñó todo y que ahora se lo imita todo.
62. Kugel.
63. Pacini Hernandez *Bachata* 210.
64. Wayne "Antony Santos".
65. ACROARTE 29.
66. Sanche entrevista.
67. Cruz Hierro "Diez figuras".
68. ACROARTE.
69. ACROARTE 29.
70. Batista Matos 80.
71. Batista Matos 80–1.
72. Pacini Hernandez *Bachata* 30–2.
73. Cruz Hierro "10 canciones".
74. Valdez "Pedro" 314.

Capítulo seis

1. Veras entrevista.
2. Veras entrevista.
3. Veras entrevista.
4. "Romantic Bachata".
5. Veras entrevista.
6. Asociación de Cronistas de Arte 28.
7. "Respuestas".
8. H. Santos entrevista; L. Santos entrevista.
9. Cruz Hierro "10 canciones".
10. "Biography".
11. Jiménez "Respuestas".
12. Jiménez "Respuestas".
13. Cruz Hierro "Diez figuras".
14. *Bachata: Música del pueblo.*
15. Sanche entrevista.
16. Sanche entrevista; Cruz Hierro "10 canciones".
17. "Diez figuras".
18. Polanco.
19. Sarante.
20. Polanco.
21. Tu Momento Newyorkino.
22. Birchmeier.
23. "Luis Miguel del Amargue".
24. "La alcaldía".
25. "Luis Miguel tiene".
26. Jiménez "Respuestas".
27. Gutierrez.
28. Gutierrez; Desde 1985 hasta 2012, la Asociación de Cronistas de Arte (ACROARTE) de República Dominicana y la Cervecería Nacional Dominicana entregaron los Premios Casandra. Desde el 2013, se llaman los Premios Soberano.
29. Jiménez "Respuestas".
30. "El Chaval lamenta"; "'Maldita residencia'".
31. "'Maldita residencia'".
32. L. Santos entrevista; Martínez entrevista.
33. Martínez entrevista; L. Santos entrevista.
34. Martínez entrevista.
35. Martínez entrevista.
36. Véase también el Capítulo nueve para más información acerca de Alexandra Cabrera.
37. Jiménez "Respuestas"; Wayne "Alexandra Cabrera".
38. Jiménez "Respuestas".
39. Este apodo surge de su participación en dicha agrupación, formada por Gerardo Díaz, "El Toro".
40. H. Santos entrevista.

Capítulo siete

1. Guitérrez 4.
2. Hoffnung-Garskof 90.
3. Levitt 238.
4. Hoffnung-Garskof 135; Levitt 238.
5. Graham 45.
6. Hume 157.
7. Hume 156; Pew Research Center.
8. Verbrigghe.
9. Duany *Quisqueya* 2.

10. Hoffnung-Garskof 196.
11. Duany *Quisqueya* 33; 40.
12. Malkki 448.
13. Hoffnung-Garskof 126–8.
14. Hume 158–9.
15. Hoffnung-Garskof 172–82.
16. Hoffnung-Garskof 166–69.
17. Levitt 248.
18. Hoffnung-Garskof 170–1.
19. Hoffnung-Garskof 230.
20. Hoffnung-Garskof 119.
21. Pacini Hernandez *Oye* 90.
22. Pacini Hernandez *Oye* 91.
23. Corniel entrevista.
24. Santana entrevista.
25. Santana entrevista.
26. Santana entrevista.
27. Santana entrevista.
28. "Ray Santana" 25.
29. Burgos entrevista.
30. Burgos entrevista.
31. Burgos entrevista.
32. El título de este tema se refiere a Burgos mismo como El Cupido que va flechando a sus oyentes.
33. Corniel entrevista.
34. Corniel entrevista.
35. Corniel entrevista.
36. Corniel entrevista.
37. J.M. Pérez 391.
38. J. M. Pérez 391.
39. Burgos entrevista.
40. *Santo Domingo Blues.*

Capítulo ocho

1. L. Santos entrevista.
2. H. Santos "Question".
3. L. Santos en Vívelohoy.
4. Pacini Hernandez *Oye* 91.
5. H. Santos entrevista.
6. Pacini Hernandez *Oye* 91.
7. H. Santos entrevista; L. Santos entrevista.
8. Wayne "The New York School".
9. Burgos entrevista.
10. Burgos entrevista.
11. H. Santos "Quote"; H. Santos "Question".
12. H. Santos "Quote".
13. L. Santos entrevista.
14. Grosjean 51.
15. L. Santos entrevista.
16. Torres 76.
17. Grosjean 52–4.
18. Grosjean 54.
19. Love entrevista.
20. H. Santos entrevista.
21. H. Santos World Debut.
22. Cáceres.
23. Como ya se mencionó en el Capítulo uno, "el grajo" se refiere al olor del sobaco. No obstante, las clases media y alta usan este vocablo para inidicar su impresión de la higiene personal de los campesinos. En el caso de la bachata, decir que esta tiene grajo significa una falta de cultura.
24. *Santo Domingo Blues.*
25. H. Santos entrevista; L. Santos entrevista.
26. L. Santos entrevista.
27. L. Santos entrevista.
28. L. Santos entrevista.
29. L. Santos entrevista.
30. L. Santos entrevista.
31. L. Santos; Rohter "Crossing Over".
32. L. Santos entrevista.
33. L. Santos entrevista.
34. L. Santos entrevista; M.C. Davis.
35. M.C. Davis.
36. L. Santos entrevista.
37. L. Santos, citado en M.C. Davis.
38. Rosen.
39. "Crossing Over".
40. Citado en Richards.
41. Aventura también sacó una versión en inglés de este tema con el mismo título, aunque esta identificación es poco apropiada ya que sus letras vienen en espanglish y se colocan palabras y un idioma en el otro con una sintaxis acertada.
42. Mientras el machismo glorifica el hombre como seductor y conquistador, el marianismo compara a la mujer con la Virgen María. Se tratan estas construcciones con detalle en el Capítulo nueve.
43. Graglia.
44. Romeo Santos en "Fiesta Latina".
45. Eva Longoria Parker en "Fiesta Latina".
46. Rohter "Crossing Over".
47. ACROARTE 28.
48. ACROARTE 29.
49. L. Santos en Vívelohoy.
50. Love entrevista.
51. Love entrevista.
52. Love entrevista.
53. Love entrevista.
54. Love entrevista.
55. Love entrevista.
56. Love entrevista.
57. Love entrevista.
58. Cobo "Prince Royce Enters 'Phase II'".
59. "Prince Royce estrenó".
60. Una referencia a su tema, *Loco de amor.*
61. "Soy un macho de hombre" de la canción "Me la pusieron difícil" de Rodríguez.
62. Le pone dos de los nombres extraídos de dos de sus propias canciones: "Mi morenita" y "Nereyda".
63. Una referencia a su disco y su canción del mismo título, *Soledad.*
64. Una referencia a su canción "Linda y difícil".
65. Hace referencias a sus canciones "Corazón culpable" y "Pena de amor".
66. Una referencia a su canción del mismo título, "La batalla".
67. Son referencias a sus canciones "El jueguito", "Qué plantón", y "Mi timidez".
68. "Biography" *Romeo.*
69. Billboard, 2007; ASCAP 2010.
70. Ortiz de Urbina y López; *Telenovelas: Love, TV y Power.*

71. World Debut.
72. H. Santos "Quote".
73. Santos y Styles.
74. Lenny Santos en Vívelohoy.
75. Citado en Vívelohoy.
76. Santos y Styles.
77. En el 2011, Romeo anunció que había aceptado trabajar en un proyecto con la compañía de Will Smith y James Lassiter, OverbrookEntertainment, en una comedia para el canal televisivo norteamericano, ABC. El proyecto, que todavía no tiene título, retrata a un joven dominicanoamericano (Romeo) que se encuentra atrapado entre las tradiciones de sus padres migrantes y sus propios sueños (Cobo "Latin Singer").
78. Cobo "Prince Royce Enters 'Phase II'".
79. Sellers 173.
80. Aparicio 108.
81. Citado en Aparicio 115.
82. Sellers 173.
83. Cobo "Prince Royce Enters 'Phase II'".
84. Rohter "Crossing Over".
85. Richards; Rohter "Crossing Over"; Rohter "Romeo".
86. Citado en Rohter "Crossing Over".
87. Aparicio 111.
88. Citado en Cantor-Navas.
89. Pew Research Center.
90. Ennis, Ríos-Vargas y Albert 3.
91. Pew Research Center.
92. Rohter "Crossing Over".
93. Rohter "Romeo".
94. Rosen.
95. Kugel.
96. Rosen.
97. L. Santos entrevista.
98. H. Santos entrevista.

Capítulo nueve

1. Silfa entrevista.
2. DaMatta 64.
3. Derby 119.
4. Derby 119.
5. Derby 119–21.
6. T. García entrevista.
7. T. García entrevista.
8. Sellers 149.
9. Aparicio 173.
10. T. García entrevista.
11. Alexandra Cabrera, del dúo popularísimo, Monchy y Alexandra (comentado en el Capítulo seis), sacó unos sencillos en ambos, los discos del dúo y los suyos después. Su trabajo como solista no es tan conocido como sus canciones a dúo.
12. "Mélida Rodríguez".
13. "Mélida Rodríguez".
14. Pacini Hernandez *Bachata*.
15. "Aridia Ventura".
16. "Aridia Ventura".
17. Silfa entrevista.
18. Silfa entrevista.
19. Silfa entrevista.
20. Silfa entrevista.
21. Silfa entrevista.
22. Silfa entrevista.
23. Bello entrevista.
24. Bello entrevista.
25. Bello entrevista.
26. Cuesta 40.

Conclusión

1. T. García entrevista.
2. I. Aponte entrevista.
3. E. Paredes entrevista.
4. E. Paredes entrevista.
5. Veras entrevista.
6. H. Santos entrevista.
7. Veras entrevista.
8. D. Paredes entrevista.
9. Calderón entrevista.
10. H. Santos entrevista.

Works Cited / Obras citadas

ACROARTE—Asociación de Cronistas de Arte. "Cien discos esenciales." *El Caribe*. 22 July 2013, sec. Gente: 28–9. Print.

Adelt, Ulrich. "Black, White, and Blue: Racial Politics in B.B. King's Music from the 1960s." *Journal of Popular Culture* 44.2 (2011): 195–216. *EBSCOhost*. Web. 27 June 2012.

_____. *Blues Music in the Sixties: A Story in Black and White*. New Brunswick, NJ: Rutgers University Press, 2010. Print.

"After Leonel: The Dominican Republic." *The Economist*. 26 May 2012: 39. *General OneFile*. Web. 11 Aug. 2012.

"La alcaldía de West New York reconoce a Luis Miguel." *Listín Diario*. 21 Mar. 2012. Web. 9 Aug. 2013.

Alix, Juan Antonio, Antonio Z. Reyes Ledesma, and José R. Heredia. *Décimas dominicanas de ayer y de hoy*. 3d ed. Santo Domingo: Publicaciones América, 1986. Print.

Allen, Dawn. "Just Who Do You Think I Am? The Name-Calling and Name-Claiming of Newcomer Youth." *Canadian Journal of Applied Linguistics* 10.2 (2007): 165–75. *Academic Search Complete*. Web. 13 Aug. 2012.

Anderson, Benedict. *Imagined Communities*. 7th ed. New York: Verso, 1991. Print.

Andújar Persinal, Carlos. *Por el sendero de la palabra: Notas sobre la dominicanidad*. Santo Domingo: Editora Universitaria, 2006. Print.

Ángel, Julio. Personal Interview. 10 Dec. 2010.

Aparicio, Frances R. *Listening to Salsa: Gender, Latin Popular Music, and Puerto Rican Cultures*. Hanover, NH: Wesleyan University Press, 1998. Print.

Aponte, Isidoro "Chichí." Personal Interview. 6 Aug. 2011.

Aponte, Rubén Darío. Personal Interview. 6 Aug. 2011.

Aquino, Miguel. *Holocaust in the Caribbean: The Slaughter of 25,000 Haitians by Trujillo in One Week*. Waterbury, CT: Emancipation, 1997. Print.

"Aridia Ventura." Artists. *IASO Records*, n.d. Web. 1 Aug. 2012.

Arroyo, Lorena, and David Botti. "Las claves de las elecciones en República Dominicana." *BBC Mundo*. 20 May 2012. Web. 11 Aug. 2012.

Arzeno, Julio. *Del folk-lore musical dominicano*. Vol. 1. Santo Domingo: La Cuna de America, 1927. Print.

"Ay." *Larousse Unabridged Spanish-English / Inglés-Español Dictionary*. Revised ed. Boston: Houghton Mifflin, 2000. Print.

The Bachata Legends. Liner notes. IASO Records, 2011. CD

Bachata: Music of the People. Dir. Giovanni Savino. The Cinema Guild, 2003. Film.

Bachata Roja: Amor y amargue. Liner notes. IASO Records, 2011. CD.

Bachata sinfónica. Dir. William Liriano, Jr. Dobleu Punto Comp, 2003. Film.

Balaguer, Joaquín. *La isla al revés*. 1983. Santo Domingo: Corripio, 1994. Print.

Baldera, Emelyn. "La bachata celebra medio siglo de amargue." *Listín Diario*. 30 May 2012. Web. 30 May 2012.

Barrios, Luis, and David C. Brotherton. "Dominican Republic: From Poster Child to Basketcase." *NACLA Report on the Americas* 38.3 (2004): 11–13. *General OneFile.* Web. 11 Aug. 2012.

Batista Matos, Carlos. *Bachata: Historia y evolución.* Santo Domingo: Editora Taller, 2002. Print.

Bello, Mayra. Personal Interview. 10 Dec. 2010.

"Biography." *Frank Reyes.* n.d. Web. 3 Aug. 2013.

Birchmeier, Jason. "Biography: Luis Miguel del Amargue." Artists. *Billboard,* n.d. Web. 9 Aug. 2013.

"Blas Durán: The Father of Modern Bachata." Artists. *IASO Records,* n.d. Web. 1 Aug. 2012.

Brito Ureña, Luis Manuel. *El merengue y la realidad existencial de los dominicanos: Bachata y nueva canción.* Santo Domingo: Unigraf, 1997. Print.

Burgos, Rafy. "Enamorar." Prestigio, 2001. MP3.

_____. "Lamentos del Cupido." MP3.

_____. Personal Interview. 10 Dec. 2010.

Cáceres, Joseph. "Los disparos del vaquero Teodoro." *Merengala.* n.p. 9 Jan. 2013. Web. 5 July 2013.

Calderón, José Manuel. Personal Interview. 2 Aug. 2011.

Calderón, José Manuel, Blas Durán, Leonardo Paniagua, Ramón Cordero, Ramón Torres, and Luis Segura. "Señora Bachta." *Señora Bachata.* Mock and Roll, 2009. CD.

Candelario, Ginetta E.G. *Black Behind the Ears: Dominican Racial Identity from Museums to Beauty Shops.* Durham, NC: Duke University Press, 2007. Print.

Cano, Guillermo. Personal Interview. 6 Aug. 2011.

Cantor-Navas, Judy. "Year-End 2010: The New Romantics." *Billboard.com.* 18 Dec. 2010. Web. 12 July 2012.

El Chaval de la Bachata. "About." n.d. Facebook. Web. 8 Aug. 2013.

"El Chaval lamenta exclusion de bachateros." *Listín Diario.* 20 Feb. 2012. Web. 12 Aug. 2013.

Cobo, Leila. "Latin Singer Romeo Santos Cast in ABC Comedy." *Billboard.com.* 12 Oct. 2011. Web. 11 July 2012.

_____. "Prince Royce Enters 'Phase II' of Career." *Billboard.com.* 9 Apr. 2012. Web. 12 July 2012.

_____. "Prince Royce: Stand by Him." *Billboard.com.* 5 June 2010. Web. 12 July 2012.

Consadine, J. D. "Latin Pop Is Spicing Up American Charts." Weekend Section. *St. Petersburg Times.* 22 Oct. 1999: 24. *Lexis-Nexis Academic Universe.* Web. 12 July 2012.

Coopersmith, J. M. *Music and Musicians of the Dominican Republic.* Washington, D.C.: Pan American Union, 1949. Print.

Corniel, Gerson. Personal Interview. 9 Dec. 2010.

Crassweller, Robert D. *Trujillo: The Life and Times of a Caribbean Dictator.* New York: Macmillan, 1966.

Cruz Hierro, Ynmaculada. "10 canciones más sonadas." *Listín Diario.* 26 June 2013. Web. 21 July 2013.

_____. "Diez figuras influyentes en los 50 años de la bachata." *Listín Diario.* 30 May 2012. Web. 30 May 2012.

Cuesta, Erick. "Leslie Grace: Un lujo de Voz." *Venue* Sept./Oct. 2013: 40–1. Web. 10 Sept. 2013.

DaMatta, Roberto. *Carnivals, Rogues and Heroes: An Interpretation of the Brazilian Dilemma.* Trans. John Drury. Notre Dame, IN: University of Notre Dame Press, 1991. Print.

Davis, Mark C. "Aventura's Lenny Santos." *Guitar Player.* n. d. Web. 11 July 2012.

Davis, Martha Ellen. "Music and Black Ethnicity in the Dominican Republic." Ed. Gerard Béhague. *Music and Black Ethnicity in the Caribbean and South America.* New Brunswick, NJ: Transaction, 1994. 119–155. Print.

del Castillo, José. "Perfiles del bolero dominicano." *El bolero: Visiones y perfiles de una pasión dominicana.* Colección Popular CODETEL. Vol. 6. Santo Domingo: CODETEL, 2009. Print.

del Castillo, José, and Manuel A. García Arévalo. *Antología del merengue / Anthology of Merengue.* Santo Domingo: Corripio, 1989. Print.

Delgado Malagón, Pedro. "Hitos del Bolero Dominicano: Una visión apasionada." *El bolero: Visiones y perfiles de una pasión dominicana.* Colección Popular CODETEL. Vol. 6. Santo Domingo: CODETEL, 2009. 211–271. 273–489. Print.

Derby, Lauren. *The Dictator's Seduction: Politics and the Popular Imagination in the Era of Trujillo.* Durham, NC: Duke University Press, 2009. Print.

"Desamor." *Larousse Unabridged Spanish-English / Inglés-Español Dictionary.* Revised ed. Boston: Houghton Mifflin, 2000. Print.

Días, Luis. "Las transformaciones del merengue y la bachata." *El merengue en la cultura domini-cana y del Caribe: Memorias del Primer Congreso Internacional Música, Identidad y Cultura en el Caribe.* Ed. Darío Tejeda & Rafael Emilio Yunén. Santo Domingo: Instituto de Estudios Caribeños, 2006. 403–405.

Diederich, Bernard. *Trujillo: The Death of the Goat.* Boston: Little, Brown, 1978. Print.

Duany, Jorge. "Ethnicity, Identity, and Music: An Anthropological Analysis of the Dominican Merengue." Ed. Gerard Béhague. *Music and Black Ethnicity in the Caribbean and South America.* New Brunswick, NJ: Transaction, 1994. 65–90. Print.

_____. *Quisqueya on the Hudson. The Transnational Identity of Dominicans in Washington Heights.* New York: CUNY, 1994. Print.

Duara, Prasenjit. "Historicizing National Identity, or Who Imagines What and When." Ed. Geoff Eley and Ronald Grigor Suny. *Becoming National.* New York: Oxford University Press, 1996. 151–177. Print.

The Duke of Bachata. Dir. Adam Taub. Perf. Joan Soriano. Horizon Line, 2009. Film.

"Eladio Romero Santos." Artists. *IASO Records,* n.d. Web. 30 June 2012.

Elliott, Richard. *Fado and the Place of Longing: Loss, Memory and the City.* Farnham, England: Ashgate, 2010. Print.

Ennis, Sharon R., Merarys Ríos-Vargas, and Nora G. Albert. "The Hispanic Population 2010." *2010 Census Briefs.* United States Census Bureau. May 2011. Web. 12 July 2012.

Fernández, Crispín. Personal Interview. 1 Aug. 2011.

"Fiesta Latina." *In Performance at the White House.* PBS. 16 Oct. 2009.

Fiske, John. *Understanding Popular Culture.* Boston: Unwin Hyman, 1989. Print.

Foucault, Michel. *Discipline and Punish: The Birth of the Prison.* New York: Vintage, 1995. Print.

Galíndez, Jesús de. *The Era of Trujillo.* Tucson: University of Arizona Press, 1973. Print.

García, Tommy. Personal Interview. 1 Aug. 2011.

García, Vicente. Personal Interview. 14 Apr. 2013.

Georges, Eugenia. *The Making of a Transnational Community: Migration, Development, and Cultural Change in the Dominican Republic.* New York: Columbia University Press, 1990. Print.

Gilman, Sander. *Difference and Pathology: Stereotypes of Sexuality, Race, and Madness.* Ithaca, NY: Cornell University Press, 1985. Print.

Godfrey, Sarah. "Prince Royce's 'Phase II:' Mixing and Matching to Expand Bachata Sound." Style. *The Washington Post.* 17 Apr. 2012. Web. 12 July 2012.

Graglia, Diego. "Güira in the Garden: Aventura to Make Bachata History at MSG." *The Los Angeles Daily News.* 8 Aug. 2007. Web. 10 May 2008.

Graham, Pamela M. "The Politics of Incorporation: Dominicans in New York City." *Latino Studies Journal* 9.3 (1998): 39–64. Print.

Gray, Lila Ellen. "Memories of Empire, Mythologies of the Soul: *Fado* Performance and the Shaping of *Saudade.*" *Ethnomusicology* 51.1 (2007): 106–130. *JSTOR.* Web. 7 Jan. 2013.

Grosjean, François. *Bilingual: Life and Reality.* Cambridge, MA: Harvard University Press, 2010. Print.

Gutierrez, Evan C. "About Zacarias Ferreira." *Artists.* MTV, n.d. Web. 5 Aug. 2013.

Guzmán, Daysi Josefina. "Raza y lenguaje en el Cibao." *Eme Eme, Estudios Dominicanos* 2.11 (1974): 3–45. University of Florida Digital Libraries. Web. 2 Aug. 2012.

Hanna, Judith Lynne. "Moving Messages. Identity in Popular Music and Social Dance." Ed. James Lull. *Popular Music and Communication.* Newbury Park, CA: Sage, 1992. Print.

Hartlyn, Jonathan. *The Struggle for Democratic Politics in the Dominican Republic.* Chapel Hill: University of North Carolina Press, 1998. Print.

Henríquez Ureña, Pedro. "Música popular de América." *Boletín de Antropología Americana* 9 (1984): 137–157. *JSTOR.* Web. 30 May 2013.

Hoffnung-Garskof, Jesse. *A Tale of Two Cities: Santo Domingo and New York After 1950.* Princeton, NJ: Princeton University Press, 2008. Print.

Hume, Yanique. "Diaspora Tourism in the Dominican Republic: Capitalizing on Circular Migration." *Canadian Foreign Policy Journal* 17.2 (2011): 155–170. *General OneFile.* Web. 11 Aug. 2012.

Itzigsohn, José. "Incorporation and Transnationalism among Dominican Immigrants." *Carribean Studies* 32.1 (2004): 43–72. *JSTOR.* Web. 7 June 2013.

Jiménez, Máximo. "Cien discos esenciales." *El Caribe.* 22 July 2013, sec. Gente: 29. Print.

_____. "Re: Respuestas a tus preguntas para el libro sobre los 100 álbumes." Message to the author. 21 Aug. 2013. E-mail.

Jorge, Bernarda. "Bases ideológicas de la práctica musical durante la era de Trujillo." *Eme Eme* 10.59 (1982): 65–99. Print.

Knights, Vanessa. "El bolero: expresión de la modernidad latinoamericana." *Actas del III Congreso Latinoamericano de la Asociación Internacional para el Estudio de la Música Popular.* n.d. Web. 30 Sept. 2008.

Krohn-Hansen, Christian. "Masculinity and the Political Among Dominicans: 'The Dominican Tiger.'" Ed. Marit Melhuus and Kristi Anne Stølen. *Machos, Mistresses, Madonnas: Contesting the Power of Latin American Gender Imagery.* New York, Verso: 1996. 108–133. Print.

Kugel, Seth. "A Latin Dance Music Sings the Blues." Music. *New York Times.* 15 June 2002. Web. 1 May 2008.

Leal, João, and Jehanne Féblot-Augustins. "*Saudade,* la construction d'un symbole. 'Caractère national' et identité nationale." *Ethnologie française* 29.2 (1999): 177–189. *JSTOR.* Web. 7 Jan. 2013.

Love, Toby. Personal Interview. 14 June 2013.

"Luis Miguel del Amaruge actuará en el Festival Latinoameriano de Milán." *Hoy.* 25 May 2008. Web. 9 Aug. 2013.

"Luis Miguel tiene otra disquera." *Listín Diario.* 17 Oct. 2012. Web. 9 Aug. 2013.

"'Maldita Residencia,' de El Chaval de la Bachata logra pegada en solo un mes." *Caribbean Digital.* n.d. Web. 13 Aug. 2013.

Malkki, Liisa. "National Geographic: The Rooting of Peoples and the Territorialization of National Identity Among Scholars and Refugees." Ed. Geoff Eley and Ronald Grigor Suny. *Becoming National.* New York: Oxford University Press, 1992. 434–53. Print.

Martínez, Elvis. Personal Interview. 16 June 2013.

Mattern, Mark. *Acting in Concert: Music, Community and Political Action.* New Brunswick, NJ: Rutgers University Press, 1998. Print.

Medina, Francisco. Personal Interview. 14 Apr. 2013.

"Mélida Rodríguez." Artists. *IASO Records,* n.d. Web. 30 June 2012.

Méndez, Alexis. Personal Interview. 1 Aug. 2011.

Mirrors of the Heart: Race and Identity. Dir. Judith Vecchione. Annenberg/CPB, 1993. Film.

Morgan, Jana, Jonathan Hartlyn, and Rosario Espinal. "Dominican Party System Continuity amid Regional Transformations: Economic Policy, Clientelism, and Migration Flows." *Latin American Politics & Society* 53.1 (2011): 1–32. *Academic Search Complete.* Web. 3 Nov. 2012.

Moya Pons, Frank. *The Dominican Republic: A National History.* 3d ed. Princeton, NJ: Mark Wiener, 2010. Print.

_____. "Modernización y cambios en la República Dominicana." Ed. Bernardo Vega et al. *Ensayos sobre la cultura dominicana.* Santo Domingo: Fundación Cultural Dominicana, 1988. 213–245. Print.

"Ñoño." *Larousse Unabridged Spanish-English / Inglés-Español Dictionary.* Revised ed. Boston: Houghton Mifflin, 2000. Print.

Ortiz, Dante. "Mejía's Neoliberal Policies Stir Cauldron of Unrest in Dominican Republic." *NACLA Report on the Americas* 35.2 (2001): 46–8. *General OneFile.* Web. 10 Aug. 2012.

Ortiz de Urbina, Araceli, and Asbel López. "Un mundo de telenovelas." *El correo.* UNESCO. May 1999. Web. 13 July 2012.

Pacini Hernandez, Deborah. *Bachata: A Social History of Dominican Popular Music.* Philadelphia: Temple University Press, 1995. Print.

_____. "La lucha sonora: Dominican Popular Music in the Post–Trujillo Era." *Latin American Music Review* 12.2 (1991):106–21. *JSTOR.* Web. 1 July 2012.

_____. *Oye Como Va! Hybridity and Identity in Latino Popular Music.* Philadelphia: Temple University Press, 2010. Print.

Pacini Hernandez, Deborah, and David Wayne. Liner notes. *Bachata Roja: Acoustic Bachata from the Cabaret Era.* IASO Records, 2007. CD.

Paniagua, Leonardo. Personal Interview. 11 Dec. 2010.

Pantoja, Adrian D. "Transnational Ties and Immigrant Political Incorporation: The Case of Dominicans in Washington Heights, New York." *Migration* 43.4 (2005): 120–144. *JSTOR.* Web. 7 June 2013.

Paredes, Davicito. Personal Interview. 3 Aug. 2011.

Paredes, Edilio. Personal Interview. 10 Dec. 2010.

Participación Ciudadana. "Segundo informe sobre el desarrollo de las elecciones presidenciales y de diputados de ultramar." *Informaciones.* Participación Ciudadana, May 2012. Web. 11 Aug. 2012.

Pérez, Juan Miguel. "De la diversion a la redención. Notas económicas sobre las funciones sociales de la bachata." *El merengue en la cultura dominicana y del Caribe: Memorias del Primer Congreso Internacional Música, Identidad y Cultura en el Caribe.* Ed. Darío Tejeda and Rafael Emilio Yunén. Santo Domingo: Instituto de Estudios Caribeños, 2006. 385–394. Print.

Pérez, Xiomarita. Personal Interview. 13 Apr. 2013.

Pew Research Center. "Between Two Worlds: How Young Latinos Come of Age in America." *Pew Hispanic Center.* 11 Dec. 2009. Web. 12 July 2012.

Polanco, Fausto. "Yóskar Sarante aún estando pegado en 1999, trabajaba en la construcción." *El Día.* 27 May 2013: Espectáculos. Web. 9 Aug. 2013.

"Prince Royce estrenó el nuevo sencillo Darte un beso." *RPP Noticias.*17 July 2013. Web. 16 Aug. 2013.

Radcliffe, Sarah, and Sallie Westwood. *Remaking the Nation.* London: Routledge, 1996. Print.

"Ray Santana 'El Pollito del Cibao.'" *Lehigh Valley Latino Espectacular Magazine.* Nov. 2010: 25. Web.

Richards, Chris. "The Bachata King." *Washington Post.* 4 March 2012. Web. 11 July 2012.

Rivera González, Luis. *Antología musical de la era de Trujillo, 1930–1960.* 5 vols. Ciudad Trujillo: Publicaciones de la Secretaría de Estado de Educación y Bellas Artes, 1960. Print.

Rodríguez, Laura. "Calderón, pionero de la bachata." *Listín Diario.* 30 May 2012. Web. 30 May 2012.

Rodríguez Demorizi, Emilio. *Música y baile en Santo Domingo.* Santo Domingo: Colección Pensamiento, 1971. Print.

Rohter, Larry. "Crossing Over, No Translation Needed." *New York Times.* 13 Nov. 2011. Web. 11 July 2012.

Rosen, Jody. "Crossover Dreams of a Bronx Bachatero." Arts and Entertainment. *New York Times.* 7 June 2009. 13 June 2012.

Sábado Gigante. Univisión. 24 Feb. 2001. Television.

Sanche, Alex. Personal Interview. 15 Apr. 2013.

Sánchez, Teuddy A. "Raffo el Soñador ... A 27 años de su muerte." *El Nacional.* 20 Jan. 2012. Web. 7 July 2012.

Santana, Ray. "el Pollito del Cibao." Personal Interview. 9 Dec. 2010.

Santo Domingo Blues: The Bachata Story. Dir. Alex Wolfe. Perf. Luis Vargas. Mambo Media, 2004. Film.

Santos, Henry. Personal Interview. 12 June 2013.

_____. "Re: Question." Message to the author. 24 Aug. 2013. Email.

_____. "Re: Quote." Message to the author. 12 Jun 2013. E-mail.

_____. World Debut of *My Way* and Interview with Laura Stylez. SiriusXM Caliente. SiriusXM Studio, New York, NY. 12 June 2013. Guest Speaker.

Santos, Lenny. Personal Interview. 12 June 2013.

Santos, Lenny, and Steve Styles. Interview by batanga.com. Batanga.tv, n.d. Web. 11 July 2012.

Santos, Tony. Personal Interview. 10 Dec. 2010.

Sarante, Yoskar. "About." n.d. Facebook. Web. 8 Aug. 2013.

Seeger, Anthony. "Whoever We Are Today, We Can Sing a Song About It." Ed. Gerard Béhague. *Music and Black Ethnicity in the Caribbean and South America.* New Brunswick, NJ: Transaction, 1994. 1–15. Print.

Sellers, Julie A. *Merengue and Dominican Identity: Music as National Unifier.* Jefferson, NC: McFarland, 2004. Print.

Silfa, Susana. Personal Interview. 2 Aug. 2011.

Slobin, Mark. "Micromusics of the West: A Comparative Approach." *Ethnomusicology* 36.1 (1992). 1–87. *JSTOR.* Web. 4 Oct. 2012.

Smith, Anthony D. "The Origins of the Nation." Ed. Geoff Eley and Ronald Grigor Suny. *Becoming National.* New York: Oxford University Press, 1996. 106–130. Print.

Tejada, Pachico. "Temática de las bachatas: Reflejo social de su entorno." *Listín Diario.* 30 May 2012. Web. 30 May 2012.

_____. "Víctor Víctor reedita parte de su discografía." *Listín Diario.* 21 Dec. 2011. Web. 7 Aug. 2013.

Tejeda, Darío. *La bachata: Su origen, su historia y sus leyendas / The Bachata: Its origin, story, and legends.* Santo Domingo: ARTISTA, 2003. Print.

_____. *La pasión danzaria.* Santo Domingo: Academia de Ciencias de República Dominicana, 2002. Print.

Telenovelas: Love, TV and Power. Dir. Alexandre P. Valenti. Films for the Humanities and Sciences, 1995. Film.

"Toby Love Bio." Artists. Myplay.com. n.d. Web. 13 July 2012.

Todorov, Tzvetan. *The Conquest of America: The Question of the Other.* Trans. Richard Howard. New York: Harper & Row, 1984. Print.

Torres, Lourdes. "In the Contact Zone: Code-Switching Strategies by Latino/a Writers." *MELUS* 32.1 (2004): 75–96. *JSTOR.* Web. 17 June 2013.

Torres-Saillant, Silvio. "The Tribulations of Blackness: Stages in Dominican Racial Identity." *Callaloo* 23.3 (2000): 1086–1111. Print.

Torres-Saillant, Silvio, and Ramona Hernandez. *The Dominican Americans.* Westport, CT: Greenwood, 1998. Print.

Tu Momento Newyorkino. "Yoskar Sarante en Tu Momento Newyorkino Premio Urbano 2012." Online video clip. *YouTube.* YouTube, 5 Mar. 2012. Web. 9 Aub. 2013.

Valdez, Pedro Antonio. *Bachata del ángel caído.* 6th ed. Santo Domingo: Isla Negra, 2009. Print.

_____. "Pedro, el musical." Ed. Médar Serrata. *El sonido de la música en la narrativa dominicana.* Santo Domingo: Instituto de Estudios Caribeños, 2012. Print.

Valentine, James. "Naming the Other: Power, Politeness, and the Inflation of Euphemisms." *Sociological Research Online* 3.4 (1998). 31 Dec. 1998. Web. Aug. 13 2012.

Van Vleck, Phillip. "Fado Music." *Nat Geo Music.* National Geographic, n.d. Web. 13 Jan. 2013.

Veloz Maggiolo, Marcio. "Ecosistema del bolero dominicano." *El bolero: Visiones y perfiles de una pasión dominicana.* Colección Popular CODETEL. Vol. 6. Santo Domingo: CODETEL, 2009. 13–209. Print.

Veras, Joe. Personal Interview. 6 Aug. 2011.

Verbrigghe, Danielle. "Dominican Immigrants Risk Death at Sea, Only to Find Hardship on a New Shore." *Puerto Rico: Unsettled Territory.* Walter Cronkite School of Journalism and Mass Communication at Arizona State University. 29 Oct. 2012. Web. 17 Aug. 2013.

Vívelohoy. "Entrevista con Vena por Vívelohoy." Online video clip. *YouTube.* YouTube, 16 May 2013. Web. 27 Aug. 2013.

Wayne, David. "Anthony Santos." Artists. *IASO Records,* n.d. Web. 3 Nov. 2012.

_____. "Edilio Paredes." Artists. *IASO Records,* n.d. Web. 30 June 2012.

_____. "Luis Vargas: Bachata Pioneer." Artists. *IASO Records,* n.d. Web 31 July 2013.

_____. "Sexual Double Entendre Bachata." *IASO Records,* n.d. Web. 31 May 2013.

Wucker, Michelle. *Why the Cocks Fight: Dominicans, Haitians and the Struggle for Hispaniola.* New York: Hill & Wang, 1999. Print.

Zavala, Iris M. "When the Popular Sings the Self: Heterology, Popular Songs, and Caribbean Writing." *A History of Literature in the Caribbean: Cross-Cultural Studies, Volume 3.* Ed. A. James Arnold. Philadelphia: John Benjamins, 197. 187–199. Print.

Recordings Cited / Grabaciones citadas

Acosta, Héctor. "Aprenderé." *Oblígame*. Venevisión International Music, 2010. MP3.
_____. "Me duele la cabeza." *Oblígame*. Venevisión International Music, 2010. MP3.
_____. "No soy un hombre malo." *Con el corazón abierto*. Dam Latin, 2012. MP3.
_____. "Perdóname la vida." *The Ultimate Bachata Collection*. Universal Latino, 2010. MP3.
_____. "Primavera azul." *The Ultimate Bachata Collection*. Universal Latino, 2010. MP3.
_____. "Sin perdón." *Mitad mitad*. Machete/Venemusic, 2008. MP3.
_____. "Tu primera vez." *Simplemente...El Torito*. Venevisión International Music, 2009.
_____. "Tu veneno." *Con el corazón abierto*. Dam Latin, 2012. MP3.
Ángel, Julio. "El salón." *Bachata Roja: Acoustic Bachata from the Cabaret Era*. IASO Records, 2007. CD.
Aventura. *Generation Next*. Premium, 1999. CD.
_____. *God's Project*. Premium, 2005.
_____. *K.O.B. Live*. Premium, 2006. CD.
_____. *The Last*. Premium, 2009.
_____. *Love & Hate*. Premium, 2003. CD.
_____. *We Broke the Rules*. Premium, 2002. CD.
The Bachata Legends. IASO Records, 2011. CD
Bachata Roja: Acoustic Bachata from the Cabaret Era. IASO Records, 2007. CD.
Bachata Roja: Amor y amargue. IASO Records, 2011. CD.
Burgos, Rafy. "Dame cabeza." *Bachata Underground*. Premium Latin Music, 2010. MP3.
_____. "Enamorar." n.d. MP3.
_____. "Lamentos del Cupdio." n.d. MP3.
Calderón, José Manuel. *20 exitos*. J.M.C. Records, 1995. CD.
Calderón, José Manuel, Blas Durán, Leonardo Paniagua, Ramón Cordero, Ramón Torres, and Luis Segura. "Señora Bachata." *Señora Bachata*. Mock and Roll, 2009. CD.
El Chaval. "¿Dónde están esos amigos?" *Ya me cansé*. Mas Music, 2007. CD.
_____. "El golpe avisa." *Por el maldito dinero*. Sanchez Family, 2012. CD.
_____. "Maldita residencia." *Por el maldito dinero*. Sanchez Family, 2012. CD.
_____. "No molestar." *I Love Bachata 2013*. Planet Records, 2012. MP3.
_____. "Por el maldito dinero." *Por el maldito dinero*. Sanchez Family, 2012. CD.
Corniel, Gerson. "Ante una flor." *Cornielísate*. Sunflower Entertainment, 2010. CD.
_____. "Ella no me quiere." *Cornielísate*. Sunflower Entertainment, 2010. CD.
Cruz, Inocencio. "Amor gitano." Online video clip. *YouTube*. YouTube, 5 Aug. 2011. Web. June 3 2013.
_____. "Amorcito de mi alma." *30 Bachatas pegaditas*. Mock & Roll, 2004. CD.
Durán, Blas.. "La arepa." *Qué candela*. Codigo Music, 2009. CD.
_____ "Consejo a las mujeres." *Qué candela*. Codigo Music, 2009. CD.
_____. "Equivocada." *Bachata Roja: Acoustic Bachata from the Cabaret Era*. IASO Records, 2007. CD.
_____. "El motorcito." MP3.

Durán, Blas, and Davicito Paredes. "A ti no te quiero." *50 años de bachata*. Mock and Roll, 2002. CD.

Encarnación, Rafael. "Muero contigo." *Bachata roja*. IASO, 2007. CD.

_____. "Pena de hombre." *Homenaje a Rafael Encarnación*. Kubaney, 1991. CD.

Enrique, Luis, and Prince Royce. "Sabes." *Soy y seré*. Top Stop Music, 2011. CD.

Ferreira, Zacarías. *Adiós*. Blanco y Negro, 2004. CD.

_____. "La avispa." *Quiéreme*. J&N Records, 2005. MP3.

_____. "Un buen amigo que un mal amor." *Mi dulzura*. ZF Records, 2013. MP3.

_____. "Como amigo sí pero como amor no." *Te dejo libre*. Sony U.S. Latin, 2009. CD.

_____. "Dime que faltó." *Dime que faltó*. Sony U.S. Latin, 2007. MP3.

_____. "Es tan difícil." *Dime que faltó*. Sony U.S. Latin, 2007. MP3.

_____. "Me ilusioné." *Mi dulzura*. ZF Records, 2013. MP3.

_____. *Me liberé*. Sunflower Entertainment, 2011. CD.

_____. "Me sobran las palabras." *Quédate conmigo*. Mayimba Music, 2011. CD.

_____. "No hay mal que por bien no venga." *Dime que faltó*. Sony U.S. Latin, 2007. MP3.

_____. "Quédate conmigo." *Quédate conmigo*. Mayimba Music, 2011. CD.

_____. *El triste*. Sunflower Entertainment, 2011. CD.

Guerra, Juan Luis. *Bachata rosa*. Karen, 1990. CD.

Love, Toby. "Casi casi." *Amor total*. TopStop Music, 2013. CD.

_____. "Llorar lloviendo." *Love Is Back*. Sony U.S. Latin, 2008. MP3.

_____. "Te parece poco." *La voz de la juventud*. Sony U.S. Latin, 2011. MP3.

_____. "Tengo un amor." *Toby Love*. Sony U.S. Latin, 2006. MP3.

_____. *La voz de la juventud*. Sony U.S. Latin, 2011. MP3.

Luis Miguel del Amargue. "Abrázame amor." *Mi regreso*. Mock and Roll, 2009. MP3.

_____. "De rodillas." *De rodillas te pido*. Mock and Roll, 2008. MP3.

_____. "Sal de mi vida." *Dispuesto a todo*. Cerro Music Group, 2011. MP3.

_____. "Se acabó lo bonito." *Mi regreso*. Mock and Roll, 2009. MP3.

_____. "Teléfono ocupado." Venevision International, 2011. MP3.

Maná and Prince Royce. "El verdadero amor perdona." *Drama y luz*. Warner Music Mexico, 2011. MP3.

Mariíta. *Bachata amargue*. José Luis Records, 1994. CD.

Martin, Ricky. "Livin' la vida loca." *Ricky Martin*. Sony, 1999. CD.

Martínez, Elvis. "Amada mía." *Directo al corazón*. Premium, 2000. MP3.

_____. "Ambición." *Esperanza*. Premium, 2012. MP3.

_____. "Así fue." *Todo se paga*. Premium, 1998. MP3.

_____. "Así te amo." *Así te amo*. Premium, 2003. MP3.

_____. "Dime." *Esperanza*. Premium, 2012. MP3.

_____. "Esta Navidad." *Directo al corazón*. Premium, 2000. MP3.

_____. "Juancito Nadie." *Descontrolado*. Premium, 2004. MP3.

_____. "La luz de mis ojos." *La luz de mis ojos*. Universal Latino, 2007. MP3.

_____. "Maestra." *Tres palabras*. Premium, 2001. MP3.

_____. "Profesor." *Así te amo*. Premium, 2003. MP3.

_____. "Triste Navidad." *Tres palabras*. Premium, 2001. MP3.

_____. "Tú sabes bien." *Directo al corazón*. Premium, 2000. MP3.

_____. "Yo no nací para amar." *Yo soy más grande que él*. Univision, 2005. MP3.

_____. "Yo te voy a amar." *Esperanza*. Premium, 2012. MP3.

Monchy y Alexandra. "Dos locos." *Confesiones*. JVN Music, 2002. MP3.

_____. "Hoja en blanco." *Hoja en blanco*. JVN Music, 2001. MP3.

_____. "No es una novela." *Éxitos y algo más*. JVN Music, 2006. MP3.

_____. "Perdidos." *Hasta el fin*. JVN Music, 2004. MP3.

_____. "Te quiero igual que ayer." *Confesiones*. JVN Music, 2002. MP3.

Ortiz, Bernardo. "Dos rosas." Online video clip. *YouTube*. YouTube, 16 Oct. 2008. Web. 3 June 2013.

Paniagua, Leonardo. "Amada amante." Online video clip. *YouTube*. YouTube, 8 Feb. 2013. Web. 5 June 2013.

_____. "Un beso y una flor." *14 Éxitos*. Kubaney Records, 1990. CD.

_____. "Chiquitita." *14 Éxitos*. Kubaney Records, 1990. CD

Paredes, Davicito. "No Speak Spanish." *30 Bachatas pegaditas*. Mock & Roll, 2004. CD.

El Pollito del Cibao. "Corazón enamorado." Online video clip. *YouTube*. YouTube, 29 May 2012. Web. 13 Aug. 2013.

_____. "La travesía." Online video clip. *YouTube*. YouTube, 29 May 2012. Web. 13 Aug. 2013.

Prince Royce. *Phase II*. Top Stop, 2012. CD.

_____. *Prince Royce*. Top Stop, 2011. CD.

Raffo el Soñador. "Cadena de tragedias." Online video clip. *YouTube*. YouTube, 23 Dec. 2010. Web. 3 June 2013.

_____. "No me hablen de ella." Online video clip. *YouTube*. YouTube, 3 Nov. 2012. Web. 3 June 2013.

_____. "El soñador." Online video clip. *YouTube*. YouTube, 27 Oct. 2008. Web. 3 June 2013.

Reyes, Frank. "A quien tú quieres no te quiere." *Déjame entrar en ti*. JVN Music, 2002. MP3

_____. "El alcohol." *Dosis de amor*. JVN Records, 2005. MP3.

_____. "Amor a distancia." *Soy tuyo*. Sony U.S. Latin, 2012. CD.

_____. "Cuando se quiere se puede." *Cuando se quiere se puede*. JVN Music, 2004. MP3.

_____. "Extraño mi pueblo." *Extraño mi pueblo*. JVN Music, 1999. CD.

_____. "Nada de nada." *Déjame entrar en ti*. JVN Music, 2002. MP3.

_____. "Princesa." *Dosis de amor*. JVN Records, 2005. MP3.

_____. "Se fue mi amor." *Si el amor condena, estoy condenado*. J&N Records, 1994. MP3.

_____. "Suspiros de amantes." *Si el amor condena, estoy condenado*. J&N Records, 1994. MP3.

_____. "Tú eres ajena." *Amor en silencio*. JVN Music, 2000.

_____. "24 horas." *Soy tuyo*. Sony Latin, 2012. MP3.

_____. "Vine a decirte adiós." *Vine a decirte adiós*. JVN Music, 1998. MP3.

Rodríguez, Melida "La sufrida." *La mujer bachata*. Palma Music, 1998. CD.

Rodríguez, Raulín. "Ay Hombre." *Si no te tengo*. JVN Music, 2004. MP3.

_____. "Culpable. *La carretera*. JVN Music, 2007. MP3.

_____. "Esta noche." 2013. MP3.

_____. "Me la pusieron difícil." *Me la pusieron difícil*. Plátano Records, 1996. MP3.

_____. Medicina de amor. *Medicina de amor*, Plátano Records, 1994. CD.

_____. "Mi morenita." *Una mujer como tú*. Plátano Records, 1993. MP3.

_____. Mujer infiel. *Medicina de amor*, Plátano Records, 1994. CD.

_____. "Qué dolor." *Una mujer como tú*. Plátano Records, 1993. MP3.

Santos, Antony. "Ay de mí, ay de ti." *Juego de amor*. Plátano Records, 2002. MP3.

_____. "Corazón culpable." *Cójelo ahí*. Plátano Records, 1994. CD.

_____. "Creíste." Anthony Santos, 2013. MP3.

_____. "Linda y difícil." *La batalla*. Plátano Records, 1993. MP3.

_____. "Lloro." *Lloro*. J&N, 2006. CD.

_____. "Por mi timidez." *Corazón bonito*. Plátano Records, 1993.

_____. "Qué plantón." *Sabor latino*. Plátano Records, 1996. MP3.

_____. "Vete y aléjate de mí." *I Love Bachata*. Planet Records Europe, 2011. MP3.

_____. "Voy pa' allá." *La chupadera*. Plátano Records, 1992. CD.

_____. "Yo quiero." Anthony Santos, 2013. MP3.

Santos, Henry. *Introducing*. Hustlehard Entertainment, 2011. CD.

_____. *My Way*. Hustlehard Entertainment, 2013. CD.

Santos, Romeo. *Fórmula, Vol. 1*. Sony U.S. Latin, 2011. CD.

Santos, Tony. "Amarilis, échame agua." Online video clip. *YouTube*. YouTube, 25 Sept. 2010. Web. 24 Aug. 2013.

Sarante, Yóskar. "Guitarra." *No es casualidad*. J&N Records, 2002. MP3.

_____. "He tenido que llorar." *No es casualidad*. J&N Records, 2002. MP3.

_____. "Llora alma mía." *Llora alma mía*. J&N Records, 2000. CD.

_____. "No tengo suerte en el amor." *No es casualidad*. J&N Records, 2002. MP3.

_____. "La noche." *Llora alma mía*. J&N Records, 2000. CD.

Segura, Luis. "Cariñito de mi vida." *50 años de bachata*. Mock and Roll, 2002. CD.

_____. "Pena por ti." *Luis Segura Disco de Oro: 20 Éxitos*. José Luis Records, 1997. CD.

Shakira. *Dónde están los ladrones?* Sony, 1998. CD.

_____. *Laundry Service*. Sony, 2001. CD.

_____. *Pies descalzos*. Sony, 1996. CD.

Silvestre, Sonia. *Yo quiero andar*. Cholo Brenes, 2002. CD.

Thalía, feat. Prince Royce. "Te Perdiste mi amor." *Habítame siempre.* Sony, 2012. MP3.

Vargas, Luis. "Carta final." *Urbano.* JVN Music, 2007. MP3.

_____. "El envidioso." *En serio.* José Luis Records, 1997. CD.

_____. *Loco de amor.* José Luis Records, 1997. CD.

_____. *La maravilla.* José Luis Records, 1997. CD.

_____. "La mesa del rincón." *Loco de amor.* José Luis Records, 1995. MP3.

_____. "No puedo vivir sin ti." *The Legend.* Planet Records, 2010. MP3.

_____. "Simplemente te amo." *Mensajero.* J&N Records, 2004. MP3.

_____. *El tomate.* José Luis Records, 1995. CD.

_____. "Veneno." *Volvió el dolor.* JVN Music, 1997. MP3.

_____. "Yo mismo la vi." *Todos éxitos.* Plátano Records, 2005. CD.

_____. "Yo no muero en mi cama." Chokolate Productions, 2013. MP3.

Vargas, Luis, and Sergio Vargas. "Dos hombres bebiendo." *Yo soy así.* Lideres Entertainment Group, 2002. MP3.

Vena. "Por mentiras." EMG/Planet, 2012. MP3.

_____. "Señora." EMG/Planet, 2011. MP3.

_____. "Ya no." EMG/Planet, 2012. MP3.

Ventura, Aridia. *20 Grandes éxitos.* José Luis Records, 1997. CD.

Veras, Joe. *Así es la vida.* Mundo, 1997. CD.

_____. "Cartas del verano." *Carta de verano.* JVN Music, 2003. MP3.

_____. "Chiquilla chiquita." *La travesía.* J&N Records, 2006. MP3.

_____. "Cirugía en el alma." *Maestro.* J&N Records, 2011. MP3.

_____. *Con amor.* Arcoiris, 1995. CD

_____. *Con más amor.* Mundo, 1996. CD.

_____. "El cuchicheo." Joe Veras / La Oreja Media Group, 2013. MP3.

_____. "Duele." *Maestro.* J&N Records, 2011. MP3.

_____. "En el amor." *La travesía.* J&N Records, 2006. MP3.

_____. "Inténtalo tú." *Carta de verano.* JVN Music, 2003. MP3.

_____. "Pido Auxilio." *Vida.* JVN Music, 2008. MP3.

_____. "Por tu amor." *Desde mi alma.* JVN Music, 2001. MP3.

_____. "Sobreviviré." Joe Veras / La Oreja Media Group, 2013. MP3.

_____. "Te solté." 2013, MP3.

_____. "Tu belleza interior." *La travesía.* J&N Records, 2006. MP3.

Víctor Víctor. "Mesita de noche." *La escencia de la bachata.* Generations, 2007. CD.

Víctor Víctor (feat. Pedro Guerra). "Debajo del Puente." *Bachata entre amigos.* Sony BMG, 2006. CD.

Xtreme. "No me digas que no." *Haciendo historia: Platinum Edition.* La Calle Records, 2007. CD.

_____. "Shorty, shorty." *Haciendo historia: Platinum Edition.* La Calle Records, 2007. CD.

_____. "Te extraño." *Xtreme.* Univision Records, 2006. CD.

Index / Índice

Numbers in **bold italics** indicate pages with photographs /
Los números que van en **letra negrita y cursiva** se refieren a fotografías

291